DUMAS ON

Alexandre Dumas in his old age: the frontispiece of the first edition of the Grand Dictionnaire de Cuisine.

DUMAS ON FOOD

Selections from
Le Grand Dictionnaire de Cuisine
by Alexandre Dumas
translated by
Alan and Jane Davidson
introduced by
Alan Davidson

Oxford   New York
OXFORD UNIVERSITY PRESS
1987

Oxford University Press, Walton Street, Oxford OX2 6DP

Oxford New York Toronto
Delhi Bombay Calcutta Madras Karachi
Petaling Jaya Singapore Hong Kong Tokyo
Nairobi Dar es Salaam Cape Town
Melbourne Auckland
and associated companies in
Beirut Berlin Ibadan Nicosia

Oxford is a trade mark of Oxford University Press

First published in a trade edition, by arrangement
with the Folio Society, by Michael Joseph Ltd. 1979
First issued as an Oxford University Press paperback 1987

British Library Cataloguing in Publication Data
Dumas, Alexandre, 1802–1870
Dumas on food : selections from Le grand
dictionnaire de cuisine.
1. Cookery—Dictionaries
I. Title   II. Le grand dictionnaire de
cuisine. English Selections
641.5'03'21   TX349
ISBN 0–19–282040–0

Library of Congress Cataloging in Publication Data
Dumas, Alexandre, 1802–1870.
Dumas on food.
Reprint. Originally published: London : Joseph, 1979.
Bibliography: p.   Includes index.
1. Cookery—Dictionaries. 2. Food—Dictionaries.
I. Title.
(TX349.D88213 1987)   641.3'03'21   87–1632
ISBN 0–19–282040–0 (pbk.)

Printed in Great Britain by
Richard Clay Ltd.
Bungay, Suffolk

CONTENTS

PREFACE

Alexandre Dumas *père* died at Dieppe in 1870. His *Grand Dictionnaire de Cuisine* was published in 1873. It was a volume of formidable weight and length, containing about 600,000 words and two illustrations. The text was often repetitive, the balance between subjects inexplicable, the punctuation and paragraphing erratic, the incubus of perfunctorily drafted recipes borrowed from other authors almost intolerable, and yet . . . it was an engaging and impressive jumble. Even a quick glance was enough to show that it was infused with the exuberance of Dumas, and that it reflected not only his quixotic attitude to life and insatiable curiosity but also his extensive and adventurous travels.

The manuscript had been delivered to the publisher before his death; and there is evidence that some editorial work was carried out on the book between his death and its publication. Yet, surveying the result, one has difficulty in believing that Dumas himself, in his prime, would have regarded the book as a finished product; or that any literate person devoted serious attention to putting the manuscript into order. It is also difficult to believe that many people have read the book from beginning to end, or ever will. This is sad. The book is the last work of one of the most astonishing and colourful authors of the nineteenth century, it is one to which he attached importance, and it is studded with passages which make amusing and instructive reading.

More is said about the history of the book in the introduction. Here, we simply wish to explain why the book has been, had to be, abridged in this edition. Our natural inclination would always be to translate a book in full, and not to meddle with its structure. But in this instance we have had no hesitation in doing acts of considerable violence, all with the aim of extracting the real Dumas, like silver, from the dross in which it is embedded. We ought to explain briefly how we have set about this bold task.

The original text consisted of:

(1) Prefatory remarks about the history of the book   (iii to vi)
(2) A letter from the publisher to M. Vuillemot, the principal adviser of Dumas on cuisine   (viii)
(3) *Quelques mots au lecteur*, an introduction by Dumas to his book   (1 to 33)

7

Preface

The introductory material is an ill-assorted collection. We have left out, for a start, the sections lifted from Victor Hugo and Grimod de la Reynière. We have also left out the letter to Jules Janin, which does not form an organic part of the book. As for the rest, much of it is repeated in the dictionary itself. We have not translated this material. We have, however, translated in full the last of the introductory items, since this provides a clear and brief introduction to the book in Dumas' own words.

The prefatory material about the history of the book has been used in our introduction.

The essay on mustard has been turned into an entry in the dictionary, which contained nothing on the subject.

This leaves us with the dictionary itself. It included much material about wines and vintages which is now of historical interest only. Moreover, Dumas says (page 299) that during fifty or sixty years of his life he drank no wine. It was not a subject on which he was personally expert. We have therefore left out all this material. We have also left out entries which are either completely trivial, or wrong (unless wrong in an interesting way), or which pertain to articles of food which are no longer in use and have no historical interest.

As for the recipes, we have been ruthlessly selective. In some entries they were so numerous that they could only have a numbing effect on the reader. Many of them come from other books. Many are of the tiresome kind which assume that the reader has a pantry full of truffles and a cellar from which he is willing to pluck bottles of champagne daily for cooking purposes. A few such recipes have been retained, to preserve part of the flavour of the original; but most of the recipes which we have translated (and in some instances tried out) are those which can be used today or which have a historical interest or a picturesque quality which makes them agreeable to read.

We have corrected Dumas, or attempted to explain what he meant, where we thought this desirable. *All passages in square brackets are additions by ourselves. So are all footnotes.*

While we have taken care thus to indicate what we have added, we have not used the device of rows of dots to indicate omissions. There would be too many of them, and they would mar the smooth flow which we have tried to give the text by taking out of it extraneous material and irrelevant interjections.

As regards the translation itself, we have done it in a fairly literal way, believing that the flavour of the original is best preserved by this means, even if the results occasionally sound odd to English ears. We have left in French a number of technical words which have no exact equivalent in English. It seemed better to explain at the outset what they mean, by means of a glossary.

This glossary (pages 27 to 36) is intended to help the reader in other ways to understand the dictionary entries. It contains three parts. The first deals with the structure of a formal French meal in Dumas' time; and also explains the great importance attached to the distinction between *maigre* and *gras*, a distinction which pervades the book. The second part names and describes and illustrates the kitchen equipment and utensils which Dumas used and wrote about in his recipes. The third part is an explanatory list of miscellaneous culinary terms, followed by a short note on weights and measures. We hope that readers will glance through this whole section, to see what it contains, before starting to read or refer to the dictionary.

We wish to add that we are well aware of the pitfalls which await anyone trying to translate a work, which is simultaneously technical and lyrical, scientific (or pseudo-scientific) and theatrical, from another language, another country and another age. French friends have kindly rescued us from such pitfalls, when we have realised that something was wrong and have appealed for help. But there are surely others into which we have fallen in all innocence and from which no one has had occasion to rescue us. If so, we shall be in the great Dumas tradition of not getting things 100 per cent right; a tradition which was followed even by the artist who designed his memorial medal and who placed on it an incorrect birth date.

ACKNOWLEDGEMENTS

We wish to thank for their help the following institutions and persons: the Bibliothèque Nationale and the Centre Pompidou in Paris; the Institut Français in London; Christiane Neave, Secretary-General of the Association des Amis de Dumas; Douglas Munro; Daniel Morcrette; Robert Landru; Jean-Pierre Leguéré; Elizabeth David; Judith Baum; Yvette de la Fontinelle and Nicole-Josette Hinton.

At the same time we should like to express our gratitude to the numerous other people in France, for example at Villers-Cotterêts, who kindly smoothed the path of research for us or solved particular problems of translation.

We should, however, make clear that responsibility for opinions expressed and for residual errors rests squarely on ourselves.

We are grateful to Penguin Books for permission to use passages from the translation by Anne Drayton of *The Philosopher in the Kitchen (La Physiologie du Goût)* by Brillat-Savarin.

The sources of the illustrations taken from other books are acknowledged in the list given on page 323.

Finally, our warm thanks go to Janet Lovelock for turning our drafts into a neat typescript; and to everyone with whom we have dealt at the Folio Society for their helpful suggestions and amiable cooperation.

INTRODUCTION

Alexandre Dumas *père*. The last word is used to distinguish our
author from his son, Alexandre Dumas *fils*, who also became a
well-known French writer. But it serves also to remind us of the
superior fecundity of the elder Dumas. He himself spoke of his
literary offspring as numbering 400 to 500, or even more (cf. pages
37 and 92). True, his collected works, as published in the Michel
Lévy frères et Calmann Lévy edition, comprised only 303 volumes;
but this collection was incomplete, lacking among other things
the very work we are now presenting.

Whence sprang a man of such prodigious activity?

His father was a French general, born a mulatto in Santo Domingo,
as the result of a union between the Marquis de la Pailleterie (who
anticipated by a century Bernard Shaw's advice: 'Marry a West
Indian negress. They make excellent wives.') and a black slave-girl
called Cessette Dumas. The child of their union was brought back to
France by the father and resolved to enter the French Army. Now,
the de la Pailleteries had hitherto provided only officers for the army,
and senior officers at that; so it was agreed that the young man should
enlist under the name Dumas. He was of striking appearance and
enormous strength. André Maurois relates that he was the only
dragoon in his regiment who, 'by taking hold of one of the beams of
the stable roof, could hoist himself and his horse off the ground'.
Within four years he had become a lieutenant-colonel of cavalry; and
had married his love, Marie-Louise Labouret, in the small town of
Villers-Cotterêts.

We thus arrive at the birthplace of Alexandre. It is a charming
town, 85 kilometres to the north-east of Paris, and was the natural
stopping-place for northward travellers, making for Belgium or
Reims, on the second night of their journey from Paris. It was therefore full of inns (one of which has recently been restored to its former
elegance and its former function, as the Hôtel le Régent); and the
countryside around it was beautiful, well wooded and well stocked
with game of many kinds.

The house where Alexandre was born, in 1802, still stands. It is a
pleasant building, but no grand mansion. His father had risen to the
rank of general, but subsequently incurred the displeasure of
Napoleon Bonaparte. He was in Cairo at the time, and had to make
his own way back to France. In doing so, he was imprisoned at

Introduction

Brindisi, and poisoned so seriously that his health was ruined. He was eventually released, and returned to Villers-Cotterêts, but remained in disgrace. When he died, still in his early forties, in 1806, he left nothing to his family, for there was nothing to leave; and the pleas made by his widow and friends to Napoleon to make some provision for his dependants met with no response.

Thus the young Alexandre was brought up in modest circumstances and without a father. It was his mother and his sister who taught him to read and write (little knowing what a flood of words they would thus release); and he spent much of his boyhood in the forests, consorting with poachers. Hence came a genuine knowledge of game, and of shooting and hunting; a knowledge which was reflected sixty years later in the *Dictionnaire*.

The small museum devoted to Dumas relics at Villers-Cotterêts possesses a pair of his boots. He had remarkably small feet. In other respects he was a large, powerful and handsome young man, with fuzzy hair and a swarthy complexion which bespoke his mixed ancestry. His intelligence was quick, but his bent was for action rather than for study and reading. He assented, when approaching the age of sixteen, to become a junior clerk in the office of the notary of Villers-Cotterêts; but even as he took up this work he found a new outlet for his energies in the pursuit of young women. Number one in a series at the extent of which one can only guess was Adèle Dalvin, the daughter of an agricultural worker. He was in the right place to win her as his first mistress. As he himself remarked in his *Mémoires*: 'There was at Villers-Cotterêts a custom, more English than French, of permitting a free and easy relationship between young people of the two sexes, such as I have not found in any other French town.' The liaison lasted two years, and seems to have been a very happy one. (I shall not attempt to chronicle Dumas' subsequent *affaires de coeur* and marriage, for they have little bearing on the *Dictionnaire*, but will merely say that his interest in women continued almost to the day of his death and that his last affair was with the remarkable Adah Menken, an American Jewess from Louisiana, who performed feats of great daring on horseback on the stage. His conquest of her—or hers of him—took place when he was sixty-five years old.)

Although the young Dumas had received very little formal education, and had shown no great interest in literature, he had had some literary education, of an informal and haphazard kind, from M. Collard, a friend of his father and a man of culture who possessed a library in which Alexandre could browse. The event which finally

Dumas as a young man

kindled his interest to a burning intensity was the performance, at Soissons, of a play by Shakespeare. Dumas attended this, and was transformed. As he himself put it: 'I was blind, and Shakespeare has brought me light.'

People will still show you, at Villers-Cotterêts, the building in which Dumas began his career as a dramatist. He constructed a makeshift little theatre in the attic of a carpenter's workshop and began to stage in it dramas, often written by himself. Ambition in a specific form now animated him, and his gaze was fixed on Paris and its great theatres, of which he heard much from his friend Adolphe de Leuven. To go to Paris meant playing truant from his clerical duties, which he was now performing in the nearby town of Crespy, and involved

Introduction

expenditure. However, he and another friend, Pierre Hippolyte Paillet, worked out a plan to be executed while Dumas' master was himself away. That was supposed to deal with the truancy problem. As for the money, Paillet knew a cheap hotel in Paris, and the two of them reckoned that they could shoot enough game on the way to meet their expenses. On this, their calculations were correct. Setting off with one horse and one gun between the pair of them, they arrived in Paris with four hares, a dozen partridges and two quails, all of which had a marketable value of thirty francs.

During this visit, Dumas contrived to be presented to the great actor Talma, after witnessing his performance in a play at the Théatre-Français. Talma asked him whence he came and what he did. Dumas was embarrassed to reply that he was a provincial notary's clerk. But Talma reminded him that Corneille had also been a clerk, and proceeded to 'baptise' him 'poet' in the names of Shakespeare, Corneille and Schiller.

'Return to the country,' said the great actor, 'resume your studies, and if you really have a vocation for the theatre the Angel of Poetry will know where to find you, wherever you may be.'

Dumas tried to kiss the actor's hand. 'Why, see,' said Talma, in an understandable understatement, 'this lad has enthusiasm and will make something of himself.'

However, the first result of the escapade was that Dumas lost the job which he had in the office of M. Lefèvre at Crespy. For once he did not run the last league of the journey home to Villers-Cotterêts, for he knew that the news would be a blow for his mother. Indeed, she now had to sell all her property in order to meet her debts. Two hundred and fifty-three francs net remained after these transactions. Alexandre took the fifty-three (which he subsequently repaid many times over, for he was an affectionate and generous son) and set off for Paris to seek help from influential persons who had known his father.

In the whole of Dumas' *Mémoires* there are few passages which make such amusing reading and throw such an agreeable light on his personality and on his ability to see himself in a comical light, as the pages about this episode in his life, when he was nearly twenty-one.

He was admitted to see General Foy, who read the letter of introduction which Dumas had brought. The general mused.

' "I must first discover what you are able to do."
"Oh, not much, I'm afraid."
"Come! You must know some mathematics."

"No, General."
"You have at least some idea of algebra . . . of geometry . . . of physics?"
The general paused between each word, and each time I blushed anew . . . This was the first time that I had really been confronted by my own ignorance.'

The questions continued. No law, no Greek, only a little Latin, some Italian, no knowledge whatsoever of accounting. The general was patently sympathetic, yet at a loss to know what he could suggest to someone so untutored. Eventually he bade Dumas write down his address in Paris, so that he could reach him if he thought of a possible opening. Dumas had hardly written his own name before the general, now beaming, declared: 'We are saved! . . . You write a beautiful hand.'

Thus it came about that Dumas, on the general's recommendation, was appointed to the secretarial staff of the Duke of Orleans. He did not forget, in thanking the general, to voice his further aspirations. 'At present I am living by my handwriting, but one day, I promise you, I shall be living by my pen.'

This was a promise which Dumas soon fulfilled. And this is the point at which the story of his life becomes quite unmanageable for all but the most skilful biographers.

Here it must suffice to say that Dumas achieved an enormous popular success as a dramatist and novelist, as everyone knows; that with Victor Hugo and Alfred de Vigny he formed a kind of triumvirate of the romantic movement in French literature; and that his fortunes waxed and waned in a bewildering way throughout the rest of his life. The zenith was the construction of a splendid mansion at Port-Marly, outside Paris, on which he lavished the huge sums earned by his plays and books and in which he gave sumptuous entertainments. The house still stands, empty and forlorn. Close by can be seen the Château d'If, a small Gothic building which Dumas built as a retreat in which he could write while his guests revelled in the main house, and which, happily, is being restored by the Association des Amis de Dumas. It is charming, and modest in scale. By its propinquity to the extravagant Château Monte Cristo (as the main house was called, after one of Dumas' most successful books) it seems to symbolize the two sides to his character; the assiduous and highly professional writer, and the devil-may-care, spendthrift, generous, amorous, gourmand lion of Paris society.

One low point came in 1852, when he left Paris for Brussels, mainly to escape from his creditors. The nadir, however, was probably the last year of his life, when he was ill, impoverished and tormented by doubts about the enduring quality of his work.

This work was vast in both size and scope. He wrote nearly seventy plays and almost a hundred novels or books of stories. *The Three Musketeers* and *The Black Tulip* are but two of these. In addition, he published more than a score of history books, and almost as many travel books. And then there are the miscellaneous works, including *Mes Mémoires*, which run to over a million words but only carry the story of his life up to the age of thirty!

This is the literary background against which the *Dictionnaire de Cuisine* is to be seen. Looked at in isolation, it seems huge, the sort of book which might represent a lifetime's study and work. Looked at in the context of what had gone before, it shrinks to modest dimensions, and seems like the last spark from a Catherine-wheel which had emitted hundreds, many of them brighter and some of them bigger, in the course of its gyrations.

During the last few decades a reappraisal of Dumas' place in French literature has been taking place. It would be out of place here to comment on this. But I have some general observations to make about his literary output; observations which are relevant to the *Dictionnaire*.

The first point is that he was accustomed to work with collaborators. Some of his detractors went so far as to allege that others did the writing for him in many instances, and that he simply applied a little polish and put his name to the work. There were ironical references to 'Dumas and Company' as a sort of literary factory. What is certain is that he used to employ others to assemble material for him, which he would then turn into a novel or play. Perhaps some of the books were partly drafted by others, rather as a painter of the Italian Renaissance would let members of his 'school' fill in, say, the landscape in one of his works. But there can be no doubt about one thing; that the finished products, or almost all of them, bore the unmistakable stamp of Dumas. Nor can there be any doubt about the fact that he did, physically, pen an almost incredible quantity of prose.

The second point is that he had only a qualified respect for facts. The qualification consisted in his overriding desire to achieve the effect he sought. Historians have taken this amiss and pointed to errors and distortions, venial perhaps in his historical plays and novels, but less so in the history books which he produced. The story has often been told of how one critic accused him of violating French history. 'Perhaps I have,' he replied, 'but see what beautiful offspring have resulted!' I had an interesting echo of all this when I found myself sitting beside a French history teacher in a bus, in 1977. I mentioned Dumas. She said that she found it truly remarkable that even today most of her pupils seemed to have derived most of their ideas about French history from Dumas. I asked whether she deplored this. She replied that it would have been helpful if Dumas had been more accurate, but that on balance his influence was beneficial, since he aroused *interest*. I think that Dumas would have been pleased by this judgment, for interest was exactly what he sought to arouse.

Thirdly, it is remarkable to see how often in Dumas' novels, and in his travel books, meals and eating habits and the subject of food in general appear. The frequency of these references bespeaks a real interest in the subject; and no one has ever denied that Dumas had such an interest. There is, however, a further question to consider, namely how much did Dumas really know about cooking?

Dumas in the kitchen

The evidence that Dumas actually did much cooking himself is surprisingly scanty. It may be that more could be brought to light by scholars willing to explore this particular point. But the biographers have either said nothing about it or repeated the few pieces of evidence set out below; while the literary critics have almost entirely, and understandably, ignored the *Dictionnaire de Cuisine* and questions pertinent to it.

There is one piece of evidence in the diary of George Sand, dated 3 February 1866.

'Fetched Marchal and went with him to dine at half-past six with the Jauberts. The parents of both husband and wife were present, Lehmann, the Dumas, father and son, and three or four friends of the family. Dumas père had cooked the whole meal, from soup to salad! Eight or ten wonderful courses. . . .'

There is also the well-known story of the lunch which Dumas improvised in the summer of 1864. He was then living in a villa near Saint-Gratien with a young lady from Naples, who charmed him, but did not charm the household staff. I give the rest of the story in the words of my fellow-clansman, Arthur F. Davidson, whose biography of Dumas was published in 1902.

'She was constantly quarrelling with the servants—sometimes inconveniently, as when one Saturday she dismissed all three who composed the establishment and left the house servantless. A Saturday of all days was the worst, for every Sunday a number of friends from Paris used to turn up. On this occasion the servants in departing had left the larder empty—a discovery only made when the guests began to arrive on Sunday morning, and it was necessary to find a luncheon for them. Once more the culinary genius of Dumas came to the rescue. By good luck one or two of the guests had brought with them slices of ham and sausage ... as a contribution to the feast. These being handed over, Dumas, after ransacking every cupboard, came upon a quantity of rice, some cooking butter, and finally—to his great delight—a few fine tomatoes. From these, with butter added, a rich sauce was made; then rice was thrown in, boiled, and interspersed with slices of fried ham. From these ingredients a savoury and sufficient *déjeuner* was prepared for the dozen guests now summoned from the garden to enjoy it, and—excepting one or two who had assisted the *chef*—quite ignorant of the peculiar circumstances. They all praised the *riz aux tomates*, and praised it still more when Dumas told them the secret. . . .'

Hmm. Even in the longer version given in Appendix 2, this seems a little thin as evidence of culinary genius. But it is the same story which André Maurois, in his preface to a recent edition of the *Dictionnaire*, selects as the outstanding example of Dumas' skill in the kitchen; and Maurois was an authority on Dumas and one of his more skilful biographers. We have, however, added in Appendix 2 some further material from published sources, showing, for example, how Dumas set about obtaining a recipe for macaroni and that he did actually go into the kitchen with his notebook for this purpose. More important, we have also added a hitherto unpublished description of Dumas' cooking when he was staying with friends at Soissons. This is both amusing and convincing.

Otherwise, there seems to be little evidence available beyond general statements by Dumas himself about his interest in cookery, and the content of the *Dictionnaire* itself, to which we now come, and in which will be found (under Lobster, page 165) a description of one whole meal for which Dumas was the chef.

The writing of the Grand Dictionnaire de Cuisine

Dumas had for many years contemplated writing this book. Towards the end of his life, he signed a contract for it with Alphonse Lemerre, a newcomer in the publishing world who dealt mostly with poets, such as Théophile Gautier, Leconte de Lisle and Charles Baudelaire, but who was open to proposals in other fields. In 1869, Dumas, now feeling old and unwell, but also in need of money and anxious to fulfil this remaining task, retreated to Roscoff on Cape Finisterre, armed with a collection of cookery books, his own material on the subject and contributions from famous restaurateurs. He chose Roscoff as a place where he could expect tranquillity and could live cheaply. He was accompanied by a cook, Marie, but she did not take to the place and left almost at once. Fortunately, the inhabitants of Roscoff made Dumas welcome and gave him much hospitality; so he was able to set about his task in favourable conditions.

In March of 1870 the manuscript was delivered to Lemerre. According to André Maurois, it was 'almost finished'. The writer who composed the very first of the various prefaces and introductions to the book, who signed himself L.T., states that a number of pages had been set in type before Dumas' death and that the setting was only interrupted by the outbreak of the Franco-Prussian war. This suggests that the manuscript was indeed almost complete.

Meanwhile Dumas had set off for the south of France, hoping to restore his failing health. But he was taken ill again at Marseilles, after hearing of the outbreak of war, and only just managed to make his way north to Puys, near Dieppe, where his son had a house. There he died, on 5 December 1870, without having seen the *Dictionnaire* again and on the very day when the invading Prussians entered Dieppe. Because of the war, some time passed before his remains could be taken to Villers-Cotterêts and reburied there. For the same reason, work on the *Dictionnaire* was suspended. L.T. says that when peace came the task was resumed and carried out with great care by old friends of the deceased author.

It is not clear to what extent further writing of the *Dictionnaire* was done after it arrived at Lemerre's establishment. The most authoritative statement on the subject appears to be that of André Maurois, who says that Lemerre charged Leconte de Lisle and Anatole France with the task of reorganizing and completing the work. This phraseology suggests that quite a lot was done to Dumas's manuscript, including the addition of new material. However, Maurois also records that Mme Maurois, when a young girl, had visited Anatole France, by then an old man, from time to time, and had asked him about his part in the composition of the *Dictionnaire*. Anatole France replied: 'I should have been proud to have written the book. But one must leave to the credit of Dumas what belonged to him. I was only a corrector of proofs—and sometimes a *commentateur*.' The last word is ambiguous; and we have no corresponding statement from Leconte

Introduction

de Lisle. A certain mystery, which will probably never be dispelled unless the manuscript used by the printers comes to light, thus shrouds the final stages in the preparation of the book for the press.

Publication of the Dictionnaire

The book eventually came out bearing the date 1873. The copy delivered to the Bibliothèque Nationale, which I have inspected, bears a notation showing that it arrived there in 1872. It thus seems clear that the printing of the book had been finished in 1872, although its official publication took place in the following year.

It never went into a second edition. Indeed I have been told on good authority that when the house of Lemerre was wound up in the 1950s there were still, in the basement, unsold copies of the first edition, and that these were not included in the sale, but destroyed.

In 1882, Lemerre published an abridged edition of the book under the title *Le Petit Dictionnaire de Cuisine*. The edition was small, and this is a rarer book than the original. It is much more compact in form and substance. A lot of the anecdotal material by Dumas was sacrificed, and the number of recipes drastically reduced. For example, only two recipes for sole were included instead of fifteen. This version of the book has never been reprinted.

The destruction of the surviving copies of the first edition seems to have provided the opportunity for a small spate of modern editions. These are listed in the bibliography. That of 1958 contained a preface by André Maurois and a foreword by Raymond Oliver. Otherwise it simply reproduced the text of the dictionary, from A to Z, reset in an attractive way. This and the similar edition of 1968 are the most agreeable versions of the book to handle. The other editions form a family. They all contain the text of the dictionary, again reset but this time in two columns to the page, with numerous illustrations from nineteenth century sources (mostly unidentified) and with a small collection of comments and corrections, by Jean Arnaboldi, added at the end. The cover design varies from maroon and gilt to white and black. These are bulky books.

The French attitude to the Dictionnaire

This has been one of polite homage, accompanied by little real interest (witness the 85 years which elapsed before a new edition came out) and virtually no analysis or criticism.

I referred above to some comments and corrections by Jean

Arnaboldi. These are discreet, almost obsequious in tone. ('Is it possible, dear Master, that in writing this entry, you somehow over-looked . . .' is the sort of thing one finds in it.) Also, by some miracle, Arnaboldi managed to single out for correction at least two points on which Dumas had actually been right; for example, the number of eggs produced by a female cod, and the statement that rays and skates are not at their best when absolutely fresh.

The preface by André Maurois, also referred to above, is an elegant and kindly piece of writing. Maurois observes that Dumas obtained much interesting material during his voyages abroad, and that *la cuisine exotique* held no more secrets, so far as he was concerned, than the cuisine of his mother and grandmother. If this meant that Dumas was fully informed about the cookery of people in other countries, it is not merely too kind a statement, but a mistaken one.

What no French admirer or critic of Dumas has ever done, to the best of my knowledge, is to subject the text of the *Dictionnaire* to a critical examination; to consider why it treats some subjects at great length and others of apparently equal importance in a few words; to analyse the source material used by Dumas (as opposed to simply listing the sources which Dumas himself acknowledges); to note what source material was available to him but not used; to make a systematic list of his errors (by which I mean errors in relation to the knowledge current in 1870, not errors which could only be detected later, when knowledge of the subjects which he treated had become more profound); or to relate the skimpy and unsatisfactory material about cookery in other countries to Dumas' own family background and personal experiences.

I hope that some French scholar will one day undertake these tasks. Meanwhile, at the risk of seeming over-bold, I offer some comments of my own.

A brief critical examination of the Dictionnaire

The first thing which struck me on reading through the dictionary was its lack of balance. A certain imbalance, reflecting the varying degrees of enthusiasm which Dumas felt for this or that foodstuff and the varying extent to which he had personal knowledge of these, was to be expected and indeed to be desired. But what are we to make of these contrasts?

Milk has an entry of half a page only. The hocco, a wild bird of South America, has nearly two pages. Cheese has one and a half pages. Cocoa has six; amber more than five.

Vuillemot, as shown in the first edition.

The section headed *Cuisine, Cuisinier, Cuisinière* occupies nineteen and a half pages. Of these, no fewer than seventeen are devoted to Spanish cookery.

A second point which quickly appears from a study of the text is that, while Dumas acknowledges his indebtedness to certain authors and attributes some passages to them, he borrowed more than he would have had his readers believe. See, for example, the first part of the entry on chocolate.

This leads me to make some general comments on his sources. The main ones which he acknowledges are the following.

(a) His friend Denis-Joseph Vuillemot, a well-known chef of English ancestry, who seems not to have published anything himself, but was Dumas' principal adviser on cookery. Lemerre, the publisher of the *Dictionnaire*, inserted at the beginning of the original edition a letter from himself to Vuillemot, which read in part as follows. 'Since Alexandre Dumas is no longer with us, to say how much you provided for his *Grand Dictionnaire de Cuisine*, just as much in the form of original recipes as in the form of advice from a skilful practitioner of the art, I think that I should discharge on his behalf a debt which he would have loved to discharge himself, and to thank you in his name.' The close relationship between Dumas and Vuillemot is illustrated by extracts from the *Dictionnaire* quoted in Appendix 1.

(b) *La Physiologie du Goût*, by Brillat-Savarin. This book appeared in 1826, anonymously. It is one of the main classics in any language in the field of gastronomy. Its construction is an impeccable piece of literary architecture. Its style is uniformly felicitous. Its content was such as to pre-empt many aspects of gastronomy from treatment by anyone else, except someone prepared to say less well what Brillat-Savarin had already said in a manner both definitive and perfect. Dumas borrowed much material from this book, sometimes acknowledging the source and sometimes not.

(c) The *Almanach des Gourmands*, by Alexandre-Balthazar-Laurent Grimod de la Reynière was an earlier work (first published in 1803 and then reappearing annually, with changed contents, until 1812). It falls into the same category as Brillat-Savarin's work, but contains a higher proportion of practical advice and a smaller proportion of what might be called 'the philosophy of gastronomy'. It too was elegant in construction, clearly written and inevitably pre-emptive on a number of subjects. Dumas often refers to Grimod de la Reynière, with a respect which the earlier author fully deserved.

(d) Urbain Dubois is given as the source of many of the recipes in Dumas' book. He is frequently described as *cuisinier de Leurs Majestés Royales de Prusse*. The main works which he had published before 1870 were *La Cuisine classique* (with Émile Bernard) and *Cuisine de tous les pays*. The latter book was published in 1868, just before Dumas set to work on the *Dictionnaire*.

(e) M. le Comte de Courchamps is often cited as the source of recipes. His work, which is now exceedingly rare, was first published in 1839 under the main title *Néo-Physiologie du Goût*. The author's name was not given. The dedication was to the author of the *Mémoirese de la Marquise de Créquy* (see below). The book reappeared in 1853 under what had previously been its sub-

Introduction

sidiary title, namely *Dictionnaire général de la Cuisine française ancienne et moderne*.

(f) Dumas makes constant references to *l'auteur des Mémoires de Madame de Créquy* (sometimes spelled *Créqui*). These memoirs, which were extensive and which contained only incidental material about gastronomy, were first published in 1834–5. Later editions were produced, for example in 1865; and it has been suggested to me that the frequency with which Dumas refers to the *Mémoires* may have been due to encouragement from their publishers. This seems possible. However, the whole matter has a further dimension. The unnamed author of the *Mémoires* was none other than Maurice Cousin, le comte de Courchamps, the very person who is mentioned above. It seems to me likely that Dumas chose to refer to him sometimes by his name and sometimes as the author of the *Mémoires*, on the principle of elegant (although in this instance rather verbose) variation, or in order to mask the full extent of his indebtedness to this single source.

(g) Carême, one of the most famous of all French chefs and cookery writers, is cited in several places by Dumas and is also accorded an entry all to himself in the *Dictionnaire*. It is evident from Dumas' 'One More Word to the Public' (page 37) that he had to negotiate with Carême's publishers for the right to reproduce some of his recipes; and this special entry may have been part of the price paid.

(h) M. de Beauvilliers, author of *l'Art de Cuisinier* (Paris, 1814), is another source frequently cited by Dumas.

The authors and works mentioned above all had to do with gastronomy or cookery. Dumas makes few references to authors who wrote on specialized subjects, such as game or fish or natural history. He was evidently aware of some such works, for he mentions natural historians such as Cuvier and Valenciennes, but he does not give the impression of having studied their writings. It is also abundantly clear that he completely neglected certain authoritative works which he could have used to make his own work more correct. A clear example of this failure is provided by his entries on freshwater fish. Émile Blanchard had published in 1866 his work on *Les Poissons des Eaux douces de la France*. This is an admirable book, written with that grace and lucidity to which the French language lends itself so readily, and combining full scientific details of the various fish with illuminating and highly readable historical and cultural material. Comparing what Dumas had to say about these fish with what

Blanchard had written some years earlier is enough to bring a frown to any brow.

Nor was Dumas accurate in dealing with sea fish, which happen to be my own subject. Given that he was writing the book at the fishing port of Roscoff, some of his errors seem very strange.

Similar faults can be found with his work in other categories of subject. We happen to have a copy of the less pretentious *Encyclopédie d'Economie domestique*, published under the direction of M. Jules Trousset from 1875 to 1879. The contrast between the knowledgeable and well-ordered entries in this work, which evidently represented the results of much hard work and careful consultation of the available literature, and the entries in Dumas' *Dictionnaire*, is striking.

We receive a similar impression if we study his recipes, and compare the presentation of his collection with contemporary works, such as those of Urbain Dubois and Jules Gouffé. The latter, in particular, who had published his *Livre de Cuisine* in 1867, was a master of the pen as well as of the kitchen. His collection of recipes, expounded in limpid prose, arranged in logical sequence, furnished impeccably with every detail which the cook need have, takes us into a world quite different from the antique anthologizing which provided most of Dumas' recipes and indeed most of his book.

However, although criticism of Dumas' work is justified and overdue, it would be wrong to make it according to criteria by which he himself was not guided. Dumas did not pretend to be either a scholar of natural history or a professional tutor in the culinary art. He implied himself that he had not taken to Roscoff a library of reference works, for 'I expected to complete my work on the simple basis of my memories, and no longer had the strength to do research or undertake fatiguing work'. In this, his last book, he was conveying to the world the miscellaneous information which he had gathered, reminiscing about the strange foods which he had met abroad, and telling all the amusing anecdotes which came back to him as he wrote at Roscoff.

His book is intimately linked with his personal experiences. Roscoff itself no doubt provided the amusing story about the onion-seller in England (page 196). England itself, which he visited on two occasions, provided interesting material (e.g. the entries on Plum-pudding and Whitebait). Tunisia was the source of one good anecdote; and Russia of several. The material about Belgian and Italian cooking is feeble, considering that he had lived in Brussels and spent several years in Naples; but his travels in Spain provided a richer vein

Introduction

of culinary lore. He drew also on his ancestral Santo Domingo, which comes up again and again. And he took advantage of his connection with the son-in-law of the governor of Java to serve up some titbits (often inaccurate) from that part of the world. All this, written in his vivid style, is irresistible reading, despite the errors.

Dumas had two aims in writing the book; that it should be used by the professionals, and read with enjoyment by the public. He made an error in trying to combine these aims; and I venture to say that the first was never fulfilled. The second can only be fulfilled if the readable material is extracted, which is what we have tried to do in this edition.

If we have helped in this way to promote his second aim, if the Folio Society now receive letters from ladies of a light disposition, stating that their fingers did not grow weary in turning over these pages (of which cf. page 38), and if sophisticated persons of both sexes find enjoyment in reading it, we shall be well content.

One result of working for eighteen months on this book has been to give us an admiration and affection for Dumas which was quite absent when we began. His genius was a warm one, which kindles a reciprocal warmth. The scale on which he operated was Gulliverian, which leaves ourselves, festooning tiny corrections and footnotes around his toes, both feeling and no doubt looking Lilliputian.

It is, however, pleasant to reflect that Dumas, during one of his visits to England, passed alongside the field on which our present house was later to be built. (He was en route to the old Cremorne pleasure gardens on the banks of the Thames, doubtless bent on some romantic or swashbuckling mission.) I have also taken pleasure in the thought that he hoped for an English edition of his book. In a document belonging to the last year or so of his life, a document which recently passed through the hands of M. Daniel Morcrette, the distinguished French antiquarian–gastronomic bookseller, he clearly expressed this hope, and the further hope that the English edition of his work would be profitable. He was nearing death's door at the time, and can scarcely have expected a financial profit for himself from an English edition. Let us construe his hope in a more general way and hope that those who read this book will derive from it some intellectual and emotional profit, such as it has afforded ourselves.

GLOSSARY

Part I—The Structure of French Meals
in the Nineteenth Century

Much of what Dumas wrote about food and many of his recipes can only be fully comprehended if one knows what a full-scale French dinner was like in his time. The pattern was variable, but markedly different from anything familiar to us today.

The first point to grasp is that a formal meal (and here we are speaking of dinners, as Dumas usually was) was divided not into courses, as we understand the term, but into *services*. Each *service* could comprise a number of what we would call courses, each of which in turn would comprise a choice of dishes from which each guest could select what appealed to him or her most. Here is an outline of a dinner of four *services*, accompanied by a commentary.

FIRST SERVICE

Potages	a choice of several soups would be offered
Hors d'œuvres	optional, and not unlike what we understand by the term, although more elaborate and possibly including hot items as well as cold
Relevés de potages	literally, what takes the place of the soups when these are cleared away—a variety of dishes which might include a *culotte* of beef, pike *à la Chambord*, etc.
Entrées	another 'course' of various dishes, usually hot and not unlike the preceding course

Glossary

SECOND SERVICE

Rôtis roast game and meats, of which several would be presented, preferably accompanied only by salads

Grosses pièces optional, but the second service could be the occasion for parading some really stunning creation like a whole sturgeon

THIRD SERVICE

Entremets a wide-ranging mixture of vegetable and other dishes (note that the word *entremets* has since assumed a different meaning, of sweets to be served after the dessert)

FOURTH SERVICE

Dessert a selection of fruits, compotes, pastries, etc., at the end of which would come ices and cheeses (if served)

During the nineteenth century there was considerable debate in France (limited, naturally, to those who were concerned with banquets and formal dinners) about the respective merits of *service à la française* and *service à la russe*. The former was the traditional French method. It involved placing on the tables all the dishes which were to be served in each *service*. The guests thus had the pleasure of seeing what they were to eat, in all the splendour of its decoration and entire. The dishes would then be taken away to be carved or otherwise prepared for distribution. All this took time, and some dishes suffered from being kept waiting. *Service à la russe* was introduced about 1860. Urbain Dubois was one of its chief proponents. According to this system the carving was done in advance and the food was brought in in relays, ready for immediate distribution. Thus people had things hot, if they were meant to be hot; and dishes which needed to be served as soon as they came out of the oven could be so served. But much of the visual pleasure was lost.

Another and more important distinction, which applied to every kind of meal, was that between *gras* (food with meat) and *maigre* (that without, which was all that Roman Catholics could eat on Fridays and other 'fast-days'). This provided a constant problem for cooks and was reflected in cookery books, where it was common to find, for example, alternative versions of a sauce, one *gras* and one *maigre*. Dumas' reflections on the whole subject are given in the entry headed Lenten fare and fast days (page 159).

Part II—Cooking Utensils and Equipment

We describe here only those utensils or pieces of equipment to which Dumas refers and which are unfamiliar, or relatively so in modern times, or which used to have different names.

Bain-Marie. At its simplest, the bain-marie is a large pan of simmering or hot water in which sits a smaller pan, the contents of which thus stay hot but do not boil. An elaborate bain-marie may accommodate many smaller pans simultaneously. A bain-marie is essential for sauces which must not boil. See the illustration on page 255.

Braisière. These were vessels designed for braising, of which a selection is shown. That on the left has a depressed lid, to accommodate hot cinders. The other two lack this feature and are designed rather for the braising of birds; but like the first they have close-fitting lids, essential for the braising process.

Casserole. This term is most often used nowadays to denote an earthenware or enamelled cast-iron cooking vessel with a lid, suitable for slow cooking of stews etc. In the nineteenth century it referred to a wide range of vessels, many of which we would call saucepans. A collection of French casseroles of various sizes and shapes is shown here. The two on the left have depressed lids for hot cinders. That on the far right is equipped with a tiny *pinceau* or brush and is in fact an early form of double-boiler; since the dotted lines show the position of an inner container, in which *glace* (meat essence for glazing) would be kept hot. This last device was also known as a *bain-marie à glace*. The vessels in

the above row are of a different kind. That on the left was for cooking saddles of venison, mutton or lamb. Its cover could be reversed to provide a receptacle for hot cinders. The other two were suited for the cooking of whole fillets of beef.

Chinois. This belongs to the family of devices for straining culinary preparations, of which another important member is the *tamis.* They are both shown here.

Chinois *Tamis*

Coupe-racine, etc. There were various devices for cutting vegetables, coring fruits and so on, some of them so constructed as to produce fancy shapes when used.

Four de campagne. Old French recipes, including many of those cited by Dumas, talk of cooking things in this 'country oven'. The drawing (right) shows what it looked like.

Marmites. Like the casseroles mentioned above, the *marmites* formed an important group of cooking vessels, which came in a wide range of sizes and were of varying shape. The picture below shows a pair of *marmites*, illustrating two different shapes, and, on the right, a single and large *marmite* made of copper. This last one was recommended with especial warmth by Gouffé (from whom the pictures come); and he also took the opportunity to advise his readers not to use *marmites* made of earthenware (which were sometimes called *huguenotes*) or of untinned cast-iron.

Pelle rouge and *Salamandre*. Nowadays, if we wish to brown the top of a dish, we place it under the grill for a few minutes. In former times the same effect was produced by using one of these two devices, which were heated until red hot in the fire and then passed to and from across the top of the dish.

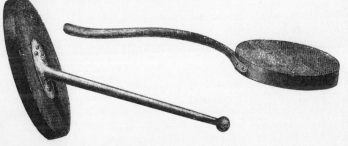

Poêlon and *Poêlon d'office*. These terms both refer to a sub-family of the category of casseroles. As shown in the drawings below they

had no lids and were equipped with pouring lips. They were not tinned, and their use was restricted to operations like blanching vegetables and (especially the small ones) melting sugar.

Terrine. This was a vessel suitable for making pâtés. It could be round in shape, or oval or oblong.

Part III—Miscellaneous Cookery Terms

This section of the glossary serves as a repository for certain short entries from the *Dictionnaire*, which are no more than culinary definitions. These are given in quotation marks, to show that they come from Dumas. Secondly, we define in our own words various culinary terms which have been left in French in our translation, either because there is no precise English translation or because the terms have become half Anglicized.

Beurre manié. Butter into which flour has been worked.

Blanquette. A white ragoût, based usually on white chicken meat or veal, cut up and cooked in a white sauce bound with egg-yolk and cream.

Bouillon. Stock or broth. See page 74.

Bouquet garni. A little bundle of herbs tied together and placed in something which is being cooked, to add aromatic flavours. The composition of the bundle varies. Parsley, thyme and a bay leaf is a common formula.

Braiser, which is to braise in English, means to cook something slowly, with a limited amount of liquid, in a tightly closed vessel.

Coulis. 'A preparation made in advance, and kept in the kitchen to finish off certain stews when the liquid needs to be thickened. A *coulis* should be neither too thick nor too light, and of a good cinnamon colour. To make it, put in a small saucepan some fillet of veal (the quantity depending on the amount of *coulis* required), some bacon cut up small and three or four carrots. Put all this on a low flame. When the juices of the meat have run out into the pan, raise the heat. When everything is cooked, remove the vegetables and meat. Add butter and flour to the pan and make a well-coloured roux. Add some hot bouillon to this, put the meat back in, cook for two hours on a low flame, sieve and then use as required.'

Court-bouillon. 'A sort of meatless fish stock, which serves as the basis of certain fish sauces. Cook together white wine, red wine, butter, chopped parsley, fines épices, bay leaves and fines herbes. Serve your fish, when it has been cooked [in the court-bouillon] on a napkin. . . . The court-bouillon called *au bleu* consists of boiling wine into which one puts the fish in order to give it a fine bluish hue.'

Croustade. This word refers to various dishes which can be described, with approximate accuracy, as pies. A flaky or puff pastry case, or a case made by hollowing out a round loaf or roll, is filled with, e.g., a ragoût or a *salpicon*.

Daube. The word is most often met in the phrase *en daube*, referring to the cookery of meat by braising in a seasoned red wine stock.

Demi-glace. A brown sauce usually made by boiling and skimming an espagnole sauce and adding to it some white stock or consommé.

Essence. A concentrate. For example, *essence de gibier* would be game stock reduced to the consistency of a jelly.

A l'étuve. This refers to cooking things in a drying oven, *étuve* being the word for drying-room (or sweating room in a Turkish bath!).

A l'étuvée. Not quite the same as the above expression. The meaning here is to cook something with no liquid, or almost none, in a tightly closed vessel. The spelling may be *étouffée*.

Feu dessus, feu dessous. Usually translated 'with heat above and heat below'. The cooking pot stands on a source of heat, such as a fire, but also has hot cinders set on its lid, which is depressed to accommodate them (as shown in drawings on page 29).

Fines épices. A pounded and sieved mixture of spices such as white pepper, red pepper, mace, nutmeg, clove, cinnamon, marjoram, sage and bay leaf.

Fines herbes. A nice problem. See page 140.

Fricassée. This term used to have a wide meaning rather like ragoût. Now it usually means a preparation of poultry in a white sauce.

Galantine. Galantines are compositions of several delicate meats arranged together in slices or in layers and cooked together.

Glace, glacer. The noun can mean meat glaze or ice, and the verb is likewise ambivalent.

Godiveau. A fine forcemeat from which quenelles are formed.

Larder. To lard. This is the culinary expression for the passing of lardoons through a piece of meat with a larding needle. In order to lard a piece of meat properly, the lardoons must be as big as half of the little finger, and well seasoned with salt and pepper. To lard the surface of meat only, thin slivers of bacon fat are used. In this case they are arranged symmetrically, and sometimes to make a design.

Lardons. Lardoons. These are small pieces of bacon fat which are used for larding meat. See above.

Liaison. This term is used in connection with the binding of a sauce by the use of a roux (flour cooked in butter) or a *coulis* (see page 32) or egg-yolks or some other binding agent.

Marmelade. See Jam, page 147, where the difference between this term and the English word marmalade is explained.

Mirepoix. A mixture of finely diced vegetables cooked slowly in butter, with seasoning. This is a *mirepoix au maigre*, so called because it has no meat in it. A *mirepoix au gras* would also contain a little diced ham or belly of pork.

Paner. To coat with breadcrumbs. This process is most frequently applied to pieces of meat or fish which are to be fried or grilled.

Paupiettes. 'These are slices of meat, covered with slices of bacon, on which a layer of stuffing is spread. They are then rolled up, skewered [to hold them together] and roasted, wrapped in cooking paper. When they are cooked, the paper is removed; and they are then coated with breadcrumbs, browned and served with a piquant sauce.'

Piment. An ambiguous word. It can mean red pepper (the fruit or the powder), or allspice (which is also referred to as *toutes épices*).

Poulette. A dish involving the presentation of such things as sheep's trotters or mushrooms in a velouté sauce bound with egg yolks and cream. Akin to a fricassée.

Praliné. Treated with a concoction of almonds and sugar.

Quatre épices. A mixture of spices pounded together; usually pepper, nutmeg, clove and ginger.

Quenelles. These may be large or small, round or sausage-shaped. They are essentially a kind of dumpling composed of forcemeat prepared from meat, game, poultry, fish or other seafood.

Ragoût. This word can be translated as stew, but this does not give exactly the right impression. We normally think of a stew as brown. However, ragoût has several meanings. It can mean a brown meat stew, with or without vegetables. But it can also be a *ragoût à blanc*, i.e. uncoloured because the meat has not first been browned. The word can also refer to a number of garnishes, which in turn can be bound with either a brown or a white liaison.

Rissole. 'A sort of pastry made with chopped meat and spices, enveloped in a pastry case and fried in lard. The first step is to make oval-shaped pieces of pastry, to be filled with a forcemeat made of the white meat of a capon, beef marrow, salt and pepper, the whole mixture being well chopped. Once the rissoles have been made, they can be conserved in lard.'

Rissoler. This verb means to cook meat or other foods until they acquire a reddish or brownish colour.

Rôt, Rôti. Two words which overlap in meaning. The first refers to a course in a meal, usually of roast meat or game, but may by extension refer to, say, a pâté or a cold roast lobster. The second can also mean the second service (see page 28) or can just mean a roast of meat, or something else which has been roasted.

Rôtie. A slice of bread which has been toasted or fried; and which may then be used as a base for various foods. A Welsh rarebit would be a sort of *rôtie*.

Roux. 'A roux is simply flour which is fried in butter or fat. It must be stirred constantly, so that it does not become lumpy. A roux is of great use in cooking meat *à l'etuvée* and in braising etc. . . . A roux is also used for colouring and binding sauces.'

Salmis. The term for a dish of game or other birds which is prepared in a complicated manner. The birds are two-thirds cooked, then cut up and finished off in a sauté dish (often at table) while the trimmings are used in the making of a sauce.

Salpicon. As the *Larousse gastronomique* puts it: in French cookery parlánce a preparation made up of one or more ingredients cut in small dice and bound with a sauce . . . *Salpicons* are used to fill pastry *barquettes*, or *croustades* or *timbales*. They can also be used as stuffing or made into croquettes. They may be hot or cold. *Salpicons* of fruit, fresh or candied, are used by confectioners.

Tarte. 'Layers of puff pastry, which may be covered with a *crème*, a compote of fruit, or jam.'

Tourte. 'A puff pastry in which various ragoûts are served as entrées.'

Toutes épices. Allspice (but see also *Piment*).

Vol-au-vent. 'A hot pastry, the bottom and sides of which should be made with puff pastry. A vol-au-vent contains either sweetbreads, chicken livers, the white meat of poultry, or mushrooms.' [Since the time of Dumas the number of possible fillings has increased.]

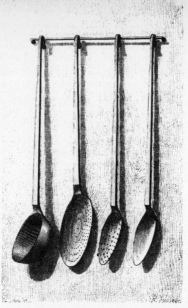

NOTE ON WEIGHTS AND MEASURES

Dumas often used weights and measures which were already obsolete when he was writing, although some of them may still have been in use in parts of France, or by elderly people. They have been converted in the recipes to modern equivalents. However, three points need explanation.

First, the meaning of the term *setier* varied considerably. If used for measuring things like grain, it meant 156 litres; whereas for liquids it meant just under ½ litre. These meanings themselves were not constant throughout the country. However, the usage in the *Dictionnaire* seems to have followed the Parisian usage, as noted above, and a *demi-setier* therefore means just under ¼ litre.

Secondly, we have normally translated *livre* as pound and *once* as ounce, since these are the approximate British equivalents. But the true equivalents are 490 grams (just over an English pound) for the *livre* and 30.5 grams (just over an English ounce) for the *once*.

Finally, Dumas often uses *une cuillerée à dégraisser* (a skimming-spoonful) as a measurement. Various skimming spoons were in use. We have assumed that what is meant is the one on the right hand side of the illustration, which holds about two of our tablespoonfuls.

ONE MORE WORD TO THE PUBLIC

[This short introduction occupies the last three of the hundred and five pages of prefatory and introductory material in the original edition.]

After I had decided to write this book and to crown with it, so to speak, in a time of relaxation, my literary work of four or five hundred volumes, I found myself, I admit, quite perplexed; not about its substance, but about the form to be given to the work.

Whatever my approach to it, people would expect of me more than I could give.

If I made of it a book of imagination and wit, like the *Physiologie du Goût* of Brillat-Savarin, the professionals, the cooks of both sexes, would pay no attention to me.

If I made of it a practical work, like the *Cuisinière bourgeoise*, the more sophisticated people would say: 'It would have been just about as useless for Michelet to tell him [Dumas] that he was the most skilful dramatist since Shakespeare, or for Ourliac to tell him that he possessed not only the French spirit but also that of Gascony, as for Dumas to come and teach us in a book of eight hundred pages how to skin rabbits and hares.'

This was not my aim. I wanted my book to be read by the sophisticated and used by the practitioners of the art.

At the beginning of the century Grimod de la Reynière had some success in publishing *l'Almanach des Gourmands*; but this was a straightforward book of gastronomy, not a book of recipes.

What especially tempted me, the indefatigable traveller who had voyaged through Italy and Spain, countries where one eats poorly, and through the Caucasus and Africa, countries where one does not eat at all, was to indicate all the ways of eating better in the former category of countries and of eating somehow or other in the latter category; granted that to achieve this result one would have to be prepared to do one's own hunting and foraging.

Here is the formula on which, after a lengthy deliberation with myself, I settled. To take from the classic cookery books which had passed into the public domain, such as the dictionary of the author of the *Mémoires de Mme de Créqui*, from the *Art du Cuisinier* of Beauvilliers, the most recent expert, from le père Durand of Nîmes, from the great collections of the epoch of Louis XIV and Louis XV, all the culinary recipes which have won citizens' rights at the best tables. To borrow from Carême, that apostle of the gastronomes, what

One More Word to the Public

Messieurs Garnier, his editors, would let me take. To take another look at the witty writings of the marquis de Cussy, and to appropriate for myself his best inventions. To re-read Elzéar-Blaz and, uniting my hunting instincts with his, to try to devise something new on the cookery of quails and ortolans. To add to all this some dishes which are unknown [here], gathered from all the countries of the world, with the most original and witty anecdotes about the cuisines of other peoples and about these peoples themselves. And finally, to deal with the physiology of all the animals and plants which are edible and which are worth describing.

In this way my book, containing both scientific knowledge and an element of wit, would not seem too daunting to the practitioners and would also perhaps deserve to be read by men of serious character—and even by women of a much lighter disposition, who would not fear that their fingers would grow weary in turning my pages, some of which resemble those of M. de Maistre [a notoriously boring writer] and others those of Sterne [the novelist].

This established, I begin, quite naturally, with the letter A.

P.S. Let me not forget to say, for such an omission would be an act of ingratitude, that I have consulted separately, for certain recipes, the great restaurateurs of Paris and even those in the provinces; such as the proprietor of the café Anglais, Verdier, Brébant, Magny, les Frères-Provençaux, Pascal, Grignon, Peter's, Véfour, Véry and, above all, my old friend Vuillemot.

Wherever they have had the kindness to place their knowledge at my disposition, there you will find their names. Let them receive here my thanks.

A.D.
(Alexandre Dumas)

ABSINTH (or WORMWOOD)   *ABSINTHE*

This perennial has very bitter leaves. It is to be found throughout Europe; and in the north a wine called vermouth is made from it.

There are two kinds of absinth, the great absinth called Roman, and the small kind called Pontic or Little absinth. The plant is also known under the name Marine absinth.* Both sorts, from the seaside and from the mountains, are eaten with pleasure. It is to the latter especially that the flavour of those animals whose meat is so esteemed by gourmands as *pré-salé* is due.

Even though all the old recipe collections vaunt absinth as a tonic for the stomach and an aid to digestion, and even though the Salerno school recommends it as a preventative against seasickness, it is impossible not to deplore the ravages which absinth has wrought over the past forty years among our soldiers and our poets. There is not a single regimental surgeon who will not say that absinth has killed more Frenchmen in Africa than the *flitta*, the *yatagan* [Arab weapons] or the Arab gun.

Some of our bohemian poets have called absinth the green Muse. Some others, not in this group, have died from the poisonous embraces of this same Muse. Hégesippe Moreau, Amédée Roland and Alfred de Musset, our greatest poet after Hugo and Lamartine, all succumbed to the disastrous effect of this liqueur.

The fatal passion of de Musset for absinth, which perhaps served also to give his verses such a bitter flavour, caused the sober Academy to fall into the near likeness of a pun. The fact was that de Musset missed many sessions of the Academy, finding himself not in a fit state to attend.

'In truth,' said M. Villemain, one of the Forty, 'do you not find that Alfred de Musset is *absent* a little too frequently?'

'You mean to say that he *absinths* himself too much.'

---

* It is not clear whether Dumas is talking of three varieties or two. In fact, there are three. *Artemisia absinthium* is the Common wormwood of Europe and North America. *Artemisia pontica* is known in English as Roman wormwood. It grows to about the same height as the Common wormwood. *Artemisia maritima* is smaller and typically grows in salt marshes. It is difficult to relate the French names cited by Dumas to these three varieties; but he must be referring to *Artemisia maritima* when he talks of *pré-salé* meat at the end of the paragraph.

ACANTHUS *ACANTHE*

This plant is very well known in art history. It has very large, glossy and pleasantly denticulated leaves which, because of their beauty and grace, have been used to adorn the capitals of Corinthian columns.

Vitruvius explains, in the following story, how acanthus leaves originally came to be used to decorate the Corinthian order. 'It happened that a young girl of Corinth died a few days before what was to be a happy marriage. Her desolated nurse filled a basket with various things which the young girl had liked, placed it on her grave, and covered it with a large tile to protect it from the ravages of the weather. By chance there was an acanthus root under the basket. In the following spring, the acanthus sprouted up so that its large leaves surrounded the basket, but were stopped by the edge of the tile. The leaves bent over and fell backwards. Callimachus, passing nearby, admired this sylvan decoration, and resolved to add to the Corinthian column this beautiful shape, which he had happened on by chance.'

The acanthus is fairly common in Greece, in Italy, Spain and the south of France, but it is only in Greece and Arabia that its raw leaves are eaten.

AGAMI (TRUMPETER) *AGAMI*

A type of bird belonging to the wader family. It is found in arid mountains and in high forests. In its wild state, this bird lives in large flocks in the forests of Guiana; but it can easily be domesticated, and its intelligence and characteristics then place it in the first rank of farm-yard animals. Daubenton says that 'the agami is the most interesting of all the birds, to judge by the praise bestowed on it. It is compared to the dog in respect to intelligence and faithfulness. It can be given a flock of poultry or a herd of sheep to guard, and will make itself obeyed, even though it is no larger than a hen. The agami is as strange as it is useful; and it is worthy of having a place in all farm-yards.'

The agami, in fact, is no more than about six decimetres tall, and seven decimetres long. Its conical beak is a dirty green; its eyes, which have yellowish brown irises, are ringed by a circle of bare reddish flesh. Short curly feathers cover its head, and the upper two thirds of the neck. The lower third is covered with bigger feathers which are not curly and are dark violet in colour. The throat and the upper part of the chest seem like a breast-plate, shining with the richest metallic reflections. The rest of the chest, the sides and the legs are black, as are the tail and wings.

One day when I was dining at a friend's in the country, just after the bell announcing the dinner hour had rung, we saw one of these birds entering the dining room.

The bird was hardly in the room when it started chasing the dogs and cats out, pecking at them with its beak, while neither dogs nor cats dared put up any resistance. Once this had been accomplished, it came to look at us, each in turn; and then, no doubt satisfied by the results of its inspection, went towards the master of the house and presented its head and neck, which the master hurried to scratch.

Unused to seeing a bird, at the very most only as large as a duck, acting in this fashion with the dogs and cats, and desirous of learning more about this peculiar animal, we bade our friend give us more information on the subject.

He then told us that, when he was travelling in French Guiana, he had noticed in Cayenne several of these birds preceding or following the colonists with every sign of great pleasure. He had then noticed others leading or shepherding flocks of ducks and turkeys, getting the birds in their charge to return at the usual hour, and then going and perching on a roof, or neighbouring tree. By this time curiosity had overtaken him and, wanting to possess two of these precious animals, he had asked his friends to let him have them, and had brought them back to France, not without fears for their safety during what was still a dangerous crossing.

Once back in the country, he was astonished to find that his foster-children were still very strongly attached to him and followed him everywhere. He had them put in the farm-yard, with the other poultry, where they lost no time in taking charge. Then, every evening, when the dinner bell rang, the two agamis could be seen arriving and chasing the dogs mercilessly right into their kennels, then returning to get their master to scratch their heads and necks, a caress of which they are most appreciative.

Our friend finished up by telling us very sadly that he had lost one of his agamis only a few days ago, when it had fallen from a roof top and broken its back. His interest in gourmandise caused him to taste its flesh, which he found delicious and certainly better than most of our chickens.

The meat of the agami is in fact very delicate, and very much sought after.

ALMONDS, SWEET AND BITTER
AMANDES DOUCES, AMANDES AMÈRES

Amande is the name given to the seed, which is enclosed in a hard skin, of all nut trees. One refers to the *amande* of the apricot, of the peach etc.; but here we are dealing specifically with the fruit of the *amandier* or almond tree which grows in Italy, in Provence, Languedoc and Touraine, and in Africa. The oil which it contains spoils quickly and is somewhat acrid. The almonds themselves are emollient, refreshing and nutritious, and they assuage coughs. Weak stomachs should not, however, be given the difficult job of digesting them in large quantities. Moreover, the skin of the almond, as it becomes older, is covered with a bitter dust which irritates the throat, brings on coughing and makes the almond more indigestible.

The bitter almond is not used as a food; it contains an acid known as prussic acid, or hydrocyanic acid. It is the most rapid and violent of poisons. One drop of prussic acid placed on the tongue or eye of an ox kills it on the spot. It is most frequently prepared from the kernel of the peach. If a case of poisoning with prussic acid occurs, but without producing results at lightning speed, because of the effects of evaporation or for some other reason, one must make the victim take a preparation of iron. In the case of indisposition following the eating of too large a quantity of bitter almonds, one should follow the same prescription.

With sweet almonds, one can make the following dishes:

Crème d'amandes · Almond cream

Blanch and grind 460 grams of sweet almonds; add just three bitter almonds, and strain the mixture after having diluted it with some boiling cream. Add some egg yolks and some double-strength orange-flower water, and let all this thicken in the top of a double boiler. One can garnish this dish with *praliné* almonds. Let us record here, in passing, that the best *praliné* almonds are those made at Bourges.

Gâteau d'amandes massif · Almond cake

Take a kilo of blanched, washed and ground sweet almonds, mixed with 15 grams of bitter almonds. Add the peel of candied lemon, angelica, sugared (*praliné*) orange blossom, a little salt, a kilo of sugar, seventeen egg yolks and only five egg whites. Mix all this together.

Butter a cake tin, line it with buttered paper, put in the mixture and cook it in a slow oven.

M. de Courchamps gives a piece of advice which I can but invite the reader to follow, which is to serve with this *entremets* a thin custard made with egg yolks into which you have poured, instead of ordinary milk, almond milk [a kind of almond paste made by pounding almonds and other ingredients with the addition of a little milk] and which you have cooked in a double boiler.

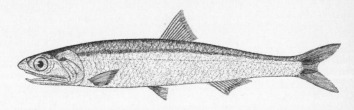

ANCHOVY   *ANCHOIS*

A sea fish, smaller than a finger, with no scales. [Dumas was misinformed. The anchovy has scales. But they come off at the slightest handling, so that when the fish reach the consumer they may well have none.] The anchovy has a big head, large black eyes, a very big mouth, a silvery body and a rounded back. It is found in abundance on the Provençal coast, and it is from there that it comes to us as *anchois confits* or as anchovies in a marinade.

The flesh of the anchovy has a delicate flavour. It may be grilled, and it is easy to digest. It may also be cured with vinegar and salt, which form a brine in which it is preserved. Preserved anchovy only appears on our tables as an hors d'oeuvre, or is used simply as a seasoning. It has, from its nature and from the way in which it is prepared, a stimulating quality which facilitates digestion when it is used in moderation.

Rôties d'anchois · Anchovy toasts

Fry long, thin slices of bread in oil, arrange them on a platter and pour over them a sauce made of virgin oil, lemon juice, coarsely ground pepper, parsley, spring onion and chopped Spanish garlic [*rocambole*, but ordinary garlic will do]. Half cover the slices of fried bread with anchovy fillets which you have dipped in white wine.

Anchovy

Anchois à la Parisienne · Anchovies in the Paris manner

Lift the fillets off some desalted anchovies. Chop hard-boiled eggs and chervil and burnet. Arrange the anchovy fillets on a platter in a pattern of lozenges, leaving a small empty space within each lozenge. Fill these spaces and the border of the platter with your chopped-up mixture of egg-yolk, egg-white and herbs, alternating them so that the colours are not mixed up. Then beat together some very fine olive oil, verjuice and coarsely ground pepper with a few drops of Chinese soya sauce. Pour this over the bottom of the dish so that it blends with the other seasonings.

ANETHUM   *ANETH*

A sort of wild celery or water parsley. There are two kinds:

Aneth ordinaire (ordinary anethum) has a single stalk which is slender, and white. The leaves are smaller than those of fennel, greenish and strong smelling; the flowers are pink, and the seeds a pale yellow. The flavour is mild, though aromatic. It is believed to have come from Germany or Italy originally. In the first of these countries it is used to season food, while in Italy the young leaves are eaten in salad like celery.

Aneth odorant (fragrant anethum) originally came from Spain or Italy, it is thought. Its stalk branches slightly, its leaves are feathery, its flowers yellow and small; and it is grown in gardens. Its smell is fragrant, though strong, and its taste is aromatic. It imparts a most agreeable flavour to fish.

The Romans garlanded themselves with aneth leaves during their banquets because of its pleasant aroma, and gladiators added it to their food to give it a greater tonic quality.

ANGELICA   *ANGÉLIQUE*

An aromatic plant, originally from Syria, which generally grows beside rivers which are close to mountains.

The Lapps regard it as a real treat. They eat the leaves and roots boiled in milk. They complete their dessert by chewing these and eating the berries, which they find under the snow.

The best angelica is made at Niort, where people have piously adhered to the tradition and methods of the sisters of the Visitation of Saint-Mary for making this excellent preserve.

44

ANGLER-FISH   *BAUDROIE*

A fish which is very common on the coast near Genoa, in the Channel and in the Atlantic. It resembles a tadpole [in shape, not in size] and is very clever at fishing for other, smaller fish, for which reason it has been given the nickname *grenouille pêcheuse* (fishing frog).

Its flesh is white and good, like that of the frog. The inhabitants of Languedoc eat it, just as they eat the frog.

ANISE   *ANISE*

An aromatic plant belonging to the family of umbelliferous plants; it is abundant throughout Europe, in Egypt and in Syria, in Italy and above all in Rome. It is the despair of foreigners who cannot escape from its taste or smell. It is put in pastries and in bread; and the Neapolitans put it in everything. In Germany it is the main seasoning of that bread which one finds accompanying figs and dried pears, and which has retained the name of *pompernick* (pumpernickel). This comes from the exclamation of a certain horseman who, having tasted one mouthful, immediately took the rest to his horse, which was called Nick, saying '*Bon pour Nick*', which with the German accent is *Pompernick*.

APPLE   *POMME*

Apples are eaten raw or stewed, in jams and *marmelades* [see page 147]. An agreeable cider, which is of good quality and keeps well, is also made from them. Sour apples, mixed with about a third of sweet apples, are mainly used for this.

The French provinces which are the most abundant in apples are Normandy, Auvergne and the Vexin français. Brittany also supplies a fairly considerable quantity.

Calville apples

Apple

The best apples to be eaten in winter are the *reinettes*, the *court-pendu*, the *pomme d'api* and the *calville*. There are three varieties of *calville*: the white, the red and the yellow. The red *calville* is the best of the three, this being the one which has red skin and flesh which is partly reddish. It contains a sweet juice and suits those who have acidity of the stomach, always assuming that only a few are eaten. *Reinettes* are particularly suitable for the bilious. But of all the apples the *court-pendu* is the best; its flavour is very agreeable, its flesh delicate and its aroma very sweet.

The *pomme d'api*, which is always eaten raw, is the smallest and the hardest of all the apples. It contains a juice which is full of flavour and very suitable for refreshing the mouth and quenching thirst; but its flesh is heavy and difficult to digest.

Bernardin de Saint-Pierre, one of the most famous of the sons of Normandy, gives in the following ingenious bit of fiction an account of the origin of apple trees in his province:

'The beautiful Thetis,' says he, 'having seen Venus carry off from under her very eyes the apple which was the prize for beauty, without herself being allowed to take part in the competition, resolved to seek revenge. So, one day when Venus had descended to part of the coast belonging to the Gauls and was searching there for pearls with which to adorn herself, and shellfish for her son, a Triton robbed her of her apple, which she had left on a rock. He then took it to the goddess of the sea; and Thetis immediately sowed its seeds throughout the neighbouring countryside to immortalize the memory of her revenge and of her triumph. This, say the Celtic Gauls, is the reason for the very large number of apple trees which grow in our land, and for the particular beauty of our girls.'

To avoid the expense incurred in weddings, Solon ordered the newly married to eat only one apple before going to bed on the first night of the marriage. This was hardly very substantial or very cheering for the poor newly-weds.

Pommes au beurre · Apples cooked with butter

With a corer remove the cores of about twenty beautiful apples. Peel nine or ten of these, as you would for making a compote, simmer them in lightly sugared water until they are three quarters cooked, and drain them. Cook the remaining apples in a casserole with a little butter, cinnamon and a glass of water until they have melted into a purée. Spread a part of this *marmelade* on a platter with a little apricot compote. Arrange the whole apples on this, fill the hole in the middle of each with butter and garnish the spaces in between the apples with the rest of the *marmelade*. Glaze with powdered sugar, and cook in the oven until they have turned a good colour. Plug the holes in the apples with cherries, or jam, and serve hot.

Charlottes de pommes · Apple charlotte

Peel and quarter about twenty beautiful French *reinette* apples. Remove the cores, and put the apple slices in a casserole with a little butter, cinnamon, lemon and a glass of water. Put a lid on the casserole, put it on a gentle fire and let the apples cook without stirring them. Let them stick very gently to the pan, to give them a slightly grilled taste. Add some sugar and some first-class butter. Let all this reduce, and keep stirring, until the *marmelade* thickens; then remove the cinnamon and the lemon. Cut some slices of soft bread, about the width of two fingers. Arrange these on the bottom and around the sides of a mould; in the middle of the mould put the apple *marmelade*, having mixed it with some apricot *marmelade* in order to make the dish more refined. Then, when the mould is filled, cover it with slices of bread and cook for about twenty minutes in an oven or on glowing coals. Let the charlotte take colour, turn the mould out on to a platter and serve. Don't forget to use clarified butter for buttering your bread. [For another version see page 93.]

APRICOT   *ABRICOT*

The tree which bears this fruit came to the Romans from Armenia; so they called it *prunus armeniaca*. To begin with, only two species of apricot were known, but a number of varieties have been obtained.

It is a fruit containing a nut. Its skin and flesh are tinged with the colour of chamois. It has a pleasant smell and a good taste, bearing some resemblance to the peach and the plum; and is such an early fruit that there are few springs when one does not hear people saying: 'There will be no apricots this year, they've all been caught by the frost.'

Apart from the various kinds of apricot which we gather in France, Chardin, during his voyage in Persia, ate excellent apricots which had red flesh and a delicious flavour. These are called *tocmchams*, meaning 'eggs of the sun'. It is at Damascus in Syria that one eats the best apricots. The people there make excellent apricot jams and cakes.

[Dumas proceeds to refer to a kind of apricot grown in Santo

Apricot

Domingo, his father's birthplace. In a footnote of a kind which occurs but rarely in his Dictionary, he says that he has taken the details from the *Dictionnaire des Aliments et des Boissons*, by M. Aulagnier, and implies that he has used this as a source of information about fruits all over the world, but especially in the French colonies.]

By means of this excellent fruit a delicious scent is given to sorbets and ices. It provides material for excellent cakes, fritters, tarts, flans, creams and conserves.

Tourte ou Gateau fourré d'abricots à la bonne femme ·
A 'tart' or 'cake' filled with apricots

Split and peel the apricots, cook them with a little sugar and let the resulting compote cool.

Arrange the half apricots on a layer of puff pastry, then cover them with a second layer of puff pastry. This upper layer should be slashed or pricked, so that it will not swell up and assume a crooked shape during the cooking. Brush the top and edges with egg-yolk, so that they will take on a golden colour, and cook the *tourte* in a *four de campagne*.

Mixing some cherries with the apricots produces an excellent effect, and this modern combination has been generally adopted in the leading kitchens of Paris.

Compote d'abricots à la minute · A quickly made compote of apricots

Make a syrup [of sugar] and, once it is thick enough, boil in it your apricots, split in half. After three minutes, skim the compote, add the juice of an orange and let it cool.

ARTICHOKE   *ARTICHAUT*

A comestible plant of which the leaves are long and wide, denticulated, non-uniform and green or whitish in colour. From its centre rises a fluted stalk, which is cottony and pithy inside, and from which spring branches, each of which bears a calyx enclosing the organs of efflorescence and fructification. Formerly this plant only grew in Italy. Today our gardeners have acclimatized it, and we have white artichokes, green, violet, red and sweet ones. The white, violet and green ones are full of flavour; the little ones, called *artichauts à la poivrade* (artichokes suitable for serving with pepper sauce), are eaten raw.

Artichokes can be preserved for winter in the following manner. Parboil them, separating the leaves and the chokes, so as to have only the hearts. Then throw these, still hot, into cold water. Afterwards, put them on racks to dry them; and finally put them in the oven up to four times, after taking the bread out. The hearts become thin, hard and transparent, but they regain their shape when they are put back into hot water, and can then be used in dressing or seasoning dishes as you wish.

Artichauts à la barigoule au gras · Artichokes *barigoule* with meat

Take some medium-sized very tender artichokes, trim them, remove the chokes and blanch them. Chop some parsley and mix it with 125 grams of butter and 125 grams of bacon, for about four artichokes. Stuff the interior of the artichokes, and arrange them so that they keep their shape. Place them in a pie dish between two thin rashers of bacon and cook slowly, with heat below and heat above. Oil them lightly. Reduce a glass of white wine in some Italian sauce [see page 256], and serve the artichokes on this sauce.

ASPARAGUS   *ASPERGE*

There is no point in describing this plant, which everyone knows. There is a white variety, a purple kind, and a green sort. The white is the earliest and its flavour is mild and agreeable, but it has little body. Those from Marchiennes, Belgium and Holland were renowned. The purple is the largest and the most substantial; it is above all the asparagus of Ulm and Poland. The green is smaller, but one eats almost all of it, and it has a good flavour. In Italy, where there is more of a taste for the unusual than for the refined, wild asparagus is preferred.

Carnivorous animals, such as cats and dogs, like this vegetable very much.

Asparagus

The best way of preparing asparagus, nowadays, is by steaming. There was a proverb in Rome relating to asparagus. When someone wanted something done in a hurry: 'Do that', he said, 'in less time than it would take to cook asparagus.'

After washing the stalks, scrape and cut them into pieces of the same length, tie them in bunches and cook them in salted water so that they remain crunchy. Serve them hot on a folded napkin, which drains them of any remaining drops of water.

Asparagus is eaten with butter or oil. On this subject we are going to tell you an anecdote about Fontenelle.

Fontenelle was very fond of asparagus, particularly when served with oil. Abbot Terrasson, on the contrary, preferred to eat them with butter. Having come one day to invite the abbot to dinner, Fontenelle said to him that he was making a great sacrifice in giving up half of his platter of asparagus, and ordered that this portion should be served with butter. A short while before going to table, the abbot felt ill, and soon had an apoplectic fit. At this Fontenelle rose hurriedly and ran to the kitchen, shouting: 'Dress all the asparagus with oil now; all of it with oil!'

Asperges au beurre · Asparagus with butter

Put two spoonfuls of flour in a pan with a little water; season with salt, coarsely ground pepper and nutmeg. Cook the flour, moistening it with the liquid in which the asparagus was cooked.

Use four egg yolks with 125 grams of choice butter to bind your sauce, taking care that the egg yolks are cooked. Strain the sauce, add some lemon juice and serve.

Asperges à la Pompadour

M. de Jarente, Minister of State when Madame de Pompadour was in favour, left the following prescription to our celebrated gourmand Grimod de la Reynière, a nephew worthy of his uncle.

'Choose three bunches of the most beautiful asparagus from large young Dutch plants, that is to say white ones with purple tips. Trim them, wash and cook them in the ordinary way, that is to say by plunging them in boiling water. Slice them afterwards by cutting them on the bias near the tip, into pieces the length of the little finger. Use only the best parts, setting aside the rest of the stems. Put the chosen pieces in a hot napkin so as to drain them and keep them hot while you prepare your sauce.

'Empty a medium-size pot of butter from Vanvre or Prévalais and put the contents in spoonfuls in a silver dish. Add a few grains of salt, a good pinch of powdered mace and a generous spoonful of pure wheat flour; and in addition the yolks of two fresh eggs diluted with four spoonfuls of the juice of sour muscat grapes. Cook this sauce in a double boiler; do not allow it to thicken excessively and thus become too heavy. Put your sliced pieces of asparagus in the sauce, and serve it all in a covered casserole as an extra, so that this excellent course does not languish on the table and can be appreciated at the height of its perfection.'

AYAPANA   *AYA-PANA*

A plant belonging to the genus *Eupatorium*, a native of Mauritius and Reunion; its leaves exude a pleasant aroma, and are supremely fortifying as an infusion. They are stomachic, aperient and sudorific. It was Admiral de Sercey who introduced them to France.

An infusion of ayapana is made in the same way as tea, but, as its aroma is very strong, twelve to thirteen leaves are enough for a six-cup tea pot. The best way to use this new aromatic is first to take it as one takes tea, and then to use it to flavour soufflés and ice creams. Ayapana blends excellently with egg yolks and cream.

M. de Courchamps tells us that nearly 300 francs were paid for 30 grams of ayapana, and this during an epidemic of cholera, for which it was an excellent remedy. At present one pays 80 to 90 francs for half a kilo.

[Ayapana was not the cure which Dumas chose for himself. The following passage is taken from the biography of Dumas by A. F. Davidson.

'One evening, when he came in, Catherine, the cook, said:

"Oh, sir! How pale you are!"

He scrutinized himself in a mirror, realized he looked terrible, and was seized with a chill.

"That's funny," he said. "I'm cold."

"Oh, sir!" cried Catherine. "That's how it always starts."

"What?"

"The cholera, sir!"

"My God! We haven't a second to lose! Quick, a piece of sugar dipped in ether, then the doctor!"

As he felt his strength was waning (perhaps from auto-suggestion), he got into bed.

Catherine came into his room. The poor girl had taken leave of her senses. Instead of a piece of sugar dipped in ether, she brought him a wineglass full of ether. Dumas, no longer knowing what he was doing either, grabbed the glass out of the servant's hands and in a single gulp downed the contents. It seemed to him he had swallowed Gabriel's sword, and he fainted dead away.

When he came to, his physician was at his side, and the cholera had disappeared. Unintentionally, this universal genius had discovered a remedy for the plague. At least this is how, in his *Mémoires*, he tells the story.']

BABA   *BABA*

'The baba is a cake of Polish origin, which should always be served in a size large enough to act as a *grosse pièce* and *entremets*, and remain for several days on the sideboard as a standby.

'As far as the origins of the cake go, it seems that it was actually King Stanislas Leczinski, father-in-law of Louis XV, who introduced it to France. When babas are served in the households of the august descendants of this good king (it is not I who recount this, but Carême), they are always accompanied by a sauceboat which contains sweet Malaga wine mixed with a sixth part of *eau de Tanésie* [the usual spelling is *tanaisie*, meaning tansy, and the product is a volatile oil obtained from the tansy plant by distillation]. Through Mme la Contesse Risleff, née Countess Potoka and a relative of the Leczinskis, we learn that the real Polish baba had to be made with rye flour and Hungarian wine.

'Sometimes one sees in Paris small babas, which have been made in small moulds, but these dry out too easily to permit approval of this economical method, which in any case is used only by commercial *pâtissiers* . . .'.

If you want to make a baba in smaller proportions, but nevertheless closely following the traditions of the Luneville* court from which neither a pastry-maker like Carême nor a gastronome like M. de Courchamps wished to deviate, take this recipe from the book on pastry-making by Audot:

Use the same sort of leavening as you would for brioche, and in the same proportions, for making the dough; but keep it a little thinner. Once this mixture is made, put the dough together, and

* The Polish court had been transferred to Luneville. Stanislas adored *The Thousand and one Nights*; hence the name.

52

make in it a well into which you put 15 grams of powdered sugar, 30 grams of Madeira or Malaga wine or rum, 45 grams of muscat raisins (picked from the bunch and cut in two), a similar quantity of currants, 8 grams of preserved citron (cut in thin strips) and a little powdered saffron. This mixture should be given the same consistency as that of the leavening, by adding either an egg or some cream. Put the dough in a buttered mould which is two or three times larger in volume than the dough. Arrange it so that the raisins do not touch the sides of the mould, where they would stick, and leave it to rise in a warm place until it is well risen. Then cook it for an hour and a half at a very low heat. The baba will be perfect when it assumes a reddish colour. It is preferably served hot.

BACON   *LARD*

The meat of the pig is usually heavy and indigestible, particularly for people who take little exercise. But when salt has hardened it, and it has been dried by smoking, it is even more harmful. This is true of bacon.

Bacon fat, moreover, which habitually becomes rancid and bitter, can only have a bad effect on the stomach, and sometimes blisters the mouth and the throat.

What is called bacon is a piece of pig which has a little flesh attached to the rind, and which one adds to the cooking pot. The bacon which comes from pigs which have been fed on acorns is firmer than that which comes from pigs fed on bran, and consequently better.

BALACHAN or BLACHAN   *BALACHAN*

This is a paste which is made in Siam and Tonkin, from shrimps. The shrimps are pounded with salt to form a sort of thick salty preparation, which is then 'cooked' in the sun for several days. Care is taken to stir it from time to time, a procedure which spreads far and wide a frightful smell.

This paste, taken in place of butter, strengthens the stomach and excites the appetite. In Tonkin it is called *nuxman* and is eaten with rice and used for seasoning meat.

[Dumas has confused *blachan*, which is a sort of fermented shrimp paste which is called by that name in Malaysia and by others in other

Balachan or Blachan

parts of South-East Asia, with the famous fish sauce of Indochina and Thailand. This is a liquid, not a paste. Its name in Vietnam is *nuoc-mam*. It is, as stated by Dumas, taken with rice and used as a condiment for meat etc.]

BAMBOO   *BAMBOU*

A large Indian reed from which canes are made. It contains a juice of which the Indians are fond; from each joint oozes a sweet syrup which the heat of the sun converts into drops of sugar. The only sugars known in antiquity were cane sugar and bamboo sugar.

Bamboo shoots, with vinegar and mustard make a pickle which is named after its inventor, Achar.

BANANA TREE   *BANANIER*

This tree is found in both the East Indies and the West Indies. In the Orient, the banana is considered to be the forbidden fruit which our grandmother Eve bit into. It serves the poor there in the same way that potatoes serve our workers here. In the Antilles and Cayenne, a wine which bears the name of banana-wine is made from bananas.

BARBEL   *BARBEAU, BARBILLON*

A fish endowed with two names, but nonetheless one fish. [This entry is given under the two names *Barbeau* and *Barbillon*. But the second is simply the diminutive of the first, and is applied to small specimens.] It is oblong in shape and of medium size. It is covered with fine scales; and owes its name to some filaments of flesh which serve as a moustache.

Its eggs act as quite a strong purgative. So it is not a bad idea to remove them from the body before cooking the fish, since their mere presence within it could produce tiresome results.

Take a barbel of middle size, enough for four people, gut it, scale it and carefully wipe it clean. Then put it in an earthenware dish with four soupspoonfuls of oil, three pinches of salt and three pinches of pepper. Half an hour later, grill it over a moderate fire. Then place it on a serving dish, cover it with 100 grams of maître d'hôtel sauce [see page 256], sprinkle some lemon juice over it and serve it thus.

You can eat barbel *en matelote*, in adding it to the carp and the eel. It is indispensable for a *matelote marinière*.

Barbillon à l'etuvée · Small barbel, stewed

Scale and gut your small barbels, then cook them with red wine (that of Burgundy is best), salt and pepper, a clove, a bouquet garni and a large lump of butter. When they are cooked, bind the sauce with a little more butter into which you have worked some ordinary flour or rice flour.

BARLEY   *ORGE*

According to Fleuri, barley was the first cereal cultivated as a food-stuff for man. The flour which comes from this grain contains practically no gluten, but a great deal of starch. This starch is united with a mucilaginous substance which results in the bread made from it being very indigestible and pretty unsavoury.

Barley, when its thin outer covering has been removed, can be used instead of rice. In Germany it is much used to garnish soups and in the making of various *entremets*.

BARRACUDA   *BÉCUNE*

A kind of sea pike, very voracious and greedy. This fish, whose voracity leads it to swallow everything, will sometimes eat even the fruits of the manchineel tree, which constitute a caustic and strong poison; and for this reason consumption of its flesh is quite dangerous.

Otherwise, the flesh of the barracuda is white, firm and fairly fat. It has the same nutritional properties as that of the pike. However, one must take great care, before preparing it as food, to assure one-self that its teeth are really white and its liver perfectly healthy, in order to avoid the risk of being poisoned.

BAY LEAF   *LAURIER*

In cooking, only the *laurier franc*, or Apollo's bay leaf,* is used; and

* According to the Greek myth, the maiden Daphne, fleeing from the lecherous advances of Apollo, was changed into a bay tree. In contrition, he, as God of Medicine, took the bay tree as the symbol of his power to protect against harm.

it is used frequently. It is put in all bouquets garnis, which are an obligatory seasoning for all stews. But it must be used in moderation, and preferably dried, so that its flavour is less strong, and less bitter.

BEANS   *HARICOTS*

Beans are eaten in three ways, and at three different stages of their development Before they are fully grown, they are eaten with their seeds, and are then called green beans. Just before they are fully mature, the seeds, which are still tender, are eaten; and they are then called flageolets. Finally, they are much eaten in dried form, and are then known, irrespective of where they come from, as beans from Soissons.

As I come from the *département* of Aisne, it is up to me to assert the worth of my compatriots and, until my last trip to Asia, I had always declared that Soissons beans were the best in the world. But I have now been forced to acknowledge the superiority of the beans from Trebizond.

But, whether from Trebizond or Soissons, dried beans have one serious disadvantage. There are some waters in which they refuse to cook. Science must then battle against nature. In this case, prepare a little cloth bag, knotted together and containing new wood ash, and put it in the cooking water; or, better still, a little bicarbonate of soda. Even the most refractory bean will be defeated by this treatment.

BEAR   *OURS*

There are few people of our generation who do not recall the sensation caused by the first instalment of my *Impressions de Voyage* when people read the article entitled 'Bear steak'. There was a universal outcry against the audacious narrator who dared to say that there were places in civilized Europe where bear is eaten.

It would have been easier to go to Chevet, and ask him if he had bear hams.

He would have enquired without a trace of surprise: 'Is it a Canadian leg or one from Transylvania which you wish?' And he would have furnished whichever he was asked for.

I could at that time have given to readers the advice which I give them today, but I took good care not to; there was a big commotion about the book, and since at that time I was just embarking on a literary career I could ask for nothing better.

But to my great astonishment, the person who should have been most pleased by the uproar, the innkeeper, de Martigny, was furious; he wrote me to upbraid me, he wrote to the newspapers to get them to state in his name that he had never served bear to his travellers; but his fury kept increasing as each traveller asked him as their first question: 'Do you have any bear?'

If the stupid man had thought to answer yes, and then served ass, horsemeat or mule instead of bear, he would have made a fortune.

Since that time we have become more civilized; bear hams have become a dish which one doesn't meet in every salted-provision dealer's premises, but which one can find without too much difficulty.

The brown bear is commonly found in the Alps; the grey bear, the most implacable of all, who first puts the horse to flight and then its rider, is to be found in America. There are in Canada and in Savoy reddish bears who don't eat meat, but who are so partial to honey and milk that they would rather be killed than let go when they are holding a honeycomb or a jug of milk. Black bears only live in cold countries. The forests and countryside of Kamtschatka are full of bears who only attack when they are attacked themselves; and a peculiar thing is that they never harm women, whom they nevertheless follow, to steal the fruit which they are gathering.

When the Yakuts, a Siberian people, meet a bear, they doff their caps, greet him, call him master, old man or grandfather, and promise not to attack him or even to speak ill of him. But if he looks as though he may pounce on them, they shoot at him and, if they kill him, they cut him in pieces and roast him and regale themselves, repeating all the while: 'It is the Russians who are eating you, not us.' (A-F. Aulagnier, *Dictionnaire des Aliments et des Boissons*.)

Bear meat is now eaten by all the peoples of Europe. Since ancient times, the front feet have been regarded as the best part of the animal. The Chinese have a high regard for them, and in Germany, where meat from the bear cub is greatly enjoyed, the front feet are a delicacy for rich people.

Here, according to M. Urbain Dubois, the cook of Their Majesties of Prussia, is the way in which these feet are served in Moscow, Saint Petersburg and throughout all of Russia. The paws are sold skinned. One starts by washing them, salting them, putting them in a terrine and covering them with a marinade cooked with vinegar, in which they are allowed to steep for two or three days.

Then line a casserole with bacon and ham trimmings and chopped vegetables. Lay the bear's feet on the vegetables, cover them with the marinade, some bouillon and some bards of bacon; let them cook for seven or eight hours on a very low flame, adding liquid as it reduces.

When the paws are cooked, leave them in the liquid until they are nearly cold. They should then be drained and wiped, divided lengthwise in four, sprinkled with cayenne pepper and rolled in melted lard. Roll them in breadcrumbs and grill them gently for half an hour. Then arrange them on a platter into which you have poured a piquant sauce (reduced, with two spoonfuls of currant jelly added as a finishing touch).

BEEF   *BŒUF*

People complain of decadence in cuisine. This decadence is much more often the work of the masters than that of their servants. Formerly, the great gastronomes like Marshal Richelieu, the Duc de Nivernais and the Comte d'Escur used to summon their maîtres d'hôtels at least once a week to ask how they were getting on with culinary discoveries. These learned conversations between master and servant brought about great advances in the science of gastronomy, by confronting the master with practical cookery on a big scale, and the cook with the theory of his art, also on a grand scale. When the Duc de Nivernais had to change his chefs, or they had learned some novelties which seemed to him acceptable, he was sufficiently patient and conscientious to have them served for eight days in a row, and to taste them each day, in order to give his directions in such a way that the new dish would finish up virtually perfect. He had such a well-developed palate that he could tell if the white of a poultry wing came from the same side as the gall.

As for M. de Richelieu, it was mainly the practical aspects which he knew better than the best maître d'hôtel. Sometimes an anecdote is more telling than the rule of three. It was during the Hanoverian war, when the country surrounding the French army was devastated for more than eighty kilometres roundabout. All the princes and princesses of East Frisia, numbering twenty-five, had been taken prisoner; and to these should be added a reasonable number of ladies-in-waiting and chamberlains. Marshal Richelieu had resolved to set them free, but before releasing them, he fancied giving them a dinner, a plan which reduced his chefs to despair.

However, when M. de Richelieu had resolved on something, it absolutely had to be carried out. He called together his chefs.

'What do you have in the canteen, gentlemen?' he inquired.

'My lord, nothing.'

'What do you mean, nothing?'

'Nothing at all.'

'But just yesterday I saw two horns pass by the window.'

'That is true, my lord, there is an ox, and a few root vegetables, but what can you do with that?'

'What I want to do, by Heaven, and what I am going to do with that is to produce the best dinner in the world.'

'But, my lord, it simply can't be done.'

'Come now, what do you mean "it can't be done"? Rudière, write out the menu which I am about to dictate to you. It is all cut and dried for these bewildered people of Chaillot. Do you know how a menu is set out, Rudière?'

'But, my lord, I swear . . .'

'Give me your chair and your pen.'

And now we see the generalissimo taking his secretary's place, and improvising a classic dinner, the menu for which has been kept in the collection of M. de la Poupelmière. Here is how this handwritten broadsheet reads:

MENU D'UN EXCELLENT DINER TOUT EN BŒUF

DORMANT

Le grand plateau de vermeil avec la figure équestre du Roi;
Les statues de Duguesclin, de Dunois, de Bayard et de Turenne;
Ma vaisselle de vermeil avec les armes en relief écaillé.

PREMIER SERVICE

Une oille à la garbure gratinée au consommé de bœuf

QUATRE HORS-D'ŒUVRE

Palais de notre bœuf à la Sainte Menehould.	Les rognons de ce bœuf à l'oignon frit.
Petits pâtés de hachis de filet de bœuf à la ciboulette.	Gras-double à la poulette au jus de citron.

RELEVÉ DE POTAGE

La culotte de bœuf garnie de racines au jus
(*Tournez grotesquement vos racines, à cause des Allemands.*)

SIX ENTRÉES

La queue du bœuf à la purée de marrons.	La noix de notre bœuf braisée au céleri.

Sa langue en civet (*à la bourguignonne*).

Les paupières du bœuf à l'estafoulade aux capucines confites.

Rissolés de bœuf à la purée de noisettes.

Croûtes rôties à la moelle de notre bœuf. (*Le pain de munition vaudra l'autre.*)

SECOND SERVICE

L'aloyau rôti (*Vous l'arroserez de moelle fondue*).

Salade de chicorée à la langue de bœuf.

Bœuf à la mode à la gelée blonde mêlée de pistache.

Gâteau froid de bœuf au sang et au vin de Juranson (*ne vous trompez pas*).

SIX ENTREMETS

Navets glacés au suc de bœuf rôti.

Tourte de moelle de bœuf à la mie de pain et au sucre candi.

Aspic au jus de bœuf et aux zestes de citron pralinés.

Purée de culs d'artichauts au jus et au lait d'amandes.

Beignets de cervelle de bœuf marinée au jus de bigarades.

Gelée de bœuf au vin d'Alicante et aux mirabelles de Verdun.

Et puis tout ce qui me reste de confitures ou conserves

Si, par un malheureux hasard, ce repas n'était pas très-bon, je ferai retenir sur les gages de Maret et de Rouquelère une amende de 100 pistoles. Allez, et ne doutez plus.

RICHELIEU

M. Vuillemot, who relates this anecdote with pleasure, never fails to accompany it with some learned comments. According to this skilful operator, the *tourte à la moelle* which the gallant marshal ordered is a heretical dish; *pied de bœuf à la poulette* is quite wrongly left out of the menu; the *beignets de cervelles* are an hors d'oeuvre and cannot become a side dish, however much the irresistible duke might wish it to be one. M. Vuillemot observes that, unfortunately for this bovine menu, *gras-double à la mode de Caen* was unknown in the eighteenth century.

Buffon has said that one would have great difficulty in living without the ox. The earth would remain a waste land, fields and even gardens would be dry and barren. It is the servant of the farm, and the support of the farming community. It constitutes the strength of agriculture; and the ancients therefore considered it a crime to eat its flesh. Pliny recounts that a citizen was banished for killing an ox. Valerius Maximus says the same thing. Greeks used not to eat it, because of their respect for this animal which ploughs the fields.

In Hindu villages anyone who eats of its meat is regarded as infamous. The Egyptians consulted Apis, the ox, as an oracle. Perhaps it is a remnant of this veneration which causes a fat ox to be paraded in Paris each year.

This animal changes its name according to its age. First it is calf, then young bullock, and finally ox. There are several species, varying in size and weight. Those in Egypt, for example, are bigger than those in Greece. The same is true in France, where our best cattle come from Auvergne and Normandy.

When America was discovered there were no cattle there. But they were brought in by the Spaniards, multiplied considerably, and have since become one of the favourite dishes in America, where they claim, as the English do, that beef is superior to all other meats in every way, and for everyone. Its meat is the one in most general use, it is very nourishing, and the digestion copes with it easily if it is of good quality. Nevertheless, it is not equally good in all countries; and its quality also varies according to the pasture. The meat is excellent when the animal is young and fat and in general suits everyone, but most of all those who have a good stomach, take a lot of exercise and require nourishing food. Sedentary persons, convalescents and people with weak digestions should not make use of it without considering whether they are up to doing so. Beef is also the meat which produces the best bouillon.

We are now going to give a few of the numerous ways in which beef can be prepared and eaten.

Beef

The cuts which are most sought after are the rump, sirloin, pope's eye, ribs and shank. The shoulder, which the butchers call *paleron*, is less good than the lean parts. Flank and chuck and the head are the least prized cuts, just as the filet mignon is the most prized. Let us leave aside the brains, which are rarely good in beef, given the French method of killing the animals by a stunning blow. A variety of fairly delicate dishes are made from the tongue and palate. The kidneys are the coarsest part of the ox, even though they are frequently used to make kidneys with champagne. Since the natural destiny of beef seems to be producing bouillon, let us start the list of beef dishes by giving that for boiled beef.

Boiled beef is much maligned by gastronomes, who call it dried out meat, but it is providential for the poor and for small households, where it provides not only today's dinner, but tomorrow's lunch.

We will explain later, in the section on bouillon, how to make the best possible sort of bouillon; but here we will just discuss the beef itself.

The most usual way to serve beef—and let us hasten to say that in this instance the most flavourful cut is the top part of the rump— the most usual way, as we were saying, is to drain it and serve it on a platter, surrounded by parsley, or fried potatoes, or a tomato sauce or glazed onions.

Culotte de bœuf à la gelée ou à la royale ·
> Rump of beef with coloured jelly decorations

(Original manuscript recipe of V. de la Chapelle, in the Imperial Library.)
'Take a rump of beef, or part of one, choosing a meaty one of good quality. Trim it, and lard it with large lardoons, seasoning the lardoons with chopped parsley and shallot, pepper and spices. Wrap it in a white cloth, tie it and put it in a braising pan. In the bottom of the braising pan you will have put the bones from the rump, five or six carrots, four onions, two cloves of garlic, a bouquet of parsley and spring onions, two bay leaves, a knuckle of veal, a glass of white wine, enough salt to give a good flavour and two or three ladlefuls of bouillon. Bring this to the boil over a good fire, cover it with three thicknesses of buttered paper, and then put the lid on the braising pan. Let this all cook gently for about four hours, with fire under and fire over.

'When the rump is cooked, take it off the fire and allow it to cool in the cloth. Strain the stock through a napkin which you have taken care to dampen, so that the fat does not pass through as well. Let it cool a little. Beat up the whites of two eggs and a little water with a fork, add this to the lukewarm stock, stir it around, put it on the fire and leave it until it comes to the boil. Remove it, cover it, place some glowing coals on the lid and leave it thus for about a quarter of an hour. Lift the lid and, if the stock is limpid, strain it once more through a cloth which has been dampened and wrung out. Let the jelly cool to see if it is too stiff, or not stiff enough. In the first case, add a little bouillon. In the second case, boil it anew with a knuckle of veal, and clarify again, as described above.

'If it is not amber enough, you can put in a little beef juice. If you want to decorate your dish with different colours, such as red and green, you can use in the first instance a little cochineal after letting it infuse on a low heat, and adding a drop at a time until you have the desired shade of red. It is best that the colour should not be too dominant. If you want to have green, take a little raw spinach juice, and likewise put in very little, in order to keep the jelly transparent. If you have no cochineal, and it is winter time, you can easily substitute a little juice from a red beetroot, by pounding it raw in a mortar, and then proceeding as with the cochineal. You pour all these jellies into containers shaped in such a way that you can cut your jellies into thicknesses of at least an inch, and in various shapes, so that you can decorate your serving platter as you choose, as if with rubies or emeralds. Next, unwrap the beef, trim it all around and gently remove the outermost skin of fat which covers it. Put it upright on the platter and garnish it with the pieces of jelly, making a coloured border, alternating red with green, as though you were setting diamonds in a crown, and serve.'

Bœuf à la mode, à la bourgeoise

Take, preferably, the middle section or the top of a rump and lard it with large lardoons. Put it in a terrine with two carrots; four onions, one of which is stuck with two cloves; garlic; thyme; a bay leaf; and salt and pepper. Pour over all this a large glass of water and either half a glass of white wine or a spoonful of brandy. Cook until the meat is very tender, skim off the fat, and pass the gravy through a sieve. Five or six hours are required to make a good *bœuf à la mode*.

Biftecks (cuits selon la méthode de M. Gogué) ·
Steak cooked according to the method of M. Gogué
Steaks should come either from the ribs or from the fillet of beef.

Beef

After having chosen a suitable piece, trim it, taking care not to leave any sinews. Then cut it into pieces of equal thickness (two or three centimetres) and lightly flatten each of these pieces, which you have made into a round shape. Dip the steaks into olive oil, if you wish, to make them more tender, or into best quality butter, which you have melted and to which you have added a pinch of salt.

Then have ready a good fire, clear and glowing, without any half-burned charcoal or any other foreign matter which could produce smoke. On these live coals, place a carefully cleaned grill, and on the grill the steaks, prepared as we have just indicated. Watch them, but don't touch them any more until the moment to turn them has arrived. This moment is indicated by the bubbles which appear on the upper surface of the meat. Once the steaks have been turned, they should not be handled any more, except for being arranged on the platter. They should be tested with the finger tip; and one can feel a certain resistance when they have been cooked just right. Arrange them then in a ring on a platter, season with salt and pepper, and put underneath them some maître d'hôtel sauce, which is simply a piece of fresh butter into which a little chopped parsley and lemon juice have been worked. Fry some potatoes which have been cut into little square sticks, about a finger in length, lightly seasoned with salt. Garnish the steaks with these, and serve hot. Steaks with anchovy butter or with tomato sauce are prepared in the same way as above, except that the maître d'hôtel sauce is replaced by the anchovy butter or the tomato sauce. You can similarly substitute cress seasoned with a little salt and vinegar, or large pickles cut in thin slices, for the potatoes.

Remark: One must take great care not to season the steaks while they are cooking. This is a grave error, and we must tell you the consequences. Salt, which becomes a solvent when heated, makes the meat bleed, and thus removes its juices, which are their most precious asset. You will notice then that the braize on which the meat is cooking is thoroughly sprinkled with its cooking juices. It is just this which gave people the idea of dealing with the inconvenience by making tilted grills, with a well, destined to receive the juices and fat which run off during the cooking process. This invention can be a way of avoiding smoke, but it has no effect on the cooking, which should be carried out in the way we have indicated.

Also, be very careful, once the steaks are on the grill, not to turn them over and over. One only needs a little experience and good sense to abstain from this routine procedure, which can only result in compromising the successful conclusion of the cooking process. In this respect, follow the method which we have given.

Pièce de bœuf à l'anglaise ·
                    Top of rump cooked in the English fashion

Take a rump of beef, weighing four kilos, and season it with salt and pepper. Take a napkin, butter it, and wrap it around the rump. Take a pot, fill it with water and bring this to the boil with a good handful of coarse salt, eight turnips, six big onions (of which one is pierced with two cloves) and a clove of garlic. When the water has come to a rolling boil, put in your rump beef, and hermetically seal the pot.

For four kilos of beef, two hours of cooking time is required; that is a quarter of an hour for 500 grams. When the proper time has elapsed, remove the vegetables, and pass them through a fine sieve. Put these in a casserole with a good piece of fresh butter, season them with salt and pepper and put them in a vegetable dish. Remove the rump of beef from the marmite, arrange it on a platter, garnish with parsley and serve. (Vuillemot)

Bouilli · Boiled meat (beef)

Any piece of meat cooked in water is what is called *bouilli.*

President Hérault tells a story, which belongs to the period of the Restoration, about a witty man who was dining at Madame du Deffand's. He said of an overcooked boiled hen that it was like a piece of honeycomb, of which the beeswax alone remained. Madame du Deffand, who was giving the dinner, thought the president was right.

Boiled meat, according to Mme de Créquy, is simply cooked meat, without its juices.

There was only one response which could be made to these illustrious gourmands, namely to ask them: 'Have you ever tasted beef or chicken from the *marmite éternelle?*'

'No!'

'Well then, try some, and you will change your opinion.'

'What is the *marmite éternelle?*'

The *marmite éternelle* is—or rather was, given that this illustrious gastronomic institution has long since ceased to exist—the *marmite éternelle* was a receptacle which was never off the fire, day or night, and in which one chicken was placed as soon as another one was removed. Likewise a piece of beef put in as soon as one was taken out, and a glass of water put in as soon as a cup of bouillon was withdrawn. Every kind of meat which cooked in this bouillon gained in palatability rather than lost, for it inherited some of the juices which had been left in the bouillon by meats which had been previously cooked, while in turn leaving some of its own. A piece of meat to be cooked in the *marmite éternelle* had to be cooked for the absolute minimum of time needed to cook it through; in this way it lost none of its good qualities.

Now that we no longer have the *marmite éternelle*, we have to make do with cooking a large dish of boiled meat.

To make a handsome remove, buy a top part of the rump, weighing from 12 to 15 kilos. Have it boned and tied in such a way that it has an oblong, curved shape. Cook it in a bouillon which you have made the night before, and in which you have put all the left-overs of the previous night's roasts, roast chicken, roast turkey, roast rabbit, etcetera, etcetera. Around your piece of beef put a garnish *à la Chambord* [large and small fish quenelles; mushrooms; fillets of sole; soft roes sautéed in butter; truffles cut to look like olives], or *à la Godard* [large decorated quenelles, small veal or poultry quenelles with truffles, sheep's sweetbreads, braised and glazed; cocks' combs and kidneys], and decorate the beef with a number of skewers holding rissoles and stuck into the meat in such a way as to resemble a porcupine. If your garnish is not to be *à la Chambord* or *à la Godard*, use instead a garnish of little pies filled with glazed onions, sauerkraut, noodles, or vegetables *à la flamande* [green cabbage (rolled) stuffed and braised, carrots and turnips trimmed into large oval shapes and glazed potatoes].

BEEFSTEAK   *BEEF-STEAK ou BIFTECK à l'anglaise*

I remember seeing the birth of beefsteak in France, after the 1815 campaign, when the English stayed in Paris for two or three years. Until then our cuisine and theirs had been just as separate as our points of view. It was therefore not without a certain trepidation that one saw beefsteak trying to introduce itself slyly into our kitchens. Yet, we are an eclectic people and without prejudice. So, as soon as we had realized that, in spite of 'coming from the Greeks, it was not poisoned,' before we held out our plates, and gave beefsteak its citizenship papers.

And yet, there is still something which separates English from French beefsteak. We prepare our beefsteak with a piece of fillet from the sirloin (*aloyau*), whereas our neighbours take something which we call *sous-noix* of beef, that is to say rumpsteak, for theirs. This cut of beef is always more tender there than it would be here, because the English feed their cattle better than we do, and slaughter their cattle younger than we do in France. They therefore take this cut of beef, and slice it in thick pieces of about half an inch, flatten these a little, and cook them on a cast-iron plate made expressly for the purpose, using ordinary coal instead of charcoal. Real beef fillet should be put on a thoroughly heated grill, with live coals, and should be turned only once in order to conserve its juices, which then marry up with the maître d'hôtel sauce. This part of English beef (and, to verify this, every time I go to England I eat it with renewed pleasure) is infinitely more flavourful than the part from which we take our steaks. One must eat it in an English tavern, sautéed with Madeira wine, or with anchovy butter, or on a bed of cress, well sprinkled with vinegar. I would recommend that it should be eaten with gherkins, if there were even one nation in the world which knew how to make gherkins.

As for French beefsteak, the best sauce to accompany it is maître d'hôtel, because one can sense the predominance of the flavour of the herbs and the lemon. But there is one observation which I will permit myself to make. I see our cooks flattening their steaks on the kitchen table with the flat side of the meat chopper; I think that they are committing a grave sin, and that they are causing certain nutritional elements to spurt out of the meat, elements which would play their role well in the process of mastication.

In general, ruminant animals are better in England than in France because, while living, they are treated with quite particular care. Nothing equals those quarters of beef, cooked whole, which are rolled along on little carts like railway wagons between the habitués of English taverns. Those pieces of beef, fat interlarded with lean, which one cuts for oneself as one wishes, from a portion of an animal weighing one hundred pounds! There is nothing to compare with them for exciting the appetite.

BEETROOT   *BETTERAVE*

A kind of beet or white beet. Its root is the colour of blood within and without, its leaves particularly so; the petioles are a dark red. The plant has a greater sugar content than any other, which at the time of the continental blockade gave chemists the idea of substituting beet sugar for cane sugar. I remember having seen in 1812 a caricature representing the little king of Rome and his nursemaid. The child was crying, and the nursemaid was offering him a beetroot saying: 'Suck, my child, your father says this is sugar.' Like all great discoveries, this one, which set us free from dependence on the colonies, was first greeted with laughter.

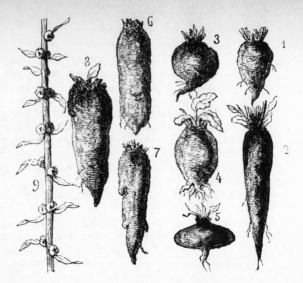

1: Betterave de Silésie. 2: Betterave rouge ordinaire. 3: Betterave rouge-globe. 4: Betterave jaune des Barres. 5: Betterave de Bassan. 6: Betterave disette. 7: Betterave jaune grasse. 8: Betterave jaune d'Allemagne. 9: Graines de Betterave.

There are five kinds of beet: the large red kind, the little red kind, the yellow, the white and the veined. This last is the one which is now known as the *betterave champêtre*.* The populace, who for such a long time were fanatically in favour of Napoleon because of his victories, which cost France a third of its blood and a sixth of its territories, do not reflect that they are beholden to him for a vegetable which is now in general use. Its leaves are mixed with those of sorrel, to ameliorate their great acidity. These large white leaves, called cardoons, are esteemed and are eaten with pleasure. In winter, the beet grows small leaves which are eaten as a salad.

Beetroots are cooked in the oven or in the embers, and thereafter preserved in vinegar. Germans eat them with soup. In the north they are fermented and used to prevent scurvy.

* This name is sometimes translated as 'garden beet'; but this is slightly misleading. Beets can be divided into those for domestic use and industrial beets. The former category was deemed, in the time of Dumas, to comprise six principal varieties, of which the names are shown in the accompanying illustration. Nowadays we would use the name garden beet for the kind then known as *betterave rouge-globe*.

When beets are cooked in the oven, which is the best way of cooking them, they must first be washed in ordinary brandy, then put in the oven on the rack, so that at no time do they touch the bricks. The oven must be heated as it would be for a large loaf of closely grained bread. Leave them in the oven until cold, and on the next day cook them in the same way, at the same heat. The beetroot is not really cooked, or rather not properly cooked, until its skin is nearly charred.

Betteraves à la chartreuse

Cut rounds of yellow beetroot, ensuring that they are properly cooked in the manner which we have just described. Put on each a round of raw onion, from the centre of which you have removed a section, the size of a one franc piece. Add some burnet, chervil, nutmeg and white salt. Cover this with another slice of beetroot the same size as the first. Press the beets and onion until they stick together, then fry in the usual way, and serve garnished with fried parsley.

Beetroot is often eaten in salad, with corn salad (lamb's lettuce), celery, rampion, but the best beet salad is made with little glazed onions, slices of purple potatoes*, fragments of artichoke hearts and steamed Soissons beans. Nasturtium flowers and cress are added, making a salad which compares with Russian salad for palatability.

Beetroot can also be served as an hors-d'oeuvre, with olives and sardines, with a dressing of tarragon vinegar, finely chopped shallots, salt and pepper, and a border of chopped white and yolk of egg. In this case, add a little oil when dressing the beet.

BLACKBIRD   *MERLE*

Throughout France there is a proverb which goes as follows: 'For want of thrushes, one eats blackbirds.' Corsica alone, after having fought without success for its political nationality, has fought more successfully for its culinary identity, and, of all our *départements*, is the only one which continues to say: 'When there are no blackbirds, one must eat thrushes.'

* This is a kind of potato which may also be met under the name 'black potato' or '*négresse*' in France. The *Larousse Gastronomique* refers to it as a gastronomical curiosity.

Blackbird

This is because the blackbirds of Corsica have an entirely different sort of flavour which they owe to the berries of the juniper, ground ivy, myrtle and buckthorn, to the seeds of the mistletoe, and to the fruits of the service tree and of the eglantine. Also, Corsica does not content itself with eating blackbirds, but sends terrines full of blackbirds all over the world. To conserve them, it suffices to pour melted lard into a container, and then to toss in the plucked blackbirds, once their gizzards have been removed. The lard congeals around them, and envelops them in a layer of fat which keeps out the air and preserves them for years.

M. le Cardinal Fesch gave superb dinners at which the blackbirds of Corsica were the principal attraction.

BLANCMANGE   *BLANC-MANGER*

According to the letters of Mme de Maintenon, it seems that Fagon* ordered this food in cases of maladies or inflammatory dispositions.

Blanc-manger (according to the recipe of M. Beauvilliers)

'Split two calves' feet in half in order to remove the large bones. Let them soak. Blanch them, let them cool, put them in a pot containing 1½ *pinte* (just over 1 litre) of water and bring to the boil. Skim, and let them cook for two or three hours. Take the fat off, and strain the bouillon through a damp napkin.

'Blanch and skin a quarter of a pound of sweet almonds and six bitter almonds. Pound them in a mortar until they are reduced to a paste, taking care to dampen them from time to time with a little water so that they do not turn into oil. Put half a *setier* (¼ litre) of water in a casserole with six ounces of sugar, the zest of half a lemon and a good pinch of coriander. Let this steep for a good half hour, then remove the coriander and the lemon and pour the infusion on the almonds. Strain it several times through a napkin, and add

---

* Guy-Crescent Fagon lived from 1638 to 1718. He became doctor to Queen Marie Thérèse, who died under his care, and then to Louis XIV. In this role he was an important figure at court, but his medical knowledge has been described as elementary. His general policy was to do nothing rather than risk doing the wrong thing. Various important people died under his care, without his taking any action (save, perhaps, giving them blancmange). These included the Grand Dauphin (1711), the Duchess of Bourgogne (1712) and the Duc de Berry (1714). After the death of the king himself, the doctor retired. (Information based on material in the *Biographie française*.)

enough of the calves' foot jelly to ensure that your blancmange will have the correct delicacy and that it will set sufficiently; a point on which you satisfy yourself by testing. When it has reached the right stage and has a good flavour, pour it either into little pots or into a mould, and put it on ice to set, as with other jellies.

'This blancmange, like every other sort of jelly, can also be made with isinglass, hartshorn or *mousse d'Islande* [a kind of lichen found and still eaten in parts of Iceland—it has qualities similar to those of carragheen, or Irish moss, which is an edible seaweed].'

M. Beauvilliers' recipe is excellent; it cannot be improved upon and one would be wrong not to follow it.

BOAR   *SANGLIER*

This is pig in its wild state; and hunting it is not without danger. The boar is quite a misanthropic animal, which on reaching a certain age seeks refuge in the thickest brambles and thickets, where it does not like to be disturbed. At this time it takes the name of *ragot* (two-year-old boar), *quartanier* (four-year-old boar) and *solitaire* (boar of advanced age). It is rare that one of these animals, armed as it is with redoubtable defences, does not turn on the hunter who has shot at him. The best the hunter can do then, if there is the branch of a tree within reach, is to hang from it until the boar has passed, for it rarely attacks the same target twice. I have retailed stories about several of the hunts of my youth, which were not without some very original anecdotes on just this point.

Young boar are skinned, and are eaten spit-roasted.

The forequarters, the head and the fillets are the best parts of the boar. Likewise, chops similar to pork chops are cut. However, since the boar is difficult to bleed one cannot always collect the blood in order to make *boudin* of it.

Quartier de sanglier à la royale · Quarter of wild boar *à la royale*
Skin and singe a quarter of a wild sow, bone it up to the knuckle and lard it with spices and aromatics, previously pounded. Put it in a terrine with a lot of salt, pepper, juniper, thyme, bay leaf, basil, onions and spring onions; and let it marinate for five days. When you want to cook it, remove the aromatics which remain within it, wrap it in a white cloth, and tie it up like a joint of beef. Put it in a braising pan with the liquid of its marinade, six bottles of white wine, the same

amount of water, six carrots, six onions, four cloves, a good bouquet of parsley and spring onions, and salt if there is not enough. Let it barely simmer for six hours. Try it, to see whether it has cooked sufficiently; otherwise give it another hour. Let it rest in the cooking liquid for half an hour and, when you remove it, leave the rind on.

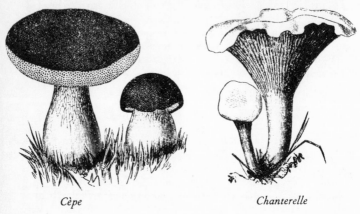

Cèpe   *Chanterelle*

BOLETUS   *BOLET*

A member of the mushroom family whose conical cap has a lower surface covered with rounded tubes or spores.

The edible boletus, the only one which one can eat,* is to be found throughout France in woods and shady places. It has a fairly stout stalk, cylindrical and sometimes swollen, and whitish or yellow in colour with a network of veins. Its cap is large, arched, and of a ferruginous colour verging on blue, or sometimes a sombre brick red or ashy red; it may also be white and yellowish, and is often wine-coloured under the skin. The tubes are first of all white, and then yellowish and greenish.

M. Dennezil, from whom we are borrowing these comments, adds that cattle, deer and pigs eat the boletus avidly, and that it is much

---

* Dumas is not quite right on this point. The following paragraph from Jane Grigson's *The Mushroom Feast* (London, 1975) gives more accurate and illuminating information about the boletus or cep. 'The true *cèpe de Bordeaux* is *Boletus edulis* (*cèpe* from a Gascon word *cep*, a trunk, because of the fat stem; *boletus* from the Greek word *bolos*, a lump: they come up like lumps in the woodlands). Other kinds of *Boletus* are common and delicious, such as *Boletus luteus* with a slimy yellow-brown cap and *B. granulatus* with a slimy reddish-yellow cap.'

sought after as a foodstuff and a seasoning in the south of France. But it is not used in Paris, even though it can easily be found in the vicinity of that town, mainly in the woods of Ville d'Avray and Meudon. In the south it is known by the name of *ceps*, *cep*, *girole*, *giroule* and *bruguet*. In Lorraine it is eaten under the name of *champignon polonais* (Polish mushroom), because it was Poles in the suite of King Stanislas Leczinski who first demonstrated that the boletus could be eaten without danger.

BONITO   *BONITE*

[Dumas is describing the Oceanic bonito, which is *Katsuwonus pelamis* (Linnaeus), but possibly incorporating a few details which refer to the dolphin. There is also a short entry under *Bonitol*, a fish which is described as 'son of' the bonito, almost as big as a mackerel and with flesh which has an excellent taste. It is likely that Dumas is here referring to *Auxis thazard* (Lacépède), the Frigate mackerel or Plain bonito; but the provenance of the name *bonitol* is obscure and the details given insufficient to make identification certain.]

A fish of the mackerel family, but larger than the mackerels. It closely resembles the tuna in appearance and feeds, like the tuna, on fish and seaweeds; but its flesh is more delicate and gourmets rank it with the mackerel. Apart from anything else, the name which it bears is sufficient indication of its merits and adequate proof of the good qualities of its flesh.

This fish lives in the Mediterranean, but is also found on the Atlantic coasts of Spain and France. It is abundant between the Tropics and, so they say, enjoys following ships.

These fish live on the surface of the water and even launch themselves into the air to seize the flying fish which constitute their principal food. Thus it is easy to fish for them, and here is the method employed. A trailing line is used, to which two white feathers are attached, near the hook, so as to look like a flying fish. The line is dangled and agitated from time to time at the height of a few inches above the water. The bonito leaps upon it to catch its prey and finds itself caught instead.

What gives a certain importance to the bonito fishery is that the bonito, like the tuna, is salted and exported thus, in barrels, all over the world. Quite often, when one thinks that one is feasting on tuna, one is merely eating bonito, which is anyway just as good.

There is no good cooking without good bouillon; and the French cuisine, the foremost of all, owes its superior status to the excellence of French bouillon. This excellence is the result of a sort of intuition given, I would not say to our cooks, but to the ordinary women of our country.

Rivarol said to some gourmands from Lübeck and Hamburg, on leaving his plate of soup three-quarters full: 'Gentlemen, there is not a single nurse or janitress in France who does not know how to make bouillon better than the most gifted cook in your three Hanseatic cities.'

We are therefore going to explain, by turning to all the various authorities on these matters, what are the elements of meat, from which bouillon derives its flavours. These elements are: fibrine, gelatine, osmazome, fats and albumen.

FIBRINE This is not soluble. The tissue of the flesh is made up of fibre and this is what the eye sees after the cooking process. Fibre is resistant to boiling water, and keeps its shape even though it loses a part of its exterior. When a piece of meat is boiled for a long time in a large quantity of water, what is left is almost pure fibre.

GELATINE is lost in proportion to the advancing of age. When man reaches ninety years of age, his bones are no more than a sort of imperfect marble; which is why they are so liable to break, and why prudence dictates to the aged the avoidance of any situation which might bring on a fall. Bones are made up mainly of gelatine and phosphate of lime.

OSMAZOME is that particularly flavourful element of meat which is soluble in cold water. It differs from the parts used to make meat extracts, which are soluble only in boiling water. It is osmazome which gives worth to good soups and which, in becoming 'caramelized', gives to meat its brown crust.

ALBUMEN Albumen is found in flesh and blood. It resembles egg white, and coagulates at a temperature under 40 degrees. It is this which is thrown out of the *pot au feu* under the heading of scum.

FAT is an oil which is not soluble in water, and is formed in the interstices of tissue cells. Sometimes this agglomerates in a mass in those animals which are thus predisposed, such as pigs, poultry, ortolans and fig-peckers.

If one wished only to draw off bouillon from a *pot au feu*, it would suffice simply to chop up the meat, put it in cold water and slowly bring it to the boil. One would thus extract all the soluble elements from the meat, and one would obtain in a half an hour a real consommé. This is what we invite people to do if they have unexpected guests, and wish to give them soup.

It is a mistake to think that poultry, unless very old or very fat, adds anything to the osmazome of bouillon. Pigeon, when it is old, and partridge or rabbit, previously roasted, and crow, in November and December, add greatly to the savour and aroma of the bouillon into which they are put. In general the flesh of these animals contains all their blood and that is what creates this good effect.

Now since it is not just for the bouillon that one prepares a *pot au feu*, but also to have meat which is edible (and not only edible on the first day as boiled meat, but capable of reappearing the following day in another form), we are going to explain what steps are to be followed in order to produce good bouillon every time without exhausting all the good of the meat.

Always choose the largest piece of meat compatible with your usual pattern of consumption. The larger, the fresher and the thicker the piece, the more the bouillon will reflect these three good qualities, without counting the saving of time and fuel. Do not wash the meat, which would rob it of some of its essences. Tie it, after removing the bones, so that it keeps its shape, and put it in a *marmite* with one litre of water for each 500 grams of meat.

Heat the pot slowly. This will result in first dissolving the albumen, and then causing it to coagulate. Since in the first state, it is lighter than the liquid, it will rise to the surface, bringing up with it whatever impurities the meat may contain. Once the albumen has coagulated, egg whites are used to clarify the other substances. The more slowly the liquid is brought to the boil, the more abundant will be the scum. An hour should elapse from the moment when the pot is put on the fire to the moment when the scum rises to the surface.

Once the scum has risen completely, it must be removed; at that very instant. Boiling would precipitate the scum, and would hinder the transparency of the bouillon. If the fire is well managed, there is no need to cool the pot to cause the scum to rise again.

When the pot has been well skimmed, and the liquid starts rolling its first waves, the vegetables are put in. These consist of three carrots, two parsnips, three turnips and a bunch of leeks and celery tied together. Do not forget to add three large onions, one stuck with half a clove of garlic, the other two with a whole clove each. In cooking of the second order, but only of the second order, colour is given to the bouillon with a half of a burnt onion, a ball of caramel, or a dried carrot. Do not forget to break with a chopper the bones which play a

75

part in the composition of your bouillon, whether they were bought at the same time as the beef, or were left over from last night's roast. The greater the number of pieces into which they are broken, the greater the amount of gelatine given off.

Seven hours of steady, slow simmering are needed to give the bouillon the requisite qualities. On an open fire, it is almost impossible to regulate this simmering; but success is easy if one uses a kitchen stove which heats the back of the pot constantly. To keep evaporation at a minimum, the pot must stay covered; and one must think twice before replenishing the liquid, even when one draws off some bouillon. However, if the meat becomes uncovered, one must pour in more boiling water until it is covered anew. When the meat is taken out of the pot, it will have lost half its weight.

BREAD   *PAIN*

In most civilized countries man's diet consists to a large extent of bread, which is made, according to the resources of the country, either of wheat or rye or corn, etc.

If the flour is to produce suitable bread, it should contain a fairly large proportion of gluten; the more it contains, the better the bread will be. When the dough, made of flour, has been suitably prepared and is put to one side in the right conditions, an alcoholic fermentation takes place. This releases a quantity of carbon dioxide. The gluten contained in the dough forms a sort of flexible network and retains in large measure the carbon dioxide, thus causing the mass to rise, and making it light and porous. When, later, the cooking process solidifies the mass, the dough retains the same characteristics and this guarantees good bread. The gluten distributed in the flour absorbs water and forms a sort of membrane which gives to the wheat dough its characteristic elasticity. It is this same membrane which retains the gas which produces the fermentation.

It is commonly said that bread should be a day old before being eaten, and that the flour should be a month old before being used to make dough. Furthermore, it is thought that the grain should be a year old before it is milled. But everybody generally finds bread good if it is fresh and has cooled completely. Only millet bread is eaten hot.

Even though systematic bread-making does not fall into the province of ordinary cooking, we feel that we should make a few precise and succinct remarks on the theory of baking. Corn, yeast and wheat flour are to be found everywhere, but there are countries where the bread made by the inhabitants is inedible. And one of our friends, M. Drouet, a sculptor, who has travelled a lot in some of these countries said to us one day that he had been obliged to eat potatoes for a long time, instead of bread, the latter being detestable.

The quality of bread depends on the yeast and the baking, but principally on the yeast. Yeast works in the following way. It is added to a little of the dough until a sort of alcoholic fermentation which is peculiar to it has taken place, and the dough has swollen and become less dense and has acquired a smell and taste which have a lively quality of piquancy and spirituousness mixed with bitterness. This fermented dough is carefully kneaded with the new dough, and the mixture promptly causes this second batch of dough to go through a similar fermentation process. But this is less advanced and complete than the first one. The effect of this fermentation is to divide and thin the new dough, and to make a lot of gas develop in it. Being unable to escape completely because of the holding power and consistency of the dough, the gas produces small cavities in it and makes it expand upwards, dilating and swelling it. This is why the name leavening has been given to the old dough which brings all this about.

When the dough has risen thus, it is ready to go into the oven. During the cooking process it dilates further due to the rarefaction of the gases. It then becomes a light bread, completely different from the heavy, stodgy, viscous and indigestible masses which are produced by the cooking of dough which has not risen properly.

The discovery that it is possible to use barm or the residue of grain-based wines for fermenting dough meant that there was another, new and very pure substance to improve bread. It is the froth which is found on the surface of these liquors during fermentation which is used by way of yeast. This froth, introduced and mixed in with the flour-based dough, causes it to rise even better and more quickly than ordinary leavening. It is by using this that the most delicate of breads, *pain mollet* [a soft bread roll] is made.

Quite often one finds that coarse bread, which has been made with a previous kneading, has a very disagreeable flavour verging on bitterness. This can happen if too large a quantity of leavening has been put in the mixture, or if the fermentation of this same leavening has been allowed to go too far.

One never meets this problem in bread made with yeast. This must presumably be because the fermentation of yeast is less far advanced than that of a previous kneading; or perhaps because one takes more care over the preparation of *pain mollet* than over the making of ordinary household bread.

Bread

Bread which has risen well and been properly baked is totally different from that which has been badly made. Not only is it much less stodgy and better tasting, but it is also better for dunking and does not become a viscous glue when eaten thus, and is therefore infinitely better for the digestion.

As for the salt which is added to the dough, it not only serves to add flavour to the bread, but also performs a chemical function in causing the flour to absorb a larger amount of water. Some other salts perform this function to an even greater degree, but only if used in very small quantities. If used in excess, these salts hinder the dough from rising so well.

Leavening and salt thus afford big advantages in bread-making. These two ingredients remove all impurities, and give a sort of pre-cooking to the flour, and a more solid consistency to the dough.

The French people, as is well known, have the highest rate of bread consumption. No doubt this is why there is less illness in France, an advantage which more than one doctor ascribes to the fact that we eat a lot of bread with our meals.

It is not the same when it comes to the English and the Germans, whose main food is meat or potatoes. That is not to say that this diet is always bad, but it is often the cause of putrefactive illnesses.

A Parisian, finding himself in a German town one day was invited to dine with one of his friends. At six o'clock he was at his friend's house. He observed a table, sumptuously laid for about a dozen people, but what struck him most was the small size of the pieces of bread which had been placed beneath each napkin.

After waiting a quarter of an hour without any other guest arriving, and feeling a pang of hunger, he said to himself: 'My goodness, I am at a friend's house, I don't have to stand on ceremony with him too much, I will eat this little bit of bread. It will keep me going until the other guests arrive, which can't be very much longer.' So he took a piece of bread, and ate it.

Another quarter of an hour passed, and he said the same thing to himself as before, and ate two more pieces of bread, since there wasn't anything else to eat.

Finally, since his friend and the guests still hadn't arrived, he ended up, while waiting, by eating all the bread on the table, so that when the guests did arrive, there was none left. The Parisian explained that it was he who had eaten it all, and they laughed a lot and asked him how he had managed to swallow so much. As for them, they did without perfectly well, and the lack of bread did not bother them. And the twelve pieces of bread which he had swallowed did nothing to stop our compatriot from doing justice to his friend's dinner.

The tardy arrival of the guests was then explained. In Germany, supper is eaten at eight o'clock, whereas the Parisian, being accustomed to dine at six, had come at his usual hour, without wondering whether this was really the time set for dinner.

How to make bread

As there are still many peasants in the countryside who make their own bread, we are going to give the easiest method of doing so.

Depending on the amount of bread required, you put out a suitable quantity of flour and make a well in the middle. In this well you put a *demi-quarteron* [about 60 grams] of yeast, or more. Beat up your mixture with tepid water, in such a way that it has the consistency of brioche dough. Knead the dough well, adding two ounces of salt dissolved in a little lukewarm water. Cover all this, and put it in a warm place to ferment and rise. One cannot repeat often enough, that the quality of the bread depends on the care given to this stage of the operation. After leaving the dough in this state for an hour or two, depending on the season, it is kneaded again and left, covered, to rise for two hours more. Then heat the oven and, when it is clean, divide the dough into as many portions as you wish to make loaves of bread, and form the bread into such shapes as you wish. Put these loaves in the oven as quickly as possible, and when they are baked, rub the crust with a little butter in order to give it a beautiful yellow colour.

BREADFRUIT TREE   *ARBRE À PAIN*

This tree grows spontaneously in the Moluccas, in the Sunda Isles, and in the Polynesian archipelago. It goes by this name because of the fruit which it bears, called breadfruit.

The breadfruit tree reaches from 13 to 17 metres in height; its trunk is very large and its cyme ample, rounded and made up of ramified branches. The fruit which it produces is greenish yellow outside, and white inside; its size depends on the variety from which it comes, but its diameter is rarely more than 21 centimetres. It contains a pulp which at first is very white, almost floury and a little fibrous, but which in maturity becomes yellowish and succulent or of a gelatinous consistency. When the fruit is ripe, it only needs to be roasted or grilled on glowing charcoal embers, or to be cooked whole in the oven, or in water. It is then scraped and the interior, white and tender like fresh bread crumbs, is eaten. This is a very pleasant and very healthful foodstuff. Its taste is comparable to that of bread made with wheat flour, with a slight flavour of Jerusalem or globe artichokes, and it keeps for seven or eight consecutive months.

We are assured that two or three of these remarkable trees are enough to provide one man with food for an entire year. As for its cultivation, it requires virtually no care, and the French, followed by the English, introduce it to Mauritius, Guadeloupe and Jamaica. The inhabitants of these places eat its fruit, make clothes with the inner growth of bark, and wrap their food in its leaves, which sometimes attain a length of one metre and a width of 40 to 50 centimetres.

BREAM   *BRÈME*

This fish is taken in the rivers and the large lakes of almost the whole of Europe. It is the object of an important fishery, which usually takes place during the months when there is ice.

In Sweden in 1749 fifty thousand bream, which together weighed more than 9,000 kilograms, were taken in the haul of a single net.

The bream bears some resemblance to the carp, but its body is not as thick, being deeper and more flattened on the sides. Its head is black, its mouth small and its lips large. Its flesh is full of bones, like that of the shad, but lacks the delicate quality of the latter.

It is possible to transport bream alive over a considerable distance by covering them with snow and placing in their mouths pieces of bread soaked in brandy.

Bream are eaten with a piquant sauce incorporating shallots.

BRILL   *BARBUE*

The shape of this fish is rhomboid. Its skin is covered with oval scales, joined together. The left side is marbled with yellow, brown and red. The brill is very abundant in the Mediterranean, on the coasts of Sardinia, as well as around the Azores. Sometimes it reaches a weight of 10 kilos. Its flesh is firm and exquisite; but, even so, one should not eat too much of it, since it is rather difficult to digest.

Instructions for cooking Brill
Gut, wash and clean out the interior of your brill. Make a cut in the

right-hand side up to the middle of the back, lift up the flesh on both sides of the cut and take out a section of the bones—three vertebrae or so—to make the fish more supple and to prevent it from splitting. Put into a large pot a quantity of water sufficient, when subsequently transferred to your *turbotière*, to cover the brill completely. Add a handful of coarse salt, two bay leaves, thyme, parsley and six to ten sliced onions. Boil all this for a quarter of an hour, strain it and let it rest.

Rub the belly side of the brill with salt and lemon juice. Place it in the *turbotière*, belly side up, and pour over it the clear court-bouillon which you have prepared. Heat it until it comes to a rolling boil, then let it barely simmer, without any further boiling, for an hour (even longer if it is a very large fish). In summer it is necessary to start the cooking over a vigorous flame, since the fish might spoil if the flame was low. While the fish is cooking, cover it with a tea-towel or a piece of cooking paper, to prevent it from darkening. When it 'gives' to the touch, it is done.

The cooking completed, take the brill out five minutes before serving it and drain it. Lay it on a platter, belly side up, and trim off the end of the tail and the outer parts of the fins. Any untidy cuts or tears can be covered by the parsley with which you surround the fish.

Serve in sauceboats a caper sauce and an olive oil sauce and, if you wish, a hollandaise sauce.

You can cook a brill in water with 500 grams of white salt, a litre of milk and a scrap of lemon. If your brill is not very fresh, put it in salted boiling water and let it simmer for an hour to make the flesh firmer.

Barbue marinée à la tomate ou à l'oseille · Marinated brill with tomato or sorrel

Clean the fish and make cuts across its back so that it will absorb a marinade made of salt, pepper, verjuice, spring onions and lemon. After two hours of marinating, sprinkle breadcrumbs, both soft and dried, over the fish, then cook it in the oven in a pie-dish and serve it on a purée of either tomatoes or sorrel.

BROAD BEAN   *FÈVE*

Broad beans are fairly digestible as long as they are young, but they become heavy when they approach maturity, and one must [then] remove their skins.

Fèves à la crème · Broad beans with cream

Take some small broad beans. Do not skin them, but blanch them in boiling water and then put them in cold water. Drain them, toss them in a lightly browned roux with salt, pepper, finely chopped parsley and savory. Add some bouillon, a piece of sugar, and a pinch of flour worked into some butter. Shortly before serving, pour a glassful of cream on to the broad beans and allow it to come to the boil just for a moment, and then bind it with egg-yolks.

BROCCOLI   *BROCOLI*

Broccoli is a type of cauliflower which flowers black instead of white and divides into separate stems instead of uniting in a single compact stem. It is an excellent vegetable, but it is little known in France, except in the Midi, where the climate is sufficiently hot for growing it. We have said that it flowers black; but in Italy it flowers purple.

Broccoli is cooked and prepared like cauliflower. The parenchyma is lighter, but it has a more exquisite flavour. Do not confuse broccoli with brussels sprouts. Our painstaking gardeners obtain the seed for this plant from the region of Milan.

Serve it with a good butter sauce, or a sauce au gratin with Parmesan cheese.

BUCKWHEAT   *SARRASIN*

Buckwheat came originally from Asia, whence it was taken to Africa, and introduced to Europe by the Spanish Moors.

This grain has certain advantages. It grows readily anywhere. It develops and ripens fairly promptly, thus allowing two harvests in good years. It is healthful and nourishing to use and easy to digest. However, one has to confess that bread made from buckwheat is the worst of all breads. The day after it has been baked it dries up, splits, crumbles, causes flatulence and is altogether detestable.

This is not the case if it is used as pap. This preparation is very nourishing and healthful. It can be eaten hot or cold, fried or grilled.

In the cantons where buckwheat is the usual food for the inhabitants, as for example in lower Brittany and lower Normandy, pap and pancakes are made with milk. This gives them a more agreeable taste and makes them lighter, more palatable, and easier to digest.

BURBOT   *LOTTE*

An excellent freshwater fish, with some resemblance to the eel and the lamprey. Its culinary preparation is as for the eel. Some people confuse it with the loach, which is not nearly as good a fish.

Lottes à la bonne femme

Scald the burbots [which have slimy skins] and cook them with white wine, sliced onion, parsley, spring onions, basil, pepper, cloves and butter. When they are cooked, arrange them [in a serving dish] and serve them in their cooking liquid.

BUTTER   *BEURRE*

This is a fatty, oily substance, made with cream taken from milk and thickened by beating.

All kinds of milk can produce butter. The richest butter, with the largest fat content, comes from goat's milk. The Scythians and the Paeonians introduced it into Greece; Hippocrates only talks of the Scythians' butter. Horace and Virgil speak of cheese, but not of butter. Werther made butter poetical. It was while watching Charlotte buttering bread for the children that he was overcome by that fatal passion which ended with a pistol shot. Goethe was right; children like nothing as much as buttered bread, except it is bread and jam.

In a few countries where I have travelled, I have always had freshly made butter, made on the day itself. Here, for the benefit of travellers, is my recipe; it is very simple, and at the same time fool-proof.

Wherever I could find cow's milk or camel's milk, mare's milk, goat's milk, and particularly goat's milk, I got some. I filled a bottle three quarters full, I stopped it up and I hung it around the neck of my horse. I left the rest up to the horse. In the evening, when I arrived, I broke the neck of the bottle and found, within, a piece of butter the size of a fist which had virtually made itself. In Africa, in

Butter

the Caucasus, in Sicily, in Spain, this method has always worked for me.

BUTTERMILK   *BABEURRE* (*Lait de beurre*)

A white watery liquid which is left when butter has been churned. This liquid is a foodstuff greatly esteemed in Holland, to the point where servants, in discussing the terms of their employment with their masters, make it a condition of their employment to be given buttermilk once or twice a week. Buttermilk is also used for making a soup; it is nourishing and refreshing, but nevertheless does not agree with everyone.

CABBAGE   *CHOU*

This genus of plant belongs to the cruciferous family.

There are different sorts of cabbage, nearly all of which originated in Europe, which is also where consumption of cabbages is greatest. In nearly all the provinces of France it is a real treat for the peasants, who for most of the time live on vegetables alone, even though it is not at all nourishing, causes flatulence and spreads an evil smell.

The ancients venerated the cabbage greatly, and swore by it, much as the Egyptians paid divine homage to the onion. History reports, however, that Apicius did not like it and that it inspired disgust in Drusus, for which Tiberius blamed his brother.

White or green cabbage. Those from Milan are the best; cabbages from Saint-Denis, from Bonneuil and those which are called the *petit pommé* (small round-headed) type, and the early curly cabbage are the first ones to appear, and are those which are generally used for eating.

Chou au lard · Cabbage with bacon

This is an excellent plebeian dish, which is made as follows. Cut a large round-headed cabbage in four pieces. Blanch them, then put them in any sort of pot with bacon, sausages, saveloy, celery, onions, large carrots, a bay leaf and thyme. Cook for an hour and a half on a low flame. Next, arrange everything on a platter, putting the bacon and the saveloy on top. Suppress the other vegetables, and make a sauce with the cooking water, after reducing it.

Chou en garbure (cuisine bordelaise) · Cabbage soup

Blanch and drain the cabbage. Remove the larger ribs of the leaves. Take a soup pot which can go on the stove. In the bottom of it put a bed of cabbage leaves, then a layer of slices of thinly cut Gruyère cheese; and cover these with slices of bread. Continue making alternating layers; cabbage, cheese, bread. Then season it, add some good bouillon and let it simmer and gratiner for an hour. Serve it as a thick soup, with bouillon in another bowl.

CAKE   *GÂTEAU*

Cakes, a sort of pastry, are almost always round in shape, and usually made with flour, eggs and butter. They can also be made of rice. Their name (*gâteau*) without doubt comes from the prodigality with which children are spoiled (*gâtés*) by having cakes given to them either as a reward, or as an encouragement of a gastronomic nature.

The most famous of all the cakes is the *gâteau des Rois* (Twelfth Night cake), a sort of broad thin cake in which a broad bean is placed. This ancient patriarchal custom has become universal, and there are few families who do not choose to have a reunion at Epiphany, and distribute sections of the *gâteau des rois*.

In certain provinces, aside from the parts to be taken by those present, a portion for God in his charity is also cut. This is given to the first beggar who passes by, and consequently becomes the portion of poverty.

Everyone knows that it is the youngest person present who is in charge of serving and distributing the slices of cake. For Barjac, the manservant of Cardinal de Fleury, it was the occasion for a bit of light-hearted flattery.

On one Twelfth Night, he managed to assemble at his master's table twelve guests of such advanced age that, even though His Eminence was already well over ninety, he was still the youngest person present and had to fulfil the tasks which are usually allocated to the children; a happening which gave him a most agreeable surprise.

Now, here are a few recipes:

Gâteau à la Madeleine · Madeleine cake

Break ten eggs, separating the yolks from the whites. Beat the yolks with three *quarterons* (367 grams) of powdered sugar, a pinch of

Cake

chopped green lemon, and a little fine salt. Add half a *livre* (245 grams) best quality flour, and mix everything together well. Incorporate a good-sized piece of best quality clarified butter in this mixture, add six well-beaten egg whites, and finish off your batter. Next, butter some little Madeleine moulds, fill them with this mixture, bake them at a low temperature, then serve them.

You can substitute for the little moulds a large baking tray covered with buttered paper, on to which you put the batter. You then cook the cake, and cut it into lozenge shapes, or whatever other shapes you like.

Gâteau au fromage de Brie · Cake made with Brie cheese

Take some fine Brie cheese, knead it with a litre of flour, 90 grams of butter and a little salt. Add five or six eggs and thin the dough well, working it with the palm of your hand. Next, let it rest for half an hour; then roll it out with a rolling pin. Shape the cake in the usual way, brush it with egg, put it in the oven to cook, and serve.

Cake; ou Kake (gâteau anglais) · English wedding cake

The practice in England, as we can read in the works of Dickens, is to make an enormous cake on the occasion of the wedding of one's offspring and to distribute a slice of this to each guest.

This is how the cake is made. Take 2 kilos of good quality flour, 2 kilos of fresh butter, a kilo of finely sieved sugar and 7 grams of nutmeg. For each pound of flour eight eggs are required. Wash and pick over 2 kilos of currants which you dry in front of the fire. Take 500 grams of sweet almonds, which must be blanched, skinned and cut into slivers; add to these 500 grams of candied lemon peel, 500 grams of candied orange peel and half a litre of brandy.

Work the butter with your hands, and then beat it with the sugar for a quarter of an hour. Beat the whites of your eggs, mix with the butter and sugar, then add the flour and nutmeg and beat all together, mixing the currants and almonds in well. Make three layers, alternating them with the lemon and orange peel. Put in a mould and place in the oven, cover with paper and leave until perfectly baked.

Gâteau à l'anglaise · English cake

Mix some flour with some milk and cream, add half a pound of dried chopped raisins, and the same amount of beef suet, some coriander, grated nutmeg, orange-flower water and brandy. Mix it all well together, butter the base of a casserole, put your cake mixture in and cook it in the oven. At the moment of serving, glaze it with sugar.

CAPON   *CHAPON*

We have already said in our preface that it was the inhabitants of the island of Cos who taught the Romans the art of fattening poultry. Because of the profusion of poultry in the dark and enclosed areas in Rome, the consul Caius Fanius was obliged to pass a law forbidding hens to be raised in the streets. What then did the Romans do to evade the law? They learned to castrate cocks, which they then raised like hens. Thus the introduction of the capon to the modern table is something which we owe to the fact that Romans were prohibited from eating fat pullets.

Chapon au gros sel · Capon with rock salt

Take a capon, draw, singe and pluck it. Truss it with the legs inside, bard it and cook it in consommé. Drain, arrange on a platter, salt it, put a sauce of reduced beef juices on it, and serve.

Chapon au riz · Capon with rice

Prepare as above. Blanch about 375 grams of rice, drain it and put it in a pot with two ladlefuls of consommé. Bring to the boil over a fast heat, then cover the pot and let it simmer on a *paillasse* [brick oven with glowing charcoal], taking care to stir the rice from time to time. When the cooking is over, skim off any fat from the rice, arrange it, and season it with butter, salt, coarsely ground pepper and reduced pan juices, if you have some, and mask your capon with this.

CARP   *CARPE*

This is a freshwater fish of rivers and lakes. It is mentioned in neither Greek nor Latin literature. [This is a puzzling statement. Aristotle, Pliny and Oppian all refer to the carp as *Cyprinus*. The French naturalist Cuvier, writing in the early nineteenth century, had explicitly compared what classical authors said about carp with the observations made of carp in his own time.]

Carp

Carp weighing 40 or 50 pounds are found in the Rhone, and their flesh is delicious. The carp lives for several centuries, a fact which it has been possible to establish by specimens which were placed by the hands of François I in the fish-ponds of Fontainebleau. Carp grow less big in the north than in the west and the south. In one female carp 18 inches long Doctor Petit found 342,000 eggs.

In the East, the Jews, who are forbidden to eat sturgeon caviar, make a caviar from the eggs of the carp.

Finding myself at Poti, at the mouth of the River Rioni (the Phasis of classical times), and being tired of eating nothing but ram, I expressed a desire for a change of food. Vasiln, who had then already been my servant for three days, suggested to me a fishing expedition in the lake. As I was compelled to wait for the Odessa boat, I asked for nothing better than to pass a day in an amusing activity. When we had travelled about a league through the forest we found ourselves on the edge of the lake, and there embarked in a fisherman's boat. It was agreed that for two roubles, that is to say eight francs, the craft would fish on contract for us. At the end of two hours we had taken three or four hundred pounds of fish.

We picked out the finest fish, left the remainder for our fishermen, and returned to the house of Maître Jacob. The biggest of our fish were a carp weighing 40 pounds and a pike–perch weighing 35 pounds. We opened up the carp. She had 13 pounds of eggs inside her. One of her scales was big enough to cover a five-franc piece completely. Twelve bottles of wine were required to cook her. This is the biggest fish of the species which I have ever seen. As she had been caught in a lake with a circumference of eight leagues and an opening to the sea, she did not smell of mud and was as pure in this regard as a river carp.

On the following day we made a present of it to the inn-keeper, who fed everybody with it.

Since we have just referred to carp smelling of mud, let us explain at once how to get rid of this smell from fish afflicted by it. As soon as the fish has been caught, make it swallow a glass of strong vinegar, and you will instantly perceive a sort of sweat break out all over its body. This you remove in scaling the fish. When it is dead, its flesh will stiffen and it will have just as good a taste as if it had been taken from running water.

Carpe à la Chambord
Take a fine Rhine carp, scale it, skin it and gut it without opening

up its belly completely. Remove the gills without damaging the tongue, then take out the sinew from the tail. Lard the fish all over with eel cut into little lardoons; or half with eel and half with truffles and carrots cut in the same way. If you are serving the carp *au gras*, lard it with bacon and either truffles or carrots. Put it in a fish kettle, pour over it a meatless braising liquid and cook it.

Next, put into a casserole three glassfuls of sauce espagnole *maigre* and half a bottle of white wine from Champagne. Reduce this sauce and skim off the fat. Add peeled mushrooms, truffles, carp roes, quenelles and sections of eel. Simmer this ragoût for a quarter of an hour, then finish it off with some anchovy butter.

Drain the carp, set it up on a platter, dispose your garnish around it, adding some crayfish to the garnish and using others to decorate the carp, pour the sauce over it, chill it and serve it. If you are serving it *au gras*, add some larded sweetbreads, pigeons *à la Gautier* or quails, if in season, and cockscombs and cock kidneys.

Laitances de carpes frites · Fried carp roes

Remove the membranes from fifteen to eighteen carp roes, then leave them to cleanse themselves in water, changing the water several times so that they come out really white.

Put into a casserole some water, a thread of vinegar and a pinch of salt. Add the roes. When you see them coming to the boil, let them boil just for a moment, then [take them out and] dip them in a light batter. Fry them until they are well coloured and serve them with fried parsley.

(?) CARPET-SHELL
CLOVIS DE SAINT-JEAN-DE-LUZ

[A question mark precedes the English name, because it is difficult to tell what bivalve Dumas has in mind. It seems likely that he is referring to *Venerupis aurea* (Gmelin), most commonly known in France as the Clovisse (not Clovis). Although the entry is confusing, we have translated it because it is one of the very few on bivalves. Dumas says nothing about several species which are well known and widely eaten in France.]

These have the name *Chirlat* at Saint-Jean-de-Luz. At Marseilles they are called *Praires*, and at Naples *Vongoli (Conca Veneris)*. Put them on the fire, in a casserole, and toss them about until they have given up all their liquid. Take them out of the casserole and reserve them. Add to the liquid in the casserole three little cloves of garlic chopped up very finely; pepper only, the juices being already sufficiently salty; and toasted bread crumbs as soon as the garlic has started to heat up. Return the bivalves to the casserole, toss them about while the liquid boils up three times, and serve hot. (Recipe given by François Frères, the excellent chef of the Hôtel de France at Saint-Jean-de-Luz.)

CARROT   *CAROTTE*

A comestible plant, belonging to the umbelliferous family, whose root is much used in the kitchen because of its strong and pleasant taste. It is a sudorific and an aperient and purifies the blood. The carrot is healthful and produces no ill effects unless used immoderately. It contains a lot of oil and essential salts and suits all ages and dispositions.

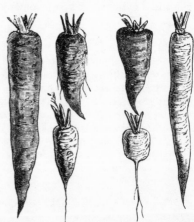

The carrot is ordinarily used in all sorts of soups, in braised dishes and *coulis*, also in meat dishes which are served in terrines and are called hotchpotch. The ones chosen should be long, large and plump, yellow or a palish white in colour, easy to snap and with a taste verging on the sweet.

Potage aux carottes · Carrot soup

Put in a pot enough water to provide a large tureen of soup. When it comes to the boil, add 250 grams of good butter to it, salt, a half-*litron* (about 4 decilitres) of dried peas and three or four crisp carrots cut into pieces. Cook it and, one hour before serving, add some sweet herbs such as sweet cicely, sorrel, etcetera; with white chicory, a little parsley root, spring onion and onion. Cook all this together, arrange and serve.

CAULIFLOWER   *CHOUX-FLEURS*

We take from the recipe books of the period of Louis XIV the best and also the royal way of preparing this vegetable.

Choux-fleurs étuvés · Stewed cauliflower

Take some tall cauliflowers and wash them in tepid water. Cook them in consommé, adding a little powdered mace. When they are properly cooked, and at the moment of serving, drain off the cooking liquid, and stir the flowers with some very fresh cold butter. As soon as the butter melts, arrange the cauliflowers and serve them at the table.

CAVAILLON MELON   *CAVAILLON*

'Cavaillon. 25 kilometres south east of Avignon. Remains of a triumphal arch. Famous winter melons.' [Dumas did not put this paragraph in quotation marks. But he is evidently quoting a real or imaginary guide book.]

The reader may presume that the town of Cavaillon is not mentioned here, because of its situation on the River Durance, nor for its proximity to Avignon, nor for its triumphal arch, but for its famous melons, which in fact are not winter melons, but green ones.

Cavaillon Melon

One day I received a letter from the municipal council of Cavaillon which informed me that they were establishing a library and were desirous of securing for it the best books which they possibly could. They therefore begged me to send them those two or three of my novels which to my mind were the best. Now, I have a daughter and a son, whom I think I love equally; and I am the author of five or six hundred volumes and believe myself to be just about equally fond of them all. So I replied to the town of Cavaillon that it was not for an author to judge the merits of his books, that I thought all my books good, but that I found Cavaillon melons excellent; and that I consequently proposed to send to the town of Cavaillon a complete set of my works, that is to say four or five hundred volumes, if the municipal council would be willing to vote me a life annuity of twelve green melons.

The municipal council of Cavaillon, I must say, replied by return of post that my request had been unanimously endorsed, and that I would certainly receive my life annuity, which in all likelihood is the only one that I will ever have.

I have now been enjoying this annuity for some twelve years, and I must say that it has never failed to arrive at the season for green melons, which become ripe a little later than the others. I do not know whether the municipal council of Cavaillon has the kindness to select from their melons and to send me those which they think are the best, but I repeat that I have never eaten fresher, more flavourful or more palatable melons than those of my annuity. I therefore have only one desire to express, which is that the people of Cavaillon will always find my books as charming as I find their melons. I thus have the opportunity both of conveying all my thanks to my good friends in Cavaillon and of pointing out at the same time to the whole of Europe that Cavaillon melons are the best that I know.

CELERY   *CÉLERI*

Celery is the plant with which, in classical times, people would garland themselves during their meals, to neutralize the strong effects of wine. 'Let us fill the goblets with the Massic wine, which causes all ills to be forgotten,' said Horace, 'let us draw their perfumes through these large *pompes* [presumably *pompes de cellier*, which were tubes through which wine-tasters could draw up a taste of wine from a barrel], and may they hurry to make us wreaths of celery and myrtle.'

Salade de céleri

Celery which is full, tender and fresh, seasoned with aromatic vinegar and with oil from Provence and a little good mustard, and then eaten as a salad is really delicious. It awakens the stomach to activity and gives one both an appetite and a sort of alacrity which lasts for several hours.

CHARCUTERIE   *CHARCUTERIE*

The art of preparing pork meat. A fair in honour of charcuterie, called *Foire aux jambons*, takes place in Paris during Holy Week. The word charcuterie comes from *charcuitier* (*cuiseur de chair*), the old name for those who engage in this trade, and who now go by the name charcutier. The products which they obtain from the pig, this unclean animal which is good from head to toe, are enormous in number: ham, all sorts of sausages, trotters, head, sausage meat, ear, tongue, crackling, brawn, *fromage d'Italie*, bacon, black pudding, *petit salé*, chops, etc.

The sale of pork has been the exclusive province of charcutiers only since 1475, when they formed themselves into a society. By their statutes, confirmed by royal decree, the sale of cooked pork was allotted to them; but such trade was to cease during Lent, when they could sell instead salt herring and sea fish. Nowadays, in most charcuteries, one finds a large number of cold dishes in which the main ingredients are veal, poultry and game, and in which pork meat plays only a subordinate role.

As charcuterie is made only from the pig, it is in the entry on the pig that we explain the different ways of preparing and serving it.

CHARLOTTE   *CHARLOTTE*

A sweet based on cream and fruit.

Charlotte de pommes aux confitures · Apple charlotte with jam

Peel and core some apples. Cut them in pieces, then stew them with sugar (about a third of the weight of the apples), a little powdered cinnamon and the zest of half a lemon until you have a *marmelade* (thick purée). Let the purée reduce.

Cut pieces of bread in the thinnest slices possible, some in oblongs and others in triangles, and dip them in melted butter. Cover the bottom of a buttered casserole with the triangles and its sides with the oblongs, which should reach up as high as will your filling.

Put a generous spoonful of raspberry-flavoured red currant jelly or apricot jam in the middle of the stewed fruit.

When the casserole is ready, put in the stewed apple, smooth the top and cover it with buttered breadcrumbs. Set the casserole on glowing embers and cover it with a fairly hot *four de campagne*, or with a lid on which you place hot coals, and let it cook until it turns golden brown.

Charlotte d'abricots · Apricot charlotte

Take twenty-four apricots fresh from the open air, reddish but not too ripe. Peel them and cut each into eight sections. Toss these in a pan with 120 grams of castor sugar and 60 grams of melted butter for ten minutes over a low heat.

While they are cooking, you cut the inside clean out of a loaf of bread of two pounds. This you will have ordered on the previous day, to be made from the same dough as ordinary soft milk rolls. You cut the crumb of this bread through its thickness with a corer of 8 *lignes* (18 millimetres) in diameter. You then soak the resulting columns of bread in lukewarm butter and use them to line the bottom and sides of your mould.

Now pour in the boiling apricots, cover the mould and let the dish cook until it takes on a blonde colour. Turn it out on a platter, glaze it with apricot purée and serve it.

[Dumas gives this recipe in abbreviated form. The whole of the second paragraph above is dealt with by a reference to a further recipe, attributed to M. de Courchamps, for a *Charlotte de pommes d'api*. However, Elizabeth David has pointed out to us that this other recipe was copied out incorrectly by Dumas or his copyist, who left out some important details. We have therefore restored the text which appeared in de Courchamps' book.]

Cheese is nothing but the curds of milk which have been separated from the serum and hardened by a slow heat. It is the coarsest part of milk and the most compact, so obviously it produces a substantial foodstuff, but one which is difficult to digest if eaten to excess.

It was the Romans who brought the art of cheese-making to Gaul. Since then it has spread widely, for there are few cantons in France which do not have their own special cheese, and few good tables where it is not served in whatever shape or form it has adopted.

Cheese can be made either with milk which has previously had the buttery part removed, or with milk which still includes it. In the latter case the cheese has a considerably better taste, because of the creamy element which is the most exalted constituent of milk and the one most full of oily elements and volatile salt.

Cheese is made from the milk of several animals, but the milk most commonly used is that of the cow. It has an agreeable taste and is highly nourishing, but difficult to digest.

Cheese for eating should be neither too old, nor too new. If it is too young, it weighs on the stomach and frequently causes wind and diarrhoea. If it is too old, it causes irritation by its great acridity; produces a bad liquid; has a disagreeable smell; and makes the stomach lazy, because the considerable fermentation which it has undergone has deprived it of its qualities of moistness and has caused it to lose its usual characteristics.

There are a considerable number of cheeses. The most esteemed are Brie, Dutch, Gruyère, Livarot, Marolles, Camembert, Roquefort, Parmesan; and finally those delicious little Swiss cheeses which are real creams both to the tongue and the eye, and which gourmands find so delectable.

We shall not indicate here all the ways of making the different cheeses, which it is anyway simpler, easier and less costly to buy for oneself from cheese merchants. We will only give the recipes for those which are made daily in the country, and whose preparation is the simplest. [Dumas gives a number of recipes, not translated here, prefaced by a set of general instructions, given below.]

To make good cheese generally, one must have good milk and good rennet.

Take milk which has been freshly drawn, and strain it. Add rennet to it while stirring it with a big spoon, then let it rest until it coagulates. Once it has turned to curd, take it out of the pot, put it in forms, drain off the whey, and arrange it appropriately on a plate.

CHERRIES   *CERISE*

A red fruit with a stone, which comes from the cherry tree. This fruit is watery and acid. If cherries are eaten in small quantities, they provide the stomach with a useful complement of aqueous juices, alkaline salts and sugary substances.

Soupe aux cerises à l'allemande · German cherry soup

We only mention this for interest's sake. It is a detestable dish of squashed cherries and pounded cherry stones, all fiercely spiced, drowned in wine and served cold.

CHESTNUT   *CHÂTAIGNE*

This is the fruit of the chestnut tree, a tree which belongs to the beech family. Chestnuts go very well with all meats and can be used as a garnish for grilled meat. They are also used in all sorts of stuffings, but only in season, for it is difficult to keep them until the end of the winter. They can, however, be preserved indefinitely when dried in a drying oven. This has been done for a long time in the provinces, especially in Limousin where chestnuts make up a considerable part of the diet. Even bread is made from them in places where wheat is very rare, but this bread is always of bad quality, heavy, and difficult to digest.

CHICKEN (and HEN and PULLET)
POULE, POULET, POULARDE

It was the inhabitants of the island of Cos who taught the Romans the art of fattening poultry in enclosed dark places. The large number of fattened poultry which were to be found in Rome compelled the consul Caius Fanius to pass a law forbidding the rearing of poultry in the streets.

The hen came originally from India; but it has spread from its birthplace to practically all points of the globe. It appears in quite strikingly different varieties. In Turkey, its feathers are almost as rich as those of the pheasant. In China, instead of feathers, it has wool. In Persia there is one entire species which lacks a tail. In India they have black flesh and black bones, which does not prevent them from being very good to eat.

Poulets de Bresse

Hens were subjected to sumptuary laws which prohibited the serving at table of any chicken other than the common farm-yard type (these being the laws which the consul Fanius invoked).

Since there are no sumptuary laws in France which prohibit the fattening of poultry, we will explain the method which produces in poultry the best possible taste and at the same time the best quantity of fat. In three weeks or a month, our hens will become fattened pullets.

Feed them for a few days with ground barley, bran and milk. Put them in a cage in a dark place, but one which is not damp. Finally, always leave within easy reach of them some barley which has been kneaded with milk.

Capons should have the same food. The Romans castrated little cocks at the age of three months, and they fattened these new capons with a paste of flour and milk, keeping them in a dark place. They also castrated hens, by removing the ovaries, in order to turn them into fat pullets. Buckwheat, even more than barley, is recommended for fattening farm-yard birds which are destined for the gourmet's table.

Brillat-Savarin had just been ill; his doctor recommended that he

Chicken (and Hen and Pullet)

should diet. A friend came and found him carving up a pullet from Le Mans.

'Is this, then, the diet of an ill man?' demanded the indignant visitor.

'My dear friend,' replied the author of *La Physiologie du goût*, 'I am living on buckwheat and barley.'

'But what about this pullet?'

'She has lived on that for two months, and now she in turn is making me live. Just think,' added the illustrious magistrate, with his pindaric enthusiasm, 'what a present the Moors gave us when they sent us buckwheat! It is the buckwheat grain which makes the pullet so seductive, so delicate, so exquisite.

When I traverse the countryside and see a field of buckwheat, I cannot prevent myself from admiring this beneficent herb which perfumes the air when it flowers. This aroma sends me into a sort of ecstasy, and I think I am breathing in the scent of the pullet for which one day this will serve as food. [Where the quotation ends, i.e. whether here or at the end of the preceding paragraph, is not indicated in Dumas' text.]

*

Chickens—There are four kinds:

1. The ordinary chicken which is normally used in a fricassée. Its meat is usually taken off the bones and serves for making stuffings of various kinds.

2. The *demi-grain* chicken [spring chicken weighing around 1½ pounds] which is put raw into marinades, and makes various entrées which do not require very large chickens.

3. The chicken *à la reine* [spring chicken weighing around 3½ pounds]. These are also very delicate and are also used for entrées and for *rôts*.

4. The large fat chicken which is more commonly used for spit roasting than for any other purpose.

It is towards the end of April that one starts to see the new chickens. They are easily recognized by the whiteness of their skin. They are usually covered with tiny quills as though they had been badly plucked. Their feet are less splayed than those of old birds, softer to the touch, and blue verging on slate in colour.

Old hens and cocks are good only for giving more body to bouillons and consommés.

After the chicken come the fat pullets and the capons.

Hachis de poulardes à la reine · Chicken hash *à la reine*

Chop up finely the white meat of pullets and chickens. Put some béchamel and some consommé, in the right proportion for the amount of meat available, into a casserole. Bring the sauce to the boil and dilute it with water. When it is time to serve, mix in the minced chicken, without allowing it to boil, and finish it off with a little butter and grated nutmeg. This hash is well received in big vol-au-vent cases or in little hot pies.

Poulets à la provençale

Take two chickens, and cut them up as for a fricassée. Have a dozen white onions and cut them in half rings, or with a little parsley. Put your onions in a casserole or a frying pan. Make a layer of onions and one piece of chicken; cover this with another layer of onions, chicken and parsley. Add a glassful of oil, one or two bay leaves and the right amount of salt. Put the remaining pieces of chicken on top of this bed. Place the casserole or pan on the stove, bring to the boil, and then leave to simmer. Once it is all cooked, glaze them, and arrange them with the onions in the middle and a little espagnole as a sauce. Then serve.

CHOCOLATE *CHOCOLAT*

It is thought that the word chocolate comes from two Mexican words: *choco*, meaning sound or noise and *atle*, meaning water, because Mexicans beat it with water to make it froth. The ladies of the New World, it seems, love it madly and make considerable use of it. There are reports that, not satisfied by having it at all times of day at home, they sometimes have it served in church. This sensual indulgence has often brought them censure and reproaches from their confessors, who nevertheless have ended up by resigning themselves to the inevitable. They found that this was in their interest, because these ladies were courteous enough to offer them a cup from time to time, an offer which they took care not to refuse. Finally, the reverend Father Escobar, whose metaphysics were just as subtle as his accommodating morals, formally declared that chocolate made with water in no way broke the rules for fasting, thus proclaiming in favour of his beautiful penitents the ancient adage: *Liquidum non frangit jejunium.*

Chocolate

Imported into Spain towards the seventeenth century, the use of chocolate immediately became popular. Women, and particularly monks, threw themselves at this new and aromatic beverage with the greatest alacrity, and chocolate was soon in vogue. Habits in this respect have not changed at all, and even today throughout the whole peninsula, it is in good taste to present chocolate on all the occasions when politeness demands that one should offer some refreshments. And this happens everywhere in all self-respecting houses.

Chocolate crossed the mountains with Anne of Austria, the wife of Louis XIII, who was the first to import it into France. With the help once more of the French monks, to whom their brothers in Spain sent samples as presents, it soon came into fashion there. At the beginning of the Regency, it was used more than coffee, which likewise had been newly imported. But coffee was regarded as a luxury drink and a curiosity, whereas chocolate was considered, quite rightly too, as a healthful and agreeable food.

M. Brillat-Savarin recommends chocolate as a tonic and stomachic substance, and even a digestive. He says that people who use it enjoy consistently good health, and he speaks of ambergris-flavoured chocolate as being excellent for people who are tired from whatever work they have been doing.

Let the illustrious gastronome speak for himself. [Dumas has in fact already allowed the illustrious gastronome to provide much of this article, although it is only at this point that he acknowledges the source of his material.]

'This is the right place,' he says, 'to speak of the properties of ambergris-flavoured chocolate, properties which I have verified myself by a large number of experiments, the results of which I am proud to offer to my readers.

'Well then, if any man has drunk a little too deeply from the cup of voluptuousness, if he has spent too much time working when he should have been asleep; if a man of spirit find himself temporarily stupid, if he finds the air humid, that time drags, and that the atmosphere is too heavy to withstand; if he is obsessed by a fixed idea which robs him of freedom of thought; in any of these situations, we say, let the person take a good half litre of ambergris-flavoured chocolate, in the proportions of 60 to 72 grains of ambergris to half a kilo of chocolate, and marvels will be witnessed.

'In my own particular way of designating things I call ambergris-flavoured chocolate "chocolate of the afflicted", because in each one of the various states which I have described, the people are subject to a kind of feeling which I cannot define but which they have in common and which resembles an affliction.'

It is still M. Brillat-Savarin who is talking:

'As for the official method of making chocolate, that is to say to make it ready for immediate use, about an ounce and a half is taken for each cup, and then dissolved slowly in water as it heats, while being stirred with a wooden spatula; it should then boil for fifteen minutes, so that the solution takes on a certain thickness, and be served hot.

' "Monsieur," Madame d'Arestrel, Superior of the Convent of the Visitation at Belley, once said to me more than fifty years ago, "when you want to have really good chocolate, have it made the night before in a porcelain coffee pot, and leave it. The repose of the night concentrates it, and gives it a velvet quality which improves it greatly. The good God cannot possibly take offence at this little refinement, since he himself is everything that is most perfect." '

COCK   *COQ*

The cock is unquestionably the most glorious, most vigilant and most courageous of birds.

As to pride, one has only to watch him parading in the middle of his harem of hens to recognize that in this respect he rivals the peacock. As to vigilance, he never sleeps more than two hours at a stretch, from one o'clock in the morning, he wrests man from sleep with his piercing cry and sends him back to his work. As for courage, Levaillant reports in his *Mémoires* that his cock was the only one of his animals to remain unperturbed by the approach or roar of a lion.

For a while, during the First Empire, there was some question of taking the ancient cock of the Gauls as emblem and insignia for the French flag. The Emperor Napoleon the First, to whom the proposal was submitted, refused, replying: 'I don't want the cock, because *the fox eats it*.' And he chose the eagle.

In cooking, the cock is used only for making consommé. The ancient recipe collections attributed heroic virtues to this consommé, known under the name of *gelée de coq*.

The virgin cock, the bachelor of the farm-yard, nevertheless owes to its continence and its virtue its particular taste and aroma. These distinguish it clearly from its uncle, the capon, who, as is well known, is not the father but the uncle of chickens. It is eaten after having been simply barded and cooked on a spit, for it would be an outrage to lard it and a dishonour to put it in a stew.

Cock

To conclude, the cock is a very handsome animal, gallant, intrepid and endowed with a sonorous voice, and highly representative of the French spirit. But it is worth very little in the kitchen, where its offspring are preferred.

COCOA   *CACAO*

A grain, the size of a small broad bean, nested in the butyraceous pulp of the fruit of the cocoa-tree. This tree grows abundantly in America and produces fluted and striped pods, of about the thickness of 7 or 8 mm, enclosing thirty to thirty-five beans fairly similar to our pistachios, but bigger and plumper, rounded and covered with a thin dry skin; the substance of these beans has a bitter, slightly tart taste.

There are different sorts of cocoa: from Cayenne, from Caracas, from the island of Sainte Madeleine, from Berbice and from Santo Domingo [now Ciudad Trujillo]; they differ from each other in the size and flavour of the beans. The big Caracas variety, the flattish beans of which resemble our big broad beans in size and shape, is considered the best of all. After this come the varieties from Sainte Madeleine and Berbice; their beans are less flat than those from Caracas, and their skins are covered by a very fine, cinder-coloured dust. The others are good only for making cocoa butter, because of their bitterness and the oil which they contain.

To obtain chocolate of the finest quality, one must blend in equal proportions cocoa from Caracas, Sainte Madeleine and Berbice; this gives it the unctuous and oily constituents which it must have; chocolate made with Caracas cocoa alone would be too dry, and that which only contained cocoa from the islands would turn out too oily and too bitter.

It is the practice to 'earth' cocoa in the ground, in order to make it lose its bitterness; and one must be careful, before using it, to get rid of this cover of earth, which makes it a bit musty. This does not prevent the cocoa of Caracas, the only one subjected to this preparatory burial, from producing the best of all known chocolate. It is necessary, however, as we have already said, to mix in other varieties so as to correct its insipidity with a certain bitterness which is not unpleasing.

These cocoas are lightly roasted; once cool, the cocoa is crushed to separate the covering, or husk, which is discarded. In Switzerland and in Germany, however, the husks are kept to make an infusion in boiling water which the inhabitants of those countries mix with milk and drink instead of real chocolate. In the Orient the aril, or covering of the coffee bean, is used in the same way, to make *café à la Sultane*.

To gather cocoa, one waits until the fruit is completely ripe and resounds, when shaken, with the rattling of the seeds within. The fruits are then stacked in piles and left for three or four days to dry in order to split them and rid them of the pulpy flesh surrounding them.

Boisson de chocolat · Chocolate drink

For each 30 grams of chocolate, put a cup of either milk or water in a chocolate pot, let this come to the boil, add the grated chocolate and stir the mixture. When the chocolate has melted and is incorporated with the milk or water, you leave it in a warm place for about a quarter of an hour; then stir the drink briskly and, when it is very frothy, pour it into cups.

COD   *CABILLAUD*

[Dumas begins this entry by explaining that he will deal in it with both fresh cod and salt cod. He remarks that *cabillaud* is the Dutch name for fresh cod. The Dutch name is in fact *Kabeljauw*. He also observes that *morue* is the French name for salt cod.]

A fish of the gadoid family. It differs from the whiting in having a barbel attached to its lower jaw. It is as fertile as it is voracious. Eight and a half million, or even nine million eggs have been found in a single cod, admittedly of the largest size, which is to say weighing between 30 and 32 kilograms. It has been calculated that if nothing happened to prevent the hatching of these eggs, and if each cod grew to its full size, it would only take three years for the sea to be full of cod, so that one could walk dry-shod across the Atlantic on their backs.

Cod spawn in December on the coasts of Spain, and in the spring on the American coasts. At these times their voracity recognizes no obstacle. Joining together in closely knit shoals, they chase their prey, especially mackerel, so vigorously as to drive them by the thousand million on to the beaches.

Cod usually live on the Newfoundland banks, at Cap Breton, off Nova Scotia and New England, in Norwegian waters, off the shores of Iceland, on the Dogger Bank and round Orkney. It is in the spring especially that they can be seen to form shoals, shaped like a parallelogram; and swarm so thickly therein as to appal those who make calculations about the number of voracious fish contained in these banks, which are several feet thick. Thus the cod fishery is one of the most important to which the European nations devote themselves. We have sure proofs that the fishery was organized from the beginning of the ninth century; for towards the end of that century we find that cod-fishing stations were established on the coasts of Norway and Iceland. From 1368 Amsterdam was conducting a fishery for cod on the Swedish coast. According to Anderson, it was in 1536 that the first French boat was despatched to the Newfoundland banks to fish for cod there. For a long time it was claimed that this first essay was made by the Maloins [fishermen of St Malo], but nowadays the honour is attributed to the Basques. Indeed, a hundred years before the expedition of Christopher Columbus, Basque fishermen who were pursuing a whale noticed the great abundance of cod at Newfoundland and carried out the first fishery for them.

In 1578 France sent 1,050 boats to Newfoundland to fish; Spain 110; Portugal 50; and England 30.

The cod fishery usually takes place in February and is most often finished in six weeks. However, it is not uncommon, in good years, for it to last four or five months. The fishing is done with lines, hooks and nets. One fisherman catches only one fish at a time; but the cod are so abundant that a single fisherman can take three to four hundred of them in a day. The fish are so greedy that all kinds of bait are suitable for catching them. The Flemish fishermen use frogs especially, the Basques use anchovies and sardines, and the fishermen of Boulogne use herrings, mackerel and even earthworms. In Ireland, mussels are used; in Holland, pieces of lamprey.

[The collection of recipes which Dumas gives for cod is a poor one. Confusion between the terms *cabillaud* (fresh cod) and *morue* (salt cod) became apparent during the above paragraphs, but without obscuring his meaning, which could be deduced from the context. But it is again apparent in some of the recipes, this time with more perplexing results. To illustrate the point, we translate one recipe below, confident that it will startle any Norwegian who reads it.]

Cabillaud ou morue à la norwégienne ·
> Fresh cod or salt cod (?) in the Norwegian style

Obtain a small fresh *morue* [i.e., according to what we have been told by Dumas himself, a salt cod, not a fresh one], cut it into four or five pieces, debone it and marinate it in warm butter, lemon juice, chopped parsley, shallots and fines herbes. Arrange it with the marinade below it and on top of it, dust it with breadcrumbs, sprinkle warm butter over it, cook it in the oven and serve it with a sauce incorporating white wine, egg-yolks and nutmeg.

COFFEE   *CAFÉ*

The plant which produces coffee is a very low, small shrub which bears fragrant flowers. Coffee comes originally from the Yemen, in Arabia Felix. At present it is cultivated in several countries. The Arab historian, Ahmet-Effendi, thinks that it was a dervish who discovered coffee, in about the fifteenth century, or in the year 650 of the Hegira.

The first European to refer to the coffee plant was Prosper Alpin, of Padua. In 1580 he accompanied a Venetian consul to Egypt. The work of which we are speaking was written in Latin, and addressed to Jean Morazini.

I have seen this tree in Cairo, in the gardens of Ali Bey. It is called *bon* or *boun*. With the berry which it produces, the Egyptians produce a drink which Arabs call *Kawa*. The taste for coffee grew to such an extent at Constantinople that the Imams complained that the mosques were deserted whereas the cafés were always full. Amurat III then permitted coffee to be consumed in private houses, as long as the doors were shut.

Coffee was unknown in France until 1657, when the Venetians first brought it to Europe. It was introduced to France through Marseilles. It became universally used, and the doctors were alarmed about it. But their sinister predictions were treated as unreal, and the result was that, despite the arguments, the cafés were no less frequented.

In 1669, the Ambassador from Mahomet II brought a large quantity to France and we are assured that coffee was being sold in Paris at that time for up to 40 crowns a pound.

Posée-Oblé, in his *Histoire des plantes de la Guyane*, written during the reign of Louis XIII, says that in Paris, near Petit-Châtelet, the decoction made of coffee and known as *cahuet* was being sold. In 1676, an Armenian named Pascale established at the market of Saint-Germain a café which he later moved to the quai de l'Ecole. He made quite a fortune out of it. But it was only at the beginning of the following century that a Sicilian called Procope re-established the coffee market at Saint Germain. He attracted the best people in Paris,

Coffee

because he only provided good merchandise. Later, he set up his business in quarters opposite the Comédie Française; this new café became both a rendez-vous for theatre enthusiasts, and a battle-ground for literary disputes. It was in this café that Voltaire spent two hours every day. In London, during the same period, more than three thousand coffee houses were established. Mme de Sevigné fought against the new fashion as hard as she could and predicted that Racine and the café would pass out of fashion simultaneously.

There are five principal sorts of coffee in commerce, without counting chicory, which our cooks are bent on mixing in. The best comes from *Moka* in Arabia Felix, and it alone is also divided into three varieties: *baouri*, which is reserved for the use of the great lords, *saki* and *salabi*.

Coffee from Reunion is highly esteemed in the trade but, even so, that from Martinique or Guadeloupe is preferred. That from Santo Domingo (Dominican Republic), which also includes Puerto Rico and other Islands of the Leeward group, is of inferior quality.

Coffee had come into general usage in France when, in 1808, Napoleon published his decree concerning the 'continental system' [blockade], which was to deprive France of sugar and coffee at the same time. Beet sugar was substituted for cane sugar, and coffee was eked out by mixing it half and half with chicory. This was completely to the advantage of the grocers and cooks who took to chicory with passion and maintained that chicory mixed with coffee tasted better and was healthier. The misfortune is that even today, when the continental decree has fallen into disuse, chicory remains a part of our cooks' repertoire and they have continued mixing a certain quantity of it with the coffee (which they buy ready ground) under the pretext of refreshing their masters. The masters responded to this situation by ordering coffee to be bought in the bean. But, in moulds made especially for this purpose, chicory paste has been made into the shape of coffee beans; and, whether one will or no, chicory has remained wedded to coffee.

It is usual for coffee made with water, and served after a meal, to be accompanied by a small pitcher of milk which has not been boiled, or cream. This can then be added to the coffee if one likes it this way.

CORN   *MAÏS*

A sort of grain, otherwise called Turkish wheat. It contains much essential oil and salt. Bread is made of it, which is difficult to digest and weighs heavily on the stomach; it only suits people with a strong and robust constitution.

A sort of porridge called *gaudes* [a kind of cornflour porridge or pudding somewhat similar to Italian polenta] is made with cornflour, sugar and milk. This is a very popular foodstuff in Bresse and Franche-Comté. When the pudding is cold, a good thing to do with it is to cut it into slices, which can be grilled and then sprinkled with sugar.

One can introduce some beef marrow or fresh butter into this pudding, thus making it more savoury; and if you then add currants, or candied citron peel, you have a dish which is quite agreeable to eat.

CRABS   *CRABES*

There are several species of crab. However, only the large crab of Brittany and the *crapelet** of the Channel are worthy to appear on our tables, despite their being difficult to digest; their eggs are better and negroes feed on them. The people of the Antilles live almost exclusively on crabs. [In this bewildering paragraph Dumas seems to have combined some jejune and partly incomprehensible remarks about crabs in the north-west of France with observations on the consumption of crabs by people in the West Indies.]

Crabs are cooked in salted water, like lobsters and prawns, with unsalted butter, parsley and a bunch of leeks. Let them cool in their cooking liquid. Then remove carefully the white meat. Take out with a spoon the creamy soft roe and mix it with the cleaned meat, adding watercress, coarse pepper, a little virgin olive oil and a little verjuice. Garnish your platter with the two big claws and serve it as a very elegant *rôt*, especially during Lent.

CREAM and CUSTARD CREAMS   *CRÈME*

Cream is what one calls the sort of skin which rises on milk either before or after boiling; it is made up of serum, a bit of cheese and of

* The 'large crab of Brittany' is *Cancer pagurus* Linnaeus, the principal edible crab of Europe, which has a range from the Mediterranean to Scandinavia. What the *crapelet de la Manche* is cannot easily be determined. If only two of the crabs found on French coasts are to be deemed edible (a proposition which millions of French people would reject at once), then the second ought to be the Spider crab, *Maja squinado* (Herbst). But it is not especially common in the Channel area. On the contrary, it is more abundant in the south of the Bay of Biscay. Nor have we found any trace of it, or indeed any crab, being called *crapelet*.

Cream and Custard Creams

butter in a state of emulsion. It is not used as a foodstuff as such because of the large quantity of butter which it contains and which would weigh on the stomach, produce nausea and even actually make one sick. Nevertheless, at Roquefort, a cheese called *crème de Roquefort* is made. This is made with milk once it has curdled and before the curd has been pounded. It spoils easily, cannot travel, and is denatured by very rapid fermentation.

This same name, *crème*, is also given to various culinary preparations of which the basis is milk and which are prepared by cooking.

We are going to indicate a few:

Crème au café blanc

Take an amount of cream which will provide the quantity you require, add lemon zest and sugar. Roast two ounces of coffee. When it is a good colour, put it in the boiling cream and cover with a lid. Let the coffee infuse in the cream, then take it off the heat. Put in a strainer the inner part of three well-washed gizzards, which have been dried and are practically in a powder. Pour the half-cooled cream through the strainer three times, while tamping the gizzards slightly with a wooden spoon.

Fill your pots promptly with the cream, taking care to stir it, and then let them set in a bain-marie, covering the recipient containing the pots with a lid on top of which you put some glowing embers. When the cream has set, take the pots out and put them, uncovered, in cool water. Wipe them, arrange and serve.

Note: Gelatine from gizzards is much better than white of egg; don't forget this.

Chocolate cream, pistachio cream, rose, orange and lemon creams, etc., are all made like coffee cream. The flavouring only is changed, and is always added in proportion to the amount of custard which you require.

Crème renversée

Take a bowl which is large enough to hold, for example, a litre of milk, six eggs and a half pound of sugar. Next, caramelize a quart of powdered sugar, add a little water to make it runny, then pour it into a mould so as to coat the bottom and sides well. Leave this to cool, and afterwards pour in the liquid custard which you have beaten well. By beating well, I mean mix the milk, the eggs, the sugar, and the flavouring which you want to use for the custard; put everything in a bain-marie, with heat beneath and heat above, until it is perfectly cooked, and has a beautiful colour. Let the custard cool in the mould for twelve hours so that it sets properly, turn it out on a platter so that it is upside down, arrange it and serve the juice around it.

Crème bachique · Bacchic cream

This is made with pink champagne, sugar and either lemon peel or cinnamon, which are boiled together. Afterwards, break a certain number of eggs. Take the yolks of these and bind them together with a small amount of the champagne, which you pour on little by little, and which you continue to stir over the fire without allowing it to boil. [When the whole of the champagne and sugar mixture has been combined with the egg-yolk mixture] strain it all into the container of your choice.

CRYSTALLIZED WHOLE FRUIT
CONSERVES DE FRUITS ENTIERS

Conserve de citrons · Conserve of lemons

You take the zest from one lemon and put it on a plate. Squeeze the juice of the lemon onto the zest, and let it steep for a while. Cook about half pound of clarified sugar to the large pearl stage. Strain the lemon juice through a cloth, or a sieve, to remove the zests. Add the juice to the sugar, and stir it thoroughly until it is very white, and then pour it into the moulds.

Oranges confites · Preserved oranges

Make incisions from place to place in the peel of the oranges. Put them in boiling syrup, half water and half sugar, let them boil until they become very soft, and then take them out.

Put more sugar in the syrup, in such a way as to bring it to the small gloss stage, let it boil, then put back the oranges and bring them back to the boil several times. Skim the syrup, remove the oranges, put them in a container, and pour the syrup over them.

Leave them until the next day, when you must boil up the syrup again several times, and pour it back on the same fruit.

On the third day, cook the sugar to just under 215°F (102.6°C); then add the oranges and let them boil, covered. The same procedure is followed on the next two days. On the last day, having brought the syrup to the pearl stage, you put in the oranges and give them three or four final boilings. Take them out, drain them, and dry them in a drying oven.

Marrons glacés

Take handsome chestnuts from Lyon and roast them on hot coals. Clarify some sugar, and cook it to the crack stage. Then put the chestnuts in the sugar one after the other; take them out again right away with a spoon, and dip each in cold water. The sugar will solidify around them immediately.

CUCUMBER   *CONCOMBRE*

There are different sorts of cucumber, but here we only need to deal with the green cucumbers which are customarily used in the kitchen, where they are prepared in different ways.

Salade de concombres

Take one or two cucumbers, which are not yet fully grown, peel them, taste them to see that they are not bitter; if they are, reject them. Cut them in very thin rounds, put them in a shallow dish, add salt, pepper, vinegar, chopped onion and let them steep thus for two to three hours. Serve this salad with beef, having removed some of the marinade.

CURRANT   *GROSEILLE*

There are two kinds of currant. The green currant (gooseberry) is vulgarly called *groseille à maquereau*, because it is used as verjuice in the season of fresh mackerel. Then there is the red currant, which is particularly used in jams, jellies, stewed fruit, etc.

Everyone knows the uses of the currant and the various preparations which can be made from it. Its juice is refreshing and, when mixed with water, and sugar or honey, it makes an acid beverage which everyone likes, and which in the north is a substitute for lemonade. By distilling it, one can also extract brandy.

The pink and white currants are less acid and more pleasant than the red ones.

We have indicated the different ways of using the currant in the section on jams and refer the reader there for information on its uses in preserves, jellies, compotes and syrup.

DATES   *DATTES*

This is the name given to the fruit of the common date tree. The best dates come from Africa. They are the principal foodstuff of the Arabs. In France they are rarely seen on the table, and are used only for making syrups or jams.

This fruit should be eaten when thoroughly ripe and very fresh; otherwise it causes indigestion and skin trouble. Pliny states that several of Alexander's soldiers died from having eaten an excessive number of unripe dates. They contain very hard stones which are ground and soaked and then given to camels and sheep to eat.

DEER   *DAIM*

A quadruped belonging to the order of ruminants in the stag family. The flesh of this animal is regarded, with good reason, as an excellent food.

The deer is too well known to require description here. In any case, we are not giving a course in natural history. We will only say here that the meat of the deer, venison, is better when the animal is killed in action.

The parts of the deer which are considered best are the quarters and the hind feet, because they are the meatiest. The brain is also a delicate morsel, according to Redi, who claims to have eaten it with bacon. One must choose a young deer, one which is tender, fat, and well nourished. Its flesh produces good meat essences and is most nourishing. When it is too old, it is tough and difficult to digest. [See also under Quarter of deer.]

DOG   *CHIEN*

Some Asian, African and American peoples eat dog meat. Negroes even prefer it to other animals; their greatest treat is roast dog. This same taste is also to be found among the savages of Canada, in the Kamtchadales and in the islands of Oceania.

Captain Cook was saved from a dangerous illness by dog bouillon.

Dog

Hippocrates says the Greeks ate dog and that the Romans served it at the most sumptuous tables. Pliny assures us that small dogs, roasted, are excellent, and that they were considered to be worthy offerings to the gods. In Rome, roast dog was always eaten at the feasts given for the consecration of pontiffs or at public celebrations.

Now this is how Porphyrus, the third-century Greek writer, explains the origin of the custom of eating dog.

'One day, when a dog was being sacrificed, a certain part of the victim (they don't say which) fell to the ground. The priest picked it up in order to replace it on the altar, but, as it was very hot, he burnt himself. In a gesture which was natural and spontaneous in the circumstances, he put his fingers in his mouth and found the juices good. Once the ceremony was over, he ate half the dog, and took the rest to his wife. Then, on the occasion of each subsequent sacrifice, he and his wife feasted on the victim. Word of this soon spread all over town; everyone wanted to taste it and in a very short while roast dog was to be found on the best tables. They started by cooking puppies, which naturally were more tender; then, when there were not enough of these, larger dogs were used.'

The official reports of the recent expedition by the English to China have given us some very strange details on the feeding habits of the Chinese. Amongst other things, we learn that they fatten dogs in cages, much as we do chickens. They feed them vegetable matter, then eat them and find them excellent. This is, it seems, one of the most choice dishes in the celestial empire. It is sold by all Chinese butchers, but it is a delicacy which, like our truffled turkeys, is reserved for the fortunate few; and common mortals are obliged to make do with the sight of it only.

DOTTEREL   *GUIGNARD*

This is a sort of plover which is to be found mainly in Loiret and in Beauce. It is the same size as the blackbird, and the top of its head is a blackish cinder colour. Its back is green in colour with reddish circles. Its flesh is much esteemed, and preferable to that of the plover. Pâtés which are much sought after are made of it. Those which were prepared for the celebrated Philippe de Chartres were made with dotterels which Collin d'Harleville immortalized in a charming epistle, his first work, which persuaded the author to follow a literary career. The result of this was that we owe *l'Inconstant* and *les Chateaux en Espagne* to the dotterels.

DRESSING (for salads)   *ASSAISONNEMENT*

We think that this is the right time to tell the story of the Chevalier d'Albignac who made his fortune in London by dressing salads. We borrow the tale from the illustrious author and philosopher of *La Physiologie du goût*:

'M. d'Albignac had emigrated and retired to London. Although his poor financial state had severely reduced his pittance, he was nevertheless invited one day to one of the most famous taverns in London. He was one of those whose systems permit dining on a single dish, if that dish is really excellent. While he was polishing off an excellent piece of roast beef, five or six young men were having a meal at a neighbouring table. One of these young men rose, approached him and said politely: "Mr Frenchman, they say that your country excels in the art of salad-making. Would you be so kind as to make a dressing for us?"

'After a little hesitation, d'Albignac agreed, and ordered everything he thought necessary for the creation of the expected *chef-d'œuvre*. He took all possible pains, and was happy to be crowned with success. While considering the proportions, he replied frankly to the questions which were put to him about what he was doing, and his current situation. He said that he had emigrated and admitted, not without blushing a little, that he was receiving financial help from the English government, a circumstance which made one of the young men feel able to slip a five pound note into his hand, which he accepted with only token resistance.

'He had given his address and, some time later, he was not a little surprised to receive a letter in which he was invited on most reasonable terms to come and dress a salad in one of the grandest mansions in Grosvenor Square.

'D'Albignac, sensing the possibility of some lasting benefits, did not hesitate a moment and arrived punctually, having armed himself with some additional seasonings which he thought suitable for making his creation as nearly perfect as possible.

'He had had time to consider the task at hand and was lucky to be successful once more. On this occasion he received such a large gratuity that he could not have refused it without damage to his interests.

'The first young men for whom he had performed, as one can guess, had vaunted, to the point of exaggeration, the excellence of the salad which he had prepared for them. The second assemblage made an even greater fuss, so that d'Albignac's reputation promptly became widely known, and he was acclaimed as "the fashionable salad maker". And in this country which is avid for anything new, the most elegant people in the capital of the three kingdoms were all dying to have a salad made like the French gentleman's. "*I die for it*," was the hallowed phrase.

> "*Désir de nonne est un feu qui dévore,*
> *Désir d'Anglaise est cent fois pire encore.*"*

'D'Albignac, like a sensible man, made the most of the infatuation of which he was the target. He soon had a coach in order to make his way more speedily to the various places to which he was summoned, and a servant to carry his mahogany work-box. In this were all the ingredients of his expanded repertoire, such as variously flavoured vinegars, oils with a fruity taste and oils without it, soya, caviar, truffles, anchovy, ketchup, meat essence, and even egg yolks, which give mayonnaise its distinctive character.

'Later he had similar work-boxes manufactured, furnished them completely and sold hundreds of them.

'In the end, by following with precision and care this line of operation, he managed to amass a fortune of more than 80,000 francs which he took back to France when times improved.

'Once back in his motherland, he did not amuse himself by making himself conspicuous on the streets of Paris, but attended to his future. He put 60,000 francs in government stocks, which at that time were at 50 per cent, and bought for 20,000 francs a small country seat in Limousin, where he probably still lives, happy and content as he knew how to set a limit to his desires.'

DUCK   *CANARD*

There are forty-two different varieties of duck, amongst which may be singled out the musked duck, whose flesh is very delicate. But one must take care to cut off its rump before cooking; without taking this precaution it takes on such a strong smell of musk that it is almost impossible to eat it. Particularly appreciated is the flesh from the stomach, vulgarly called *aiguillettes* [long thin strips of meat].

---

* 'The desire of a nun is a devouring fire, that of an Englishwoman is a hundred times worse.' Mrs. Fisher, in a gloss on this passage in her own translation of Brillat-Savarin, remarks that the original jingle, of about 1750, went as follows:

> A maiden's lust is a burning curse,
> But a nun's, in truth, is a hundred times worse.

Canard Musqué

Of all birds, the duck is most like the goose, but it is more delicate and easier to digest. Geese, like ducks, can be wild or domesticated, the latter being larger. There are varieties within these species, for example that from Barbary, which is the biggest, less delicate and more likely to smell musky. But if one crosses this sort with another, the result is a hybrid which lacks the disadvantage of having the bad taste of the Barbary type. It is with this sort of cross-breed that *les canetons de Rouen* (duckling of Rouen) are prepared, so highly esteemed for their size and quality. Wild duck is almost always eaten after being cooked on a spit; but there are ways of presenting it as an entrée which I shall endeavour to make known.

DUCKLING   *CANETON*

Canetons de Rouen à l'échalote · Rouen duckling with shallots

Take the whitest duckling which you can find. Cook it on a spit, covered in paper, and on a low heat. Chop up some shallots very fine, put them in some good meat juices, and pour over the duckling with orange juice.

Canetons à l'orange · Ducklings with orange

Take two ducklings and truss them as for a spit-roasted entrée. Line a casserole with a good *mirepoix* [see page 34], add the ducklings and cover them with a piece of buttered paper. Let them sweat gently, then add half a bottle of champagne, with a ladleful of good consommé, and let all this simmer until perfectly cooked.

Take the zest from two oranges, cut it up into fine strips and blanch these in boiling water. Separate the orange quarters, removing the skin, and blanch these likewise. Strain the duck stock through a napkin, and carefully remove the fat. Clarify it, using two egg whites and

a little black pepper, then strain it again through a napkin, into a bain-marie. Add lemon juice, a piece of meat jelly the size of a nut, and a little black pepper. Add the ducklings and arrange them with the orange quarters around them, orange juice poured over them and the pieces of zest on top. (Recipe from Vuillemot.)

I must confess my great partiality for this dish, particularly when confected by the skilful operator from whom I have taken the recipe.

DUMPLING   *DUMPLING*

Foreign cooking, an English dessert.

Dumpling aux pommes ou aux prunes · Apple or plum dumpling

Roll out your hot pastry-dough thin and lay on it peeled apples or plums from Damascus. Having dampened the edges of the dough and closed the edges, boil the whole thing in a cloth for an hour. Pour hot melted butter over it, sprinkle it with sugar and serve.

[We have done our best, with the help of pastry experts on both sides of the Channel, to make sense of this recipe, but have concluded that it can only be presented as an example of how Dumas could go astray in dealing with dishes with which he was not familiar.

An apple dumpling made in England in the nineteenth century would have been made with suet-crust pastry, and would have been wrapped in a cloth, and boiled or steamed (for two hours, not one). But the use of the word '*chaud*' seems to show that Dumas meant hot-water crust pastry (the same as raised pie pastry) to be used. This would have been totally unsuitable for boiling!

A possible explanation of the confusion is that in certain parts of England, e.g. Nottinghamshire and Gloucestershire, fruit pies were made with hot-water crust pastry in the eighteenth and nineteenth centuries. Dumas might have come across such a recipe and somehow amalgamated it in his mind with the recipe for apple dumpling. But this seems rather unlikely.

Dumas' suggestion that plums could be used instead of apples is interesting. It may be the result of his interest in English plum puddings. These, however, do not contain plums.]

Dumpling de Norfolk · Norfolk dumpling

This dish, which owes its name to the Duke of Norfolk, who had a great affection for it, is made in the following way. You add to a fairly thick dough a big glass of milk, two eggs and a little salt. Cook it for two or three minutes in quickly boiling water. Discard the water, drain the dumpling and serve it with slightly salted butter.
[Norfolk dumplings are named for the county, not for any Duke thereof. They are not made in the manner described; and if they were, they could not possibly be cooked in 'two or three minutes'. Nor are they served with slightly salted butter. What people in Norfolk and many other English counties used to do was to keep back some of the dough from bread-baking, make large dumplings therewith (say, ¼ lb each), boil them for about fifteen minutes and serve them in the meat gravy. See, for example, Elizabeth David's *English Bread and Yeast Cookery*, Allen Lane, 1977.]

DURIAN   *DURION*

This is the name given to a fruit which grows on a very tall tree, which is remarkable for its size, and resembles our melons. The tree comes from India originally, and the Siamese like the durian so much that they keep it available, preserved, all year. By cooking it with fresh cream they make a *marmelade* which they put into pots.

The durian is enveloped in a skin which is harder than that of chestnuts, and covered with very sharp spikes. The smell of the skin is disagreeable and has the taste of roasted onions, but the flesh of the fruit has an exquisite taste. In this flesh there is a small nut containing a kernel which people toast and then eat. It tastes like our chestnuts.

The Egyptians ranked eels as gods, devoting a religious cult to them. They reared them in special ponds or tanks, whither priests were charged to bring them cheese and animal entrails daily. They tamed these sacred eels and adorned them with jewels in the form of necklaces.

The eel reaches an enormous size. In Italy, and especially in the salt-marshes of Comacchio, eels more than two metres long, weighing up to ten kilos, have been seen. In Albania their thickness sometimes equals the thickness of a man's thigh. But the countries where they attain the greatest size are Poland and Scotland. The peoples of those countries regard them as snakes and do not eat them. The Jews also abstain from eating them, because of religious scruples. One eel which measured six metres in length and 65 centimetres in circumference was found in Scotland. The sailors who caught it ate it and found that it had a very delicate flavour.

[This anecdote, for which no source is given, is baffling. The maximum length of *Anguilla anguilla* (Linnaeus), the common eel, is reckoned to be under 1 metre 40. Even Couch (*British Fishes*, 1878), who lost no opportunity to cite reports of exceptionally large fish, goes no further than to report, on the word of a Mr Daniel, that an eel taken in Kent was five feet nine inches long. Nor can we solve the mystery by supposing that the eel to which Dumas refers was a conger eel for which the maximum length is not much more than four metres. Given the mystery of the Loch Ness monster and the special interest which many people have in any unusually large and eel-like creature found in Scotland, one can only lament for the umpteenth time that Dumas was so sparing in his citation of sources.]

River eels are the best and therefore the most sought after. Their backs are of a brown colour mixed with blue, their bellies of a bright and pure silvery white colour; while eels in ponds, stagnant pools or ditches are always earth-coloured.

The general practice of our cooks, whether they are men or women, is to make a circular incision round the neck of the eel and then pull its skin off. A better way of skinning an eel is to expose it first to the heat of a charcoal brasier, which causes its skin to wrinkle and puff out. One can then remove this grilled skin by pulling it from head to tail, using a cloth with which to grip it. This method removes from the eel the oil belonging to its skin, gives it a better taste and makes it easier to digest.

EGGPLANT   *AUBERGINE*

The fruit of a sort of solanaceous plant. It is shaped like a large egg.
The white and the purple ones are the best. They are eaten in salads
or cooked, and here are the best ways of preparing them:

Aubergine à la languedocienne

Split the eggplants lengthwise, remove the seeds and chop up the
flesh. Salt and pepper them, sprinkle them with nutmeg and grill
them on a low heat, basting them with good oil.

Aubergine à la parisienne

Remove the flesh from four purple eggplants [which you have cut in
half lengthwise], but keep the skin intact. Chop the flesh up with
some white poultry meat, or the meat from a roast lamb, or the lean
meat of a sucking pig or any other well-cooked white meat. Put 180
grams of marrow in this chopped mixture or, if you prefer, season it
all with a pinch of nutmeg, 180 grams of bacon fat and a little salt.
Add to the mixture some stale breadcrumbs and moisten it with four
egg yolks. Fill the half eggplant-skins with this stuffing and cook
them in a pie-dish, sprinkling marrow or melted bacon fat over them.

EGGS   *ŒUFS*

An organic body, laid by female birds, which encloses the growth of
a germ. Hens' eggs are those most frequently used for human
nourishment.

'It is obvious', says M. Payen, 'that this foodstuff contains all the
essential elements for the formation of animal tissues, since it suffices
without any external nutriment for the evolution of the germ, which
little by little is transformed into a small animal composed of muscle,
tendon, bone, skin, etcetera.'

In fact, one finds in the egg nitrogenous substances, fats and sugars,
sulphur, phosphorus and mineral salts. The white is formed of
albumen.

Eggs are one of the foodstuffs which are most difficult to find
fresh in winter. Now, everyone knows that there is no taste more
disagreeable than that of an egg which is not fresh. Almost all
cookery books advise you to lay in your supply between the two

Eggs

feast days of Our Lady, that is to say between 15 August and mid-September. [The Assumption of Our Lady is celebrated on 15 August and her Nativity on 8 September.] The best way to preserve them then is to bury them in fresh wood ash in which have been mixed branches of juniper, bay and other aromatic woods. It is good to mix some very fine, dry sand into these ashes.

Moreover, there is one very simple way of knowing whether an egg is still good. Place it in a cup full of water. If one of the ends rises, and tends to stay upright, that shows that the egg is one third empty, and consequently inedible. If it stays plumb on its middle, that shows that it is fresh.

When an egg is fresh, we do not say that the only way to eat it is soft-boiled; but merely that this is the best way. Cooked thus, it loses none of its delicacy. The yolk is flavourful, the white milky; and if one has been sufficiently sybaritic to cook it in broth, and to see that it is neither over- nor under-cooked, one will eat a perfect egg.

There are people for whom an egg is an egg. This is a mistake. Two eggs which are laid at the same time, one by a hen which runs about in a garden, the other by a hen which eats straw in a farm-yard, can be very different in taste and palatability.

I am one of those who wants his egg cooked by putting it in cold water which is then gently heated. In this way, all the egg is cooked to the same degree. If, on the contrary, you drop your egg into boiling water, it is rare that it does not break; and it can happen that the white is hard and the yolk uncooked.

If you are served with overdone eggs, as often happens, use this method: mash your eggs on a plate with salt and pepper and a piece of butter, sprinkle over them some of those chives which are called *appétits* and, if you don't have time to have other eggs cooked, you will have lost nothing on the deal.

Œufs pochés · Poached eggs

Here is the recipe from the *Cuisinier Imperial* of 1808 and the *Cuisinier Royal* of 1839. It's up to you whether to use it.

Have fifteen poached eggs, taken out of the cooking water and waiting on a platter. Have twelve ducks on the spit and, when they are 'green', that is to say nearly cooked, take them off the spit. Slit them down to the bone, take the juices, season these with salt and coarsely ground pepper, and, without allowing them to boil, pour them over your fifteen poached eggs.

Twelve ducks for fifteen eggs! What do you say to that?

Œufs au gratin

Mix together some breadcrumbs, butter, a chopped anchovy, parsley, spring onions, shallots, three egg-yolks, salt, coarse pepper and nutmeg. Sprinkle a layer of nutmeg on the bottom of an ovenproof dish, add the above mixture and let it cook gently. Break on to this gratin the quantity of eggs which you wish to serve, and cook gently. Move a hot iron ladle (*pelle rouge*) gently over the dish to make the whites set. When they are cooked, sprinkle them with salt, pepper and nutmeg.

Œufs à la tripe · Hard-boiled eggs with fried onions

Gently fry in butter some sliced onions, without allowing them to brown. Mix in half a spoonful of flour with the onions; and add a big glassful of cream, salt, pepper and nutmeg. When this mixture has slightly reduced, add the sliced hard-boiled eggs and heat through without allowing to boil.

Œufs aux champignons · Eggs with mushrooms

Poach eight fresh eggs in water. Take some mushrooms (the quantity which you would need for making a stew) and peel, wash and dice them. Cook them in water with a bouquet garni, a piece of butter into which you have worked some flour, and a little salt. When the mushrooms are cooked and the sauce reduced, bind it with four egg-yolks and cream. Add some lemon juice and serve the sauce around the eggs.

One can make the same dish with St George's agaric or with morels.

FENNEL   *FENOUIL*

A very aromatic plant of the umbelliferous family, whose seeds smell of aniseed, especially in southern Italy. Fennel is eaten like celery. It is not unusual to see working people with a bunch of fennel under the arm and making their lunch or dinner of this, accompanied by bread.

The smell, which to begin with is pleasant, becomes unpleasant because of the excessive use made of it by the Neapolitans who put it in everything.

FIG-PECKER or BECCAFICO (GARDEN WARBLER) *BEC-FIGUE*

In classical times this bird was called *Avis Cypria*, meaning the bird from Cyprus, because the Greeks and Romans had it brought from Cyprus, preserved in brine.

'The beccafico, like the quail and the ortolan, when cooked in buttered paper in the embers, leaves nothing to be desired as far as flavour is concerned' (Vuillemot).

Brillat-Savarin, who has a great affection for the beccafico, says:

'The beccafico incontestably ranks first in excellence amongst the small birds.

'It becomes quite as plump as the robin and the ortolan. Besides, nature has endowed it with a slight bitterness and a unique flavour which engage, fulfil and beatify all the digestive powers. If the beccafico were the size of a pheasant, one would certainly pay as much for it as for an acre of land.

'It is a great pity that this privileged bird is seen so infrequently in Paris; a few do come here but they are lacking in the fat which is all important. One can say that they hardly resemble at all those which are to be seen in the eastern and southern provinces of France.'

I have heard stories in Belley, in my youth, of the Jesuit Faby who was born in this diocese, and of the particular partiality which he had for beccaficos. As soon as one heard the shout 'To the beccaficos! To the beccaficos!'—the beccafico being, as one knows, a bird of passage —everyone said: 'Father Faby is about to arrive.'

On 1 January, without fail, he appeared with a friend, and they regaled themselves during the entire period of the birds' passage. It was everyone's pleasure to invite them. Towards the 25th they left; when the beccaficos had gone, of course. As long as Father Faby was in France, he never once missed his gastronomic trip. By misfortune he was sent to Rome, where he died as Grand Pénitencier [a priest of the rank of cardinal who could grant special dispensations]. His own greatest penitence was, indubitably, being unable to eat the beccaficos of Provence any longer.

Few people know how to eat small birds: ortolans, beccaficos, warblers, robins. Here is the recipe which has been given me in confidence by the Canon Charcot, a gourmand because of his position,* but who by dint of his studies lifted himself from gourmandise to gastronomy.

'Start by removing the gizzard of a very plump bird, then take it by

* '*Vie de chanoine*' (a canon's life) is a French expression meaning an easy life.

the beak, sprinkle it with a little salt and pepper and pop it adroitly into your mouth, without allowing it to touch either your lips or your teeth. Bite into it close to your fingers, and chew vigorously. The result of this is to produce enough juices to spread throughout the mouth, and in masticating you will enjoy a pleasure which is quite unknown to the common people.'

King Ferdinand of Naples, a great hunter and great gourmand, having noticed that the beccaficos, when flying over ancient Parthenope, alighted especially on the hill of Capodimonte, had a castle built there, which cost him five millions.

The order was given that when a flight of beccaficos came down at Capodimonte, the king was to be fetched, wherever he was, even in the Council Chamber.

On the day when the question of war against France was brought up in the Council, a war which the queen wanted but the king did not, the king arrived with the firm intention of opposing this sad piece of braggadocio with a firm veto. But hardly had the question been raised when the king was informed that a magnificent flight of beccaficos had begun to alight at Capodimonte.

The king tried to hold himself firmly in check, but failed. He rose, and left the council chamber shouting: 'Do whatever you want, and go to the devil!'

War was declared, and the beccaficos, which had already cost the king five millions, all but cost him his throne.

FIGS   *FIGUES*

Despite the reputation of figs from Argenteuil, the only good figs to be had in France come from the south. The only figs which are better than those from Marseilles are those from Capodimonte, and Sicily, than which there are none better.

Figs are eaten both fresh and dried.

People who have travelled in Italy know that the biggest insult you can make to someone from Milan is to display the thumb pressed between two fingers. This is known as *faire la figue* (to flout); and this aversion to the fig derives from an occurrence which Rabelais relates as follows:

'The people of Milan, having revolted against the Emperor Frederick, expelled the Empress, his wife, from the city, forcing her to mount an old mule, facing backwards.

'When Frederick reconquered Milan, and took the rebels prisoner,

Figs

he had the idea of making the executioner place a fig under the tail of this very same mule. Each of the vanquished was made to remove it from there, and present it to the executioner while saying, "*Ecco il fico!*", and then to replace it; all this under the threat of being hanged.

'Several people preferred to be hanged rather than to submit to such a humiliation, but fear of death decided most of them to do so. This is what causes the fury of the Milanese when someone "makes a fig" at them.'

It was also a fig which caused the Roman senate to decide to destroy Carthage. Every time that Cato gave his views to the senate he finished with the words, 'Carthage must be destroyed!' (*Delenda est Carthago!*).

During one session of the senate, when they were deliberating on war with Carthage, Cato showed his colleagues a fig. 'When do you think,' said he, 'this fig was picked? To judge by its freshness, very recently. Well then, only three days ago this fig was hanging from the tree, and it comes from Carthage. Judge from this how close the enemy is to us!' It was immediately decided to go to war.

Thouin, the nurseryman at the botanical gardens, ordered a very simple-minded servant to take two beautiful early figs to Buffon. On the way, the servant allowed himself to be tempted and ate one of them. Buffon, knowing that he was to have been sent two, asked the man for the other one. The latter admitted that he no longer had it.

'Well, what did you do with it?' exclaimed Buffon.

The servant took the remaining fig and, swallowing it, said: 'This is what I did with it! . . .'

FISH   *POISSON*

'Fish', according to Cuvier, 'are vertebrate aquatic animals, which have cold blood and breathe through gills.'

We are only concerned here with fish as food; so we will not enter into an anatomical discussion of the nature and mode of life of the different species of fish, but will limit ourselves to drawing the attention of our readers to those fish which we consider to be the best.

Fish deserve to be counted as a major food resource. At all times in the past, man has sought out this wholesome and delicate source of nourishment; and Montesquieu attributes the large population of China to the frequent consumption of fish by the Chinese.

The people of ancient Greece, fortunate in having the sea close by, devoted themselves to fishing and took pains to distinguish the best species. Greek cooks knew how to prepare fish in various ways, which are mentioned by those classical authors who wrote about dietetics. There were several ways of preparing fish with salt and of marinating them in olive oil with aromatic herbs; and the fish *en escabèche* which Italians and Spaniards prepare is undoubtedly just an imitation of the classical practice. [The term *en escabèche*, which is the equivalent of the old English word caveach, refers to marinating fried fish so that they will keep for a while. The practice has spread to Latin America, from Spain and Portugal, and even as far as the Philippines.] We also know, despite the scant nature of the information which has come down to us about Greek cookery, that people in those times used to prepare swordfish with mustard, conger eel with salt and oregano, and gilt-head bream with olive oil, vinegar and prunes.

Gallienus was the first to recommend salting tunny, since in salted form its flesh is less compact. Athenaeus has passed on to us several precepts about seasoning fish; and Xenocrates, Aeschylus and Sophocles all mentioned sauces for fish. Fondness for seafood was carried to such lengths at Athens that a police regulation bade people summon the vendors of seafood on the spot, by the sound of bronze drums, so that each person could secure fresh fish at the moment of its arrival in the market. We are even told that, to make the vendors sell as quickly as possible, they were instructed to remain standing up, with the intention that this requirement would make them easier to deal with and more anxious to sell their fish at a reasonable price.

Among the fish most highly esteemed in Roman times was the parrotfish [*Euscarus cretensis* (Linnaeus), still plentiful in the Aegean, but no longer in great demand]. Gourmets preferred it to all other species. The liver of the angler-fish [*Lophius* spp., highly prized at Venice and elsewhere, but not so much for the liver as for the tail end of the body] also enjoyed a high reputation, although the rest of this fish's body was held in low esteem. The mullet had the reputation of providing a very delicate dish, and has [presumably] degenerated since then, for we regard it as an ordinary fish. In those days gastronomes took pleasure in watching the mullet expire on the table, so

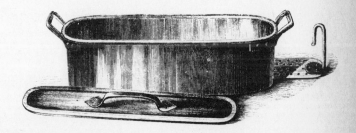

that they could enjoy seeing it change colour. [Cf. page 241. Dumas may again be confusing the red mullet and the grey mullet. It was the red mullet which Romans watched changing colour. The grey mullet, on the other hand, could be described as an ordinary fish.]

[In France] it was only towards the twelfth century that the fish merchants, joining together, undertook the supply of seafood to our capital. It was at that time that the difference was established between *harengères*, who attended to the sale of sea fish, and *poissonières*, who sold freshwater fish.

The annual value of the freshwater fish sold in Paris is about two million francs; that of sea fish, six million francs. Although considerable quantities of sea fish arrive at Paris while they are still fresh, thanks to the city being close to the sea, there are many others which cannot be successfully transported thither, however fast the journey is made. In the last century Louis XV offered by way of encouragement a reward of 9,000 francs to whoever could bring a gilt-head bream, in a state of freshness, to Paris. No merchant succeeded in winning the prize—which it would be easy to win today, when we have the railway—and it was this situation which caused deep dismay to the great epicures of the eighteenth century.

FLOUR   *FARINE*

A powder extracted from the seeds of graminaceous plants, especially wheat. Wheat flour is frequently used to make white sauces and roux, and also in the preparation of various foodstuffs. Have a light hand when you use flour; it is tricky to cook and can detract from the flavour of your sauces, and make them heavy. The very best quality should therefore be used, particularly that called *gruau* [finest wheat flour], in making pâtisserie, both thick and thin. To make biscuits, use potato flour.

If you want to avoid some of the disadvantage of flour, dry it out in a warm oven, until it has changed colour slightly. It will then be excellent for mixing with butter to add to sauces which are too thin and require thickening.

FONDUE   *FONDUE*

Take the number of eggs which you need to use, according to the number of guests whom you expect.

Next take a piece of good Gruyère cheese, which weighs a third of the weight of the eggs, and a piece of butter which weighs a sixth of their weight.

Break the eggs into a casserole and beat them well, then add the butter and the cheese (grated or chopped into small pieces).

Put the casserole on a well-heated stove, and mix with a spatula until the mixture is suitably thick and light. Add a little or no salt, depending on whether the cheese is more or less old, and a good helping of pepper, which is one of the principal characteristics of this ancient dish. Serve on a dish which has been gently heated; have the best wine brought forth, which will be roundly drunk; and marvels will be seen. (Recipe for fondue, extracted from the papers of M. Trollet, bailiff of Mondon, in the canton of Berne.)

[This recipe appears in *La Physiologie du Goût* by Brillat-Savarin, (who gives the name of the bailiff as M. Trolliet). Its authenticity has been questioned, courteously but effectively, by Dr A. Gottschalk, contributing to *L'Art d'être Gourmand* by Gaston Derys (Albin Michel 1929).]

FRITTER   *BEIGNET*

The name *beignet* (fritter) comes from a Celtic word meaning swelling or tumor. It was during the crusades that we first met fritters. The Sire de Joinville relates that the Saracens offered fritters to Saint Louis when giving him his freedom.

A fritter is a sort of dough, fried in a pan, which usually encloses a slice of some sort of fruit.

Pâte à la provençale · Provençal fritter batter

Put 360 grams of flour into a bowl with 2 yolks of egg, 4 table-spoonfuls of oil from Aix-en-Provence and enough cold water to mix the flour into a soft paste. Add two stiffly beaten whites and use.

Beignets de pommes · Apple fritters

Once you have peeled and cut your apples into slices, steep them for two hours in brandy, sugar and cinnamon. Drain them and put them in moderately hot oil. When the apples are cooked, sprinkle them with sugar and glaze them.

(The same recipe does for pear, peach, apricot and nectarine fritters.)

There are many types of frog which differ in size, colour and habitat. Frogs which live in the sea are monstrous, and are not used as a food-stuff, nor are frogs which live on the land. The only frogs which are good to eat are those which live in the water. They must be taken from very clear water, and those chosen should be well nourished, fat and fleshy, and should have a green body marked with little black spots. Many doctors in the Middle Ages were opposed to the idea of people eating this meat, which nevertheless is white and delicate and contains gelatinous matter which is more liquid and less nourishing than that of other meats. Bernard Palissy, in his *Traité des pierres* (Treatise on Stones) of 1580, expressed himself thus:

'And in my time, I have observed that there are very few men who have wanted to eat either tortoises or frogs.'

And yet in the sixteenth century frogs were served at the best tables, and Champier complained of the taste for these, which he found odd. And it is just about a century ago that a man named Simon, from Auvergne, made a considerable fortune on frogs which were sent to him from his part of the country, which he fattened and then sold to the best houses in Paris, where this food was very much in style.

In Italy and Germany, there is a very large consumption of these batracians, and the markets are covered with them. The English are horrified by them, and no doubt for this reason they used to make, about sixty years ago, caricatures showing the French eating frogs. They should read this passage from the history of the island of Santo Domingo, written by an Englishman named Atwood:

'There are', said he, 'in Martinique many toads which are eaten. The English and the French prefer them to chickens. They are fricasseed and used in soup.'

Frogs are prepared in several different ways, mostly in soups which are very health-giving and which are even used by some women to maintain the freshness of the complexion.

FRUITS   *FRUITS*

Fruits have played an important part in man's nourishment from the earliest times, when he lived only on roots and fruit, until today, when fruit still appears on our tables.

Fruits are eaten fresh and raw, cooked and dried.

Cooking makes fruits more digestible without changing their laxative properties. When dried, they are more difficult to digest, but are sweeter and more nourishing. Dried figs used to be an important element in the diet of athletes.

Fruits are nutritious in varying degrees, depending on the number and nature of their constituent elements. In general, those which form the basis of the diet for all civilized peoples are the feculent fruits, which contain varying proportions of gluten, sugar, starch, albumen,

Fruits

mucilage, resin and salt. The principal ones can be classed as follows: wheat, rye, barley, oats, rice, corn, beans, peas, broad beans, lentils, chestnuts, etcetera.* To make these edible, they must be given a variety of treatments, which all come within the province of the kitchen and which will be described in the articles about these particular fruits or grains.

Next come the fruits belonging to the *mucoso-sucré* group [an obsolete term, the general sense of which was 'containing a kind of sugar which cannot be crystallized']: plums, apricots, grapes, figs, cherries, etcetera. These are much less nutritious than those in the first group and would not alone suffice to give man his daily nourishment. *Marmelade*, jelly and preserves are usually made of these. They are also eaten raw, but they must be very fresh, in order not to upset the digestive system.

We also have almonds, walnuts, coconuts, hazelnuts, etcetera, which are called *oléagino-féculeux* [oleaginous-starchy] fruits. These are difficult to digest, because of the oil which they contain, and can only be eaten in small quantities.

Finally, the *acides-mucilagineux* [acid-mucilaginous] fruits, the least nourishing of all, are nevertheless an important asset during the hottest periods of the summer, when they are used to make very refreshing drinks as well as jams, preserves, etcetera. The principal ones are the orange, the lemon and the currant.

Fruits were always prominently featured on the table in ancient times. The Emperor Claudius Albinus is reported to have loved fruit so much that one day at lunch he ate five hundred figs, a hundred peaches, ten melons and a large number of grapes.

Of all the early fruits, the wild strawberry is the first to appear. Everyone knows that it is the best and the most natural. It has been a useful and agreeable ornament of our tables for a long time. Next come cherries, of which the finest, those known as cherries from Montmorency, arrive later than the others. Currants in bunches and raspberries also follow the strawberries, and just as quickly have their place taken by apricots, plums, green almonds, melons, pears and figs. The peach from Montreuil, a fruit so delectable that all gourmands want to eat it, is another arrival at this time; as are the dessert grapes of Fontainebleau, which are the best in the world. And then, finally, come the winter fruits, the pear, the apple, and the fruits with shells, walnuts, hazelnuts, chestnuts, etcetera.

* Elsewhere, e.g. in his article on wheat, Dumas draws a distinction between cereals on the one hand and fruits on the other. Here he includes cereals among fruits.

GAME   *GIBIER*

The name *gibier* (game) applies to anything which is taken by hunting, and which serves as a foodstuff for the hunter. Boars, stags, deer, roebuck and other similar animals are what are called big game. Small game is made up of much smaller animals, such as hare, rabbits, partridges etcetera.

Game, fish and poultry all keep perfectly when wrapped in a thin linen covering, placed in a charcoal burner and covered with fine charcoal. Alternatively, the body of the game is gutted, filled with wheat, sewn up and placed in a pile of corn in such a way as to be entirely covered.

GARLIC   *AIL au singulier, AULX au pluriel*

A bulbous vegetable whose cloves are used as a seasoning.

Everyone is familiar with garlic, and particularly conscripts, who use it to obtain a discharge. Its bulb contains a bitter and volatile juice, which brings tears to the eyes. If put on the skin, it reddens it and even produces a grazed effect on it.

Everyone recognizes the smell of garlic, except the person who has eaten it and who has no idea why everyone turns away when he approaches. Athenaeus recounts that those who ate garlic never entered the temples consecrated to Cybele. Virgil talks of it as a plant which is useful to harvesters in increasing their strength during periods of great heat; and the poet Macer as a deterrent against their falling asleep when there are snakes to be feared. The Egyptians adored it; the Greeks, on the contrary, detested it. The Romans ate it with pleasure, but Horace, who on the very day of his arrival in Rome ate and got indigestion from a dish of sheep's head with garlic, hated it.

Alphonso, King of Castile, disliked garlic to such a point that in 1330 he founded an order, the statutes of which laid down that those knights who had eaten garlic or onion could neither appear at court nor communicate with the other knights, for at least one month.

Provençal cooking is based on garlic. The air in Provence is impregnated with the aroma of garlic, which makes it very healthful to breathe. Garlic is the main seasoning in *bouillabaisse* and in the principal sauces of the region. A sort of mayonnaise is made with it by crushing it in oil, and this is eaten with fish and snails. The lower classes in Provence often lunch on a crust of bread sprinkled with oil and rubbed with garlic.

GHERKIN   *CORNICHON*

These are young cucumbers which are usually preserved in vinegar in the following way.

Take very small gherkins, brush them, cut off the tail ends and put them in an earthenware container with two handfuls of salt. Turn them over several times so that they are well impregnated with the salt, and leave them for twenty-four hours. Then drain them thoroughly and pour enough boiling white vinegar on them to cover them well. Put a lid on the container and allow the contents to infuse for twenty-four hours, by which time the gherkins will have taken on a yellow colour.

Decant the vinegar into a cauldron, which must not be tinned, and put it to boil over a very hot fire. Toss in the gherkins, stir them, and at the moment when they are about to come to the boil remove them from the cauldron and let them cool, when they will become green again.

Put the gherkins in storage containers and cover them with condiments such as sea-samphire, tarragon, pimento, little onions and garlic. Fill the containers with vinegar, so that everything is submerged, and cover them carefully. The gherkins should be good to eat eight days later.

If you attach more importance to the taste of the gherkins than to the green colour, brush them in small batches at the time of gathering, salt them, drain them of their liquid as described above, and put them in cold vinegar with seasonings.

GILT-HEAD BREAM   *DORADE*

A fish which takes its name from the golden reflections of its scales. It is found in all [our] seas, and periodically comes up rivers. Its flesh is white, firm and of an excellent taste.

The preferred ways of eating it are either roasted or cooked in a court-bouillon and accompanied by a white sauce with capers. It can also be served fried or with a purée of tomatoes.

[It seems likely that this entry refers to *Sparus aurata* Linnaeus, the finest fish of the marine bream family in French waters. Its French name is *Daurade*, sometimes spelled *Dorade*, and often confused, whether by mistake or by design on the part of fishmongers, with *Pagellus bogaraveo* (Brünnich), which is also known as the *Dorade* or *Dorade commune*. The former species enters brackish waters and has

a golden spot on each cheek and a golden crescent between the eyes.
It therefore answers fairly closely to the description given by Dumas.]

GINGERBREAD   *PAIN D'ÉPICE*

Since olden days the best gingerbread has been made in Reims. At
the end of the fifteenth century, in the reign of Louis XII, it enjoyed
a great reputation, and that made in Paris was second in rank.

Towards the end of the reign of Louis XIV and at the beginning
of the reign of Louis XV it was customary to make presents of crisp
biscuits and gingerbread nuts from Reims. Only children eat them
now, but even so the business remains considerable.

Gingerbread is made with the best rye flour, sugar foam or yellow
honey and spices. You cook it all together and then divide it up into
such shapes as you wish. It stimulates the appetite and restores and
sustains the digestive processes; but one must only eat it in moderation. Sailors do well to make use of it.

The invention of gingerbread goes back a long way; there is no
doubt but that it followed on the heels of that of bread. Encouraged
by the success of the process which produced bread, people tried
combining the flours of different cereals with anything which could
enhance their flavours, such as butter, eggs, milk, honey, in order to
discover what the results would be. It was no doubt these experiments which gave birth to all the pastries with which the ancients
regaled themselves. Our forefathers brought back the recipes for
them from Egypt and Asia at the time of the Crusades; and these
recipes have served to shape the art of the pastry-maker and the
confectioner.

The Romans had their gingerbread; it was the offering made by
the poor to the immortal gods. The Greeks ate it at the dessert course.
Our own ancestors appreciated it greatly and even made use of it as
gifts. It took a prominent place in meals at court. Agnès Sorel, the
beautiful mistress of Charles VII, called the Lady of Beauty (because
of the Château de Beauté which she owned on the banks of the
Marne, and which was a present from her royal lover), never tired of
this delicacy. Several authors in the last century have even suggested
that the Dauphin poisoned her with gingerbread; since Louis XI
liked her not at all, because his father liked her all too well. But this
conjecture is based solely on the cruel and vindictive character of
this prince.

Marguerite de Valois, the sister of François I, also revelled in it.

Gingerbread

But under Henri II people suddenly took a dislike to it, because rumour had it that the Italians were putting poison in it. It only came back into favour at the end of the reign of Louis XIV, as we said above.

Rye flour makes this bread a bit heavy, but when it is well prepared and properly cooked the aromatics which are used make it more digestible. Good gingerbread, preferably made with good honey and lightly spiced, has laxative qualities, quenches thirst and promotes expectoration.

In order to prevent it from becoming soggy, as a result of humidity, and from becoming stale, it must be cooked correctly and exposed from time to time to the heat of a fire or the sun.

GOOSE   *OIE*

Geese were sacred for a long time in Rome. This was because, while the dogs slept, a goose who had remained awake (history does not tell us why) heard the noise made by the Gauls in scaling the Capitol. This goose woke her friends, who all took fright and started screeching so loudly and to such good purpose that they in their turn awoke Manlius.

But as soon as Julius Caesar had defeated the Gauls, members of the Roman army started to eat geese (following in this the example of the Gauls, who had no reason to respect Manlius' allies, the cause of their downfall).

Word soon spread, even as far as Rome, that the geese from Picardy made a delicious dish. From that time on, men of Picardy, who are born traders, could be seen conducting flocks of geese to Rome on foot. Along the way, the geese devoured everything in sight.

The ancient Egyptians regarded the goose as one of the most delicate of dishes. Rhadamanthus, King of Lycia, thought so highly of them that he ordered people to stop swearing by the gods, and to swear by the goose instead, in all his lands. This was also the usual oath in England at the time when Julius Caesar conquered it.

According to Pliny, it was a Roman consul, named Metellus Scipio, who discovered the art of fattening geese and making their livers delectable.

Jules César Scaliger, doctor and celebrated scholar, has a particularly soft spot for geese. He admires them not only from the physical, but also from the moral point of view.

'The goose,' says he, 'is the most beautiful emblem of prudence.

Geese lower their heads in order to pass under a bridge, no matter how high its arches are; they are decent and reasonable to such a point that, when they are ill, they purge themselves without a doctor.

'They have so much foresight that when they pass over Mount Taurus, which abounds in eagles, each goose will take a stone in its beak. Knowing what chatterboxes they are, they ensure, by thus constraining themselves, that they will not emit the sounds which would cause their enemies to discover them.'

Geese can even be taught a little. Mémery, the chemist, saw a goose turning a spit on which a turkey was roasting. She was holding the end of the spit in her beak; and by sticking out and pulling back her neck, produced the same effect as the use of an arm. All she needed was to be given a drink from time to time.

GRAPE *RAISIN*

Since the time of Noah, who was the first to plant and make use of the vine, innumerable varieties of grape have been produced. It would take too long to enumerate them all here, so we will limit ourselves to mentioning the principal ones, which is to say those customarily seen on our tables.

These are the *chasselas* [a fine white table grape] of Fontainebleau, which stands in the top rank. The large Corinthian and the black *chasselas* come afterwards, and a few muscats such as the one from Frontignan, the early muscat from Piédmont, that from Rivesaltes, the coral red, the big black muscat, the purple from Gascogne and the *passe-musqué* of Italy. There is also the big grape, elongated and purple, of the Madeira type, famed for its beauty, size and excellence. But the best of all the muscat grapes is that which has been given the name of *l' Enfant-Jésus* (Infant Jesus), after the beautiful painting by Mignard; unfortunately this excellent fruit has become very rare.

According to Gallienus, the grape is the best of all autumn fruits, the most nourishing of those which do not keep, and the one whose juice is the least harmful when it is completely ripe. Tissot has reported that some soldiers, attacked by an obstinate dysentery, recovered rapidly when they were conveyed to a vineyard, where they ate grapes in abundance.

Richard Lion-heart, when he was still only the Duke of Guienne, called together the notables of his Duchy, and proclaimed this memorable edict: 'Whosoever takes a bunch of grapes from another's vineyard will pay five sous or will lose an ear.' This edict teaches us that in 1175, at the time when it was given, an ear was very little valued in Gascony, since it was worth only five sous. Since then they have appreciated in value very considerably, because today there is not a single Gascon, no matter how young, who does not value his ears a great deal more than all the vineyards in the world, even though he is still very fond of the grape.

People have noticed that certain small game, such as little foxes, the hare and some small birds, become much plumper in autumn. At that time their flesh becomes more tender, delicate and better to eat, but as soon as the grape harvest is completed they become completely thin, and their flesh loses the good taste which it acquired through the grape.

The drying of grapes, in removing most of the liquid element from them and in lessening the acid which they contain, makes them more nourishing, and at the same time gives them an emollient quality very suitable for curing any acridity of the stomach, and for soothing the abdomen. So anyone suffering from a weak stomach will do well to chew two or three raisins, including the seeds, after the meal. This contributes greatly to the digestion of the food.

Grapes are dried either in the sun or in ovens. The first method keeps them very sweet, whereas the second method gives them a certain tartness. The famous Damascus raisins come from vines with large grapes, or long, oblong grapes, and are named according to the name of the place where they are grown: French raisins, Calabrian, Spanish or Levantine. Amongst Spanish raisins a distinction is made between those from the muscat grapes, sun-dried grapes (dried on the vine, in the sun), the blossoming grape, Malaga grapes and grapes from Lexias. The best raisins in France come from Languedoc and Provence; these are called *jubis*, *pcards* etc. So far as the raisins of Italy are concerned, those from Calabria are much acclaimed because of their excellent flesh and delicate flavour.

The very small raisins which are called *raisins de Corinthe* (currants) come from a variety of vine which grows mostly in the Ionian islands and in Greece. The alcoholic liqueur which is made by fermenting raisins and wines together was already known in the ancient world, under the name *vinum passum*, and was one of the favourite drinks of the Romans.

GRAVY (MEAT JUICES) *JUS*

The name *jus de viande* is given to a concentrated decoction of veal, mutton and beef juices etcetera which form the basic stocks in the kitchens of great houses. These meat juices, which are eminently warming and refreshing, suit those temperaments and those tired stomachs which are in need of being restored.

Formerly, roasted white meats were always served without gravy. Nowadays, it is usual to serve all platters of roast meat with a kind of beef juice which our contemporary cooks put with all possible meats, making no distinction between them. This is a revolutionary practice which seems to have prevailed over the good habits of yesteryear.

GUINEA HEN   *PINTADE*

Guinea hens are a kind of bird belonging to the gallinaceous order. They came originally from the Orient, and were called *pintades*, painted birds, because of the rounded white spots which are scattered on the background of their greyish-blue plumage. These are placed so regularly that they seem to have been marked out by the brush of a painter, especially on the ordinary guinea hen (*Meleagris numida*). Their Latin name, *meleagris*, stems from a belief embodied in Greek mythology, that guinea hens were the product of the metamorphosis of Meleager's sisters; the spots on their feathers being the traces of tears. Finally, the word *numida* is due to the name which they were given by the Romans, *poules de Numidie* (Numidian hens).

The head of the guinea hen is bare, like that of the turkey. It has a fleshy wattle which stems from the upper mandible, and a horny comb on the top of the head. Its feet are without spurs. The feathers grow all the way from the top of the neck to the bottom of the body, and are thicker over the rump, which gives the bird a convex, rounded appearance. The tail, which is short and hangs down, makes the shape of the body even more rounded. Guinea hens are the same size as the biggest hen.

Guinea Hen

The ordinary guinea hen looks like a partridge. It has a shrill and quarrelsome cry, and makes itself so difficult in the farm-yard that people who raise them finally give up, despite the excellence of their flesh and their abundant broods. 'It is', says Buffon, 'a lively, restless and turbulent bird, which does not like to keep its place, and which knows how to become master of the farm-yard. It makes itself feared even by the turkeys. Even though it is much smaller than they are, it imposes its will on them by its petulant behaviour. The female broods for from three to four weeks. Whatever else may have been said about these birds, the mother does look after and bring up her family well, so long as circumstances permit her to stay in good health herself, and so long as she is not troubled by too frequent visits around the scene of incubation. But her young are much more difficult to raise than chickens in our temperate climate. They are first fed on small grains and insects. What suits them particularly well is chopped meat, either raw or cooked; ants' eggs; or a mixture of breadcrumbs, parsley and hard-boiled eggs. Later they manage with millet.'

When the guinea hen is reared at liberty in a park, its flesh is equal in delicacy to that of a pheasant. It is prepared in exactly the same way. (See under Pheasant.)

HADDOCK   ÆGLEFIN

A species of fish of the gadoid family, which resembles the cod. It frequents our coasts, where it is fished in the same way as the cod. Its flesh varies according to its age, the ground where it is fished, its sex and the time of year. It is usually from six to seven metres long and weighs from five to seven kilos.* It spawns at sea and at certain times of year is found in such large numbers that, within a mile from the English coast, three fishermen can fill their boats twice daily.

Additional remarks

[These appear in the Dictionary under the heading *Anon*. Dumas evidently supposed that the fish called by this name were a separate species. In fact, the name is or was applied in certain localities to young haddock or, less often, young hake.]

* Something has gone wrong here. The haddock never attains a length of more than about one metre. The normal maximum length is around 80 cm and the normal maximum weight about three kilos.

The *Anon* is a little fish with a strong resemblance to the whiting. It is abundant in the Channel in January and February. The flesh is white, firm and flaky, with a good flavour and easy to digest. It has the same nutritional qualities as the whiting, and the coastal fishermen treat it as something special. It is prepared like the whiting, either roasted on the grill or fried in butter.

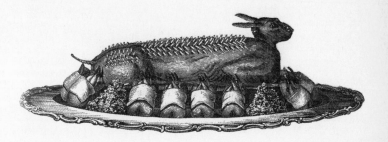

HARE   *LIÈVRE*

This quadruped is already too well known to necessitate our giving a physical description of it. I will simply add something about its intelligence, which sometimes shows up that of the hunters and even the dogs.

The hare is hunted with the pointer, but more often with the beagle.

If a beagle is used, the hare circles the plain or the forest twice, the first time for 25 or 30 minutes, the second time for three quarters of an hour to an hour and a half. These are what are called the hare's small circuit and its big circuit.

What stroke of fate causes the hare to return to the point from which it shot away, after either the first circuit or the second? The fact that it does this means that it is almost always near to the place where it took flight that it returns to be killed.

The hare's first circuit is made quite openly and without doubling; but on the second it feints and, although its repertoire of tricks is not as complete as that of the fox, sometimes succeeds in putting the dogs on the wrong track and disappointing the hunter. One of its first tricks is this. When it arrives at a place where there is long grass or brambles which offer a refuge, it makes a circle of 25 to 30 paces in diameter, as exactly as though with a compass. It then makes three or four turns along the track of its first circle and, summoning all its strength, leaps to one side and squats close to the ground.

The dogs, once they have arrived at the point where the hare has ceased following a straight line in order to take a curving one, do the same. They follow the hare's tracks in a circle. But at this point the trail eludes them. The huge leap made by the hare interrupts the scent; and the dogs, thrown off the track, continue to bay, but in the manner of dogs calling the hunters to their aid. The hunter will arrive, in fact, but as soon as the hare hears him it leaves once more, rested and altogether prepared for a chase longer than any of the previous ones.

I once observed a hare employing these same tactics; but this hare, instead of looking for refuge in the brambles, leapt on to a bent tree and tried to hide itself in a cluster of leaves.

It was my pointer who routed the hare from its 'nest' and denounced it to me by the fixety of its stare. And so it came to pass that I killed a hare on the branch of a tree, as I would have a pheasant or a grouse.

HAZELNUTS (also called FILBERTS)   *AVELINES*

A kind of large purplish nut. They say that the best kind comes from the lands of Foix and Roussillon, but I am inclined to think that the best are those from Avellines, which has given them their name. Hazelnuts grow wild in the ravines and ruins which surround Avellines. Victor Hugo all but killed himself when he fell into one of these ravines while he was picking hazelnuts as a child.

HERBS   *HERBES*

The twenty-eight herbs* which are used in the kitchen are divided into pot-herbs (*herbes potagères*), herbs for seasoning, and herbs to accompany salads.

---

* Dumas does not list twenty-eight, but twenty-five. Tarragon, chives and thyme appear twice. The number of herbs listed for seasoning is nine, not ten.

    It may seem odd that parsley is not listed among the fines herbes. The *Larousse Gastronomique* states that nowadays fines herbes usually means parsley, and parsley alone, but adds that in the past it meant mixed chopped herbs, sometimes with the addition of chopped mushrooms and truffles.

Pot-herbs are six in number. One should know that these are: sorrel, lettuce, white beet, orach, spinach and green purslane.

The herbs for seasoning are ten in number: parsley, tarragon, chives, spring onion, savory, fennel, thyme, basil and tansy.

Herbs to be mixed in with salad, or *fines herbes*, are twelve in number: garden cress, water cress, chervil, tarragon, burnet, samphire, buck's horn plantain, bush basil, purslane, *cordioles* of fennel, thyme, young balm and chives.

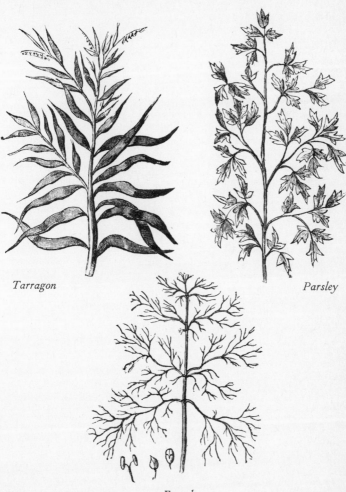

Tarragon   *Parsley*

Fennel

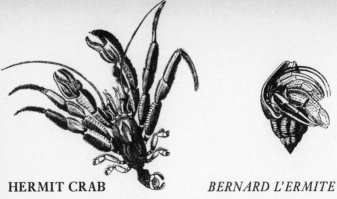

HERMIT CRAB   *BERNARD L'ERMITE*

A species of crab of which the meat is regarded as a delicious morsel.
It is usually grilled in its shell before being eaten.

There is nothing more comical than this little crustacean. Nature
has furnished him with armour as far as the waist—cuirass, gauntlets
and visor of iron, this half of him has everything. But from the waist
to the other end there is nothing, not even a shirt. The result of this
is that the hermit crab stuffs this extremity of himself into whatever
refuge he can find.

The Creator, who had begun to dress the creature as a lobster, was
disturbed or distracted in the middle of the operation and finished
him off as a slug.

This part of the hermit crab, so poorly defended and so tempting
to an enemy, is his great preoccupation; a preoccupation which can at
times make him fierce. If he sees a shell which suits him, he eats the
owner of the shell and takes his place while it is still warm—the history
of the world in microscopic form. But since, when all is said and done,
the house was not made for him, he staggers about like a drunkard
instead of having the serious air of a snail; and so far as possible he
avoids going out, except in the evening, for fear of being recognized.

HERRING   *HARENG*

Everyone knows the herring. I would even say that there are few
people who do not like it.

In life, the herring is green on the back, with white flanks and belly;
after death the green of the back changes to blue. It is the offspring of
the pole. From its birthplace to the 45th degree of latitude, it is found
in all the seas. From 25 June onwards, when one begins to see in
Holland [i.e. in Dutch waters] what is called 'herring lightning', the

herring form long shoals which are several leagues wide and so thick that the fish which constitute them stifle each other by the thousand in shallow waters. Sometimes the nets which they fill, too weak to lift such a weight, tear apart and released their half-captured prey. By means reminiscent of the columns of fire and smoke of the Hebrews, one can keep track of the movements of the herring by day and by night; at night by the phosphorescent glow which they diffuse, during the day by the groups of fish-eating birds which follow them, swooping down from time to time and ascending again with a flash of silver in their beaks. Whales, sharks, porpoises, bonitos and sea bream pursue them, biting at the shoal itself, and consume enormous numbers of them.

The herring fishery is the most important of all, now that the fishery for cod is diminishing. This is demonstrated by Le Havre, which used to send forty vessels to fish for cod and only sent one this year. The herring industry provides a livelihood for 800,000 people and earns for Europe about 4,000,000 francs [annually].

Of the fresh herrings eaten in Paris, the most handsome and those of the best quality are the ones which come to us from the coasts of Normandy. We shall explain further on how they are prepared for table.

The freshly salted herring known as *hareng pec* should always come from Rotterdam, Leeuwarden or Enkhuizen, in Holland. This kind of herring is cut into rounds and eaten quite raw, without undergoing any kind of preparation beyond that given to a salad.

The finest *harengs saurs* (red herrings), the biggest, the most succulent, those of the most beautiful gold colour, the ones which have received the best smoking over juniper wood are the *saurets* of Germuth in Ireland [presumably a mistake for Yarmouth in England, which has for centuries been famed for its red herrings and bloaters].

Salt herrings hardly ever appear on the table of the masters; but in countries where they are plentiful they are very useful for workmen and poor people. In certain provinces people make of them an extremely appetizing and fortifying dish, thus: they do not de-salt them, but fry them in small pieces, in lard, with a mass of raw, chopped leeks, mixed with potatoes of the large floury kind, which have been cooked in well-salted water with sprigs of rosemary.

A fresh herring is an excellent fish, about which one would make the greatest fuss if it was expensive and rare. It is necessary to choose fresh herrings which have their gills red and their scales shining, and which are well rounded on the underside, for then they are full of meat; but it is only at the end of August or in mid-September that they have the fullest flavour.

Herring

In the sixteenth century there still existed, among the canons of the cathedral of Reims, quite a peculiar custom. On Ash Wednesday, after evening prayers, they used to process to the church of Saint-Rémi in two files, each trailing behind him a herring attached to a cord. Each canon tried to step on the herrings of the canon in front of him, and to save his own herring from being trodden on unexpectedly by the canon behind. It was inevitable that this extravagant practice should be suppressed, along with the procession.

The herring fishery, as is well known, is one of the most productive branches of trade for England, which exports a lot of herring, especially to Italy for Holy Week. At the time when Pope Pius VII had to leave Rome, which had been conquered by the revolutionary French, the committee of the Chamber of Commerce in London was considering the herring fishery. One member of the committee observed that, since the Pope had been forced to leave Rome, Italy was probably going to become a Protestant country. 'Heaven preserve us from that!' cried another member. 'What,' responded the first, 'would you be put out to see the number of good Protestants increased?' 'No,' replied the other, 'it isn't that, but if there are no more Catholics, what shall we do with our herrings?'

Harengs frais au fenouil · Fresh herrings with fennel

Split your herrings open along the back and anoint them with warm butter and salt, using a feather or a small brush. Wrap them up in fennel leaves, grill them and serve them with a *sauce rousse* to which you add some thin stalks and leaves of fennel, previously blanched in white wine and chopped very finely.

Harengs frais en matelote

Put your herrings in a casserole with a piece of butter, parsley, mushrooms, spring onions, a touch of garlic, two good glassfuls of Burgundy or Bordeaux wine, salt and pepper. Cook them over a high heat, serve them with the sauce reduced and with a garnish of fried croûtons.

HONEY   *MIEL*

This is the syrupy sweet substance which bees gather from flowers, render edible, and then deposit in the honey-comb cells in their beehives in order to nourish themselves with it during the winter. Honey is to be found in almost all the countries of Europe, because there are flowers and bees almost everywhere. In classical times, it was on Mount Hymettus that the most highly esteemed honey was gathered. Today the best is to be found in Narbonne.

According to Laertius, Pythagoras lived exclusively on bread and honey. He lived to the age of ninety, and died inviting all those who wished for a long life to eat the same food as he had.

Honey took the place of sugar, over a very long period of time, for our ancestors, the Gauls, and our French forefathers. Sugar was not known then, except under the name of 'honey from the reed', and was used only in medicine, but honey has now taken its place with the apothecaries, and sugar has replaced honey on our tables.

HOP   *HOUBLON*

A climbing plant with large leaves whose flowers and fruit contribute to the making of beer. In Belgium, where hops are very common, and where the usual drink is beer, young hop shoots are eaten in spring. The flavour of these is very close to that of asparagus, and they are prepared in the same way, and produce the same effect.

HORSE   *CHEVAL*

Eating horse is the proverbial phrase which means eating hyperbolically tough meat. Horsemeat is indeed closer grained than that of beef. It is red and oily. Even though it is highly nitrogenized, and consequently very nutritious, it is very doubtful that it could ever become daily fare. M. de Sainte-Hilaire has tried in vain up to now through his *agapes** of horse to get this animal firmly established in Parisian butchers. It is probable that this noble animal, which man associates with his military glories, will never serve him as a foodstuff save in the exceptional circumstances of blockade or famine. As long as the horse is not reared, fed and fattened like beef, specifically for consumption, it should not appear on the table except during such difficult times. Then, and then only, use horsemeat as beef, and prepare it as you wish or as you can.

* The name *agape*, applied to a meal, originally referred to a meal which early Christians would hold in church, in commemoration of the Last Supper. This practice was abolished by the Council of Carthage in AD 397. The word subsequently came to denote an important family meal, a meaning consonant with the sense of the word in classical Greek, which was 'brotherly love'.

HORSERADISH   *RAIFORT*

There are considered to be two sorts, the cultivated and the wild. The root of the cultivated horseradish is large, fleshy, blackish-brown outside and very white inside. The flesh has such a spicy flavour that it seems biting and hot.

To improve horseradish, it is cut into rounds two or three hours before being served. Each round is covered with pounded salt and the rounds are then piled one on top of another. This treatment causes them to emit a bitter fluid and makes them less pungent to eat.

Sometimes horseradish is used as a garnish around a roast sirloin of beef or a large fish cooked *au bleu*. It is also used to garnish *barquettes* [small boat-like pastry cases] for hors d'oeuvre; and to prepare a flavoured butter which is used for making sandwiches and *craquelins à l'écossaise* [a crisp biscuit, known as cracknel in English].

Horseradish has the same disadvantages as the true French turnip. It is equally apt to bring on flatulence, causes a heaving of the stomach and even provokes headaches, when too much of it is eaten.

Horseradish is put in ragoûts when one wishes them to be highly seasoned.

ICE, ICES, ICE CREAM   *GLACE*

In the sixteenth century the use of ice was still unknown in France, and when François I had conferences at Nice with Pope Paul III and the Holy Roman Emperor, Charles V, his doctor was astonished to see that the wine was chilled with ice brought down from the mountains which are close to that town.

But ices, as we know them, were unknown in France until about 1660, when a Florentine called Procope first proffered tastes of these attractive sweets and dainties to the subjects of Louis XIV. The café which he established in the rue de l'Ancienne-Comédie still exists today. Nowadays, ices are very widespread and, during the summer, they are to be found on all good tables.

Glace à la fleur de cédrat · Citron flower ice cream
   (recipe from the Château de Bellevue)

Take one *pinte* (nearly a litre) of cream, the yolks of 8 eggs, 3 *quarterons* (367 grams) of sugar and 2 ounces (60 grams) of citron flowers which have been crushed into a powder.

Mix all this together and cook it in a bain-marie. Sieve it and allow it to cool. [Freeze it.]

All other flowers may be used, following the same procedure.

INDIAN PICKLES   *ACHARDS*

A well-known mixture which comes to us from the East Indies, bearing the name of its inventor. The best pickles come from Reunion Island. All that has to be done is to chop finely slices of pumpkin and white beet. Add to this white onions, mushrooms, palm cabbage, cauliflower, corn which has only grown a third of the way to maturity, etc. Colour it all with saffron, and pickle it with salt and vinegar from Orléans, salting and peppering the mixture as for gherkins. You complete the operation by adding ginger root and a few red peppers.

Indian pickles are eaten in three ways. They may be taken straight out of their jar. Or they can be cut into pieces and mixed with all sorts of roast or boiled meats. They are also eaten after being drained on a napkin, and then impregnated with good green oil.

Finally, they are eaten dressed with cream cheese made with goat's milk, instead of with green oil. This is what is called in the colonies *à la cucoco*. This last recipe has been given to European gastronomes by le Marquis de Sercey, Vice-Admiral, and former Governor of the French Indies, to whom we are indebted for the ayapana which he first brought to France. (See under Ayapana.)

Achiar · Bamboo Pickle

A sort of jam made with vinegar and bamboo shoots which are still green. The Dutch use this a great deal for seasoning their dishes from the East Indies, where it is made in earthenware urns. This condiment is very bitter and hot; it agrees only with people of phlegmatic temperaments and with the elderly.

JAMS   *CONFITURES*

[It may be helpful to preface this entry by observing that under French regulations, brought into force since Dumas' time but no doubt reflecting past practice, a distinction is made between *confiture* (jam), of which the maximum permitted moisture content is 40 per

Jams

cent, and *marmelade* (a term which is not the equivalent of the English marmalade, but means a thick fruit purée), which can have up to 45 per cent. Dumas treats *marmelades* as a subdivision of *confitures*.]

There are two sorts of jam, the *confitures sèches* ('dry' jams) and the *confitures liquides* ('liquid' jams). The first are composed of the fruits, the stems and the roots of certain plants and the peel of certain fruits. The second are made with fruits preserved in a liquid, and their preparation demands the greatest care.

Marmelades (see above), *gelées* (fruit jellies) and *pâtes* (fruit 'pastes') also fall into the category of jams. However, the term *marmelade* only applies to a confection of apricots or plums. As for jellies, they are made from fruit juice in which sugar is dissolved and then boiled until it reaches a syrupy consistency.

We are going to give, by categories, the different recipes for *marmelades*, jellies, fruit pastes etcetera. [A small selection of the recipes is given below.]

JELLIES

Gelée de groseilles · Currant jelly

It is important in making this jelly to use currants which are not too ripe and which are still acidulous, so as to keep the jelly really clear. Otherwise, it would have to be clarified, which cannot be done without detracting from the flavour of the fruit.

Usually, to make a good jelly, 500 grams of sugar should be used for each 500 grams of fruit; but this proportion is not *de rigueur* [i.e. it can be varied].

[Dumas proceeds to give his own recipe, which departs from the principle just stated. He then announces that, even as he was writing, a note on the subject arrived from 'a master of the art'. We give the latter, since it comes from Dumas' principal adviser on cookery, and seems to be a better recipe than Dumas' own.]

Dear illustrious master,

My experience, acquired in front of kitchen ranges, suggests to me the following reply on the point which you seek my advice.

To make good currant jelly, take fruit which is barely ripe and which is gelatinous. Remove the stalks, toss the currants into a pot and add likewise a few raspberries. For 2 kilos of fruit, take 2 kilos of sugar, which you melt in a basin containing half a litre of water. Five minutes later, when it first comes to the boil, add the currants to the sugar. Boil vigorously for a quarter of an hour, remove the pulp and pour your currant jelly through a fine strainer. Next let it flow boil gently for a further two minutes, then pour the strained liquid into your pots. In this way you will obtain excellent jelly with a strong fruit flavour. Unfailingly successful.

Vuillemot

Gelée de pommes à la façon de Rouen · Apple jelly as made at Rouen

Reinette apples are normally used to make this jelly, because of the larger amount of acid which they contain, which prevents the jelly from being insipid. Even so, it is usual to add some lemon juice.

Peel the apples with a silver knife, so that their juice will not become discoloured. Wash them well in hot water, drain them and put them in a pan with water to cover. Boil them until they are cooked, but have not become squashy; then put them in a strainer and let them drain. To the juice thus extracted, add two spoonfuls of clarified sugar which has been cooked to the large gloss stage. Put all this into a pan and let it boil until it reaches the small pearl stage. Add some thin strips of lemon peel and let it boil for a minute or two more. Then remove the strips of lemon, reserving them to be put on top of the pots when you have filled these with the jelly.

Marmelade de pêches · Peach jam

[Dumas is now using the term *marmelade* for a jam made with fruit other than apricots or plums, which he had previously said were the only fruits with which a *marmelade* could be made.]

Jams

Choose ripe autumn peaches, peel them and cut them into pieces. You will also need sugar in bulk, which you clarify and cook to the large pearl stage, after which you add your peaches to it. Be sure to stir continuously with a spatula until they have had the desired amount of cooking. Add a few almonds, as for apricot *mermelade*.

Marmelade sans nom · Nameless jam

This is made with the fruit of the eglantine, or dog-rose, picked after the first frosts. It is very agreeable and very tart. And it is a good remedy, which should not however be used to excess, for stomach troubles.

After having removed stem and calyx from each of the fruits, you split them and take out all the seeds. Put the cleaned fruits in water to cover and cook them gently. Then sieve them and add their weight in sugar. Reduce the mixture and boil it until the jam, when cold, sets more firmly than other jams.

An elaborate Coupe-Julienne

JULIENNE   *JULIENNE*

This is the name given to a soup made from various sorts of herbs and vegetables, particularly carrots cut up fine. People have managed to preserve these chopped vegetables by means of drying them, thus enabling this soup to be made at any time.

From the recipes of Marc Heliot, we learn that formerly the julienne was not made exclusively of vegetables. In fact, it had among its ingredients a shoulder of mutton, which was half roasted and then put in a pot with a slice of beef, a fillet of veal, a capon and

Parsley Roots (often called Hamburg Parsley)

four *pigeons fuyards* [a small, pale variety of domesticated pigeon]. All this was cooked for five or six hours to make a rich bouillon. We also learn that three carrots, six turnips, two parsnips, three onions, two parsley roots, two heads of celery, three bunches of green asparagus, four handfuls of sorrel, four white lettuces and a good pinch of chervil were to be cut in pieces, with the addition, if the season permitted, of a *litron* (nearly a litre) of small green peas; all to be cooked separately from the meat in a large *marmite* containing the bouillon in which would be simmering the bread crusts which are also ingredients in this soup of olden times.

KANGAROO   *KANGUROO*

Kangaroos come originally from Australia and the surrounding islands. Essentially fruit-eaters in their wild state, kangaroos are very easy to feed when tame. They decide to eat everything which is offered to them and, it is said, even drink wine and brandy when these are given to them.

Among the mammals, the kangaroo is without question one of the animals which would be the most useful and easiest to breed in Europe, either in captivity or wild. In fact, the taming of the kangaroo, as several experiments have already shown, requires practically no trouble. This is particularly true of the large kinds of kangaroo which inhabit the southern regions of Australia and Van Diemen's Land. The climate of these provinces, although temperate in general, is often very cold, and the abundant warm hair which covers the kangaroo would allow it to withstand the most rigorous winters in France without suffering too much.

The flesh of the kangaroo is excellent, especially when it has grown up wild. The rapid growth of these animals, coupled with their considerable height, produces a substantial amount of meat in very little time. In addition, the peculiar structure of these animals, which gives them back legs much larger in size than their front ones, is eminently favourable to the production of good quality meat, greatly preferable to that of the cow or sheep in that it is much more tender than the first and much more abundant and nutritious than the second.

The kangaroo is timid and gentle. It is not in the least destructive, as several authors have claimed. In this respect it can be compared to the hare. It is very easy to feed.

The lifespan of the kangaroo is from ten to twelve years. In the final period of its existence, it very often becomes blind, because of cataracts which develop. At this stage these unfortunate creatures, no longer able to see their way, sometimes crash into the walls of their enclosures and shatter themselves to pieces.

KIDNEY   *ROGNON*

It is under the name *rognons* that the culinary art has seized on the kidneys of animals. They are characterized by a flavour of urine, which is what the connoisseurs of this sort of dish are seeking.

The meat of the kidney is distinguished by the fact that cooking never makes it more tender. It usually has a soft and compact consistency which makes it difficult to digest and which produces obstructions. There are some young animals, however, whose kidneys are fairly tender and which have a good flavour, such as lambs, calves, suckling pigs and a few others.

Since beef kidneys are always slightly gritty and have too strong a flavour, we recommend our readers not to use them too much.

Rognons de mouton aux mousquetaires ·
                                        Mutton kidneys, musketeers' style
Take some kidneys, remove the fat, split them in two and put them on skewers. Season them with salt, pepper and a little finely chopped shallot. Grease a casserole with some butter, bacon fat or other fat, arrange the kidneys in it, and put it on the fire or hot embers for a moment, with heat above and below. Leave them for just a moment, for this is enough to cook them. Arrange them on a platter. Into the casserole in which they were cooked put a little water, a few fresh bread crumbs, salt, pepper and a dash of vinegar. Put the kidneys on to this and serve as an hors-d'oeuvre.

Rognons de veau sautés · Sautéed veal kidneys

Remove the skin and fat from the veal kidneys and chop them up. Put them in a frying pan with butter, salt, pepper, nutmeg, chopped shallot and parsley, and cooked mushrooms. Sauté all this on a very high heat. Add a little flour, some white wine and a few spoonfuls of reduced espagnole sauce. Then, just at the moment of serving, put a little very fresh butter and lemon juice on the kidneys.

If you cook veal kidneys on a spit, or in the oven, you leave the fat on.

KINGFISHER (or HALCYON) *ALCYON*

Few people realize that this bird, whose gentle name recalls to us the unhappy love of Ceyx and Halcyon, is none other than the swallow which lives on the shores of Cochin-China, bearing the name *salangane*, the bird whose nests are eaten by the Chinese with such relish. The finest variety is found in Mauritius and Reunion, in the Moluccas and in the Philippines.

These birds produce a gelatinous small font-shaped nest made of a semi-transparent white substance which is hard like horn and mixed inside with light layers of cotton. Outside, this substance looks like very white gelatine, dried up into filaments which are carefully joined together.

These nests are made up of a resin which is unknown in Europe and which is called *Calambac*. This resin, which is the same as the *Timbach* of the Indians, is a substance which can be crushed by the teeth, and whose flavour is delicious. In China, it is sold for its weight in gold because of its perfume. It is burned on embers in the most famous pagodas on the most solemn occasions, and at the homes of the famous in the Celestial Empire. The price of these birds' nests is extremely high; they are called S*acaïpouka*. Today it is known that several sorts of swallows produce these gelatinous nests, but the white kind are the most sought after.

Sumatra despatches the nests, in numerous small consignments, to Canton, where the Chinese show great enthusiasm for them. They are found in the crevices of mountains, rooted in little cups which are stuck all along the mountain-face. They are gathered twice a year; and the swallows take over a month to build them.

For a long time it was thought that these nests were nothing but sea foam mixed with fish spawn.

Kingfisher (or Halcyon)

I have seen lots of these nests, and I must say that I have perhaps eaten more of them than any other Frenchman, having been connected with the son-in-law of the governor of Java, who received whole case-loads every year. He had them gathered from a hollow cavern, not far from Java, among the rocks battered by the sea.

The substance of which these nests were made, and which we tried to have analysed, resembled strong glue which had been diluted to half strength. They were two or three inches in diameter, and some still contained eggs which had been laid in them. These weighed no more than ten grams. They cost eight to ten piasters the half kilo there.

Here is how they used to be cooked, according to the recipe which was sent to us from Java. After having cleaned them, we let them soak; this softens the filaments, which separate from each other. Afterwards they are placed under roasted birds, whose juices, they absorb, or else cooked with a small capon for twenty-four hours, on a very low heat, in a hermetically sealed earthenware pot. We also make bouillons, soups, and quickly prepared, highly nourishing stews with them.

LAMB   *AGNEAU*

It is in the period from December to April that the meat of lamb is good. Lamb must be at least five months old and should be entirely milk-fed.

The name of this charming little animal is said to have a most poetic origin. According to the bucolic etymologists, it comes from the verb *agnoscere*, to recognize, because when it is tiny it recognizes its mother. In fact, when it can barely walk it follows its mother, tottering and bleating.

The lamb has been from ancient times and still is today one of the most sought-after dishes in the Orient. The Greeks thought highly of it, and few feasts were given without roast lamb being the most important dish. Eating too much of this meat was one of the excesses of gourmandise for which a certain prophet reproached the Samaritans. The flesh of lamb, which is white but moist, was eventually forbidden to the Athenians.

In primitive times, when barter often took the place of money, Abraham gave Abimelech seven lambs as a token of their covenant [Genesis 22]. Jacob gave two hundred lambs to the children of Hemor, in payment for a field.

Lamb

Agneau à la Hongroise · Lamb cooked in the Hungarian way

Cut a dozen large Spanish onions in round slices; add a piece of butter suitable in size for the quantity of onions, and make a roux by adding a little flour to the butter and onions. Make sure that the onions brown, but that they do not burn. Put in mixed herbs, salt and pepper; add a good pinch of Hungarian red pepper or, if this is not available, a few specks of Cayenne pepper instead. During this time you will have cut your breast of lamb into pieces the size of tablets of chocolate, and you will have browned them in fresh butter. When you judge that they have browned enough, pour on to the lamb and fresh butter the contents of the casserole in which you have made your roux with the onions and mixed herbs. Then, since the onions will not cook unless moistened with water or bouillon, and will only brown in butter, you must pour in, every quarter of an hour, a drinking glassful of good consommé. Let this simmer for five quarters of an hour, and serve.

This is one of the best dishes which I have eaten in Hungary.

Grosse pièce d'agneau aux tomates farcies ·
                        Large piece of lamb with stuffed tomatoes

Take the lower half of a lamb, truss it, wrap it in buttered paper, roast it until done, take it off the spit, arrange it and glaze it. Put oiled paper around the bone at the end of the leg, garnish the half lamb with stuffed tomatoes, and serve separately a *sauce à la Uxelles*.

The thing which earned M. le Maréchal d'Uxelles the honour of giving his name to a sauce was not to have lost the Battle of Rosbach, like M. de Soubise, or to have won the Battle of Fontenoy like M. de Richelieu. It is quite simply an anecdote, related I think by Saint-Simon.

Mlle Choin, the mistress of the Grand Dauphin, had a little dog which she adored, who particularly liked the heads of roast rabbits. Every day Mlle Choin received a visit from the Maréchal d'Uxelles, at the end of which he pulled from his pocket a batiste handkerchief, startling in its whiteness. Enfolded in this were two heads of roasted rabbits.

The good Mlle Choin could not have been more appreciative of this mark of attention, and she was able to help not a little in restoring the Maréchal d'Uxelles to favour, after the surrender of the town of Mayence.

One fine day, the Grand Dauphin died. The following day, and

Lamb

the one after that, and on all the subsequent days she waited for the marshal in vain. She never saw the Maréchal nor his batiste handkerchiefs, nor his rabbits' heads. It was not for her dog that he had been bringing them, not at all, but for the Grand Dauphin.

Selle d'agneau rôtie à l'anglaise ·
Saddle of roast lamb in the English way

The double fillets joined together are the best part of the lamb. This is roasted, and served either after the soup or *en flanc de table* (on the side of the banquet table). It is accompanied with a *sauce anglaise*, very much relished by those Parisian gourmets in whom our two hundred and seventeen years of war with England have not inspired an invincible horror for everything which comes from the other side of the Channel.

Put a quarter of a litre of consommé in a casserole with a pinch of chopped green sage, boil for five minutes, add two pounded shallots, two or three spoonfuls of vinegar from Orléans, 60 grams of sugar and a little black pepper. Salt, strain, and serve separately in a sauce boat.

LAMPREY   *LAMPROIE*

This fish, which resembles the eel, lives in the open sea and ventures up rivers in the spring. Some lampreys weigh up to seven pounds. Their shape is that of an adder, their colour greenish-yellow marked with patches of gold and black spots. The skin is less dark on the belly.

Platinus reproached the Popes and the seigneurs of Rome for feeding lampreys to their guests. They would pay up to twenty gold pieces for them, and would kill them by plunging them into wine from Cyprus, having first put a nutmeg in the mouth of each and stopped up all the gill openings with cloves. After this preparation the lampreys were put in a casserole and cooked with pounded almonds and all sorts of spices.

In England, at times when the lamprey is scarce, people pay up to a guinea for one. The City of Gloucester makes an annual present, on Christmas Eve, of a lamprey pie to the king or queen.

[The tradition has since lapsed, but was revived on the occasion of the Queen's Jubilee in 1977, when the authorities at Gloucester prepared a lamprey pie in the traditional way and sent it to Buckingham Palace. The recipe which they used is being published in my book on *North Atlantic Seafood* (Macmillan, 1978). A.E.D.]

Baby lampreys, called *lamprillons*, are a great delicacy. The fry, called *sept-œil* [seven-eyes, a name often applied to adult lampreys, since these fish have one eye and six eye-like gill-openings on each side of their heads] constitute an hors d'oeuvre of the utmost delicacy. The fry are mainly received from Rouen and Barfleur, whence they are despatched already prepared and packed in jugs, with unsalted butter, a purée of sorrel and fines herbes.

Large lampreys are still prepared today as they were in the sixteenth century. The manner of doing this is called *à l'angevine*.

LAPWING   *VANNEAU*

A bird remarkable for the beauty of its feathers and the delicacy of its flesh. There is a proverb which goes as follows: 'You haven't eaten anything really good if you have not eaten woodcock or lapwing.'

The eggs are even more highly prized. In the months of April and May they are eaten, or rather gulped down, by the thousand in Belgium. In Poland, they are used to make excellent omelettes. In Holland, where the lapwing is very common, they are eaten with all kinds of sauces.

LARK   *ALOUETTE*

Larks have the double advantage of being liked by gourmands and lyricized by the poets. Juliet says to Romeo,* who wants to leave her before dawn:

Juliet   Wilt thou be gone? it is not yet near day:
It was the nightingale, and not the lark,
That pierc'd the fearful hollow of thine ear;
Nightly she sings on yon pomegranate tree:
Believe me, love, it was the nightingale.

Romeo   It was the lark, the herald of the morn,
No nightingale: look, love, what envious streaks
Do lace the severing clouds in yonder east:
Night's candles are burnt out, and jocund day
Stands tiptoe on the misty mountain tops:
I must be gone and live, or stay and die.

* Romeo and Juliet, Act III Scene V.

Lark

Larks were in great demand on the table of the Athenians; they were sacred at Lemnos, because they had saved the island from the locusts. The lark is very delicate, and much esteemed for its taste. It is only really good in the month of November and those which follow, up to February. It gets fatter during the periods of fog at an amazing rate; it has that in common, we might add, with its purveyors, but it becomes lean more quickly than they.

Barded and roasted, larks are very pleasant, but only after a substantial dinner. Grimod de la Reynière is of the opinion that the biggest lark and the best robin, in the hands of a man of good appetite, are no more than a little packet of toothpicks, of more use in cleaning the mouth than in filling it. The illustrious gourmet adds:

'The lark pâtés of Pithiviers are amongst the most delicious dishes which can brush against a worthy man's palate; the pastry covering is excellent, and the seasoning without parallel.'

Plucked, arranged, trussed, ready to put on the spit, the lark finally changes its name and is called *mauviette*. Lister, the gourmand doctor of a gourmand queen [Queen Anne], established the principle that if twelve larks, ready for the spit, do not each weigh 30 grams, they are not edible, but if together they weigh 400 grams or more, they are excellent.

Be careful, therefore, to weigh your larks before putting them on the spit.

LEEK   *POIREAU*

The leek originated in Spain and is cultivated throughout all the temperate parts of Europe. Poor people eat it raw with bread; and it is used in all households to give taste to soups, for it is endowed with diuretic properties which can be of use in the diet.

It is rare for the leek to have any use except as a seasoning in French soups, and in court-bouillons of foreign provenance. But there are countries in which people make ragoûts of leeks, and a certain meat soup, made with white leeks, which merits particular attention.

Leek tarts are made in Lorraine.

LEGUMES   *LÉGUMES*

What is meant by the word legumes are the seeds which come in pods and are picked by hand. The name has wrongly been given to a whole lot of [other] vegetables which serve as foodstuffs for man and animals; it has been applied not only to the fruits, but to all the parts of vegetables, such as roots, stems, leaves, etcetera. The name should, however, be applied only to those plants belonging to the leguminous family, such as peas, lentils, broad beans, beans, etcetera.

Among these legumes, all of which serve to nourish men, some are healthful and easy to digest. Others, on the contrary, are difficult to digest, and should not be used exclusively in one's diet; for as a food-stuff they are heavy and indigestible, and only suit the most robust stomachs, workers and country people who are used to a difficult and laborious life.

We will explain in each individual entry the way in which the various legumes should be prepared and eaten.

LEMON   *CITRON*

The fruit of a tree which, like the orange tree, is an evergreen. Its leaves are wide and long like those of the bay tree. It originated in Asia, and the Hebrews were the first to naturalize it in the beautiful valleys of Palestine. What proves this is that even today they present themselves in the synagogues, on the day of Tabernacles, with a citron in the hand.

Virgil has extolled the lemon under the name of 'apple of Media'. Aristophanes, who calls the lemon *axioma persicum* because of its bitter flavour, says that in bygone days people used to make crowns of the leaves of the lemon tree, to place on the heads of the immortal gods.

The lemon is frequently used in the kitchen as the seasoning for various sauces. A very refreshing and good-tasting drink is also made from it.

LENTEN FARE and FAST DAYS   *MAIGRE*

The word *maigre* has been given to those foods which it is permissible to eat during days of fast, in contrast to those labelled *gras* which are forbidden during this period.

Lenten Fare and Fast Days

Various people have claimed that abstaining from meat is incompatible with good health. This is a mistake, and it has been proved that a meatless diet is in no way incompatible with our bodily requirements, providing, however, that proper attention is paid to the choice of foods, and that their quality is not perverted by the excessive use of seasonings which are very often the reasons for the deleterious influence of these foods on the human body.

It is likewise a mistake to claim that the use of these foods is more healthy than the eating of meat because they are easier to digest and more nourishing, because they are more fattening and strengthening, because they make the blood more rich, more 'milky' and more abundant, therefore cause greater plumpness. But all of this depends more or less on the strength or weakness of the stomach. From this point of view, the most perfect foodstuff would be the one whose constituent parts had the greatest disposition to convert themselves into our flesh and bones, and not to those superfluous substances which only tend to make our bodies uselessly large and which, far from maintaining or increasing our strength, only serve to overwhelm them.

There is no connection between a meatless regime and bodily thinness, and the proof of this is that one sees emaciated men devouring large quantities of meat without becoming plump, whereas soft and languorous women remain fat despite a vegetarian diet of the lightest kind.

Nevertheless, we are not denying that most meatless foods, and in particular fish, are good foods; but it does not follow that they are therefore better than meat, and that they nourish better. The learned Nonnius, who wrote a treatise for the express purpose of defending fish, still agrees that meat is the healthiest foodstuff and the one which produces the best blood. The reason for this, says he, is that it has the greatest similarities with the elements of our bodies. Man, he adds, only abandoned grasses and fruits because he found out by experience that meat sustained him better.

As for the foods whose use is permitted in the collations and luncheons served during Lent, there are so many, and they change so much, depending on the climate and habits, that we would be unable to indicate them all here; and the church gives dispensations so readily, that we refer our gourmand readers to it.

In the *département* of the Seine, the use of butter, of milk and milk products were forbidden in general.

'You will not permit any of the following to be served to me,' said Louis XVIII in 1815, referring to Lenten collations and luncheons, 'you will not serve me at the castle either flesh or fish, or the leftovers of meat or fish. You will serve neither eggs nor butter, nor soft cheese, cooked or melted, M. le contrôleur. Aside from these things, you may give us anything you wish to eat.'

But today the Archbishop of Paris has been happy to authorize the use of milk products and eggs for Lenten meals, and this has been a great source of food for poor people, who, lacking the means to buy fish, which is very expensive throughout the Lenten period, saw themselves obliged to eat meat, and because of that, felt themselves threatened with God's anger.

LENTILS   *LENTILLES*

There are two sorts of lentils, the large and the small. The latter is called *lentille à la reine*, and is considered the better.

Lentils are prepared like beans, but one must be careful to choose light blond ones which cook well, because there are some kinds which do not cook easily, even in the purest water.

Lentils are used to make purées with which to garnish soups or coat meat which has been cooked *à l'étuvée*.

LEPORIDE (BELGIAN RABBIT)   *LÉPORIDE*

For something like six thousand years, people have reproached scientists for fighting against God, without themselves succeeding in creating even the smallest animal.

Tired of these reproaches, they set to work, and in the year of grace 1866, they answered back by inventing the *léporide*.

This time, they not only played a trick on God, but also on M. de Buffon.

M. de Buffon had said, seeing the antipathy which exists between hares and rabbits, despite the resemblance between the two species: 'These types will never approach each other.'

M. de Buffon was wrong.

The antipathy which exists between the hare and the rabbit is not a racial antipathy, but a simple antipathy of character. If it is true that nothing resembles a hare physically more than a rabbit, it is also true that in point of character nothing resembles it less. The hare is a dreamer, or rather a day-dreamer, who has chosen the surface of the earth for his abode. He only leaves his form after taking the greatest precautions, after having turned his ears, which are like mobile funnels, in all directions. It is especially during the day that he goes on expeditions, and he will not return to his form if he has been chased from it two or three times.

The rabbit, on the other hand, digs a long underground gallery, of which he alone knows all the twists and turns, and uses this as his resting place. He leaves it in imprudent fashion, not bothering about the noise which he makes in going out; and it is almost always at dusk that he risks his incautious sorties. Then, being very partial to green wheat, clover and fragrant wild thyme, he goes to look for these elegant hors d'oeuvres in the plain, as they are not to be found in the forest. It is there that the hunter lies in wait for him, and makes him pay for his lack of caution.

It has been said that the antipathy which exists between rabbits and hares is such that a warren which is invaded by rabbits is immediately abandoned by hares, and vice versa. This is perfectly true; the reason being that the rabbit, wayward and rowdy, sleeps all day and stays up all night, whereas the hare sleeps during the night and is awake by day. It is obvious that such a difference in habits makes it impossible for creatures with such dissimilar ways of life to share the same dwelling.

This, on the other hand, was just the point on which the scientists were counting. They put a litter of rabbits and hares together, before either of them had opened their eyes, and they fed them on milk from a cow, an animal which, having no connection with them, could not inculcate in them by means of their first nourishment any preconceived hatreds.

They put the two litters in a dark room so that, when the infant creatures opened their eyes, they could not distinguish the slight differences which exist between the two species.

The animals thought they all belonged to the same family and, being well fed and having no reason to quarrel, lived together in fraternal friendship until the first stirrings of love were felt by them, and were substituted for brotherly tenderness.

The scientists took turns watching, so that nothing would be missed of the coupling thought by M. de Buffon to be impossible. One day they saw, with great pleasure, a doe rabbit and a buck hare approaching each other with more than fraternal tenderness, after which the little colony promised to increase soon in such proportions as would leave no doubt at all but that the two families, which supposedly would never approach each other, were cross-breeding.

About twenty little ones were the result of this mysterious scientific experiment. However, nature prevailed, in that the female rabbits gave birth to eight or ten little ones, whereas the female hares only produced two leverets to see the light of day.

It was only a matter of continuing the experiment to give the lie completely to M. de Buffon.

M. de Buffon had said: 'If, as a result of a mistake, weakness or violence there were to be a coupling between the two species, the result would be cross-breeds who would be impotent to reproduce themselves.'

This abnormal litter was isolated from all other members of their species and, to the great satisfaction of these learned persons, the children followed the example of their fathers and continued cross-breeding.

It was left to give a name to this new species; it was called *léporide*; and steps were taken to see that the cross-breeding continued. So today we have some completely new animals, much to the delight of the learned men who created them and gave them this name.

They share at the same time the qualities of the hare and the rabbit, but they are bigger than their progenitors and weigh thirteen or fourteen pounds. Their flesh is lighter than that of the hare, but less light than that of the rabbit; they can be accompanied as you please by any of the sauces which are usually served with the two quadrupeds who took part in their creation. It seems certain that in two or three years they will become common enough to take an honourable place in our forests and in our markets. I have even been assured that some have already been seen in the market places of Le Mans and Anjou. One was sent to me by the *Société d' Acclimatation* [see page 195] on the express understanding that I would eat it. I can confirm that whether it was the son of a buck rabbit and a doe hare or of a doe rabbit and a buck hare, it was in no way inferior to either its mother or its father.

[No more has been heard of the leporide. Expert opinion suggests that M. de Buffon was right and that the animal never existed; or that, if it did, it was unable to reproduce. Work in this field in the present century is thus summed up by Annie P. Gray (*Mammalian Hybrids*, Commonwealth Agricultural Bureaux, Slough, 2nd edition, 1972): 'There are conflicting opinions on the possibility of this cross, but controlled experiments have invariably given negative results.']

LETTUCE   *LAITUE*

A comestible plant, which according to Tournefort received its name (*laitue*) because it was thought to have the faculty of increasing the secretion of milk (*lait*) in nursing women. According to Pythagoras, it was given the name *eunuchinus* because it is as effective as castration in causing frigidity.

There are several different types of lettuce: the hearted, the round-headed, the crispy-leaved, the romaine with straight leaves, the romaine with frizzy leaves, the lettuce with leaves like those of the oak, lettuces of variegated colour and white cos lettuces.

The two best kinds of lettuce are the imperial lettuce and the Silesian lettuce. These can provide salads throughout the year, besides which they can be made into ragoûts, stuffed, braised, cooked with cream, marinated, fried and used as a garnish for all *grosses pièces de relevé*.

LOACH   *BARBOTE*

[This entry appears under the heading *Barbote*. At the time when Dumas was writing, the name *Barbotte* was, according to Blanchard (*Les poissons des eaux douces de la France*, 1866), used in the vicinity of Paris for the species *Nemachilus barbatulus* (Linnaeus), for which the correct French name was, as it still is, *Loche*. *Barbotte* was also used in certain places for the burbot, for which the correct French name is Lote or Lotte. See also under Burbot. It is clear from what Dumas says in this entry that he means the loach.]

A fish of rivers and lakes. Loaches which live in lakes are less delicate than those which are fished in rivers, since their flesh smells of mud and is hard to digest. Their liver, on the other hand, has a highly agreeable taste. It is very large in relation to the total volume of the fish. Some gourmands even claim that the liver is the only part of this fish which is worth eating.

Scald your loach under boiling water to clean it, then gut it and discard the eggs. Make your court-bouillon ahead of time, since loaches only need to be in it long enough for it to bubble up once, by which time they are cooked.

LOBSTER   *HOMARD*

The lobster is a crustacean much used in cooking. The *langouste*, or spiny lobster, is less flavourful and less prized; its meat can be chopped and put in a mayonnaise, to produce an excellent white sauce for bass and turbot.

Lobster

In Paris one must, so far as possible, buy only live lobsters. Choose, moreover, the heaviest that you can find; and put it to cook in a copper pan or casserole with salted water, a big piece of fresh butter, a bunch of parsley sprigs, a red pimento and two or three white leeks. After a quarter of an hour's cooking, add a goblet of Madeira or Marsala, and leave the lobster to cool in the court-bouillon. The segments of shell must then be cut along the whole length of the tail; and you will already have made a sauce, for which the following is the best recipe.

Take out in a single piece the whole of the interior of the lobster known as the *tourteau* and detach all the white meat with a sharpened quill. Take out the 'stuffing' or creamy roe which is to be found attached to the carapace. Add the eggs of the lobster, if it is female, and mix all this together with green olive oil, a generous spoonful of good mustard, ten or twelve drops of Chinese soya sauce, a handful of chopped fines herbes, two crushed shallots, a fair amount of black pepper, and finally a liqueur glass of *anisette* from Bordeaux or simply of aniseed ratafia. Beat it all together with a fork as you would an omelette, and, depending on the size of the lobster, add the juice of two or three lemons to the sauce.

Homard à la broche · Lobster on a spit

Take a large lobster or spiny lobster, alive and vigorous, and fix it on a stout skewer, which you then tie with string on to a spit. Expose it right away to a hot fire, having sprinkled it with champagne and melted butter, salt and pepper. The shell will quickly become crisp, that is to say apt to crumble between the fingers, like chalk. When it becomes detached from the body, this is the sign that the lobster is sufficiently cooked; it must then be sprinkled again with the juice from the dripping pan, from which the fat has been skimmed and to which has been added the juice of a Seville orange and a pinch of mixed spices.

This ragoût, which is peculiar to Normandy, never fails to create an impression when it appears on the table.

[Dumas gives, under the same heading of Lobster, an account of a whole meal which he prepared at the seaside.

'Oh sea, the only love to whom I have been faithful'

This line from Byron may become my motto, and I love the sea and hold it as necessary to our pleasure and even to the happiness of our

Lobster

existence. When a certain period of time has elapsed since I have seen the sea, I am tormented by an irresistible desire and, under some pretext or other, I take the train and arrive either at Trouville, Dieppe or Le Havre. On one particular day, I had gone to Fécamp.

I had hardly arrived before a fishing expedition was proposed for the following day.

I know all about fishing expeditions where nothing is caught, but one buys the fish which forms the basis of the dinner after the fishing expedition. On this occasion, however, contrary to the usual practice, we caught two mackerel and an octopus, but we bought a lobster, a plaice and about a hundred shrimps. A woman selling mussels, whom we encountered on our way, added to this lot about a hundred of her bivalves.

We had been having long discussions to establish to whose house we would repair and who consequently would be in charge of the dinner. Finally the choice fell on a wine merchant from Fécamp who had put his entire cellar at our disposition. He assured us en route that his cook had got the *pot-au-feu* going, and that we would find at his house the wherewithal for two or three dishes which the cook would have gotten together for his own dinner.

But his cook, even though he claimed her to be a cordon bleu, was unanimously demoted and I was elected in her place. She was free to

The *Pot-au-Feu*

keep the title of vice-cook, but only on condition that she would not oppose the chief cook in any way.

As we had been promised, we found a *pot-au-feu* which had been simmering since ten o'clock that morning, which meant that it had had about eight hours of cooking time. And it is after eight hours of cooking that a *pot-au-feu* comes of age.

France, I have already said, is the only country which knows how to make a *pot-au-feu*; furthermore, it is probable that my janitress, who has nothing to do but look after her *pot-au-feu* and unlatch the door, eats better soup than M. Rothschild.

To come back to our cook, she had the *pot-au-feu* which was simmering, two chickens already plucked and awaiting the spit, a beef kidney still ignorant of the sauce for which it was destined, a bunch of asparagus which was starting to run to seed, and at the bottom of her basket some tomatoes and white onions.

I had everything spread out on the kitchen table, and I asked for pen and ink. For the approval of my table companions I presented the following menu:

Potage aux tomates et aux queues de crevettes.

Entrées.

Homard à l'américaine.
Carrelet sauce normande.
Maquereaux à la maître d'hôtel.
Rognons sautés au vin de Champagne.

Rôts.

Deux poulets à la ficelle.
Poulpe frit.

Entremets.

Tomates à la provençale.
Oeufs brouillés au jus de rognon.
Pointes d'asperges.
Coeurs de laitue à l'espagnole, sans huile ni vinaigre.

Dessert de fruits.

Vins.

Château-d'Iquem, Corton, Pommard, Château-Latour.

Café.

Bénédictine. Fine champagne.

Lobster

As I said, I presented the menu, which was greeted with enthusiastic cheers. The only question which arose was how long it would take me to prepare such a dinner.

I asked for an hour and a half, which was granted me with some astonishment. They had thought it would take three.

The great talent of a cook who wants to be ready on time is to prepare as much as possible in advance and to have all the necessary ingredients readily to hand. This takes but a quarter of an hour. Now, as it is impossible in writing about the meal to set going a soup, four entrées, two roasts, two side dishes and a salad, all at the same time, allow me to take up and explain my courses dish by dish.

Potage aux tomates et aux queues de crevettes ·
Tomato and shrimp bisque

In one pan, heat salted water for the shrimps, with assorted herbs and two slices of lemon. When it is boiling, throw in the shrimps.

In a second pan, put twelve tomatoes from which you have pressed out the excess liquid, four big onions cut in rounds, a piece of butter, a clove of garlic and assorted herbs. [Cook all this together.]

When the shrimps are cooked, drain them in a colander, keeping the cooking water. Peel the shrimps and put the peeled tails aside.

Once the tomatoes and onions are cooked, press them through a fine sieve, put them back on the fire with a little jellied meat stock and a pinch of red pepper, and let this thicken into a purée. Then add an equal quantity of bouillon, and half a glass of the water in which the shrimps were cooked, and bring to the boil while stirring. When it has boiled up three or four times, toss in the shrimps, and the soup is ready.

By the way, although I am giving each recipe separately, it will be obvious that everything has to be cooking at the same time.

*

Homard à l'américaine · Lobster à l'américaine

We are choosing Vuillemot's method from the various different methods for preparing lobster à l'américaine.

We beseech our readers, and above all the ladies, to pay great attention, as the dish is very complicated.

1. Prepare in a casserole two large onions cut in quarters, a bouquet of assorted herbs and two scraps of garlic; add a bottle of good white wine, half a glass of ordinary cognac, a ladleful of good

consommé, salt, ground pepper and several grains of good cayenne pepper from Spain. Then toss in your lobster. Half an hour of cooking will suffice.

But wait a minute! The most difficult part is still to be done.

2. Let your crustacean cool in the cooking water, if you are not in a hurry; and the less hurried you are, the better it will be. Then remove the meat from the lobster, including the meat from the claws, and cut it all up into neat slices. Put all this in a sauce-boat, moisten it with a little of the bouillon in which the lobster was cooked, cover with a piece of buttered paper and keep it in a warming oven. You must wait before serving it.

3. Take eight beautiful tomatoes and cut each in half. Press out and discard the watery part. Butter a casserole and lay your tomatoes on this, seasoning them with salt, ground pepper, a little cayenne and fresh butter. Put the casserole in the oven and, after cooking, keep it hot.

4. Take two big onions, dice them, squeeze them in a cloth to extract the gluten, sauté them in a casserole with a little butter until they are golden, add a tablespoon of flour and then add half the bouillon in which the lobster was cooked. Let your sauce refine at the side of the stove and reduce it by half, adding two generous spoonfuls of tomato purée. Reduce again by a third, adding some jellied meat stock. Next, strain the sauce, add a bit of lemon juice, a nut of fresh butter, and wait.

5. Finally, take the lobster's coral, and the eggs if it has any, pound all this in a mortar with some butter, sieve it and add a little cayenne. Take a vegetable dish and arrange the pieces of lobster in it in the shape of a crown, with the tomatoes on top. Pour the lobster butter into the gaps between the pieces of lobster, glaze with some meat essence and serve.

As this dish is somewhat complicated, it should not be attempted by novices; one must be a real cook, equipped with a certain skill, in order to attack it.

*

Carrelet à la sauce normande · Plaice with *sauce normande*

Put the plaice on a silver dish, which must be buttered, season it with salt, pepper and a glass of white wine and put it in the oven.

Put a piece of butter in a casserole and stir in a little flour, until it becomes golden. Moisten this with the butter and white wine from the plaice, leaving behind only enough liquid to ensure that it does not dry up. Reduce by half.

Lobster

Cook about thirty mussels and ten or twelve mushrooms. Put the juice from the mussels in the sauce, reduce it all by half, then bind it with four egg yolks and half a glass of fresh cream. Arrange the mussels and mushrooms around the plaice and pour the sauce on top. Dot the dish here and there with some little pieces of very fresh butter, let the fish sit in the oven for two minutes, then serve it.

*

As to the mackerel *à la maître d'hôtel* and the sautéed kidneys with Burgundy wine, I can't teach anyone anything about making these two dishes. They are the ABC of cooking. The only thing is, take care to make the sauce for the kidneys rather thin, and put half a glass of this to one side at the time of serving. You will see why later.

*

Poulets à la ficelle

Up to the time when I came to make my chicken *à la ficelle*, I had put up with the comments of my vice-cook, but once we arrived at this decisive moment her comments turned into opposition.

As I had no time to waste, I threatened her with a *coup d'état*, offering to have her wages paid and then to have her sacked immediately. This threat had its effect. She obeyed passively, and five minutes later, my two chickens were turning side by side like two spindles.

But, as I have more time today, listen to me and let me explain why chicken cooked *à la ficelle* is superior to spit-roasted chicken.

All animals have two orifices, the upper and the lower. The chicken, in this respect, is the same as man. Diogenes said it two thousand four hundred years before me, on the day when he threw down in the Agora at Athens a feathered cock, shouting: 'Here is Plato's man.'

Well, first one must stop up one of the orifices, the upper one. This orifice is blocked up in the Belgian fashion, by poking the head of the bird into its stomach and sewing up the skin on top.

Let us move on to the second orifice, the lower one, which is much more important than the first.

You will have removed (and when I say you will have removed, I mean that your cook will have removed) the intestines and the liver. She will have thrown away the intestines, chopped up the liver with fines herbes, spring onions and parsley, and worked this together with a piece of butter. She will have replaced the intestines, which now are not only useless, but actually harmful, with this minced mixture which is destined to give the chicken added flavour.

Now, what should the aim of the cook be? To preserve the greatest possible quantity of juices in the animal which is to be cooked. Now, if you pass a skewer lengthways through the animal and, to keep it in place, pass another one through the animal crossways, then instead of stopping up one of the two holes which nature has made you have added two more holes, from which all the animal's juices will escape.

If, on the contrary, you tie its feet with a string, and hang it up vertically by this string, with the lower orifice up in the air and the upper orifice stopped up, and if you baste the chicken with best quality fresh butter into which you have worked salt and pepper, taking care to tip some into the lower orifice with the basting spoon, you will have fulfilled all the logical requirements for having an excellent chicken. The only thing left for you to do is to keep an eye on it while it is cooking, and then, when you see a few little cracks appear in its skin, from which issue jets of steam, cut the string. At this point put the chicken in the dripping pan, and pour the pan juices over it.

Never, never allow a single drop of bouillon to be mixed with the butter with which you baste the chicken. Any cook, as I think I have said elsewhere, any cook, I say, who puts bouillon in the dripping pan deserves to be thrown out of the door ignominiously and without mercy.

*

Pieuvre frite · Fried octopus

Cut your octopus into pieces, roll these in flour, slip them into boiling fat, remove when cooked, and you will have something similar to fried calves' ears, with a light taste of musk.

*

As for the scrambled eggs with kidney gravy and asparagus tips and tomatoes stuffed *à la provençale*, that is child's play.

Put twelve egg yolks and six egg whites into a soup tureen. After having beaten them, add a piece of butter, fines herbes, half a glass of bouillon (chicken bouillon if you have any) and the half glass of kidney juices which you have kept, and turn all this over to the cook, who has nothing more to do than to pour the mixture into a casserole, put it on the fire and stir.

Lobster

Essential advice: serve the scrambled eggs soft, as they will continue to cook on the platter.

*

As for the tomatoes, cut them in half, let the liquid drain off, remove the seeds, put the tomatoes side by side in a *four de campagne* and pile in a pyramid, in the middle of each tomato, a mixture of chopped chicken, veal, game from the night before if you have some, and mushrooms.

Over all this pour a whole glass of olive oil, the best quality you can find; sprinkle with salt, pepper, parsley and garlic chopped up together and add a dash of pimento. Cook with heat above and below, basting the pyramids of meat three or four times with the oil in which the tomatoes are cooking.

*

As for the salad of hearts of lettuce, without oil or vinegar, this is a reminder of our trip to Spain. In Spain, the vinegar does not smell at all; but, in contrast, their oil is foul. As a result it is impossible, even when the heat from the sky and the dryness of the air give you the most violent longing for fresh greenery, to eat salad there.

Well, we remedied all that by substituting egg yolks for the oil, and lemon for the vinegar. This mixture, seasoned sufficiently with salt and pepper, produced an exquisite salad. We finished up by preferring its flavour to that of our French salads.

*

At the end of an hour and a half, the meal was on the table. The only thing was that four hours later we were still at dinner!

So, what a reputation did I leave at Fécamp, and what a reception was given to me when I arrived there for my most recent visit.

*

Allow me to add one more recipe which can perfectly well come after those given above, without being out of place. This is scrambled eggs with shrimps.

Take twelve eggs and break them into a salad bowl, using all the yolks, but only eight of the whites. If there is too much egg white, it detracts from the delicacy of the dish.

In a separate pan boil the bodies [minus the tails, which you reserve] of the shrimps, adding a glass of Chablis wine. Have it all bubble up two or three times, then pour everything into a mortar to make a purée of it. This you then press through a fine sieve, to remove even the smallest bits of carapace.

Blend this fine purée with the eggs to which you have already added salt and pepper and which you have lightly decorated with finely chopped spring onions and parsley. Next add to this the [peeled] shrimp tails, beat them up with the eggs and pour everything into a frying pan which has been buttered with good fresh butter. Cook, and turn out carefully on a platter.

MACARONI   *MACARONI*

Macaroni was brought to France by the Florentines, probably at the time when Catherine de Medici came to marry Henry II. But fashion did not go wild over it; everyone knows those long tubes of farinaceous matter which are like big hollow vermicelli, and whose name gives a sufficient indication of their origin.

Italy, Naples in particular, is the native land of macaroni. There, people prepare it in a thousand different ways, as we do potatoes. It is used in soup and prepared au gratin, always accompanied by grated Parmesan cheese, and it appears on all tables, those of rich and poor alike. The Neapolitan *lazzaroni* [the name given to the lowest class of people in Naples] exist on macaroni, figs, garlic and iced water.

All the sorts of flour used in breadmaking can be used equally well to make macaroni; but the best sort to use is the very small-grained wheat from Odessa, turned into semolina. This semolina is then converted into dough, pounded and crushed and put in a metal cylinder surrounded by a heating apparatus. At the bottom of the cylinder is a sort of sieve, pierced with little slits of the same size as one wants the strips of macaroni to assume. By means of pressure, the dough is forced out of this mould and appears in long narrow bands, whose edges are then brought together and adhere, thus forming the tubes which are then ready to be used. Real gourmands introduce fish or meat juices into these tubes with the help of a little syringe.

Now let us go on to the way in which these farinaceous tubes are prepared for consumption.

One should not choose overly large tubes, but those about the size of a large piece of straw. These are put in salted water, or better still in bouillon. They should be three quarters cooked, in such a way that they swell in volume—*ché cresca in corpo.*

Macaroni

[The rest of the recipe, which is ascribed to Mme Ristori, is evidently based on the notes taken by Dumas when he watched that lady's cook prepare macaroni. See Appendix 2, where a better description is given than that provided here.]

Macaroni à la ménagère

Boil a pound of macaroni in water for three quarters of an hour, with a piece of butter, salt and an onion with a clove stuck in it. Drain it well, and put it in a casserole with a little butter, a quarter *livre* (122 grams) each of grated Gruyère cheese and grated Parmesan cheese, a little nutmeg, coarsely ground pepper and a few spoonfuls of cream. Toss this all together. When the macaroni flows smoothly, arrange it and serve.

Macaroni au gratin

Having prepared the macaroni as above, sprinkle it with breadcrumbs and grated cheese, and brown it under a *four de campagne*.

MACEDOINE   *MACEDOINE*

This name is given to a mixture of foodstuffs about which we have already written in the entry for Chartreuse [not translated, but Dumas explains that a classic chartreuse is a dish of vegetables in their prime].

Macédoine de légumes printaniers · Macedoine of early vegetables

First quality vegetables must always be chosen: carrots, turnips, green asparagus tips, green beans, garden peas, and small white beans which are just starting to grow bigger. One can also add a few small broad beans from the market garden, artichoke hearts and cucumbers.

Cut the carrots and turnips in such a way as to give them varied and attractive shapes. Cut the green beans in lozenge shapes, and the asparagus into little sticks. Blanch all these vegetables and drain them. Melt a good piece of fresh butter in a casserole and toss in the vegetables, adding a little powdered sugar. Stir gently on the fire, finish off the macedoine with a few spoonfuls of béchamel and arrange it in a pyramid on a platter. This dish of early vegetables is a most agreeable and excellent one to eat.

One of the most handsome and one of the bravest fish in existence. When it is brought into the boat, alive, from the line, it seems to be made of azure, silver and gold.

The mackerel often attacks fish much bigger than itself, and even man. A Norwegian historian tells the story of a sailor who was bathing and suddenly disappeared. When he was fished out of the water ten minutes later he had already been largely eaten by mackerel.

These fish gather together each year to make extensive journeys. Towards the spring, they skirt the coasts of Iceland, Shetland, Scotland and Ireland and rush headlong into the Atlantic Ocean, where one column, passing in front of Portugal and Spain, goes on to enter the Mediterranean, while another column enters the English Channel, in April and May, and passes on from there, in June, to the waters off Holland and Friesland.

Mackerel are found in all the seas, in uncountable numbers. They pass the winter in the Arctic, their heads buried in the mud and fucus —that, anyway, is what people used to believe. However, Bloch, Noël, Lacépède and others think that the migrations of the mackerel are like those of the tunny and the herring, and that the former, like the latter, simply withdraw into the depths of the sea, at the surface of which they are seen to reappear in the spring.

Maquereaux à l'anglaise

Take three or four extremely fresh mackerel, gut them through the gill-openings, tie up the head of each and cut off the small tail-end; but do not cut their backs at all. Put a good handful of fennel into a poissonnière which has its removable rack in place, and place the mackerel on top, adding some lightly salted water. Cook them over a low fire. Once they are cooked, lift out the rack, drain the fish, arrange them on your serving platter and pour over them a fennel sauce or the sauce called *à groseilles à maquereau*. [The latter sauce is gooseberry sauce. Dumas gives a recipe for it, which we have not translated, in his entry for Sauces, and describes it as an English sauce. This is interesting, since it has been known in both France and England for a long time as a suitable accompaniment for mackerel, and there are those who think that it was originally French. Dumas' method of making it, in summary form, is to take two good handfuls of half-ripe gooseberries, cut them in two, seed them, blanch them in lightly salted water and drain them. They are then added to a sauce which has been made by combining equal quantities of velouté and butter, heating the mixture and blending it well.]

MADELEINE   *MADELEINE*

As for the excellent cake which is called madeleine, and which well deserves the great reputation which it enjoys, there befell a little adventure to one of our friends which we are going to relate.

A few years ago, one of our friends was going to Strasburg. Since he was travelling as a tourist, he gladly stopped in the towns and villages through which he was passing, first of all to rest, and then to observe the different manners and customs of the inhabitants.

One day he got back on the road rather late, thinking that he would reach before nightfall the next town where he was to rest, but he hurried in vain; he could not see any sign of any sort of dwelling. Finally, towards eleven o'clock, he saw in the moonlight the dark and thrusting spire of a church.

Everything was dark and quiet, not a single light was still shining and our traveller was at a loss to know where he would find a good table to cheer his stomach and a good bed to rest his limbs, benumbed with fatigue.

Suddenly he saw through the night a glimmer which seemed to come out of the ground. He approached this ray of light, the only one which he could see, and which represented salvation to him. He knocked at a door which was beside him and from under which shone the gleam of light which had made his heart beat faster. At first a grunting answered him.

He knocked a second time, but harder, and then heard a strange, seemingly subterranean voice ask:

'Who is there, and what do you want?'

'I am a traveller, plagued with weariness and dying of hunger,' answered the voyager, 'in the name of God, open the door, and you will not regret it.'

Then he heard footsteps approaching the door. Someone pulled back an enormous iron bar, the door opened and he saw a man whose wild face was completely besmeared with flour, and whose bristling hair and beard contributed even more to his frightening appearance; the man was naked to the belt.

'Come on in and hurry up,' said he to the traveller, in this same sepulchral voice.

Our friend did not feel at all reassured, and at one moment he rather wanted to turn back and go and knock at another door; but the man had replaced the iron bar, and there was no way of retreating, so he put on a brave face and entered a large room where there was a huge baker's oven giving off enough light to illuminate it entirely.

'Excuse me, Monsieur,' said the traveller very politely, 'I have just covered sixteen or eighteen leagues, almost without eating, could you get for me, on condition, of course, that I pay you, something to stay my hunger and to rest my body?'

'I only have my bed,' answered the man in his gruff voice, 'and as for something to eat we are not lacking that here; it remains to be seen if you will like it.'

'Anything will please me, if only I can eat something. Look, what do you have to offer me?'

The man went towards a cupboard, opened it, and took out a little basket in which were about a dozen beautiful, golden, oval cakes.

'Here,' said he to the traveller, 'just taste that and you'll have something to say to me.'

He put the basket on the table, near the traveller and, placing his hands on his hips, surveyed him.

Our friend took a cake and bit it hungrily; in a second he had swallowed it whole; he took a second, then a third, then a fourth and at each cake which he swallowed the man kept smiling with pleasure.

Finally when not one was left in the basket, he said to him: 'Well, what do you think of my "madeleines"?'

'Give me something to drink first,' said the traveller in a strangled voice.

Once more the man went to his cupboard and brought out a bottle covered with a venerable layer of dust. He uncorked it and then, taking two glasses, filled them and offered one to the stranger.

'Drink,' he said to him, 'I don't want to see you choked to death by my precious cakes.'

The stranger drank in one gulp what was an excellent Bordeaux wine, and then, stretching out his glass a second time, said: 'Your good health, my good chap, you have just given me one of the best meals of my life. But, tell me, what do you call these succulent cakes?'

'What, you don't know the madeleines of Commercy?'

'Am I then at Commercy?'

'Yes, and you may be sure that you have just eaten the best cakes in the world.'

Without entirely sharing the good fellow's enthusiasm for his cakes, the traveller was forced to admit that they were excellent and that, being in need, he had supped very well.

Madeleine

The man then offered him his own bed, saying that he would manage with a mattress. The traveller protested a bit, but finally accepted and went to bed, falling asleep directly. Next morning he breakfasted more copiously than he had supped the night before, which didn't stop him on leaving from providing himself with a certain number of madeleines, which the good man forced him to accept as a souvenir of the fright which he had felt at first.

The madeleines of Commercy are in fact famous. It is thought that their reputation was made by King Stanislas Leczinski, when he came to France.

Here now is the recipe which comes from Madeleine Paumier, pensioner and former cook of Mme Perrotin de Barmond.

Grate the zest of two little citrons (or two lemons or Seville oranges) on a sugar lump, crush the sugar lump fine, mix it with some powdered sugar and weigh out nine ounces of this mixture. Put it in a casserole with eight ounces of sieved flour; four egg yolks or six whole eggs; two spoonfuls of eau de vie from Andaya and a little salt. Stir this mixture with a spatula. Once the dough is worked, continue to stir it for only a minute. It is absolutely necessary to observe this rule if you want to have really good madeleines; otherwise the excessive workings of the mixture will have an adverse effect on the cooking and will incline the madeleines to be heavy, to stick to the moulds and to be ragged or to crinkle up, which would make this sweet look pretty sad.

Next, clarify ten ounces of butter from Isigny in a little casserole. As the milk progressively rises up, skim it off carefully. When it no longer bubbles, that shows that it is clarified. You thereupon decant it into another casserole and when it has cooled slightly, you fill one madeleine mould with it. You then pour this same butter into another mould and continue thus until you have done eight, after which you pour the butter back into the casserole. Once more you fill a mould with hot butter and pour it in turn in another eight moulds. Finally you do this twice more, which gives you 32 buttered moulds.

One must not turn the moulds upside down once they have been buttered, as they must hold the little bit of butter which has run back into the bottom of each.

Afterwards, you mix the rest of the butter into the dough mixture and then put it on a range at a very low heat. Stir the mixture so that it does not stick to the casserole and, as soon as it starts to become liquid, take the casserole off the fire, but without allowing it to become tepid. Then fill each of your moulds with a spoonful of this mixture and put them in the oven, at a moderate temperature.

MELON
MELON

An annual creeping plant belonging to the cucumber family. Depending on the species, the fruit is as big as either an apple or a pumpkin. Those from Honfleur sometimes weigh up to 24 pounds. They say that it grows wild in the country of the Kalmuks; but I have been there during the months of October and November without ever seeing a single melon, even though 50 leagues away they were being harvested by the thousand beside the Caspian Sea, where the biggest and the best only cost 4 sous.

The melon probably came originally from Africa. It certainly originated in hot countries and is only good when it has been caressed by the sun's rays. The best melon is the cantaloup, brought back from Armenia by the Romans; it was named thus from the village of Cantaloupo, where it was cultivated. Throughout all the southern part of France, we have the water melon or the green melon, which, for some gastronomes, equals the cantaloup.

Naples has its national melon, which is called *Cocméro*, and which is eaten almost exclusively, along with macaroni, by the *lazzaroni*. Its flesh is red, with black seeds; actually, however, it has no body, and is just cold water.

To make the melon digestible, gastronomes say that one must eat it with pepper and salt, and drink on top of it a half glass of Madeira, or rather Marsala, since Madeira has disappeared. There is no other way to prepare it but to cut it in slices and to serve it between the soup and the beef or between cheese and dessert.

MILK
LAIT

A white, mild and slightly sweet liquid, which is an animal substance formed in the udders of female animals, and which constitutes man's first nourishment.

The only kinds of milk which we use are those of the cow, the goat and the ewe; and, as a remedy for certain cases of consumption, that of the ass.

I have had occasion to drink camel's milk, and mare's milk, and have not found them inferior in any way to those of the goat and the cow.

MULBERRY   *MURE*

This is the fruit of the mulberry tree.

There are two kinds of mulberry tree. The white mulberry, whose fruits are used for feeding farm-yard animals, which eat them with pleasure, is one; but we do not need to discuss it here. The other is the black mulberry tree, which bears large, soft fruits called mulberries, whose smell and sweet flavour delight gourmets. It is thought to have come from Persia or China originally, but it has been grown for a long time in the Orient, whence it no doubt travelled to Italy.

The poets of antiquity have praised this plant, whose foliage enchanted them. Ovid, in his fable about Pyramus and Thisbe, causes those two unfortunates to perish under one of these trees. The story goes that their blood, besprinkling its roots, passed a purplish black colour on to its fruits, which had previously been white; and that, because of Thisbe's prayer, the gods preserved this sinister colour as a reminder of the catastrophe which befell the two lovers. Virgil was pleased to describe, in one of his Eclogues, a Naiad smearing the face of Silenus with purple mulberry juice. Horace, in his verses, recommends the eating of mulberries at the end of the meal, as a means of staying in good health during the sweltering days of summer. Pliny, on the contrary, says that it is unhealthy to eat them at that stage of the meal. He states that the mulberry tree is known as 'the wisest of the trees', because it does not sprout until the cold weather is past; and that its sprouting, which takes place in the course of one night, is accompanied by an audible noise.

Mulberries are refreshing, nourishing and laxative. The Romans made a medicine from them which was given for all ailments. Today, a syrup is made of them, which doctors recommend in general for inflammatory illnesses.

MUSHROOM   *CHAMPIGNON*

The generic name for a large number of spongy, cryptogamous plants which have caps but no branches or leaves. Mushrooms grow in damp places. There are many poisonous ones. Even those which are good are capable of being mildly intoxicating to persons who, like the Emperor Claudius or Trimalchio of whom Petronius wrote, are tempted to use them to excess.

I must confess that nothing terrifies me more than the appearance of mushrooms at table, particularly when I find myself by chance in a small provincial town. I see in a newspaper this short paragraph:

'Yesterday, Mr X., his wife and eldest daughter, having been out walking in the forest of . . . , brought back from there a dish of mushrooms which they ate for their dinner. This morning the husband and wife were dead, poisoned, and people were giving up hope for the daughter.'

The great tragedy about mushroom poisoning is that when the first symptoms of intoxication are felt it is already too late, as the poisonous food is by that time already half digested.

Properly speaking, an antidote for poisonous mushrooms does not therefore exist. One starts by administering a vomitive. Then, if this is not sufficiently effective, a gentle purgative should be given: 30 grams of castor oil, 60 grams of manna [the sweetish exudate of the European flowering ash], an enema with 60 grams of cassia, 15 grams of sulphate of soda and of magnesia. As well as this, several spoonfuls of a potion made of ether and orange flower water should be given. During this period, the doctor should arrive and will appraise the situation.

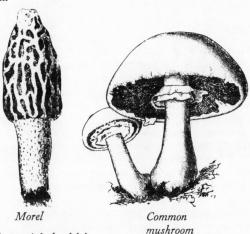

Morel　　　　　*Common mushroom*

Champignons à la bordelaise

Take the biggest *cèpes* (esculent boletus) which you can find, choosing the driest, thickest and firmest. It is most important that they should not have been picked a long time previously. Wash them, rinse them, and carefully incise their undersides in a lozenge pattern. Put them in an earthenware dish, and sprinkle them with best quality oil, and with a little salt and coarsely ground pepper. Let them marinate for two hours, and then grill them on one side. When they have finished cooking, which you can easily judge by seeing if they give when pressed with the finger, arrange them on a serving dish and dress them with a sauce in the following manner.

Put in a casserole a quantity of oil which will be adequate for making the sauce. Chop parsley, spring onions and a clove of garlic very fine, and put them in the oil. Heat this all together, pour the sauce over the mushrooms, then squeeze over them the juice of two lemons, or sprinkle them with verjuice, which is even better.

Croûtes aux morilles

Peel, split, wash, blanch and drain your morels. Put them in a casserole with butter, parsley and spring onions. Put them on the fire and sauté them. Sprinkle with flour, add a little consommé, cook and reduce. Remove the bouquet, bind with diluted egg yolks, add some sugar and serve with a garnish of black truffles.*

MUSTARD   *MOUTARDE*

[There is no entry for mustard in the dictionary itself. However, as we have explained on page 8, there is an annex devoted to the subject. It is an elegant essay of more than five thousand words, supposedly written in response to an anonymous correspondent who had conveniently requested Dumas to deal with the subject historically, etymologically, botanically and in the context of cookery. Dumas did so, in such an orderly and coherent way as to startle any reader familiar with the looser and more jumbled essays in the dictionary. Extracts only are given here; but we have taken care to include the final page, in which the purpose of the whole essay is revealed as an advertisement for Bornibus mustard.]

You ask me, my dear anonymous correspondent, how far back in history mustard goes. Let me, then, deal with the egg before I come to the chicken, and with the seed before the plant.

The Greeks and Romans, who were not familiar with mustard in pots or in 'bricks', as it is sold nowadays, knew it in the form of mustard grains, which they used in stews, and as a powder, which

---

* Dumas says nothing in this recipe about the *croûtes*. However, it is clear from another recipe (not translated here) that you are to take round bread rolls which have been hollowed out, buttered and grilled until dry, and that the morel mixture goes into these.

they employed with roasts, just as we use our modern mustard.

Greeks and Romans had but the one word for mustard, which proves clearly that this condiment came from Greece to Italy, from Athens to Rome. They used the name *sinapis* without distinction for both mustard grain and powdered mustard.

[After further comments on mustard in classical times, Dumas describes the Dark Ages when much knowledge and many recipes were lost.]

Dijon alone, the city which the Romans called Divio, had kept the original recipe of Palladius, and can be credited, if not for inventing mustard, at least for restoring it to us.

Since when have the Dijonnais had the honour of providing this indispensable condiment for our table?

It is impossible to say. All that is known is that Etienne Boileau, who was Provost of Paris under Saint Louis, granted to the vinegar-makers, in his regulations about guilds and corporations, the right to make mustard.

In the *Cris de Paris* of the thirteenth century, we find:

> '*Vinaigre qui est beau et bon!*
> *Vinaigre de moutarde.*'

During that period, the sauce-vendors (*sauciers*) used to carry sauces to people's houses at dinner-time, and would run through the streets of Paris, crying: 'Mustard sauce! . . . Garlic sauce! . . . Onion sauce! . . . Verjuice sauce! . . . Ravigote sauce! . . .' Anyone who was disinclined to eat his meat without sauce would open his window or door and summon the vendor, whereupon he would be served at once with the sauce of his choice.

It is readily understandable that these sauce-vendors resorted to imitation in an effort to make mustard their own product and to exploit it; but Dijon maintained her supremacy in its manufacture.

[After explaining that attempts in the south of France to supplant the vinegar in mustard with wine-must were unsuccessful, Dumas returns to the Paris scene.]

At nine o'clock in the morning and six o'clock in the evening the only people one met in the streets of Paris were children on their way to buy a pennyworth of mustard. If one asked what time it was, the reply would not be 'nine o'clock' or 'six o'clock', but 'it's the time for children to be fetching the mustard'.

The first cookery book to appear in France, *Le Viandier* by Taill-event, head chef of King Charles VII, contains a long and unaffected eulogy of mustard. Here is what he wrote, in French which is difficult to read, but which we render in a manner comprehensible to all.

'One evening, following a great battle against the English, King Charles VII and his three inseparable companions, Dunois, La Hire and Xaintrailles, came to lodge for the night in the little town of Sainte-Menehould, in which only five or six houses survived, the town having been burned. The king and his suite were dying of hunger. The ruined and ravaged countryside was lacking in everything. Finally, they managed to get hold of four pig's feet and three chickens.

'The king had with him no cook, male or female; so the wife of a poor edge-tool maker was charged with cooking the chickens. As for the pig's feet, there was nothing to do but put them on the grill. The good woman roasted the chickens, dipped them in beaten egg, rolled them in breadcrumbs with fines herbes, and then, after moistening them with a mustard sauce, served them to the king and his companions, who devoured the pig's feet entire and left only the bones of the chickens.

'King Charles, who had supped to perfection, asked on more than one occasion subsequently for *des poulets à la Sainte-Menehould*. Taillevent, who knew what he meant, served him chickens like those which the wife of the poor tool-maker had prepared for him.'

Louis XI, who liked to invite himself to supper at short notice with his cronies, the *bons bourgeois* of Paris, used almost always to carry with him his own pot of mustard. According to the *Contes* of J. Riboteau, the Receiver-General of Bourgogne, he ordered from an apothecary of Dijon, in 1477, twenty pounds of mustard for the personal use of the king.

Finally, and to end this chronological history of mustard with an anecdote which I believe to be little known, we shall relate that among the various Popes who held such a brilliant court at Avignon, Pope John XXII was one of those who did not disdain the pleasures of the table. He was passionately fond of mustard, put it in everything, and not knowing what to do with one of his nephews who was a good-for-nothing, made him his *premier moutardier* (head mustardier). Hence comes the practice of saying of a conceited fool that he thinks himself 'the Pope's head mustardier'.

[Dumas explains how the dominant position of mustard was threatened by the influx of new spices and condiments from, e.g., the East Indies.]

Mustard, attacked by this invasion of eastern and western spices, fought a brave battle. Dijon, the great centre for its manufacture, thought that the product needed statutes which would completely reassure the public about the way in which mustard was handled and about the ingredients of which it was composed. As a result, the mustard-makers and the vinegar-makers of Dijon were given, in 1634, statutes which brought them into line with the other trades of the town and gave to them alone the right to make mustard.

Twenty-three vinegar-mustard makers of Dijon adhered to the new regulations. Among their signatures is to be seen that of Naigeon.

But, despite all this, the fashion for mustard was continuing to decline. People found that it left something to be desired, as a source of acidity and variety in their food. Then there arrived on the scene Jean Naigeon, great grandson of the one who had signed the regulations of the twenty-three. By changing one single element in the manufacture of mustard he brought about a recrudescence of sales and a renewal of the favour which mustard had enjoyed.

What did he need for this? An inspiration, a flash of genius. He was the first to substitute verjuice for vinegar, verjuice being the juice pressed from the grape before it is ripe. The result of this was that mustard no longer contained any sugar or acetic acid, but only tartaric, citric and malic acids.

[Meanwhile, however, there was a new development.] Paris had begun to be a serious competitor of Dijon. This revolution began in 1742. A vinegar-maker of Paris, called Capitaine, began to use white vinegar instead of red vinegar for his infusions, and to introduce capers and anchovy essence into mustard of high quality. These innovations found great favour.

Ten years later, another vinegar-maker, called Maille, established a European reputation for his speciality. Having been named purveyor 'by appointment' to the Marquise de Pompadour, he assumed the title, just a shade ambitious, of vinegar-maker and distiller to the King of France and the emperors of Germany and Russia. A man of ready wit, who understood his own epoch, which was one of full sensuality, he began by composing some vinegars for the use of women and others for men. His clientele soon included all the smartest people and the dandies of the aristocracy, duchesses, marquises, countesses, young beaux and abbés who moved in society. To work for the boudoir was a sure means of arriving in the kitchen. Before the emergence of Maille there were only nine kinds of vinegar. He added ninety-two, all of fine quality and good for the health.

He multiplied to a similar extent the number of vinegars used at table. He had twenty-four mustards: red mustard, fine mustard with capers, fine mustard with anchovy, mustard powder, garlic mustard, tarragon mustard, nasturtium mustard, lemon mustard, Choiseul mustard, Choisy mustard, mustard *à la conserve, aux fines herbes, à la*

Mustard

grecque, *à la maréchale*, *à la marquise*, *à la reine*, *à la romaine* and finally mustard with truffles. These were all his own, except for the versions with capers and with anchovy. The most fashionable were mustard *à la ravigote*, with garlic, with truffles, with anchovy and with tarragon.

Bordin flourished at the same time as Maille and, like him, had his role in the period. He invented the mustard called *de santé* (for the health) and composed recipes for forty different kinds of mustard—imperial mustard, mustard *au vin de Champagne*, *à la rocambole*, *aux champignons*, *à la rose*, *à l'italienne* and *à la vanille*.

In 1812, counting the twenty-nine new kinds of mustard invented by Acloque, the pupil and successor of Maille, but not counting the mustards of Capitaine and of Dijon, France possessed eighty-four kinds of mustard. At this point Grimod de la Reynière announced three new mustards, which brought the total up to ninety-three [?]. These three were those of Châlon-sur-Saône, Besançon and Saint-Brieuc.

Here is what was said about them by this famous connoisseur, on whose part we must notice a marked preference for Messieurs Maille and Bordin, who were, I suspect, regular and profitable subscribers to the *Almanach des Gourmands*.

'An apothecary and chemist of Saint-Brieuc has recently constructed a factory for the production of a mustard which is not without merit and which has above all great strength and pungency. It is beginning to penetrate the old region of Armorique and to arrive as far as le Contentin. M. Maout (for this is the name of the manufacturer, who was predestined to make mustard, since his name includes the first five letters of *moutarde*) plans to set up an establishment at Paris.'

However, this brief comment on the product of M. Maout was enough to attract attention to him. Doctor Gastald, Portalis and Cambacérès declared themselves in favour of the mustard of Maout, and wherever one supped in France, that is to say wherever one ate with a certain delicacy, this 'Celtic' mustard appeared on the table beside those of Maille and of Bordin. This triumvirate reigned for more than half a century on the tables of France.

[Dumas next deals with his anonymous correspondent's question about the etymology of the word *moutarde*, before proceeding to treat it from the botanical point of view; and then passes to its role in cuisine.]

You ask me, finally, which of the preparations I prefer from the culinary point of view.

Mustard

Until I tasted and appreciated the mustard of M. Alexandre Bornibus, I used to prefer to all others the aromatic mustards of Maille and Bordin. But once chance had caused me to taste the Bornibus mustard I realized that the day would come when it would be the champion.

I speak of chance, for here is how it happened. I was writing a novel of which the main scene took place at Bourg-en-Bresse. I obtained information about the shortest way of visiting this town, the stage on which my characters were to perform, and was told: 'Go to Mâcon, a branch line from there will take you straight to Bourg.'

I arrived fast asleep at Dijon, heard the cry 'Dijon! Dijon!' and then fell into confusion. Was it at Dijon or was it at Mâcon that there was a branch line to Bourg? I no longer had any idea. Since I had only one travelling-bag with me, I jumped down on to the platform from my coach, made for the exit and asked for the branch line to Bourg. The ticket-collector, who did not understand what I was trying to say, did not reply, and I found myself outside in the courtyard. I addressed myself to a coachman who was conveniently waiting there.

'The branch line for Bourg?' I asked him.

'For what *bourg* (place)?'

'For Bourg-en-Bresse.'

'Ah, well, you're not in the right place. That is at Mâcon.'

I made to re-enter the station. The ticket-collector asked me for my ticket.

'My ticket? I've just given it to you. Look among the tickets which you've just collected and you'll find one for Mâcon.'

While he was looking for it, the locomotive coughed, spat, sneezed and departed.

'Goodness me,' laughed the ticket-collector, 'you'll be the first arrival for tomorrow's train.'

'But still,' said I, 'if I'm going to leave tomorrow you'll have to give me back my ticket.'

'And here indeed it is,' quoth he. 'My goodness, yes! It's for Mâcon, all right. Bah! . . . Stay the night here.'

'So be it,' I replied, 'and I'll take the opportunity to visit the cathedral and to pay a call on my poor friend Louis Boulanger.'

Louis Boulanger, one of those painters whose first works were the most promising, was director of the museum at Dijon, and I was delighted to have this opportunity of seeing him. The only trouble was that I could hardly burst in on him at eleven o'clock in the evening. So I had myself taken to the Hôtel du Parc.

I asked for supper. They served me two mutton cutlets and

Mustard

half a cold chicken.

'What mustard do you want?' asked the waiter.

'That of Dijon, of course.'

'I know,' said he, with the air of someone who was saying to himself 'what an imbecile!', 'but I'm asking whether you prefer men's mustard or ladies'.'

'Oh, oh,' said I in turn, 'and what difference is there between men's mustard and women's?'

'Ladies'.'

'All right, ladies'.'

'The fact is, sir, that since a lady's palate is more delicate than a man's, the ordinary mustard of Dijon is too strong and too pungent for the ladies, so much so that M. Bornibus has invented a separate mustard for them.'

'Who is this M. Bornibus?'

'Oh, sir, he's all the rage as mustard-maker. People here talk of no mustard but his.'

'It's true, I know him by reputation, but I don't yet know his mustard. It would be interesting to taste it here in Dijon. Will you give me some, then?'

'Which of the two?'

'Both of them.'

'So monsieur will eat the ladies' mustard?'

'Yes, on the principle of *a fortiori*.'

And the waiter served me the two mustards with my cutlets.

I am not a great lover of mustard. Since nature has furnished me with an excellent stomach, I have never made much use of this 'preface to the appetite', as Grimod de la Reynière calls it. But I must say that on this occasion, prompted only by the fine canary colour of this good apéritif, I plunged the wooden spoon into the mustard pot and made two pyramids on my plate, one of the men's mustard and one of the ladies'. And I must also say that from this moment I shed my former self and joined the supporters of Bornibus mustard.

On my return to Paris, I went to visit the premises of M. Bornibus at 60, Boulevard de la Villette. He gave me a tour of the establishment, in the most obliging manner, and explained to me that the superiority of his products derived from the perfection of the handling machinery which he had himself invented, and above all from the way in which he chose and combined his primary ingredients.

There, my dear anonymous correspondent, I think you have all that you sought from me, chronologically, etymologically, botanically and from the culinary point of view.

MUTTON   *MOUTON*

There exists in the mountains of Greece and in the islands of Cyprus, Sardinia and Corsica a race of sheep—now exceedingly rare, thanks to the bullets of huntsmen—which is believed to be the primitive form of the present species of sheep.

The sheep of the Cape of Good Hope, of the Caspian Sea and of Astrakhan have tails so thick that they weigh up to twenty pounds. Some of them trail behind them little carts on which their tails rest, so that the wool will not be spoiled by dragging along the ground.

It was to Don Pedro, King of Castile, that Spain was indebted for the introduction into that country of the sheep of Barbary, which have given such renown to the wool of Castile. The profits brought in by these valuable animals induced the Spanish noblemen, following the example of their king, to visit their flocks and attend to their rearing; while the shearing days were celebrated as festivals. This was why these sheep, which brought Spain thirty millions in revenue, were called the jewels of the royal crown. A ram of the finest pedigree had no price; and sums of up to 500 piastres were seen to be paid for a single animal.

In the fifteenth century, Edward the Fourth, King of England, obtained through the generosity of the King of Spain three thousand

Mutton

of this fine breed of sheep. The only result of the change of climate was to make the wool longer and less fine; but the extreme care which the English took of their flocks and the complete extermination of the wolf in England made it possible to keep these sheep continuously in the open air. Since that time there has been a general demand for English wools. In order to remind the nation continually of the importance of this industry, a sack of wool used to serve as seat for the Chancellor in the House of Lords, and I think it still does today.

In France, the sheep whose meat is most prized are those from the Ardennes, Langres, La Crau and the salt marshes. When young, a sheep is called lamb; its flesh is then very tender, but less succulent. Later, if it has not been castrated, its flesh is less appreciated than that of the ewe.

Sheep are an important resource in all countries, but particularly in those where one finds neither shelter nor kitchens; I am speaking of Spain, the banks of the Nile and Arabia. When one crosses tracts of desert with four or six Arabs, one agrees in advance (and this influences the price) whether one is going to provide them with food or whether they will look after themselves.

When one agrees to provide their food, they are always hungry, and it is impossible to fill them up; when one agrees not to be responsible for their food, they lunch off a date, dine on two, tighten their belts one notch after each meal, and that's the way it is.

In 1833 I was going from Tunis to a Roman amphitheatre, twelve or fifteen leagues deep in the desert; I bargained with four Arabs to escort me to El Djem, which is the name of this ruin. The Arabs were responsible for providing me with my mount, that's to say a camel, and for supplying their own food. I had taken in a sort of tin suitcase a piece of roast meat, dates, wine, water and brandy. When we had arrived at our first overnight stop, we got ready for dinner and, to my great astonishment, I saw my Arabs dine off a few dates and a banana. I was embarrassed to have my relatively splendid dinner, when they had hardly eaten at all; so I gave them three quarters of my bread, all my roast meat and half my fruit, keeping only the wine and water for myself. I announced to them that on the following day we would all eat together and have a sheep, and that they should therefore procure one, which seemed to me an easy thing to do, as I had seen groups of five or six grazing wherever there was some grass.

One would be wrong in thinking that the desert starts at the coast; it is only ten or fifteen leagues inland that one find solitude, starvation and thirst. The next day I was awakened by the bleating of a sheep; during the night one of my men had gone and acquired for a consideration of five francs a beautiful lamb weighing about fifty pounds. Two hours later we were at El Djem, where we had agreed to lunch.

I had heard a lot about the way in which sheep are cooked in the desert, and I did not want to miss any stage in the preparations. Since it wasn't to be ready for two hours, and since it didn't take more than two hours to visit the amphitheatre, I was present for all stages of the cooking. The Arabs started by slaughtering the lamb, following all the religious rituals prescribed by the Koran, then they opened the stomach and threw away the intestines. They kept the heart, liver and lungs, then rummaged in the sack of provisions and stuffed the stomach with dates, figs, dried raisins, honey, salt and pepper; after which the stomach was carefully sewn up. During this time, the two Arabs who were not busy with the sheep were digging a pit two feet deep with their sabres. This they filled with dry wood, which they set alight after having prepared another armful of dry wood near to that which was now being reduced to embers. They then laid the lamb, in its skin, on the bed of glowing charcoal, covering it with the second armful of wood which they had got ready and which immediately caught fire. When this armful was also burned, the sheep found itself buried like a chestnut under the embers. The Arabs then threw back on it some of the earth which they had taken from the pit in which it was now cooking; after which they told me to go and look in a leisurely way at the amphitheatre, and that the sheep would be cooked in an hour and a half. I returned after an hour and a half because I was very hungry, and was particularly looking forward to tasting my guides' cooking. They were undoubtedly looking forward to it just as much, for they had hardly spotted me talking to the Arab who spoke a little Italian, whom I had taken with me, before they started rummaging around in their subterranean fire, and pulled out the sheep.

It was roasted like a potato whose skin is burnt; when scraped with a dagger, its skin took on the beautiful golden colour of a browned roast which has just been done to a turn. The burnt wool disappeared completely, and one could guess that beneath the skin, from which not a crack had allowed any fat to escape, lay succulent meat, full of savour. I didn't know how to cut up the sheep, and so I motioned to the chief of our escort to be the first to attack it.

He needed no encouragement. He brought his thumb and first finger together and, like a vulture stabbing with its beak, shot his hand forward and pinched and tore off a strip of meat. The others did likewise immediately and, as I could see that if I didn't hurry, the whole sheep would be gone when I asked for my share, I indicated to them in signs to let me have my turn. I then cut off a shoulder at the front with my dagger and, little wishing to participate in this rush for the spoils with my bare hands, I placed my shoulder of mutton on one of the plates from my kit and, like a child in disgrace, had my meal alone. My Arab had returned my flask full of cool water, as he had promised.

I must say that I have eaten lamb from some of the most famous kitchens of Europe, but never have I eaten more delectable meat than this which was cooked under the embers. I recommend this to all travellers in the Orient. [See also Quarter of roast lamb.]

NIGHTINGALE   *ROSSIGNOL*

In vain does the nightingale charm us with its melodious song. It does not stop our cruel hunters from killing it for its meat, which yields only to that of the fig-pecker in delicacy.

It is said that Lucullus had several platters of a large quantity of nightingales' brains served to him in the course of a sumptuous repast; an exquisite dish if this was so.

NOODLES   *NOUILLES*

An alimentary paste of German origin. A very thin type of vermicelli with which vol-au-vent cases are sometimes filled.

When you want to make noodles, rather than buying them ready-made, you take half a litre of flour and add to this four or five egg yolks, a little salt and a little water. Make a well-mixed, fairly stiff dough with all this; then roll it out with a rolling pin so that it is about five millimetres thick. Cut this into strips and sprinkle them with flour so that the noodles will not stick to each other. Throw the noodles into boiling bouillon, and leave them to cook for a quarter of an hour. Give them a little colour with a spoonful of gravy, or a little caramel. If you are afraid that they will dissolve in the cooking, use whole eggs instead of using just the yolks and add a little infusion of saffron to the dough.

NOUGAT   *NOUGAT*

White nougat, called nougat of Marseilles, is made of sweet almond slivers and shelled pistachios which are cooked with honey from Narbonne. White nougat is served and eaten with the dessert.

Brown nougat, with which temples, domes, and porticoes are built is made as follows. Take five hundred grams of sweet almonds, shell, skin and wash them, then drain them on a white cloth. Cut each of these almonds in slivers, which you then allow to turn golden in a very slow oven. Melt 75 grams of powdered sugar in a pan on the stove. When it has completely melted, toss in your hot almonds, and mix everything together well. When you have taken the pan off the fire, put the almonds in a mould which you have wiped out and oiled. Arrange them around the mould by using a lemon to press them in place. If you use your fingers, they will stick to them. Mount them as thinly as possible, unmould them, arrange them and serve.

NUTMEG   *MUSCADE*

In French we give the name *noix muscade*, or simply *muscade*, to the kernel, or central part, of the fruit which comes from the nutmeg tree.

Two kinds of oil are obtained from nutmeg; a thick one which is called nutmeg butter and which is extracted from nutmeg by boiling it in water, and a volatile oil which is sometimes prescribed in certain medicaments.

It is preferable to use mace when cooking sweet dishes. This is a sort of husk which envelops nutmeg, and whose flavour is more delicate.

OIL   *HUILE*

Oil is mostly made from olives, but it can also be made from a host of other seeds, such as colza, nuts, beechnuts and rape.

Beechnuts, nuts and rape all produce oil which is very acceptable when fresh, but becomes rancid as it ages. After the olive, it is the beechnut, fruit of the beech tree, which produces the best oil.

Amongst olive oils, there is a choice to be made. My opinion is that Lucca oil is the freshest, the lightest and the one which keeps best. Next come virgin oil, green oil, and the best quality oil from Aix, Grasse and Nice.

Although Italy and Spain are covered with olive trees, it is these two countries which produce the worst oil. The proprietors let their olives become rancid, in order to obtain two harvests. The advanced age of the olives causes the oil extracted from them to have an intolerably rotten smell. This applies likewise to the oil which is produced in Greece, Syria and Egypt.

OLIVES   *OLIVES*

Olives picked straight from the tree are acrid and have a disagreeable taste, even when they are completely ripe. It is therefore necessary to keep them in oil and brine to make them lose this natural bitterness and become pleasant to eat. They should retain only a slight bitter taste tempered by the admixture of oil and the effect of the brine.

The Greeks, who attributed a divine origin to olives, venerated them so much that for a long time the only people who were employed in the cultivation of this small tree were virgin women and pure men. An oath of chastity was required by those who were charged with harvesting the crop.

Olives which have been added to stews, and which for that very reason have been subjected to a more or less prolonged cooking, are always better and more digestible than raw ones.

OMELETTE   *OMELETTE*

Omelette aux fines herbes

Break some eggs into a salad bowl, and beat them with a wicker beater. Add parsley, tarragon and chives to the eggs, and beat until the whites and yolks are completely blended. Pour half a glass of cream into the mixture, and beat it once more. Then, when your butter starts to bubble in the frying pan, pour the mixture in. The eggs will spread foaming to the whole circumference of the frying pan. When this happens, use a fork to keep bringing the edges back into the middle, while taking care that the omelette remains liquid, and that the cooked mixture does not become thick.

Have a platter ready which has been buttered with the freshest possible butter and sprinkled with some more fresh fines herbes. Turn out the omelette on to this platter and serve it while it is still dribbling.

Excuse the use of this last word, but each art has its own language which must be employed to make oneself understood by the initiated.

Omelette arabe · Arab omelette

I have said that my first preoccupation in writing this book was to demonstrate the cuisine of peoples who have none. Here, for example, is a recipe which the Bey's cook was kind enough to give me.

Ostrich and flamingo eggs, full and fresh, are now to be found almost everywhere, thanks to the zoological societies which have been founded even in towns of secondary importance. [The Société d'Acclimatation was founded in 1854. In 1874 the magazine which it sponsored expressed, among other aims, the intention of domesticating exotic animals and of selling to members of the society unusual products such as, one would suppose, ostrich and flamingo eggs.] Thus an ostrich egg is today sold for one franc, and is equal in content to about ten hen's eggs.

This is how to make an Arab omelette.

Chop a fresh onion, put it in a frying pan with half a glass of olive oil, let it soften without colouring, and add the flesh of two large sweet peppers, after having grilled them for a few moments in order to remove the skin. Add two good peeled and seeded tomatoes, cut in small pieces. Season this first preparation with a little salt and a touch of cayenne. Reduce some of the liquid given off by the tomatoes, then take the frying pan off the fire and add to its contents four anchovy fillets.

Now, as a separate operation, rub the bottom of a terrine with a clove of garlic. Pierce an ostrich or flamingo egg at both ends, so that you can blow out the white and the yolk, causing them to fall into the terrine. Season, and beat with a fork.

Finally, pour a quarter of a glass of olive oil into an omelette pan. When it is thoroughly hot, pour in the eggs, let the omelette set, and add to it the mixture which you prepared earlier. Turn it over, keeping it flat; sprinkle a little more oil over it; and two seconds later slide it on to a round platter.

195

Omelette

Omelette aux fraises · Strawberry omelette

Choose big *ananas* strawberries, which are very fresh and sweet smelling. Remove a score of the most beautiful, and cut them into quarters. Put them in a bowl with sugar, a little orange zest, and two soupspoons of rum.

Press the remaining strawberries through a fine sieve. Make enough purée to fill a glass, sweeten it sufficiently, add a little orange-flavoured sugar, and chill it on ice.

Break ten eggs into a pan. Mix into them two soupspoons of castor sugar, and two spoonfuls of good cream. Beat all this together for a few seconds with a whisk.

In a frying pan melt 150 grams of best quality butter. When it is hot, add the eggs, and let the omelette thicken with the help of a spoon. Bring it back to the front of the stove and put the strawberries which have been cut up in the middle of the omelette. Fold the omelette back at the two edges to give it a pretty shape. Sprinkle it lightly with vanilla sugar, and then place it like an island in the middle of the strawberry purée.

ONION   *OIGNON*

If it is necessary to have the subject right under one's eyes in order to write properly about it, it was providential that I was taken to Roscoff, just as the word onion was about to flow from my pen.

In fact, the Cape of Armorica reminds one, even more than ancient Egypt, of how, in the war of the gods against Jupiter, the vanquished were chased to the end of the continent and, seeing that there was no more land on which to continue their flight, changed themselves into onions to escape Jupiter's wrath. In no other part of France is this bulb, so vaunted in antiquity that poets sang about it and Egyptians worshipped it, to be found in such profusion.

In some years Roscoff sends up to thirty or forty ships laden with onions to England. It was a native of this region who first had the idea of speculating in this trade. But in order to familiarize the English immediately with the French onion and to exhibit its superiority over the British bulb, it was necessary to strike an audacious blow which would have reverberations.

This Roscovite came one day to find M. Corbière, the author of several nautical novels and a long-term officer, living in Roscoff, and asked him how to say in English: 'L'oignon anglais n'est pas bon.'

The person to whom the question was put replied: 'The English onion is not good.'

'Be so good as to write that on a piece of paper, Monsieur,' asked the Roscovite.

M. Corbière took a pen and wrote down the required phrase. The Roscovite thanked him. Three days later he was seen leaving for London with a sloop laden with onions.

Once he had arrived in the capital of England, he went straight to the busiest market, spread out a placard on which was written in big letters the following maxim; THE ENGLISH ONION IS NOT GOOD. And underneath his placard, he put a little barrow full of French onions.

One knows the English; they are not the sort of people to put up with this sort of insult. One of them came up to the foreign merchant and spoke to him; he, knowing not a word of English contented himself with the reply: THE ENGLISH ONION IS NOT GOOD.

This reply exasperated the Englishman, who approached the Roscovite, putting up his two fists. The Roscovite did not know what the Englishman was trying to say, but saw clearly that he was being threatened. He took the Englishman by the elbow and, setting his body in motion like a top, swung him around himself three times. At the end of the third turn, the Englishman fell; he got up, furious, and turned back on his adversary, who stood ready to defend himself.

The Roscovite was nearly six feet tall, and as strong as his god Teutates. He grasped the Englishman with his arms, lifted him up and threw him down flat on his stomach. This was contrary to all the rules of wrestling; the shoulders must touch the ground before one of the combatants is declared defeated. So the Roscovite realized that he was in the wrong.

'It's true, it's true,' said he, acknowledging with a motion of his head that he had made a mistake; and he raised his fists again, much as the Englishman had done. The Englishman came back at him. This time, the onion seller took him by his shirt collar and by the skin of his stomach and laid him gently on the ground, in such a way that not just one shoulder, but both shoulders, touched the ground squarely. He repeated this movement several times, but increasing the violence each time, until the Englishman shouted: 'Enough! Enough!.'

Then the cries, the hurrahs and the bravos broke out. The English are the fairest in appreciating merit when it comes to a show of strength; they wanted to carry the onion seller shoulder high.

'No, don't, no don't!' shouted he, putting himself on the defensive, 'while you carry me in triumph you will steal my onions.'

Onion

There was some truth in what the poor devil said. However, they bought all his onions that very day, and the evening was entirely spent carrying him around in triumph. From that moment, French onions obtained their right of freedom of the city in England.

Soupe à l'oignon à la Stanislas

During one of his trips between Luneville and Versailles, where the ex-king of Poland, Stanislas, went each year to visit his daughter, the queen, he stopped at an inn in Châlons, where he was served a soup so delicate and carefully prepared, that he was unwilling to continue his journey without having learned how to prepare a similar one.

Wrapped in his dressing gown, His Majesty descended to the kitchen and absolutely insisted on seeing the chef perform before his eyes. Neither the smoke nor the smell of onion, which brought great tears to his eyes, was able to distract him from paying the closest attention. He observed everything, took a note of everything, and only got back into his carriage when he was sure that he now possessed the art of making an excellent onion soup.

Here is the recipe for onion soup à la Stanislas.

Take off the top crust of a loaf of bread and break it into pieces, which are to be heated on both sides. When the crusts are hot, rub them with fresh butter and put them once more near the fire until they are lightly toasted. Then put them on a plate while the onions are fried in fresh butter. Usually one uses 30 grams of butter for three large onions, diced very small, which are left on the fire until they have taken on a beautiful, slightly dark, golden colour; a colour which is obtained only by almost constant stirring. Then add the crusts and continue to stir until the onions become brown. When they are sufficiently brown, moisten them with boiling water to unstick them from the casserole, season as necessary, then leave them to simmer for at least a quarter of an hour before serving.

It is a mistake to think that this soup is improved by using bouillon; on the contrary, this addition makes it too rich and lessens its delicacy.

ORACHE or MOUNTAIN SPINACH   *ARROCHE*

A vegetable also known by the name of *belle-dame* (beautiful lady) *bonne-dame* (good lady) and *follette* (wanton).

Orache leaves, mixed with other herbs which have a strong taste, such as mint, cress, sweet marjoram, etcetera were formerly much used in salads in France; and these salads are still in great demand by other peoples in Europe. With sorrel and spinach, they make up the mixture known as *herbe cuite* (cooked herbs) and go into the making of *bouillon aux herbes*.

Orache provides hardly any nourishment. It is refreshing and slightly laxative, but it does not suit weak stomachs, unless it is seasoned with salt, pepper and vinegar, that is to say served in a salad of the kind described above.

ORANGE   *ORANGE*

The fruit of the orange tree is globular in shape, like a globe which has been slightly squashed, and its colour is a beautiful golden yellow. Its peel varies in thickness; the inner white layer is not fleshy like that of the lemon, but practically devoid of flavour and somewhat cottony in texture.

The gourmands of ancient Rome hated the smell and taste of oranges.

The best orange, without any doubt, is the one called *Mandarine*, which comes to us from China. It is smaller than our billiard balls. Indeed there are some mandarins the size of a walnut, which are yellow, verging on red, in colour, have a thin peel, and a smell approaching that of the lemon. The flesh of the fruit is very sweet, and contains little juice.

ORTOLAN*   *ORTOLAN*

One day the following dialogue took place between Antoni Deschamps, a great poet and Pythagorean philosopher, and Elzéar Blaze, who was a hunter like Nimrod and as witty as Méry.

'Do you think,' asked Antoni Deschamps of Blaze, 'that man should be allowed to kill a partridge, a fig-pecker, an ortolan, one of these charming birds which after all does no harm to anyone and whose looks and whose song bring joy to our eyes and ears?'

'Certainly,' replied Blaze, 'when a man is furnished with arms, and if the hunting season is open and he is hunting on his own land, or on land where he has permission to hunt.'

'You don't understand. I am asking you if you think that man,

* Ortolans are garden buntings. The name ortolan comes from the Latin *hortus*, meaning garden.

Ortolan

bearing in mind the above conditions, has the right to kill a partridge, a fig-pecker, an ortolan—inoffensive creatures, made like himself by the hand of God?'

'Yes, without a doubt, but only on the condition that he eats it.'

'So one can then eat partridges, fig-peckers and ortolans?'

'With pleasure, if they are cooked to perfection.'

'But the abbé de Saint-Pierre . . . but Pythagoras . . .'

'Said the opposite, I know. Too bad for them, we should pity them. Listen to me, I put this dilemma; either we must eat the animals, or the animals must eat us.'

'Are you frightened that the partridge will eat you?'

'Listen. Partridges produce each year, on average, twenty or twenty-five little partridges. Let ten years go by without killing any and they would be as numerous as wasps and gnats: then there would be no more wheat, no more oats, no more grapes. So let us eat partridges, since we must have horses; let us eat partridges, since we like the wine of Burgundy; and, if only because we must have bread, let us eat partridges. The right to eat partridges comes from God himself, who at the time of the creation said to Adam, our ancestor, and after the flood said to Noah, our grandfather: "You will be master of all the animals." *Manui vestrae traditi sunt.* That is to say, I put them in your hands. Why? So that our hands can take them to our mouth, of course. So, eat everything which seems good to you. Man was not made to graze upon the grass: his teeth prove that. Pythagoras and the abbé de Saint-Pierre were very decent men, but they didn't understand a thing about cooking. Let them do the talking and you do the eating. Moreover it is indisputable that if one were to listen to everyone, one would finish up by eating nothing at all.'

I don't know if Antoni was completely convinced by Blaze's logic; but what I do know is that he continued eating, and that at one meal he played his part very well, even though the business at hand was a dish of ortolans. It is true that the dish was *ortolans à la toulousaine*, and that in Toulouse they have a special way of fattening ortolans which is better than anywhere else; when they want to eat them, they asphyxiate them by immersing their heads in very strong vinegar, a violent death which has a beneficial effect on the flesh.

Ortolans à la toulousaine

Pluck your ortolans, get rid of the crop, singe them lightly, rub them with half a lemon, thread them on a little iron skewer and spread them with butter into which you have worked some lemon juice. Dredge the birds all over with breadcrumbs, and roast them for seven or eight minutes over a hot fire. Baste them with the butter which runs into the dripping pan. At the last minute, salt them, take them off the skewers, arrange them on a hot platter, pour the pan drippings over them and send them immediately to the table with some cut lemons.

OSTRICH   *AUTRUCHE*

This is the biggest of birds, and one of the best known. It is also one of those which have been known for the longest time in the context of food, since it is discussed in the Old Testament, in particular in Deuteronomy, where Moses forbids the Hebrews to eat its flesh. This same flesh became very popular with the Romans. Heliogabalus is reported to have had the heads of 600 ostriches served to him at one meal, so that he could eat the brains.

Ostrich meat is not very good; it is tough and tasteless. Nevertheless, the wing, which is the most tender part, and well seasoned fillets can be eaten.

Ostrich eggs are very big. Some have been seen which weigh as much as thirty hens' eggs. Some travellers who have eaten these eggs have found them very good. There is a considerable trade in them at the Cape of Good Hope. People even make gigantic omelettes with them. They are also prepared with fat. Finally, they are used to clarify coffee.

The Arabs of today, like the Hebrews of yore, abstain from eating the meat of the ostrich, but they take pains to seek out its fat and use it in the preparation of their dishes, also to rub into their bodies if they have rheumatism and other illnesses. The fat fetches a very high price, perhaps because it is so rare.

OYSTERS   *HUITRES*

The oyster is one of the most deprived molluscs in the kingdom of nature.

Being acephalic, that is to say having no head, it has neither an organ of sight, nor an organ of hearing, nor an organ of smell. Its blood is colourless. Its body adheres to the two valves of its shell by a powerful muscle, with the aid of which it opens and closes the shell.

It also lacks an organ of locomotion. Its only exercise is sleep and its only pleasure is to eat. Since the oyster cannot go and look for its

Oysters

food, its food comes to find it or is carried to it by the movement of the waters. This food consists of animal matter suspended in the water.

It has been said that 'the Gods are going away'; an eloquent exclamation and one which has been admired. But recently a cry has made itself heard that: 'The oysters are going away!' There is, to be sure, no connection between the hermaphrodite mollusc which lives in its shell at the bottom of the sea, attached for ever to its rock, and the inhabitants of the worshipful Mount Olympus. However, the famous cry of Bossuet, his famous and eloquent cry—'Madam is dying! Madam is dead!'—did not produce an impression as terrible as this gastronomic call of distress: 'The oysters are going away!' And the first effect of this cry was to make the price of oysters go up from 60 centimes a dozen to 1 franc 30 centimes.

Feelings ran deep. The oyster, this treasure of the gourmands, was on the point of escaping from them; the oyster which, according to Dr Reveillé-Paris, is the only alimentary substance which does not cause indigestion.

We first hear of oysters among the ancient Greeks, and the very first time, I think, was in connection with the proscription of Aristides. 'I am tired of hearing him called Aristides the Just,' said an honest Athenian; and Aristides was proscribed by a majority of oysters, each oyster-shell [which was put in the ballot-box] carrying its sentence and representing the casting of a vote.

The Greeks had oysters brought from the Hellespont. They used to be gathered around Sestos, the place where Leander leaped into the sea to make his nocturnal visit to Hero. This place is known now as Boralli-Calessi. I ate some oysters from Sestos while crossing the Bosphorus, and found them nothing special.

The Romans, whose gourmandise was quite different from that of the Greeks, rendered almost divine honours to the oyster. There was no good dinner without raw oysters chilled with ice, or without cooked oysters seasoned with *garum*, a kind of brine [in fact a kind of salty fish sauce] of which Pliny has preserved the recipe for us.

The Romans graded oysters by number, according to their excellence. The first in quality were those from the Lucrine lake; then came those of Tarentum, followed by those of Circei. Later, the Romans came to prefer the oysters from the coasts of Great Britain.

Apicius, the famous gourmand who cut his throat because he only had between six and eight million sesterces left, that is to say between fifteen hundred thousand and two million francs, had discovered a way of preserving oysters. In our time, he would have patented this and lived off the patent.

In France the oysters are fished with a dredge, and the fishermen used to make a practice of dividing the oyster banks into several zones, which were opened successively to fishing, so that the banks would not be exhausted. While one of these zones was being exploited, the other, that is to say the reserved area, would be producing more oysters which could reach marketable size.

During the months of May, June, July and August, the fishery was forbidden. Gourmands say that oysters should not be eaten in the months without an 'R'. By way of compensation, these are the months when mussels are in a state of perfection.

Oysters straight from the sea are never eaten. At least, no disciple of Lucullus or apostle of Brillat-Savarin would commit such a heresy. Oysters must be kept in special 'parks', at a depth of one metre and on sand or shingle, before being eaten.

It was a Roman called Sergius Orata, who lived 250 years before Jesus Christ, who first had the idea of putting oysters in the Lucrine lake, to fatten them. He conducted a trade in oysters, brought to a state of perfection by his careful treatment, and became a rich man.

The oyster which we eat is the *Ostrea edulis*. The Ostend oyster, the green oyster, the oyster of Marennes, all these are only varieties of the same species. [This was true, but other species, especially the Portuguese oyster, are now cultured in France and may also become, for example, *vertes de Marennes*.]

We had oyster parks at Marennes, Tréport, Étretat, Fécamp, Dunquerque, Le Havre and Dieppe. We shall come in a moment to that of Régneville. [This moment, quite a long one, is taken up by recalling the origins of pisciculture in China, its development by the Romans, and subsequent advances in the art; all portrayed as providing inspiration for M. de Chaillé and Madame Sarah-Félix, who set up an oyster park at Régneville, and whose initial problems in the enterprise are described. These lead to an account of reproduction in the oyster.]

The eggs of the oyster are almost invisible. Leuwenhoeck has worked out that about a million of them would be needed to constitute the volume of a child's marble. The tiny oysters, when they come out of their mother's shell, are capable of movement. Nature provides this faculty for the larvae of all stationary animals, and thus allows them to affix themselves where they wish. Only they must choose their abode with care; for, once fixed in it, they are stuck with it for the rest of their lives.

In the park at Régneville, they began by using ordinary tiles and bundles of sticks; thus offering the oysters a choice between a position on the sea bed and one of suspension between high and low tide. But our oyster-rearers quickly saw that they had made a twofold mistake. The bundles of twigs became coated with a mucus which made it impossible for the little oysters to attach themselves. As for the tiles, they on the contrary allowed the oysters to affix themselves too securely. The oysters found it convenient to use the tiles as one of their shells; and, when one plucked an oyster from its beloved tile, its shell was either broken or left behind on the tile. The oysters' motto was becoming that of the ivy: 'Where I attach myself, there I die.'

Our oyster-rearers then stuck old newspapers on to the tiles, so that they adhered to the tiles only by their ends. The oyster, admittedly, was now stuck to the newspaper; but the newspaper was not effectively stuck to anything. Besides, not all newspapers, in our opinion, are suitable for being used in this way. I know some which would bestow on the innocent molluscs the toxic properties which oysters at Venice contract when they attach themselves to the copper parts of boats.

What is the length of an oyster's life? This is still a mystery. To begin with, few oysters die of old age. And those who do, perish unknown.

Oysters are usually eaten in the simplest way in the world. One opens them, extracts them, sprinkles a few drops of lemon juice on them and swallows them. [Dumas does not mention the advice offered by many experts, which is to bite an oyster before swallowing it, thus releasing the flavour which is in its liver.] The most refined gourmands prepare a kind of sauce with vinegar, pepper and shallot and dip the oysters in this before swallowing them. Others—and these are the true oyster-lovers—add nothing at all to the oysters, but eat them raw without vinegar, lemon or pepper.

PANCAKES (recipe of M. de Courchamps)
PANNEQUETS

Put in a pan two tablespoonfuls of flour, three egg-yolks and two whole eggs, a little salt and a few drops of orange flower water. Mix it all well and finish thinning it with some milk, so that the mixture is light in colour.

Take a small round and shallow frying pan, heat it and wipe it. Put

a bit of butter in several thicknesses of paper, so that it is in a sort of little sachet, and rub the frying pan all over with this. Put two table-spoonfuls of your batter in the frying pan, tipping the pan in all directions in order to spread out the pancake well; the pancake should be thin and even throughout. When it is cooked, turn it over on to the serving platter, spread it out and sprinkle it with sugar. Continue thus until you have completely used up your pancake mixture.

These pancakes are sometimes smeared with jam; but this masks their taste and is an affectation of which we could not approve.

Thus speaks M. de Courchamps. But if you do not add any sort of jam as a filling what you have are not *pannequets* but simply thin *crêpes*. Red currants or apricots are necessary for the confection of true *pannequets*.

PANTHER   *PANTHÈRE*

We mention the panther because there are people in India who eat its flesh.

A panther may be subdued rather than tamed; it never entirely loses its ferocious character. Those who use it for hunting need to use the most elaborate means to train, lead and exercise it. The panther's special habitat is that part of Africa which extends along the Mediterranean, and Asia. It is in India that it is trained for hunting purposes. It is taken, blindfolded, in a little cart, until the game is in sight. There it is freed and the blindfold removed. It springs forwards and seizes its prey; then after it has had its fill of blood, it allows itself to be recaptured and tied up again.

Indians and negroes who eat the flesh of the panther find it good. Gallienus says that it is nevertheless inferior to the flesh of bear, and claims that its liver has a detestable flavour and even develops into a poison.

PARMESAN CHEESE   *PARMESAN*

Despite the designation under which it is generally known, this cheese is not made in Parma, but at Lodi and the surrounding vicinity. Thus its correct name is *formaggio lodigiano*, or *formaggio di Grana*. Much cattle is raised in the vicinity of Lodi, where more than thirty thousand cows are fed for the preparation of the cheese.

As for the culinary uses to which parmesan is put, see Macaroni, and Fondue.

PARSLEY   *PERSIL*

Parsley is the obligatory condiment for all sauces.

'Parsley', says the learned author of the *Traité des plantes usuelles*, 'makes dishes more healthful and more agreeable; it stimulates the appetite and aids the digestion.' Bosc's opinion of this plant is even more positive. 'Take away parsley from the cook,' says he, 'and you render it virtually impossible for him to practise his art.'

Parsley, we repeat, is essential for all stews and all sauces; but there are two dressings in which it is the principal ingredient, that of *Watter-Fisch* and Parsley Sauce *à la Hollandaise*.

PARSNIP   *PANAIS*

This plant belongs to the same family as the carrot. Its root is white, its stem long, straight, thick, firm, ridged, hollow and branching. The flowers are of a generous size; the flavour is mild and sweet.

There are two kinds of parsnip, the long sort and the round sort. This root vegetable goes into broths; and it is also fried in butter. Its taste is not generally pleasing. Ray says that the English think that when the parsnip is too old it produces delirium and even madness; and so they call it the mad parsnip. This same plant was also said to be an aphrodisiac. It is not to be confused with hemlock, whose leaves have red spots at the base of the stems.

In Thuringia, a syrup which replaces sugar is extracted from the parsnip. It is a plant which has a composition similar to that of the beetroot and the carrot; sugar is a constituent part. Drappies says that he has extracted 12 per cent of sugar from it.

In Germany they grow and often eat a sort of farinaceous and sweet parsnip of small size. It is used to make a stew with fresh loin of pork and fillets of hind.

PARTRIDGE, YOUNG PARTRIDGES
PERDRIX, PERDREAUX

Besides several other varieties of partridge, there are four which are greatly esteemed and which are served at table because of their delicacy and excellent taste. These are the common grey partridge, the red-legged partridge, the red partridge and those from the crags.

This bird was unknown in France prior to the year 1440. It was

René, King of Naples, who brought some from the island of Chios to Provence.

Partridge shooting is usually carried out with the help of setters or pointers. These dogs follow the scent, and sink into the pointing position when they have come near to the partridge. The hunter makes the dog move, thus causing the partridges to rise and fly away, and then discharges his weapon at them. Outstanding hunters affirm that the most suitable hours for partridge shooting are from ten o'clock until noon, and from two o'clock until four, since at other times the partridges are always moving about, looking for food, and do not stay still in one place.

Partridges are caught in the snares known as *collets*; and they are also caught in nets such as poachers use, which are called *traînasses* (drag-nets) and *pantières* (draw-nets). These devices are mostly used at night. The partridges, driven by the beaters and frightened by the light, go and get themselves entangled. The drag-net kills a prodigious number of these birds each year.

Male partridges are also attracted with the help of tame females. These have been reared in cages, which are then taken to districts where there are many cocks. Such partridges are called decoy birds. The cock partridge is likewise lured by imitating the call of the female.

Young partridges are distinguished from mature ones by the last of the big wing feathers. The tip is sharp at the end for young partridges, but is rounded in adult partridges.

Epicures of the last century took the supreme decision that among young partridges the grey were better than the red; whereas among mature partridges the red were better than the grey. The mature grey partridge is always more esteemed in countries where the red partridge is more common; and it is precisely the contrary in countries where there are only grey ones. The two kinds are almost equally good, but the red ones are always plumper.

The flesh of the young partridge is mildly stimulating, full of flavour and easily digestible. That of old partridges requires lengthy cooking, but as it is impregnated with osmazome it is more flavourful than that of young partridge. An old partridge boiled with other meats gives an excellent flavour to the bouillon and makes it more tonic.

Perdreaux rôtis · Roast young partridge

Lightly singe your young partridge, fold the feet on to the legs, and cover them from in front with a vine leaf covered with a bard of bacon. Roast in a moderate heat, and serve with a Seville orange and no sauce.

Perdreaux à l'anglaise · Young partridge in the English style

Stuff the partridge with a stuffing made of their livers, butter, coarsely ground pepper and some salt. Cover them in paper, and put them on the spit, without barding them. Let them cook until they are three quarters done. Then lift the legs and wings, without separating them from the body, and place under each a little butter into which you have worked some breadcrumbs, chopped shallot, parsley and spring onions, salt, coarsely ground pepper and a little nutmeg. Put the partridges in a casserole with a good glassful of champagne and four tablespoonfuls of consommé. Boil them gently until they are cooked to perfection, without covering them, so that the sauce is reduced, and serve with the juice and zest of Seville oranges.

PASTRY   *PÂTISSERIE*

The character of pastry varies according to the taste and customs of the various peoples who consume it. Each people, each province, each locality has contributed successful methods to this art. They have made contributions to its enormous success by providing inventions of greater or lesser originality; but each one of these has its own distinctive character. France marches at the head of pastry making, in the present state of civilization, followed by Italy and

Switzerland. Even the position of the pastry cook in our society has changed. This artist, who earlier belonged to a low class, now enjoys considerable respect. In bygone days it was proverbially said of an impudent person that he had 'passed through the *pâtissier*'s front door'. This stemmed from the fact that pastry cooks kept an inferior kind of tavern. Because it was shameful to frequent them, prudish people only entered by the back door, and it was a brazen act to go in through the shop or the front door. Today it would be an insult to equate our pretty and elegant *pâtisseries* with inferior taverns. Men of the highest breeding and women from the best social classes do not blush in entering a pastry shop, in tasting quite openly the products of the pastry-cook's labours, in savouring the excellent wines and liqueurs which he has chosen to accompany them, and in leaving his premises without shame or pretence.

PEACH   *PÊCHE*

The peach tree comes originally from Persia. Its fruit is agreeable to regard, to touch, to smell and to taste. Its skin is fine and delicate, and adorned with a light velvety down which preserves it from attacks by insects. In some varieties the colour is a light greenish-yellow, of varying degrees of paleness; in others it is a rosy yellow, tinged with some orange. The side turned to the sun is always reddish-purple, darker and more purple in some than in others. The stone is oval and pitted and so solid that it is extremely difficult to crack. It usually contains one almond, and occasionally two.

The peach is famous in China and has been from the earliest times. Poets depicted it as having the power sometimes to give immortality and sometimes to cause death. As a sign of goodwill or friendship, either a real peach or one made of porcelain is exchanged; and Chinese artists use this motif in all their interior decoration.

In Persia, it was thought for several centuries that the peach was a deadly fruit; so people did not eat it, and even tried to avoid touching it. But people introduced peaches into Egypt, and the climate there sweetened them and made them better. Since then the Persians have eaten a lot of peaches.

The best peaches are to be found in the environs of Paris. Montreuil, especially, is justly famous for the beauty, enormous quantity and excellence of its peaches; after it come Dauphiné, Angoumois and Touraine, etcetera. To have firm, fine and sweet flesh is the most important quality for a peach. This can be seen as soon as one re-

Peach

moves the skin, which should come off easily. The second quality which a peach should have is that its parenchyma should dissolve as soon as it is put in the mouth. The third and last quality is that the taste of the fruit should be piquant, winey, and sometimes a little musky. In addition, the stone should be very small. Peaches which are not smooth, such as the cling-stone and the nectarine, should have only a moderate down, because a thick velvety coating is always a sign of an inferior peach. In contrast, the down falls off those of superior quality, and especially those which have ripened in the open air.

Pêche de Montreuil · Montreuil peaches

The Montreuil peach owes its origin to a character called Girardot, who was an ancient musketeer, a chevalier de Saint Louis and also, finally, a gardener.

This man Girardot, after having been seriously wounded several times, was constrained to leave the corps of musketeers, and retired to his small property in Malassis, which is situated between the villages of Montreuil and Bagnolet. He devoted himself to the culture of fruit trees, helped by the advice of La Quintinie, the director of the king's gardens at Versailles, where he frequently went to visit the espaliers.

Girardot having a favour to ask of Louis XIV, and not knowing how to go about it, his friend La Quintinie announced to him one day that the king was to have gone to Chantilly to hunt with the Prince de Condé, but that the prince was ill. He said that he would now try to arrange that the hunt should go in the direction of Montreuil, and invited Girardot to prepare himself for this august visit.

The next day a basket containing twelve magnificent peaches was deposited in the pantry by an unknown hand, with this inscription: 'For the king's dessert'. These peaches were admired by everyone. A few days later, Girardot saw the king arriving, preceded by La Quintinie, just as had been promised. The king was coming to inspect the espaliers which had produced such magnificent peaches, and at the same time to thank the gardener who had tended them. The ancient musketeer, once more clad in his uniform, then made his request to the king, which was very well received. The king also granted him a pension and the honour of supplying each year, for 'the dessert of the king', a basket filled with his most beautiful peaches, as a souvenir of those which he had supplied to Chantilly.

This custom was continued by his descendants and by the people of Montreuil, whom he had favoured, until 1789.

Except in a few countries, the custom of serving peacocks as an ordinary roast dish has been lost.

I have only eaten peacock once in my life, but as it was a very young peacock it was similar to what is called corn-fed chicken and seemed excellent to me. I was going to the celebrations taking place at Saint Tropez on the occasion of the unveiling of the statue of the Bailiff of Suffren. We had been obliged to abandon the train and to take a private coach. Three or four leagues from Saint Tropez, the coach paused in a charming village, the name of which I have forgotten. It was situated on the top of a hill covered with chestnut trees. During this stop I stuck my head out of the window, attracted by a game of bowls which some young men were playing with the same enthusiasm which I have observed in Paris, before this noble game, which is no less ancient than *le jeu de l'oie* [a game similar to snakes and ladders], was banned from the Champs Elysées. The young men looked up at the coach to see what stranger was taking such an interest in their game, and recognized me. Hardly had my name been pronounced before the coach was surrounded, so that we had to get out and were pulled along towards a café, where we were obliged to have a grog with the local people.

At the end of ten minutes we had become such good friends with our new acquaintances that they did not want us to leave and insisted on keeping us for dinner. We were only able to obtain a reprieve on condition that we returned for dinner on the following Wednesday, that is to say three days later. It was then Sunday.

By dint of giving our word of honour and after an exchange of bevies of handshakes, consent was secured for our departure, while they told us that they would wait on the following Wednesday until 8 o'clock for dinner or, failing that, until 10 o'clock for supper.

We took part in the festivities at Saint Tropez and at 2 o'clock, despite the pleadings of our new acquaintances there, we boarded the coach to keep our promises to our former ones.

Once we were on our way, we ourselves began to fear that our invitation might have been forgotten by our prospective hosts. We decided that, if this proved to be the case, we would shame them by stopping and dining at the inn, throwing doors and windows wide open. But this fear did not last long. A hundred paces before the village, we saw a sentinel making telegraphic signals, the significance of which became even more clear when they were concluded by the firing of a gun.

Peacock

As soon as the gun had been fired, the church bell rang and we saw the whole village coming out in front of us. It was quite impossible to remain in the coach. The mayor took my daughter by the arm. The notary, the very same player of bowls who had originally recognized me and who, unfaithful to one of the greatest passions which exist, had quit his game in order to drink grog with us, gave me his arm. Surrounded by all the women, and with all the children gathered together round about us, we made our triumphal entry into the village.

Our astonishment, when we arrived, was great. Our table was set in the public square, as in the heyday of Sparta. But the first thing which made us rejoice was to see that instead of the thin broth of Lacedaemonia the table was laden with dishes which had a most appetizing appearance and probably a most excellent taste also. In the middle of these, a roast peacock, with all its feathers, was spreading its tail in a fan and raising its sapphire neck.

The table was set for thirty or forty. They had not been sure of the time of our arrival and that was the reason why the guests were not more numerous. Also, I must admit, they may not have been sure that I would return. But when they saw that all was set fair and were sure that I had in fact arrived, everyone came out with their tables all laid and put them in front of their doors, or beside others. A quarter of an hour later, 300 guests were animatedly gesticulating, the better to celebrate my arrival, which had been heralded by warm cheering.

At the time of this event I wanted to tell the world about it; but there was not a single newspaper which found the tale worthy of its columns and deigned to afford me space. Newspapers sometimes display this kind of goodwill!

It is understandable that the memory of the taste of the flesh of the peacock should have been lost in the middle of the noisy reception given to me. My only recollection is that in the excellent dinner each course reached the height of distinction and flavour.

Paon rôti à la crème aigre · Roast peacock with sour cream

Gut and truss a young peacock and put it on a spit, sprinkling it with butter which has been seasoned with salt and pepper. Then, when it starts to cook, take two glasses of sour cream and sprinkle them over it. Next, untruss the bird and arrange it on a platter, paying the same attention to its toilette as to that of a pheasant; that is to say, restoring to it its tail, head and wings.

PEANUT   *ARACHIDE*

This is also called *pistache de terre* (the pistachio of the earth), because it exhibits a very remarkable characteristic; as the pods succeed the flowers they bend over towards the ground, and embed themselves in the soil to complete their development.

This plant came originally from Mexico. Spaniards brought it to Spain, where it produces a very large crop nowadays. In 1802 it was introduced into the *département* of Les Landes, and grew there perfectly well; but the lack of outlets for the crop soon made a complete failure of its cultivation, which has now been quite abandoned.

The peanut produces a fruit which is no larger than a hazel-nut and looks like a pistachio. The nut is both nutritious and oily and is eaten either raw or cooked. It produces half of its weight in excellent edible oil, which is wholesome and cheap and has siccative properties which make it a useful material for artists. The stalks are well liked by cattle, and its roots taste of liquorice.

The Americans call this fruit *Mani* [a Spanish word, used in Latin America]. They make pralines of it, and pies, and they find its flavour more agreeable and delicate than that of the pistachio.

The consumption of raw peanuts will sometimes, apparently, provoke violent headaches and sore throats. Cooking and torrefaction remove these injurious properties.

The Spaniards call the peanut *Cacohuette*, because it tastes of cocoa, and use it, mixed with a little cocoa, to make a chocolate for the poor which is not at all bad for the health.

PEAR   *POIRE*

The pear which comes from cultivated stock is one of our best fruits; there are more than three hundred varieties to be found in our gardens. If we compare the small size, hardness and bitter taste of the wild pear with the huge size, sweetness and softness of many of our beautiful fruits, we realize what a marvellous influence cultivation has had. The wild pear is inedible; it is used only to make a thin wine of rather poor quality. So it is with justice that it has been called the *poire d'angoisse* (pear of anguish).*

Pears, like apples, enclose five compartments filled with soft little seeds; but those of the pear are browner, and most of them black.

* *Avaler des poires d'angoisse* means to go through hardships or to eat humble pie. A *poire d'angoisse*, in medieval times, was a pear-shaped gag.

Pears, which are about the same size as apples and equally varied, come in more than three hundred types, as we have already said; so we will limit ourselves to indicating those which we think are the best. They are divided into three classes: pears which 'melt in the mouth' (*poires fondantes*); pears which are crisp but sweet; and pears with firm or crisp flesh and impregnated with an astringent quality which even cooking fails to make disappear completely.

Nearly all the summer pears, such as the *Bon-Chrétien*, the *Petit-Muscat*, the *Madeleine*, the *Rousselet* from Reims etc. belong to the first class. One can equally include in this category a few which flourish in autumn, such as the *Beurrés* and the *Doyennés*; and of winter pears the *Saint-Germain*, the *Virgouleuse*, the *Crassane* and a few others.

Those in the second class are less digestible than those in the first, but they too can be eaten raw. Examples are the golden *Messire-Jean*, the *Rousselet*, the Spanish *Bon-Chrétien* etc.

Those in the third class, when raw, are suitable only for the hardiest of digestions. It is best, therefore, always to cook them with sugar.

PEAS   *POIS*

We are talking here only about the little peas which are picked before they are fully grown, when they are still tender and full of sweet juices.

Without question, young peas are one of our best vegetables. When they are very fresh, and cooked as soon as they are shelled, they are always well received.

Dried peas are also of value, but they are more difficult to digest than fresh ones. They are prepared in the same ways, with butter, with bacon, with sugar; but they are hardly ever used except in puréed form.

Petits pois à l'ancienne mode (a recipe from the Abbey of
Fontevrault) · Peas cooked in the old style

Pod two litres of young green peas just before you are going to cook
them, and wrap them in a damp cloth. Next, take the heart of a
cabbage lettuce and separate the leaves of this in such a way that you
can insert a branch or stalk of freshly picked green savory. Tie up the
lettuce and put it in a pot with the peas, a pinch of salt, half a glass of
water and half a pound of fresh butter. After cooking for a quarter of
an hour, take out the lettuce; and just before serving the peas bind
them with three spoonfuls of double cream which you have blended
with the yolk of a newly laid egg, a pinch of white pepper and a small
spoonful of powdered sugar.

PEPPER   *POIVRE*

As we have already said in our preface, pepper has always been, of all
known spices, the most widespread and the one most used in cooking.

For a long time pepper was an item of very great luxury, and a
pound of pepper was a very considerable present to give anyone. It
has been reported that, when Clotharius III founded the monastery of
Corbie, thirty pounds of pepper figured among the various com-
modities which he required his customs authorities to pay to the
monks annually.

When Roger, Count of Béziers, was assassinated in a riot by the
citizens of that town in 1107, one of the punishments which his son
imposed on these citizens, after he had subdued them by force of
arms, was the exaction of a tribute of three pounds of pepper annually
from each family. Finally, at Tyre, the Jews were obliged likewise to
pay over two pounds of pepper a year to the archbishop. According
to the *Annales de l'Eglise d'Aix*, it was Bertrand and Rostang de
Noves, who were Archbishops of Tyre in 1143 and 1283 respectively,
who imposed this obligation on the perfidious Jews.

Pepper, much used as a condiment, facilitates digestion.

Before the advent of cubeb it was frequently used in dispensaries.
In hot countries, tremendously strong fermented sauces are made of
it. As it is one of the most powerful stimulants, it is only used in
moderation in good cooking; and nervous, susceptible people should
even abstain from using it. This does not apply to country people,
the sensibility of whose stomachs has become dulled by their habitually eating coarse food, and which therefore needs to be strongly

excited. Pepper is just right to produce this effect; so it is much used in all provincial cooking. There are three kinds of pepper; black pepper, white pepper and long pepper.

PERCH   *PERCHE*

An excellent river fish, whose flesh is as light as it is nutritious. The perch of the Seine are especially esteemed.

The perch was given its name from the Latin word *perca*, because it is marked with black spots. [In fact, the perch is marked by vertical dark bars, which fade after death. The Latin name is derived from the corresponding Greek word, of which the meaning seems to be varied in colour, rather than spotted.] Gourmands in the sixteenth century called the perch 'fresh-water partridge'. It is a very voracious fish and, if put in a fish-pond, will kill and eat almost all the other fish.

The eggs of the perch are also very tasty.

PHEASANT   *FAISAN*

This type of bird belongs to the order of gallinaceous birds.

King Croesus, seated on his throne encrusted with diamonds and precious stones, wearing his diadem and clad in gold and purple, asked Solon if he had ever seen anything more beautiful.

'Yes,' replied the philosopher, 'I have seen pheasants and peacocks.'

The pheasant was discovered by the Argonauts, and brought back by them from the banks of the river Phasis, from which it draws its name. From Greece it went to Rome, and from Rome to the rest of Europe.

The meat of the pheasant is perhaps the most delicate and flavourful which it is possible to find. It is served roasted, braised, its fillets sautéed, or as escalopes or as a *salmis*. When it is prepared by braising, it can be served with a truffle sauce, or *à la Perigueux*, or on a ragoût of very ripe olives, or on a bed of sauerkraut. The author of the *Henriade* [Voltaire] has written a poem about the pheasant which is even better than his poem on the Béarnais King [Henri IV]. It consists of one line only:

'The bird from the Phasis is a dish of the gods.'

Brillat-Savarin wrote one of his best *méditations* on this splendid bird:

Pheasant

'The pheasant is an enigma, the answer to which is revealed only to the initiate; they alone can savour it in all its excellence.

'Every substance has its esculent apogee; some attain it before they reach their full development, such as capers, asparagus, grey partridges, spoon-fed pigeons, etc.; some when they reach their natural prime, such as melons, most kinds of fruit, mutton, beef, venison, and red partridges; and some when they begin to decompose, such as medlars, woodcock, and, above all, pheasant.

'This last bird, eaten within three days of its death, has an undistinguished taste. It is neither as delicate as a fowl, nor as fragrant as a quail.

'Cooked at the right time, its flesh is tender, sublime, and tasty, for it partakes of both poultry and venison.

'This desirable stage is reached just as the pheasant begins to decompose; only then does its fragrance develop, combining with an oil which, to be formed, requires a period of fermentation, like the oil of coffee, which is only obtained by roasting.

'This moment is made manifest to the senses of the profane by a faint odour, and by a change in the bird's belly; but the inspired few divine it by a sort of instinct which moves them on certain occasions, as, for example, when a skilled cook decides at a glance to take a fowl from the spit or to leave it for a few more turns.

'As soon as the pheasant has reached this stage, but no sooner, it is plucked and carefully larded with the freshest and crispest bacon.

'It is not for nothing that we say that the pheasant must not be plucked too soon; careful experiments have shown that those kept in feather are much more fragrant than those which have been kept plucked for a long time, either because contact with the air neutralizes part of the flavour, or because a part of the juice which nourishes the feathers is re-absorbed, and helps to enrich the flesh.

'After the bird has been plucked and larded, it is now ready to be stuffed; and this is done in the following way:

Have ready a brace of woodcock; bone and draw them, laying the liver and entrails on one side and the flesh on the other.

'Take the flesh, and mince it with steamed ox-marrow, a little grated bacon, pepper, salt, herbs, and a sufficient quantity of good truffles to produce enough stuffing to fill the interior of the pheasant.

'You will be careful to insert the stuffing in such a way that it cannot escape; quite a difficult business sometimes, when the bird is fairly high. There are various methods, however, one of which is to tie a crust of bread over the opening with a piece of thread, so that it serves as a stopper.

217

Pheasant

'Then cut a slice of bread two inches longer at each end than the pheasant laid lengthwise; take the woodcocks' livers and entrails, and pound with two large truffles, an anchovy, a little grated bacon, and a piece of good fresh butter.

'Spread this paste evenly over the bread, and place it beneath the pheasant prepared as above, so that it is thoroughly soaked with all the juice which exudes from the bird while it is roasting.

'When the pheasant is cooked, serve it up gracefully reclining on its bed of toast; surround it with bitter oranges, and have no fear of the result.

'This savoury dish is best washed down with good wine from Upper Burgundy; I derived this truth from a series of observations which cost me more trouble than a table of logarithms.

'A pheasant cooked in this way would be worthy to set before angels, if they still walked the earth as in the days of Lot.

'But what am I saying? The thing has been done. A stuffed pheasant was prepared before my very eyes by the good chef Picard, at the Château de la Grange, the home of my charming friend Madame de Ville-Plaine, and carried to the table by her steward Louis, stepping with processional dignity. It was as carefully scrutinized as one of Madame Herbault's hats; it was studiously savoured; and throughout this learned work the ladies' eyes shone like stars, their lips gleamed like coral, and their faces were pictures of ecstasy.

'I have done more: I have offered such a dish to a group of judges of the Supreme Court, who know that it is sometimes necessary to lay aside the senatorial toga, and to whom I proved without much trouble that good cheer is Nature's compensation for the cares of the bench.

'After careful consideration the president announced in a grave voice the word *Excellent*! All heads bowed in agreement, and the verdict was unanimous.

'I had observed, during the period of deliberation, that the noses of those venerable men were agitated by marked olfactory twitchings, that their august brows shone with calm serenity, and that about the corners of each judicial mouth there played something which might almost have been a smile.

'But these remarkable effects are in the nature of things. For a pheasant cooked in accordance with the foregoing recipe, already distinguished enough in itself, is impregnated from outside by the savoury juices of the roasting bacon, while from inside it absorbs the fragrant gases given off by the woodcock and truffles. Meanwhile, the toast, richly garnished already, is also soaked with the three varieties of gravy which exude from the roasting bird.

'Thus of all the good things brought together, not a single particle escapes appreciation; and such is the virtue of this dish that I consider it worthy of the most august of tables.'

Faisan braisé à l'angoumoise · Braised pheasant

Remove the skin from some truffles and cut them into strips. With these strips lard all the meaty parts of the pheasant. Put in a casserole 125 grams of grated pork fat and a similar quantity of butter. Toss some chopped truffles in this, and the trimmings of those which have been used for larding the pheasant, after chopping them up too and seasoning them with salt and pepper. Let all this partially cook for a few minutes, then let it cool and add twenty-five or thirty roast chestnuts. Stuff the body of the pheasant with this mixture.

Wrap the pheasant with thin slices of veal and bards of bacon. Tie it up and place it in a braising pan which has been lined with bards of bacon. Moisten with a glass of Malaga or white wine and two spoonfuls of caramel and cook on a low flame. Once the pheasant has been cooked, remove it and undo the string, skim off the fat from the cooking liquid, add a few chopped truffles, and boil the liquid for a few seconds. Bind the sauce with chestnut purée, and put the pheasant on top.

After the swallow, the pigeon is the bird which flies the fastest; it does sixteen leagues (64 kilometres) an hour. My friend Vuillemot had the annual task of releasing from his hotel, l'Hôtel de la Cloche, at Compiègne, the pigeons sent by the royal stage coach for the competition which used to take place at Lille, about twenty years ago.

I have been present on several occasions at the departure of these male travellers, who sped away in their race towards the desired female, and who, thanks to the power of instinct, managed to accomplish the trip between Compiègne and Lille in four hours.

The wild pigeon is called wood-pigeon or ring-dove, and the manner in which it abounds in all the royal or imperial parks proves that it becomes tame very easily. It differs from the domestic pigeon not only in its flesh and feathers, but also because it perches on trees. The youngest are called *ramereaux* and are usually eaten from the spit, but they can be used as an entrée.

Pigeons aux petits pois · Pigeons with fresh garden peas

Remove the feathers from three or four pigeons and clean and gut them. Put the liver back in the empty cavity and tuck the feet inside. Leave the tips of the wings on the birds, but singe and clean them. Put a piece of butter in a casserole, brown the birds in this and then remove them.

You will already have cut some lightly salted belly of pork into large dice, and soaked them for half an hour to remove the salt. Put them in the butter and brown, drain and remove before putting a good tablespoon of flour in the butter to make a little roux. This should be light in colour. Then put back the browned pork and the pigeons, and coat them in the roux. Add some bouillon little by little until you have a sauce-like consistency. Season with parsley and spring onions, half a bay leaf, half a clove of garlic and a clove of nutmeg. Put the casserole at the side of the stove so that the pigeons barely simmer.

When the cooking is half over, put in a litre of tiny peas and let them cook, taking care to stir them frequently. When they are cooked, taste and add salt if necessary. Skim off the fat; and remove the peas, so that you can reduce the sauce if it is too thin. Once the sauce has been reduced, arrange the pigeons and cover them with the mixture of peas and pork and serve.

This fish is the shark of fresh waters, just as cunning and just as ravaging in its behaviour as the sharks of the sea. In the Lake of Zirkmitz in Carniole there are pike weighing 20 or even 25 kilograms, in the stomachs of which may be found whole ducks. A pike, if allowed to remain alive, can reach any size and attain any age. In 1749, at Kaiserslautern, one was taken which was more than 6 metres long and weighed 175 kilograms. Its skeleton was preserved at Mannheim. (Aulagnier, *Dictionnaire des aliments et des boissons*.) [These figures are implausible. It is possible that some pike may have attained a weight of 50 kilograms or even a little more, but even this is deemed unlikely. The skeleton was probably that of another kind of fish.]

In the time of Charles IX there was a pike in the fish-pond of the Louvre which used to come when people called 'Lupul'; it would raise its head out of the water to receive the bread which was thrown to it.

The Emperor Frederic II put a pike in a pond on 5 October 1230, and this same fish was taken in the same pond 267 years later. [The story was that the fish taken in 1697 or 1698 carried a ring which bore an inscription in Greek saying that it had been put into the lake on 5 October 1230, by the master of the universe, Frederic II. There is a similar story about a pike caught in the Meuse in 1610, which bore a ring dated 1448. However, these tales are doubted. The present opinion of scientists is that the normal life span of a pike is about fifteen years, and that even twenty would be highly exceptional.]

Brochet à la genevoise · Pike in the Geneva style

Take a pike and tie a string round it at intervals of two fingers' breadth. Put it in a fish kettle with salt, pepper, an onion which has had two cloves stuck into it, and a bouquet garni. Pour over it an equal mixture of red and white wine, allowing half a litre for each 500 grams of fish.

Put the fish kettle on a very hot fire and stimulate the flames to such an extent that the vinous vapours which are arising from it catch fire. When the fire has thus played its part, put 250 grams of butter in the kettle, add some mixed spices and let everything cook gently for about an hour. When the court-bouillon has been sufficiently reduced, add some lumps of butter to the kettle, stirring the whole time. Then take out the fish, drain it and bind the sauce.

The pike-perch is a common fish throughout the north of Europe. There are two kinds; the one lives only in lakes and large rivers, while the other lives in the sea, close to the mouths of rivers.

This fish is known under different names. In Russia it is called *soudac*, in the south of Germany *schills*. In Prussia, pike-perch are very abundant and usually of a perfect quality, especially those fished in the large rivers.

[Dumas gives a separate entry, unconnected with this one by any cross-reference, for *Soudac*, which he describes as a good fish to be found all over Russia, resembling the pike in form, and to some extent in taste. The duplication of entries was no doubt due to the fact that the pike-perch had, in Dumas' time, no French name. It has subsequently been introduced into France, and is known as the *sandre*.]

PILAU   PILAU

This is a dish which is very widespread in the Orient. It consists in rice which is cooked in water or bouillon, but in such a way that the grains remain whole and a little hard, and on which melted butter is poured. Nevertheless, there are as many different ways of preparing a pilau as there are provinces.

Pilau turc · Turkish pilau

Wash the rice in tepid water. Put it in a container which can be hermetically closed, with three times its own volume of water or bouillon, on a high heat. When it starts to boil, dilute a little ordinary saffron, or saffron from Gâtinais, in a saucer or in a cup, and pour it into the container. Next, let it boil very vigorously, keeping the container tightly shut. The rice will harden and thicken as it becomes cooked.

Take the rice out of the pot, and serve it in a pyramid on a platter. The whole operation should have taken about an hour and a half.

PIMENTO (and ALLSPICE)   PIMENT

The pimento, also called 'coral of the gardens' because its fruits are of a reddish colour when fully developed, appears in a wide variety of shapes and sizes. These are distinguished from each other by the names long pepper, Guinea pepper and Cayenne pepper. The big long pimento which is grown in European gardens is usually preserved with salt and vinegar, like olives and capers. In the Antilles and other hot countries, much smaller but very much hotter pimentos grow wild. One of these varieties is known under the name of *piment enragé* (violent pimento), is about the size of a clove and cannot be tolerated by the human tongue. Yet thrushes and other birds are very partial to it and fairly stuff themselves with it. For this reason it is also known as bird pimento. It is to be found in great abundance in woods and forests.

Another type of pimento, the Jamaica pepper, is the fruit of a tree belonging to the order *Myrtaceae*. It is quite well known in the Antilles, where it grows in abundance, under the incorrect name *bois d'Inde*. This tree is covered with numerous flowers which are replaced by purple berries when they have matured. These are succulent and sweet, and highly scented, but cause people who eat them to become very overheated. Wood pigeons, thrushes, blackbirds and other birds who are avid eaters of these berries acquire a very delicate flavour and become very plump through the consumption of this food. It is these same berries, picked before they become fully ripe and dried in the sun, or kiln dried, and then pulverized which constitute the allspice found in the shops. In the Antilles, and particularly on the island of Jamaica, these provide a fairly lucrative crop.

The name allspice is an indication that these berries combine something of the flavour of the four most important commercial spices; cinnamon, pepper, cloves and nutmeg.

PISTACHIO *PISTACHE*

The name is given to the kernels of the fruits of the pistachio tree. The nut is small and oblong, and rather difficult to break because of its flexibility. It is yellowish in colour, punctuated with white when it is nearly ripe, and with a reddish tinge on the side turned to the sun; and it encloses an oily seed whose meat is a delicate green and whose taste is more agreeable than that of the filbert.

Pistachios can be substituted to advantage for almonds and filberts in all preparations of haute cuisine and other culinary dishes, and likewise in the confection of sugared almonds and pralines. But most of the 'sugared pistachios' which are to be found in confectioners' shops are seeds taken from the conical fruits of a sort of pine.

PLAICE   *CARRELET*

A sea fish. It is called *carrelet* [a name applied to various square objects] because, more than any other fish, it has a shape like a lozenge with rounded corners. [It is also called *plie*. Dumas, oddly, has a separate, although nugatory, entry under that name, evidently believing it to be a different fish. It is also odd that he does not mention the most obvious feature of the colouration of the plaice, namely the orange spots on its upper side, which are for most people the distinguishing characteristic of the species. And he makes a surprising mistake in saying that the plaice has eyes on the left side of its head. It is true that 'reversed' specimens sometimes occur, but all normal plaice, like the one in the illustration, have eyes on the right side. In what follows, read 'right' for 'left' throughout. I should add that Dumas was not alone in making this error. It recurs in a number of later books, including even the *Larousse gastronomique* (English language edition, 1961). I have yet to establish whether Dumas put the mistake into circulation, or himself inherited it from some earlier reference book. It does not occur, of course, in any scientific works about fish.]

The plaice has eyes on the left side of its head, and a mouth which opens very wide. The left-hand side of its body is ash-coloured with an admixture of black; the right-hand side is white.

The flesh of the plaice is white, tender, distinctly moist and delicate. It is better than that of the dab, but deteriorates easily in being transported.

Filets de carrelets à la Orly

Lift the fillets from four small plaice and marinate them in lemon juice with salt and coarse pepper.

Use the bones and débris of the fish, with white wine, to make a good consommé.

Flour the fillets and fry them until they are well coloured, then sprinkle over them the consommé which you have made and which, having been clarified, will serve as the sauce.

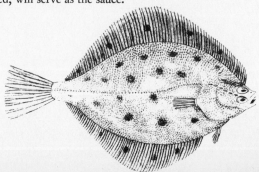

PLOVER   *PLUVIER*

There are two kinds of plover; the golden plover, whose feathers are yellow, and the grey plover, whose feathers are ash-coloured. Several writers have confused the plover with the lapwing, because these birds live in the same places, eat the same foods and have flesh which is fairly similar in taste and effect. However, that of the plover is more delicate.

Plovers are sociable, migratory birds who live principally on earthworms. It is claimed that they make these come up out of the earth by tapping their feet constantly on the soil. They also eat coleopterous insects and some molluscs.

The plover stimulates the appetite and is easy to digest, but is not a very substantial foodstuff.

PLUM PUDDING   *PLUM-PUDDING*

A farinaceous dish without which one cannot have a really good meal in England. It has also become much more widely served in France during these last years. For making this, the ingredients which stand first in line, as essential and constituent elements, are flour, eggs and butter, the flavour of which is enhanced by the addition of various other ingredients. Thus there is pudding with cherries, pudding with sago, lemon pudding, cauliflower pudding, frothy pudding, etc.*

PLUMS   *PRUNES*

Plums were brought from Syria and Damascus by the Crusades, and their different names, as one would suppose, have special significance. Thus, those called *Reine-Claude* owe their name to the first wife of Francois I, daughter of Louis XII. One reads that this good Queen Claude had grafts taken from this tree in her garden in order to give some to everyone. Those called *Mirabelle* were brought first to Provence, and then to Lorraine by King René. As for those called *Monsieur*, they were thus named because Monsieur, the brother of

* Dumas follows this astonishing description, which appears to be for 'pudding' rather than 'plum pudding', by giving a recipe for plum pudding. This, he says, was translated from the English by the late M. de Cussy. The recipe does not call for butter (one of Dumas' three essential ingredients), but for beef marrow or beef kidney suet, which is in fact correct.

Plums

King Louis XIV, liked them enormously, and could never have enough.

Plums are an excellent fruit, very sweet, and very nutritious. Most varieties are a little acidulated and capable of being made into a fermented beverage superior to that which is drunk by farmers in some of our departments. In a few types, the sweet matter seems to be blended with a slightly tart element which disappears in cooking. And as these types have an abundant parenchyma, they are the ones which, subjected to an incomplete desiccation, make the best prunes.

Excellent compotes are made of plums; as are jams, *marmelades*, fruit pastes, ratafias and puddings.

POMEGRANATE   *GRENADE*

This is what the fruit of the pomegranate tree is called. Outside the country where it is grown it is little sought after, and is used only for embellishing dessert fruit baskets, where it creates an excellent effect.

This is what M. Cohier de Lompier has to say about it:

'There are no beautiful dessert fruit baskets without pomegranates; likewise there are none without oranges. A pomegranate which has been cut open, looking like a rich treasure of rubies or sparkling garnets, is one of the most beautiful jewels of our majestic fruit baskets. Nothing else can equal the effect of a few half-open pomegranates on the sides of a pyramid of fruit. Even though one sees the dazzling vermilion of the most beautiful apples, and the variegated enamel sheen of our plump pears, with the gold of the orange, and the supreme beauty of the pineapple, one senses something missing in this fruit basket offered by the god Vertumnus [god of the seasons] to the court of Pomona [goddess of fruits and gardens]. But we must equally admit that, aside from playing this splendid role in the decoration of the tables at a buffet, the pomegranate is a fruit which does not even match the currant in quality. It is not worth any more than the barberry, and it must be agreed that it is practically worthless in temperate countries where the "four red fruits" are abundant and at their best.'

A syrup called grenadine is made of pomegranates. This is very good for dry coughs or irritation. It is made from those pomegranates called *d'épine vineuse* (of the wine-coloured thorn).

One of the most beautiful towns, if not the most beautiful one, in Andalusia has taken its name from its resemblance to a half-open pomegranate. Chateaubriand has put this comparison in the mouth of

his 'last Abencérage'. [The reference is to a Moorish tribe in the kingdom of Grenada in the fifteenth century. Its history inspired Chateaubriand to write *Les Aventures du dernier Abencérage* (1826).]

PORK   *COCHON*

'It is the king of the unclean animals,' says Grimod de la Reynière of the pig, in the eulogy which he bestows on this animal. 'It is the one whose empire is the most universal, and whose qualities are least in dispute. Without it, there would be no bacon, and consequently no cookery; without it, no ham, no sausage, no *andouille*, no black pudding and therefore no *charcutiers*.

'Corpulent doctors,' continues Grimod de la Reynière, rising to a lyrical style, 'you condemn the pig and yet in relation to indigestion it is one of the brightest jewels in your crown.'

Then, returning to a more familiar style, he goes on to say: 'Dressed pork is much better at Troyes and Lyon than anywhere else. Pork loins and shoulders have made the fortunes of two towns, Mayence and Bayonne. Everything about the pig is good; what culpable lapse of memory can have transformed its name into a vulgar insult?'

The pig was the principal foodstuff of the Gauls and they kept it in sizeable herds.

The Romans cooked them whole, and in varying fashions; one method consisted in boiling one side and roasting the other.

The second was called *à la Troyenne*, an allusion to the Trojan horse whose interior was filled with warriors. The pig's interior was stuffed with fig-peckers, oysters and thrushes, the whole basted with good wine and delicious juices; these dishes became so expensive that the senate passed a sumptuary law to prohibit them.

Athenaeus talks of a wild boar, half boiled, half roasted, prepared by a cook who knew how to clean and stuff one without eviscerating it; he made a small hole under one of the shoulders, and the animal, washed out within by wine, was then stuffed through the mouth.

The Egyptians considered the pig an unclean animal and if by mischance someone touched a pig, he had to bathe, fully clothed, in the Nile, to purify himself. On one day only, and under one circumstance only was it allowed to eat pork; this was at full moon, and the animal was then sacrificed to Bacchus and Phoebe.

Everyone knows that the Jews regard the flesh of the pig as unclean flesh, but everyone also knows that this designation stems more from reasons of hygiene than those of religion.

The country where pigs achieve the highest degree of delicacy is China. No doubt this is because of the frequent occasions which they have (if one believes, wrongly, the Jesuit Fathers) for eating human flesh. Moreover, the Chinese use pork as the basis of all their banquets and their hams are superior to those of any other country.

Cuvier was irritated by hearing that the internal structure of the pig was similar in all respects to that of man, and that surgeons in olden days, who did not have the right to dissect the dead, studied the anatomy of pigs as the equivalent of that of men. He wrote these few lines to redress the error into which historians of medicine have fallen. 'The stomach of man and that of pig are in no way similar. In man, this visceral part is shaped like a bagpipe; in the pig it is globular in shape. In man, the liver is divided into three lobes; in the pig, it is long and flat. In man, the length of the intestinal canal is seven or eight times that of the body; in the pig, fifteen to eighteen times. The epiploon, that is to say the part whch is popularly known as the *toilette* (caul), is much more stretched out, and fattier. And what is very consoling to those delicate souls who want to have nothing in common with the pig's nature is that the pig's heart shows notable differences from that of man.

'I would add, for the benefit of scientists and wits, that the pig's brain is also much smaller in size than man's, which proves that its intellectual faculties are much inferior to those of our academicians.'

The pig, along with the rabbit, is the most prolific animal in the world. Vauban, who was, as is known, an excellent mathematician wrote a treatise on pigs which he entitled *Ma Cochonnerie*. He calculated the descendants of a single sow over a period of twelve years; these descendants added up to 6,434,838 pigs, counting children, grand-children, and great-grand-children.

The pig has long been regarded as a sacred being in Naples; it was the only street cleaner which existed in this modern Parthenope; there were few houses where a pig was not tethered by a rope long enough to allow it to clean an area 24 feet in dimaeter. Likewise the pig, anyway those who were let loose, assisted at all the celebrations.

One of the brothers of the King of Naples, called Prince Anthony (whose reputation will be explained by a word from his brother), said in front of the king, in speaking of the Marquis de Sal . . . 'We are friends like pigs.' And the king replied to him, shrugging his shoulders; 'You are more pig than friend.'

The same Prince Anthony was surprised in a peasant girl's bedroom by one of her brothers, armed with a broomstick. He wanted

Pork

to escape by the window, against which a ladder was propped, but at the bottom of the ladder he found a second brother armed with a second broomstick. He did not merely have to run the gauntlet of the broom, but that of its handle. The two brothers delivered themselves so well, and revenged their sister's honour so gallantly on Prince Anthony's back that the latter died from the blows some twelve or fifteen days later. He was given a great state funeral which left the King's palace and wended its way towards Sainte-Claire, the church where the Royal tombs were. But astonishment was great when an enormous pig, the ownership of which was disclaimed by everyone, took up position on the wall side of the pavement and served as leader of the cortège. Everything possible was done to chase it away, but nothing in the world succeeded in making it deviate from its path. Once it arrived at the church of Sainte-Claire, it stopped by itself and mounted the six or seven steps which lead to the interior of the church. Then more efforts were made to remove the unclean animal, but the latter seemed to be defending what it appeared apparently to regard as its right: the beadle advanced, menacing it with his halberd, with which he was perhaps about to pierce it, when a voice from the crowd shouted: 'Unhappy man! Do you not see that it is the soul of Prince Anthony?'

It only needed this enlightenment to make the rights of the pig recognized. The church was then opened to it, and the pig participated in the whole funeral ceremony with all the tranquillity of a spirit which knows it can depend on prayers.

Of all animals, the pig is the one most used in cooking; for in practically all dishes, be they entrées or roasts, bacon and ham are used. The other parts of the animal are less esteemed, yet *hure* [potted pig's head brawn or 'cheese'] is a very distinguished dish when prepared by a man who knows his trade. Pig's trotters are served *à la Sainte Menehould* [p. 184], or are stuffed with truffles. The ears appear on the menu of kings; and breast of pork is used in many stews. Young, fat pork should be chosen, but care must be taken to ensure that its flesh is not invaded by the parasite called trichina.

There is nothing in the pig which has to be thrown away. Black pudding is made of the blood; *andouilles* of the intestines; while the trimmings of the meat provide sausage and brawn.

Jambon au naturel · Cooked ham

Procure a good ham; those from Westphalia are the best and in general more esteemed than those from Bayonne. Trim it; that is to say, remove the top layer of the flesh and anything yellowish from the edge. Remove the bone from the chump end, cut the end of the hock and put the ham to soak. When you drain it, stick a larding-needle into the pope's eye which will allow you to decide whether it needs to soak for a longer time.

That done, put the ham in a cloth, tie the four ends together, and put it into a *marmite* or braising pan which is a close fit. Pour in some water and add four or five carrots, the same number of onions, four cloves, three or four bay leaves, two or three cloves of garlic and one or two bouquets of parsley, thyme and basil. Bring to the boil, and then cook it over a low heat according to the number of half-kilos of weight. When you think it may be cooked, test it with a larding needle; if it goes in easily, this shows that it has been cooked enough. Take it out of the pan, untie the cloth, and then retie it more tightly. When the ham has partly cooled, remove the rind. Trim it and dredge it with sieved dry breadcrumbs. Put a napkin on a platter, and place the ham on this.

Cochon (petit salé au chou) · Salt belly of pork with cabbage

We can evoke the shades of the Greeks and Romans to prove that the cabbage has merited the commendation of the earliest nations on earth. Cato, for example, an irreconcilable enemy of doctors and himself a medicaster, treated everybody in his house with cabbage, regardless of the illness. And the wonderful thing was that no one felt any the worse. With the exception of Augustus, all the emperors up to Vespasian were gourmands. But it must be said to the credit of the stupid Claudius that it was he who raised the status of the cabbage, because of the love he had for salt pork. 'Roman Senators,' he shouted, on entering the Senate one day, 'Tell me, I pray, is it possible to live without salt pork?' And the honourable company instantly replied: 'No, my Lord, better die than give that up.'

From that moment on, to curry favour with Claudius, the senators feasted on salt pork with cabbage.

In order to make *petit salé* you cut belly of pork in pieces, rub them with fine salt as you would bacon, add a little saltpetre and arrange them as you go along one after the other in a pot. Be sure to press them down carefully to prevent them from taking on a stale taste; fill up any holes in the covering of salt, put a white cloth over the container and then its lid, making the seal as nearly hermetic as possible. Use it after eight or ten days, laying the pieces on a bed of cabbage or whatever you wish.

231

This excellent vegetable was brought from Virginia by the English admiral Walter Raleigh in 1585, and since then has preserved people from famine.

This admiral was better known for his enterprising spirit and the vicissitudes of his life than he has been for the importation of the potato. This, at first, drew very little attention. Walter Scott reports that one day when Raleigh found himself taking a walk with Queen Elizabeth and her suite she had to walk a short distance through a small pool of mud. He unfastened his velvet cloak, which was embroidered with pearls, and spread it over the mud so that the queen could traverse it without wetting her feet. She rewarded him for this by naming him admiral.

As for the potato, absurd prejudices prevented it from being duly appreciated for a long time. Many people thought it a dangerous foodstuff, or at least a coarse one and at best suitable for pigs. This was the position at the end of the last century, when Parmentier began a series of practical and theoretical works which bore on the cultivation of the potato. He was sufficiently successful to overcome the prejudices, and everyone became convinced of the advantages of potato cultivation.

In 1793 potatoes were considered so indispensable that a decree of the Commune, dated 21 *Ventôse*,* ordered a census to be taken of luxury gardens, so that they could be devoted to the cultivation of this vegetable. As a result, the principal avenue in the Jardin des Tuileries and the flower beds were turned over to potato cultivation. This is why potatoes were for a long time given the additional name of 'royal oranges'.

The potato is a real nourishment and one which is healthful, easy and inexpensive. Its preparation has this agreeable and advantageous aspect for the working class, that it involves practically no trouble or expense. The alacrity with which one observes children eating baked potatoes, and feeling all the better for them, proves that they suit all dispositions.

The choice of potatoes is neither in doubt, nor unimportant. The grey ones with gritty skins are the less good; the best, without question, are the purplish ones, known in Paris by the name *Vite-lottes*, and preferable even to the red ones.

---

* *Ventôse* is the sixth month of the calendar of the first French republic; 19 or 20 February to 20 March in our calendar.

Pommes de terre à la parisienne

Melt a piece of butter or other fat in a casserole with one or two onions cut in small pieces. Add a glass of water, and put in your carefully peeled potatoes, with salt, pepper, and a bouquet garni, and cook on a low flame.

Pommes de terre à l'anglaise

Carefully wash some potatoes, cook them in salted water, and then peel them. Soften a good piece of butter in a casserole, put in the potatoes (which you have sliced), add salt, pepper and *mignonette* [a muslin sachet containing red pepper, nutmeg, coriander, cinnamon, ginger and cloves], but without the nutmeg. Toss the potatoes with this and serve on a very hot platter.

Pommes de terre à la provençale

Put six soupspoons of oil in a casserole with the zest of the skin of half a lemon, parsley, garlic, and well-chopped spring onion, a little grated nutmeg, salt and pepper. Then peel the potatoes, and cook them with these seasonings. When the moment to serve arrives, sprinkle them with the juice of a lemon.

POULTRY   *VOLAILLE*

It is well to recommend to people who work in the farm-yard, and the cook as well, never to kill poultry when the birds' stomachs are full. One should also always take care never to shut them up when dead (we are still speaking of the birds), until they have become cold and stiff.

To fatten capons, pullets, etcetera, they are put in a closed hen-house full of barley and wheat; and care is taken to see that water and boiled bran mush is given to them from time to time.

In Normandy and in Maine, areas reputed for providing Paris with the finest pullets and the best capons, they are put in tubs, covered with a cloth, and fed on a mash of millet, barley or oats. These pieces of mash are dipped in milk to make the birds' flesh a delicate white. To begin with, not very much is given, in order to accustom the birds to this diet. Day by day the amount is increased, and they are forced to eat as much as they can swallow. They are fed with this mash three or four times a day; morning, mid-day and evening. Ducks and turkeys are fattened in a similar fashion with the feeds which suit them best—usually corn meal and potatoes which have been boiled with oats and buttermilk.

PRICKLY PEAR (or INDIAN FIG)   *FIGUES D'INDE*

Any tourist who has travelled in Sicily or Calabria will be grateful to the prickly pear for services rendered to him. It is the fruit of the cactus called *raquette*.

The fruit is either yellow or pink, and the pulp which it contains is icy cold, even though the fruit is exposed to the sun. It is true that it is protected by a thick skin, which must be opened with caution because of the prickles in it. Once they have penetrated your skin, these prickles obstinately refuse to come out. As for the other characteristics of this fruit, however hot it is and however many one may eat, I never heard of anyone being given indigestion by the prickly pear. Along with the *cocomero* (water melon) the prickly pear is the eminently national dish of the Neapolitans.

Neapolitans are in the habit of saying, in boasting about their country, that for a farthing's worth of *cocomero* they can eat, drink and get it all over their faces.

PRUNES   *PRUNEAUX*

This is the name given to plums dried in the oven. Their fabrication is the very simplest. It consists in picking plums when they are properly ripe, placing them on racks and exposing them to a low heat in the oven three or four times successively. After all this the prunes are deposited in a dry place, and keep without spoiling for one or two years. The plums most often used for this purpose are those from Damascus.

Prunes from several regions, from Tours, from Nancy, from Brignoles, and from Agen, have deservedly acquired a reputation and are the source of important revenues. Moreover, they are prepared with considerably more care than ordinary commercial prunes.

Prunes are usually cooked with sugar, except for those from Brignoles, which are sweet enough by themselves and therefore do not need any. To enhance these compotes, a little Bordeaux wine is mixed in.

PUDDING   *PUDDING*

An English dish about which we have already written in the entry on
Plum Pudding. We are going to give a few French recipes here.
[Dumas does give some French recipes, although the two chosen for
translation here are avowedly English.]

Cabinet pudding (an English dish)

Have some big biscuits or pieces of Savoy cake which you have cut
into pieces. Butter a mould, put in the bottom a few seeded *raisins de
caisse* [grapes which have been stored in drawers or boxes], and the
same quantity of currants washed and picked over. Add to this a few
pieces of candied citron which have been cut into small dice.

Arrange one layer of biscuits and then one of fruit, alternately,
until the mould is full. Prepare a custard cream, pour it into the
mould so that it becomes incorporated with the biscuits, put the
pudding in a bain-marie for an hour, sprinkle with a little currant
jelly and serve.

Pudding au pain (or Bread-Pudding)

Take a shallow fireproof dish, arrange on it some slices of buttered
bread and sprinkle over them currants which have been well washed
and picked over. Mix two whole eggs with a litre of milk, which you
have flavoured with powdered sugar and the zest of a lemon. Pour all
this on to the slices of bread, cook in a slow oven for half an hour, and
serve.

PUFFER-FISH   *BAKU*

A fish of Japan, sought after for the delicate quality of its flesh. The
Japanese discard the head, intestines and bones. They also wash and

clean it with great care. However, despite these precautions, some people are poisoned by it and die. When a Japanese is fed up with life, he chooses this fish in preference to any other instrument for his own destruction. Scheutzer, in his *Histoire du Japon*, says that five persons of Nangasaka, having eaten a dish of puffer-fish, were seized with convulsions, delirium and vomiting of blood in such violent fashion that they died of it within a few hours. Despite this, the Japanese are unwilling to abstain from eating a food which they regard as such a delicacy. There is an edict of the emperor which expressly forbids soldiers and employees of the empire to eat it. It costs much more than other fish.

[Although this entry is given under the heading *Baku*, the fish referred to is evidently what the Japanese now call Fugu. There are regulations which forbid anyone who is not qualified to prepare this fish for human consumption, so great is the risk of eating it when it has not been properly prepared. The official manual for fugu-cooks is a little book in itself.]

PURÉE   *PURÉE*

Purées which are the products of farinaceous or other substances have two completely distinct uses. They constitute a dish in themselves; and they serve as a garnish or a bed to accompany roasts or entrées. They differ from sauces by their firm consistency, and their thickness.

Purée de marrons · Chestnut purée

Remove the first and second skins from roast chestnuts, toss them in a casserole with some butter, and moisten them with bouillon and white wine. Soften the chestnuts over a low heat, pound them in a mortar and press them through a sieve. Elsewhere cook half a dozen sausages, add to the purée the juices and the fat from the sausages, and serve the purée as a bed for the sausages.

Chops may be substituted for the sausages.

Purée des quatre racines · Purée of four root vegetables

Take a few carrots, onions, turnips, one or two parsnips. Chop them all up, put them in a casserole with a good bit of butter, moisten them with bouillon and stir until the vegetables start to soften. Let them cook for two or three hours, then take them off the stove and press them through a hair sieve or a fine strainer. Moisten them from time to time with a little of their bouillon, then return the purée to the casserole, add some meat essence or a little stock, or a little reduced cooking water. Add a little light-coloured caramel and serve as a separate dish, or as a garnish.

QUAIL   *CAILLES*

The quail holds a distinguished place among the very best dishes. It is a traveller which breeds in temperate countries, but rarely stays there. For a long time people have tried to find out how the quail, which possesses none of the characteristics of birds which fly long distances, could fly over the highest mountains and cross seas. Everyone knows that the quail, which is rather a fat bird, is straining itself when it takes to the air for a third time and that the hunter can then catch it either with his hand or with his hat, right under his dog's nose. The question how the quail and the swallow, which have wings and tails so dissimilar, can carry out equally long journeys, has for long been unanswered and the problem has remained unresolved.

The quail, of all the creatures which can properly be classed as game, is the daintiest and most attractive. A plump quail pleases equally by its taste, its shape and its colour. One is guilty of performing an act of culinary ignorance whenever one cooks a quail in any way other than by roasting or *en papillote* [in buttered paper]; the reason being that its flavour is very transient and that any contact with liquid will cause this to be dissolved, to evaporate and be lost.

QUARTER OF DEER, ENGLISH STYLE
QUARTIER DE DAIM À L'ANGLAISE

This is what Walter Scott calls venison in his novels. Who is there who has not wanted to eat Walter Scott's venison and Fenimore Cooper's bison's hump?

Unfortunately, bisons live at a considerable distance from us. The same is not true of the deer which we have in all our forests; but it is true that these are reserved for the royal pleasure, and that our deer are less good than the English ones.

When you have a quarter of deer, wash it in tepid water, wipe it with a cloth, salt it and wrap it in buttered paper. Then enclose it in a large sheet of pastry, made simply with flour and lukewarm water, to the thickness of a centime. Carefully seal the joins, and support the pastry by covering it in turn with buttered paper. Roast the quarter for three hours, basting it every ten minutes. When it is cooked, unwrap it and arrange it on a hot platter. Prick the quarter of deer with the point of a knife in order to have the meat juices run out. Serve immediately, with a sauceboat of currant jelly and with a dish of white beans which have just been drained and buttered.

QUARTER OF ROAST LAMB
QUARTIER D'AGNEAU RÔTI

The leg, the loin and the four cutlets from the best end of neck nearest the loin constitute a quarter of lamb.

Saw off the projecting bone of a quarter of lamb, and tie up the skirt. If you do not have an English-style spit, impale it with an iron skewer. Cover it with greased paper and cook it, basting it with butter or lard. After three quarters of an hour, uncover it, sprinkle it with breadcrumbs and let it take colour. Salt it, take it from the spit and arrange it on a platter with a paper frill. Send in some good gravy in a separate dish.

In England it is customary to serve a sweet and sour sauce with a quarter of lamb. This is made with shallots chopped with fresh mint, a little water and vinegar which has been seasoned with salt and sugar.

QUINCE   COING

This is the fruit of the quince tree. A syrup is made from quinces which is administered in cases of persistent diarrhoea, as is the mucilaginous water obtained by soaking quince seeds. The quince is used for making bandoline, which is used by hairdressers for making hair glossy. It is also used for making jams.

RABBIT   LAPIN

Rabbits originated in Africa, whence they passed to Spain, and then to France. Pliny and Varro relate how, in the Spanish town of Tarragona, the large number of rabbits which had dug their burrows under the houses of the town caused the collapse of twenty-five or thirty of them. Bazilazzo, one of the Liparian islands, was deprived of all its crops and was reduced to famine by the large number of these animals. They were so abundant in the southern provinces of France that Beaujeu tells of a provincial gentleman who, in 1551, went rabbit hunting with a few of his vassals and three dogs and returned with 600 rabbits. In the islands near Arles, they say that there are so many that a hunter who fails to kill a hundred in a day comes back discontented.

The rabbit has been regarded as a symbol of fecundity. It is so prolific that calculations suggest that ten doe-rabbits could produce from 800 to 900 rabbits each year. They carry their young for thirty or thirty-one days, and furnish the hat-making trade with something in the region of fifteen to twenty million skins annually.

Winter is the best season to eat them; and to eat them at their best they should be neither too young nor too old. To distinguish the mature rabbit from the young rabbit one taps the exterior of the front paws above the joint. If one cannot feel a protuberance the size of a lentil, it is proof that the animal is definitely young.

One can tell the wild rabbit by the reddish colour of the hairs on its feet and of those beneath its tail. This colour is spuriously given to tame rabbits by singeing the hairs on these parts. It is easy to spot this deception by the smell; or, if they have been dyed, by washing the affected parts.

On the scale of digestibility, the meat of young rabbit ranks just after that of poultry which is not too fat, and just before that of poultry which is too fat.

Lapereaux aux petits pois · Young wild rabbit with peas

Make a small quantity of roux. Joint the rabbits. Turn the pieces of rabbit in the roux, which should be very light, and add a little diced ham and some good bouillon. Dilute the roux well with this, then add a bouquet of parsley and spring onions with a clove; a bay leaf; and half a clove of garlic. While the rabbit is boiling, put in a litre of garden peas, seasoning it all with the correct amount of salt. When the ragoût has reduced considerably, remove the bouquet and serve.

RADISH   *RADIS*

There are more than ten varieties of radish, and it is unnecessary to say that they are eaten raw. Radishes are shaped like turnips, but unlike them do not have a sweet taste. On the contrary, they have a sharp taste, and stimulate the appetite. There are white, pink and red ones, and the small summer grey one, whose flavour is more pronounced than that of the other sorts.

The radish came originally from China; and we read in Charlemagne's *Capitulaires* [capitularies, i.e. collection of ordinances] that it was among the vegetables which this monarch recommended his farm managers to cultivate.

The radish is eaten as an hors d'oeuvre with butter and salt. It is a diuretic, an attenuant and an antiscorbutic.

RASPBERRY   *FRAMBOISE*

There are two kinds, red and yellow ones. The red are the more common. Connoisseurs of raspberries think that although the two kinds have much the same taste, the aroma of the yellow ones is more delicate.

RAY   *RAIE*

Since this fish needs to be 'mortified' to make it more tender, its carriage from the seaports to Paris improves its quality. It is also the only fish which can be kept for two or three days, even in thundery weather.

The two best species are the *turbotine* and the *raie bouclée*.* The best way of eating them is to cook them in salted water with vinegar and slices of onion. They should then be drained, skinned and served with either a white sauce incorporating capers or a *beurre noir noisette* [butter which has been heated to the point at which it is between brown and very dark brown], and with a garnish of fried parsley.

The liver of a ray should only be left for two or three minutes in boiling water, in order to be cooked.

---

* There is no problem about the latter of these. The *raie bouclée*, or thornback ray, is *Raja clavata* (Linnaeus) and is generally regarded as the best ray. However, the name *turbotine* is baffling. We have found no trace of this name being applied to any ray. On the other hand, *turbotin* is the name for a small turbot; and *turboden* is a Breton name for turbot generally. It seems hardly possible that Dumas could have confused the turbot, for which he anyway provides a separate entry (page 285) with a ray. Yet no other explanation presents itself; and he may have made the confusion in a moment of aberration.

Raie frite · Fried ray

Skin a ray and cut it into pieces like fillets, without taking out the
bones. Put the pieces to marinate with seasonings, adding a piece of
butter with flour worked into it, vinegar and fines herbes. Warm the
marinade a little, so that the butter melts, and leave the pieces of fish
in it for four hours. Then take them out, flour them, fry them and
garnish them.

RED MULLET   *ROUGET*

This fish is also called *mulet*.* It is a marine fish, which has a red body
and a very large head. It is most common in the Mediterranean,
where it is fished in every locality, usually over muddy bottoms. It is
also met in Atlantic waters, notably in the Channel, but is becoming
rarer and rarer there.

The red mullet was greatly sought after by the Greeks and the
Romans, as much for the excellence of its taste as for the beauty of its
colours. The Romans especially made it into an item of great luxury
and did not hesitate to buy it at absurdly high prices. Suetonius,
among the ancient authors, tells us that red mullet were so sought
after in his time that three of them were sold for 30,000 sesterces
(5,844 francs), an incident which obliged the Emperor Tiberius to
pass sumptuary laws and to impose a tax on foodstuffs brought to
market.

Nowadays the red mullet, while not achieving that degree of
admiration which the Romans felt for it, is still highly esteemed by
gourmets. Its flesh, which is white and firm, flakes easily and is
pleasant to eat. It is highly digestible because it is not fat.

* There is evidence of confusion here. The red mullets which are found in
French waters are *Mullus barbatus* (Linnaeus) and *Mullus surmuletus* (Linnaeus).
The latter, but not the former, may be called *surmulet*. Neither is called *mulet*,
which is the name for grey mullet, which are fish of a different family.

On top of this confusion between red and grey mullet, there is a symptom of
a different and additional muddle. Dumas says that the red mullet has a very
large head. It does not. But the red gurnard, which again is a fish of a completely
different family, related neither to the red mullet nor to the grey mullet, does have
a very large head and is sometimes called *rouget-grondin*. This appellation is no
doubt the invention of fishmongers who wished to give their customers the idea
that the red gurnard, which is a fish of only moderate quality, is comparable with
the red mullet, which is an extremely good fish. Dumas, or his collaborators,
may have been misled here too; although it is fair to add that the last three
paragraphs of the entry are patently about the true red mullet.

Red Mullet

The best way of preparing red mullet, says M. de Courchamps, is to gut them through the gills, without scaling them, to grill them over red coals and to serve them with a white sauce to which capers and preserved nasturtium seeds have been added, as well as the livers of the fish, crushed.

Red mullet are often cooked in a court-bouillon, but we do not recommend this, since grilling them, of all the different methods which have been tried, is the most successful.

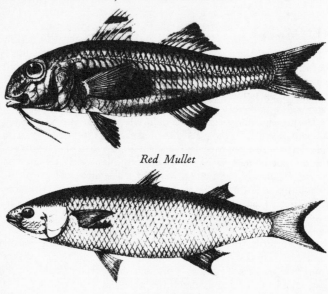

Red Mullet

Grey Mullet

RICE   *RIZ*

Originally from the Orient, rice ranks immediately after bread as the healthiest, most abundant and most universally known food. The peoples of Asia, Africa and America are big consumers of rice and thrive on it. Rice is much used in many European countries too.

An amber-tinted white wine is also made from rice in some countries and tastes as good as Spanish wine. This inebriating wine is much used in China, where rice forms the basis of the people's diet.

The rice which we eat in France comes from Italy, from Piedmont and from the Carolinas.

Riz à la chancelière (a recipe of la présidente Fouquet) ·
Rice in the Lady Chancellor's style

Put the following ingredients in a big earthenware *marmite*, which must be higher than it is wide: half a pound of rice which has been rinsed six times in tepid water, half a pound of powdered sugar, a quarter pound of fresh butter, three spoonfuls of white honey, a small spoonful of finely ground cinnamon and, finally, two *pintes* (a little less than two litres) of very fresh milk. Put the *marmite* in the bread oven at the same time as the bread and let the rice cook until the time comes for your big twelve-pound loaf to be taken out.

Take good note that the *marmite*, which must be of a good height, should be more or less empty in its upper part, so that the milk, when made to boil by the great heat of the oven, cannot escape from the pipkin and is obliged to keep falling back on the rice.

Madame la chancelière de Pontchartrain has lived for a long time on this food, which is both agreeable and light and which is very salubrious for inflammations of the chest and stomach.

ROAST MEAT   *RÔTI*

These are meats cooked on the spit or in the oven. The roast is served as second course in well-ordered meals. The big roast is the large roasted meat, such as beef, veal, leg of mutton etcetera; the small roast is poultry, game and small birds.

Some people consider roast meats less healthy and less nourishing than boiled meats. 'The heat,' they say, 'acting immediately on the meat which it is roasting, dissipates all the moisture which made it so wholesome. It dries out the fibres and, in concentrating the juices of the roast meats, ferments and magnifies them to the point of increasing all the salts and thus forming a saline and spirituous essence, suitable for fermenting the blood and increasing the bile.

'On the other hand' (still according to these same persons) 'boiled meat receives the effect of the heat only through water, which tempers and corrects it. It is like what happens when you use a double-boiler, not a hot dry heat which burns, but a gentle, moderate heat which cooks without hardening, and penetrates without drying. Now nothing else so resembles the body's digestion, and better prepares it for the nourishment which is being provided.'

This is wrong: nothing, on the contrary is better able to rob meat of its juices than water. Water is the most powerful of solvents. It empties the pores of the meat, and makes it capable of absorbing all sorts of salts and whatever is most spirituous, most oily, and most earthly in the animal body. More compounds are dissolved and more juices are extracted by liquid solvents than by any other medium. How then can meat, when it has been boiling in water for a long time, not lose the best part of its juices? It loses them so completely that bouillon removes all the gelatinous matter from it. It is therefore an error, we repeat, to suggest that boiled meat is more nourishing. And, if the roast is more flavourful than boiled meat, it is because, as a learned doctor of the last century has said, it still has all its juices, instead of losing a part of its juices to the water, as boiled meat does.

Meats to be roasted should not be seared too rapidly by the heat, any more than they should be done too slowly. Dark meats should remain reddish, so that their juices are retained, but white meats require a more even cooking, and any trace of pinkness should disappear.

As for fixing a definite rule in respect to cooking roast meats, this is somewhat difficult because it all depends on the quality, and the weight of the meat to be roasted. But there are two essential points to bear in mind about the procedure which must be followed to roast successfully. First of all, the management of the fire; and then the quality of the meat, which must be differently treated depending on whether it is red meat, or white.

ROCK PARTRIDGE   *BARTAVELLE*

One of the names for the Greek partridge. This bird is much larger than the red partridge which it greatly resembles. Its back is a reddish grey, its breast grey, and its stomach red.

The rock partridge, which can be found throughout the Orient, as in Sicily and at Naples, never descends to the plains. Its flesh is white and greatly esteemed, even though it has a slightly resinous bitter taste. It is found principally in the Alps, sometimes in the valleys of Grésivaudan, of the Viennois and Valentinois. It is of Attic origin, and it was the good king René of Anjou who endowed his dear province with this excellent game. One of the Scaligeri adds that the rock partridge originated on Mount Olympus, and that it has retained a feeling of its own grandeur, given that it only enjoys high places, where it has sovereign reign. [Giulio Cesare Scaligero (1484–1558) was an Italian philologist and doctor. His son, Joseph (1540–1609), has been described as a humanist and Protestant philosopher.]

Father Poiré has said that there is the same difference between rock partridges and partridges as there is between peaches and chestnuts. Cyrano de Bergerac reckons that the rock partridge bears the same relationship to the partridge as cardinals do to simple mendicant monks. Finally, M. de la Reynière has said that rock partridges are worthy of such great respect that one should only eat them on one's knees. The author of the *Mémoires de madame de Créqui* recommends that one should lard them with very thin bacon strips, or bard them if they are very young, and serve them as a superb roast dish. But M. Vuillemot has stated the principle that game should never be larded, and we defer to his authority.

ROEBUCK (VENISON)   *CHEVREUIL*

A small species of the family of the deer, an animal which it much resembles although it is more elegant and seems more agile and lively. The roebuck is very wild and exceedingly difficult to tame. People have tried to tame them by taking them very young, but their impetuous and independent bent reappears at the first possible moment. They are then capable of capricious and dangerous behaviour towards those to whom they have taken a dislike.

The age of the roebuck, like that of the deer, can be recognized by the number of antlers on its horns. If its meat is to be tender and flavourful, it must be caught when it is between eighteen months and three years old. At this time its flesh is very good, although the quality does depend to a large extent on the place from which it comes. The best come from the Cévennes, the Ardennes, Rouergue and Morvan. However, the very best, without doubt, is that of the *chevrotin* or fawn of the roebuck, when it is only nine or ten months old.

Roebuck (Venison)

Gigot de chevreuil rôti · Roast leg of venison

After trimming a leg of venison and larding it with narrow strips of larding bacon, leave it to marinate for several hours in salt and olive oil. Cook it on a spit for an hour, basting it with its marinade, and then make a sauce of the marinade and the juice of some shallots.

ROQUEFORT   *ROQUEFORT (fromage de)*

A cheese which is made at Roquefort-en-Rouergue in Aveyron.

This cheese is made of a mixture of goat's and ewe's milk, heated and put in a mould under pressure. Next, each little mass of cheese is encircled with bands to prevent it from cracking open. It is dried in cellars where there is plenty of movement in the air. The cheeses are then salted. This is done by covering them with a layer of salt and then, after the salting has lasted for three or four days, stacking them on top of each other. They are left for a while to become refined; and care is taken to scrape and clean them whenever a slightly coloured bloom appears. As soon as this bloom is red and white, these cheeses are good to eat. This is usually after three or four months in the cellar.

We recommend Roquefort cheese, which is considered with good reason to be the best of all our dry cheeses.

SAFFRON   *SAFRAN*

This is the name given to the pistils of a plant belonging to the genus *Crocus*, when they are detached from it. These are gathered in the environs of Paris and in Gâtinais, where the quality is superior.

The smell of saffron is extremely strong; it can cause violent headaches, and even bring about death. Its bitter, aromatic taste is not at all disagreeable. Its colour is pronounced, and the yellow which it produces immediately tints anything with which it comes in contact. Saffron is one of the most prized colouring agents, and the ancients esteemed it greatly as an aromatic. The Romans made an alcohol-based tincture of it which they used to scent their theatres. There are some countries where this flower is used as a seasoning, and to colour cakes, vermicelli, butter etcetera.

Nowadays it is only used for making babas, pilaf, rice in the African style and scubac [a kind of whisky with aromatics, which Sir Walter Scott, for example, called usquebaugh].

Mousse au safran

Boil some double cream with a little dried powdered orange-flower, and mix into this a fairly strong decoction of saffron from Gâtinais. When this mixture is cold, beat it vigorously with a box-wood whisk. Arrange it in your dessert goblets, put these on ice and keep them there until serving time.

SAGO   *SAGOU*

A sort of starch which comes from the Indies, and which is found in several types of palms. It has no smell and tastes insipid. It is used in soup and then becomes transparent and swells greatly. It is usually consumed as pap, or is cooked in milk, with sugar and aromatics.

Sago is a very pleasant, light, but not very nourishing food. It is recommended as a food in early infancy, extreme old age, convalescence, consumption, and for all people suffering from weakened digestion. An artificial sago is made with potato flour.

SALAD (see also Dressing)   *SALADE*

This word is used principally to designate those culinary preparations which require, beside salt and pepper, oil or butter and cream, and usually vinegar as well.

In discussing salads in relation to our physical well being, it would seem at first that they ought to have a bad effect on health: raw herbs, irritating spices and vinegar should, one would think, be difficult to digest and might even irritate the stomach. And yet experience does not justify this judgement. There are few dishes which are used so widely in all classes of society as this one. There is almost always some on hand, and it generally tastes good. For all that, it is only occasionally that they cause upsets, and it would therefore be unfair to arouse mistrust of them.

Whatever is used to prepare salads, it is also necessary to use vinegar in strict moderation. In the preparation of a dressing it is worthwhile to make the acidity of the vinegar disappear by blending its flavour with that of the herbs, oil and other ingredients. To achieve this, an egg yolk is a very effective agent. One should also use wine vinegar exclusively. Nowadays it is too often replaced by an acid obtained from the combustion of wood. This is a distinction to which insufficient importance is attached, and we must draw the attention of the public to it. The accompanying fines herbes which are drawn from stimulating plants should be served separately, as they are more difficult to digest than the salads. If this were done, it would be possible for many more people to eat salads.

Salads vary according to the season. Towards the end of autumn chicory starts to be eaten. It is seasoned with nothing more than a crust of stale bread rubbed with garlic, placed in the bottom of the salad bowl and then tossed with the salad so that the latter becomes well impregnated with the flavour. No other herbs are added to this salad.

Later, endive is used. This is a sort of chicory which is less tender and flavourful than the first sort, and which is likewise prepared without additional herbs.

Winter salads are almost always made with lamb's lettuce, rampion and celery, cut in matchsticks. Celery is sometimes used alone as a salad, but then it must be seasoned with beaten oil, mustard and soya sauce. Watercress is also a winter salad, and it is usually garnished with slices of beetroot and a few slivers of olive.

Wild chicory appears towards the end of the winter and it is presented like white chicory by mixing it with sliced beetroot.

Lettuce usually appears towards Easter. Of all the salads, it is the best liked. It is usually dressed with herbs and quartered hardboiled eggs. But it is sometimes dressed with marinated oysters, tails of shrimp, turtle eggs, anchovy fillets or stuffed olives; and sometimes also with Indian pickles or Chinese soya sauce. This salad requires a lot of oil; the green oil from Aramont is the best which one can use for its seasoning. After this comes cos lettuce, less tender and less watery than the last mentioned, but endowed with a sweet flavour. It is not served with hardboiled eggs.

Salads are also made with all sorts of cooked vegetables, as we have mentioned in the places where the various kinds of these are discussed.

M. Chaptal has given a way of dressing salad which has always been commonly used in northern Europe; a fact which in no way prevents us from giving due credit to this illustrious academician. The method consists in saturating the salad with oil seasoned with salt and pepper, before adding the vinegar. The vinegar then slips off each of the oily leaves so that if one has put too much vinegar on a salad, which happens often as we all know, one never has to rue this, because the vinegar falls to the bottom of the salad bowl. M. Chaptal has most judiciously calculated that it must do this because of the laws of specific gravity and the relationship between its specific gravity and that of oil.

We should also mention that since salt is not soluble in vinegar, it is useless to try to blend the one with the other; it is preferable to mix the salt with the oil first and then to pour it on the salad.

M. Chaptal was rewarded for his gastronomic service by the adoption of *salade assaisonnée à la Chaptal* as a culinary term.

Without any ambition to receive such a valuable reward myself, I am going to tell you how I season my own salads.

First of all, I place a plate over my salad bowl [, in which the salad has already been installed,] and turn it upside down. I then put the plate, now heaped with salad, at my side, and the empty salad bowl in front of me. I put into the salad bowl one [hard-boiled] egg-yolk for two people, that is to say six for a dozen diners. I mash them up in olive oil so as to make a paste, to which I then add: French parsley, mashed tuna, pounded anchovies, the mustard of Maille, a generous tablespoonful of soya sauce, tiny gherkins (chopped up) and the whites of the eggs (also chopped up). I dilute all this with the best vinegar which I have been able to procure.

Finally, I put the salad back into the salad bowl and let my servant toss it. And I let fall on it, from a height, a pinch of paprika.

SALAD HERBS   *FOURNITURE*

The mixed herbs which accompany chicory or lettuce, the main body of the salad, come under this heading. These are: garden-cress, chervil, spring onions, tarragon, samphire, balm (when it is young), buck's horn plantain, burnet, flowering nasturtium and the flowers of the violet, the great mullein, borage and bugloss.

SALMON   *SAUMON*

A fish which belongs to both the north and the south. It is a freshwater fish during the season of fine weather, and a sea fish during the rest of the year. It leaves the sea in the spring, for the purpose of spawning; and travels in large groups. There is a remarkable orderliness about the salmon on their nomadic journeys. They form themselves into two lines, joined at the front to make a 'corner' [i.e. in arrowhead formation]. It is the same arrangement that one observes among migratory birds.

Salmon

They usually make their ascent of the rivers at a slow pace and play games along the way. Their mode of travelling makes quite a noise. However, the moment they think themselves in danger, they move so fast that the eye cannot follow them; their speed is equalled only by flashes of lightning.

Neither dams nor small waterfalls halt their progress. They lie on their sides on stones, arch their bodies strongly, and then, straightening themselves out in a violent movement, are projected up into the air and pass over the obstacle. In this manner they make their way up the rivers, sometimes to a distance of eight hundred leagues from the sea-coast. The fishery for the salmon takes place between October and February.

Queue de saumon grillé · Grilled tail end of salmon

Clean the tail end of a salmon, put it on a plate and marinate it in a little olive oil, with fine salt, a bay leaf, parsley and spring onions cut in half. After it has been in the marinade, turn it over, using for this purpose the cover of a casserole, and put it in place on the grill. Baste it from time to time with the marinade. The cooking time will depend on the thickness of the piece. To check whether it is done, part the flesh slightly from the backbone; and if the flesh is still red let it cook further. When the cooking is completed, turn the piece of salmon over, using the cover of the casserole again, remove the skin, add a butter sauce to it and sprinkle over it either preserved capers or nasturtium flowers which have been kept in vinegar.

Saumon fumé · Smoked salmon

Take some smoked salmon and cut it into thin slices. Put some olive oil on a silver platter. Sauté your 'fillets'. When they are cooked, add the oil, sprinkle them with lemon juice and serve them. [This recipe is not clear, but has been translated to show that in the view of Dumas smoked salmon should be cooked before being eaten.]

SALSIFY   *SALSIFIS*

A root vegetable. There are two kinds, one grey, and the other, which is the better, black. They are scraped until white and thrown a few at a time into water which has a little vinegar in it. Then, when they are well washed, they are cooked in plenty of water with salt and vinegar. They can be crushed under the finger when they are cooked enough. One should then take them out, drain them, and serve them with a butter sauce.

To serve them fried, cook them in water to which a greater quantity of vinegar has been added, dip them in a good batter and fry them in butter in the usual way.

SAMPHIRE   *BACILE*

This is a plant which belongs to the umbelliferous species. It grows on the sea shore, amongst the rocks. I have picked it on all the shores of Normandy. The stems are tough, green and embellished with fleshy leaves. The folioles are narrow, the flowers white, with a salty, piquant and aromatic flavour, but for all that still very agreeable. The stems are preserved in vinegar and are eaten like gherkins and Indian pickles.

SANDWICHES   *SANDWICHS ou tartines à l'anglaise*

Take twenty-four very thin slices from close-grained, day-old bread and butter these. Put twelve on a white cloth, and cut slices of any of the following: lean roast veal, fillet of beef, roast beef, cooked ham, cold ox tongue, roast poultry, game, cured fish. Arrange these slices of meat on your twelve pieces of bread, sprinkle them with a little white salt, and then cover the meat with the other twelve slices of bread. Serve these at dinner as an hors-d'oeuvre; and as a light repast when taking tea.

SARDINE   *SARDINE*

A small marine fish with a delicate flavour. It is found all over the place, but especially off the coasts of Brittany, where it is very abundant. Thus the fishery for the sardine is a source of wealth to the Bretons. Records show that from the seventeenth century this fishery was producing an enormous revenue, and that in the town of Port-Louis alone 4,000 barrels of sardines were produced each year.

The sardine is also very abundant in the Mediterranean, especially in the waters around Sardinia, whence it takes its name.

Only people living on the coast can eat sardines fresh; and it is still necessary to salt them [i.e. all the catch, including what is to be eaten fresh] at once, since of all fishes this is the one which keeps least well. The sardine is barely out of the water before it dies, and putrefaction quickly assails it. The accumulation of such a large number of individual fish hastens their decomposition; so the fishermen take care, as they empty the sardines out of the nets, to mix a generous quantity of salt with them. Despite this precaution, enormous quantities of sardine spoil.

Sardines are cured, by salting them and smoking them, in the same way as herrings. The sardines from the north [of France] are much more highly esteemed than others, because aromatics and spices, which produce a very pleasant flavour, are added to the pickle. However, these sardines do not keep for long. When they spoil, they are used as bait in fishing for mackerel, whiting, rays and other marine fish.

Our good King Henri IV, who used to prize the titbits, seems to have had a particular liking for fresh sardines. After his act of abjuration, he usually made his lunch of them on fast days.

Pisanelli claims that the sardine likes the sound of musical instruments, and puts its head out of the water to listen to this.

Drinkers have an especial liking for sardines, for eating them excites their thirst and, so they say, makes them enjoy their wine.

Sardines en caisse · Sardines baked in a pastry case

Take some fresh sardines and cut off their heads and tails. [Gut them.] Put some fish stuffing in the bottom of a pastry case, arrange the sardines on this and cover them with more of the same stuffing. Mix in a beaten egg, sprinkle soft breadcrumbs on top, cover them with a sheet of cooking paper and bake the dish in the oven. Then drain off the fat, pour over the dish a clear *coulis* made without meat; and serve it when you need it as an hors d'oeuvre.

SAUCE   *SAUCE*

This is the name for a liquid seasoning, to which salt and mild spices are added, to bring out the flavour of certain dishes.

The methods of preparation vary greatly. We are going to give the recipes for those most used in cooking.

[Dumas gives 88 recipes, only two of which are attributed to any source. The arrangement is poor, no clear distinction being made between the basic sauces and the variations of them. In some instances instructions are repeated in two places, in a contradictory manner. Consistency in the nomenclature of the sauces is lacking, so that it is sometimes difficult to relate a reference to a sauce in another entry to any sauce given here. This whole section is of disappointing quality. We have therefore translated only a small number of the recipes, placing three basic preparations at the beginning and then proceeding in alphabetical order.]

Velouté, ou coulis blanc

Into a buttered casserole put a topside of veal, or a knuckle of veal, or part of a leg of veal, with some strips of ham, a spoonful of consommé, carrots and onions. Bring this to the boil over a good fire. When the liquid has reduced, and the solids are in danger of sticking to the casserole, add some more consommé, taking into account the amount of meat being used and the strength of the consommé. When all this has come to a good boil, draw it off the fire and add shallots and mushroom trimmings (but no lemon). Add also a well-seasoned bouquet, which you remove when cooked, pressing it between two spoons to extract all the flavours. Remove the meats likewise, when they are cooked.

While your sauce is cooking, prepare a white roux with which to thicken it. This is how you should go about it. Melt 500 grams of best quality butter and clarify it in a casserole. Add some wheat flour, of the finest quality, to the butter and stir until the flour has completely absorbed the butter. Next, put the casserole over a low flame and keep stirring so that the roux does not take colour. Watch it carefully and, once you think the flour is cooked, dilute either some or all of it with the velouté liquid [i.e. what you made in the preceding paragraph]. Continue to stir the mixture so that the flour does not fall to the bottom of the casserole and stick. Skim off the fat, strain the sauce, put it back on the fire, skim off the fat once more, reduce the sauce and remove it from the fire. Finally, put it in a container, sieved and strained.

Glace, ou Consommé réduit · Glaze, or reduced consommé

Take one or two knuckles of veal and—either in addition or as a substitute for them—the trimmings of a breast of veal or veal leftovers. Put all this in a newly tinned *marmite*, with four or five carrots, two or three onions, and a bouquet of parsley and shallots.

Sauce

Moisten it all with some first-class bouillon or other good stock. Skim the pot and add some cold water several times. Then put the pot on the side of the stove. When the meat comes off the bone, strain the consommé through a napkin which you have previously wrung out in cold water.

Let the consommé cool, clarify it, and then let it reduce until it has the consistency of a sauce, taking care to stir it all the time, since there is nothing more given to sticking and burning. Take care also, with this in mind, not to put it on too high a heat; this could darken it, whereas it ought to be of a beautiful golden colour and very transparent. Do not add salt; it will be salty enough.

This reduced consommé serves to give body to your sauces and ragoûts, which might otherwise lack it.

It is also used to glaze meats. You make a little brush with the tail feathers of old hens, removing the bristles and leaving only the ends of the feathers, about two inches in length. Arrange them evenly so that none protrudes more than another, and tie them together tightly. This will be your brush. Wash it in tepid water, squeeze it out and use it. But take care not to let it boil in your glaze, for fear that tufts of feather will then fall off into what you are preparing.

Espagnole

Line a casserole with some bacon and, even more important, with ham too, proceeding in this respect as for a *grande sauce* [i.e. you butter the casserole first and cut the bacon and ham into strips]. Put a knuckle of veal on top, with a spoonful of consommé, five or six carrots and onions. Bring to the boil as for an ordinary *coulis*, and then simmer until the veal has released its juices. When the process of reduction has produced the meat 'glaze', which you will recognize in the bottom of the casserole and which should be a beautiful yellow, take the casserole off the fire.

Stick a knife into the knuckle of veal, so that the remaining juices run out, and provide additional liquid in the form of consommé in which you have cooked a sufficient quantity of partridge, rabbit or chicken. Add a bouquet of parsley and shallots, two cloves, half a bay leaf, a clove of garlic, a little basil and thyme. Bring all this to the boil, then put it on the side of the fire and skim off the fat.

At the end of two hours, bind the espagnole sauce with a roux, as for an ordinary *coulis*. When it is bound in such a way as to be more light than thick, let it boil for half or three quarters of an hour, so that the roux is properly incorporated. Then skim off the fat, strain the espagnole through a sieve into another pan, and reduce it by a quarter.

The espagnole can be used for all brown ragoûts. You will add some madeira, champagne or burgundy, depending on which little sauce you require. My habit is not to put wine in the basic espagnole, given that wine does not go with everything (and that it can go off from one day to the next, if it has not been used up in one day, which would be wasteful).

Sauce à la béchamel

Put as much velouté as you need, and a little consommé, in a casserole. Let us suppose that you are using half a litre of velouté. Bring it to the boil on a high heat, stirring it carefully, and let it reduce in volume by one third. At the same time reduce a pint of double cream to one third of its volume. Then blend the cream, little by little, into the sauce and keep stirring until the sauce has been reduced to the same volume as it had before the cream was added.

Once the sauce has the consistency of a light gruel, wring it through a very white piece of cheese-cloth. Place it in a bain-marie before serving it.

Brède sauce · Bread sauce [not a sauce from Breda in the Netherlands, as one might imagine from the French spelling]

Take some breadcrumbs, moisten them with milk and let them cook for about three quarters of an hour, until the mixture has the consistency of a thick porridge. Add twenty grains of white pepper to this, and the right amount of salt. To finish it off, add a piece of best butter, the size of a nut.

Serve the sauce in a sauceboat, beside your pieces of venison.

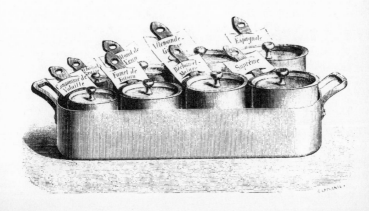

Sauce

Sauce italienne

Into a casserole put some chopped mushrooms, small cubes of ham and slices of lemon (free of pips). Add a tablespoonful of chopped shallots which, like the mushrooms, should have been washed and then squeezed dry in a cloth. Put in also half a bay leaf, two cloves and a quarter of a litre of oil.

Put the casserole on the fire. When you see that the lemon and other ingredients are nearly cooked, remove the lemon. Add a spoonful each of chopped parsley and of espagnole sauce, and half a litre of good white wine; also a little pepper. Reduce the sauce, skim off the fat, remove the ham and then, when the reduction of the sauce has been carried far enough, remove it from the fire.

[These instructions produce what Dumas calls a *sauce italienne rousse*, i.e. it is reddish-brownish in colour. He explains that a *sauce italienne blanche* is made in the same way, but using velouté instead of espagnole.]

Sauce à la maître d'hôtel froide · Cold maître d'hôtel sauce

Put a piece of butter in a casserole and add to it some chopped parsley, a few tarragon leaves, one or two leaves of balm, a sufficient quantity of fine salt and the juice of one or two lemons (or a trickle of verjuice). Blend all this together with a wooden spoon until it is thoroughly mixed.

Sauce piquante

Chop an onion and soften it in butter in a casserole, without allowing it to brown. Add half a glass of vinegar, a sprig of parsley, two bay leaves, a little thyme, pepper and a clove. Reduce the liquid by half; then add to the reduced liquid a glass of bouillon or meat juice and an equal amount of sugar. Bring the liquid back to the boil, and move it to the side of the fire [to simmer]. After a quarter of an hour, skim the fat off the sauce and strain it. Add to the strained sauce two table-spoonfuls of whole capers and an equal amount of chopped gherkin.

Sauce poivrade

Dice a slice of ham into twelve little cubes. Put these in a casserole with a piece of butter, five or six sprigs of parsley, two or three shallots cut in half, a clove of garlic, a bay leaf, a little basil, thyme and two cloves. Stir all this over a good flame and, when it has softened, add a pinch of pepper, with two tablespoonfuls of vinegar and eight of unreduced espagnole sauce. Stir the sauce, bring it to the boil, put it on the side of the stove to cook gently for three quarters of an hour, skim off the fat, strain it and serve it.

Sauce à la purée d'oseille · Sorrel sauce

Take two handfuls of sorrel, or more if required. Remove the stems, wash the sorrel, drain it and chop it very finely. Put it in a casserole with a piece of butter, which you allow to melt. When the sorrel is cooked, force it through a strainer and then return it to the casserole. Use the back of a knife to scrape off any purée left on the outside of the strainer [and return this to the casserole too].

Tip one or two spoonfuls of espagnole sauce into this preparation and let it cook for a further three quarters of an hour. Take care to keep stirring it, skim off any fat and add plenty of salt. Once the sauce has attained the consistency of a thick porridge, remove it from the fire and use it as required.

Sauce au suprême

Put two or three spoonfuls of reduced velouté into a casserole, with the same quantity of chicken consommé. Reduce all this to the volume of three spoonfuls of velouté. At the time when you are ready to use the sauce, put in a piece of butter the size of an egg, put the casserole over a lively flame, stir and then strain the sauce. It should be well bound without being too thick. When it is done, take it from the fire, add the juice of a lemon or a thread of verjuice, strain it again and use it as required.

Sauce tomate

Take ten to fifteen very ripe tomatoes, of a good red colour. Remove the stems, cut them in two with a knife and remove the seeds. Squeeze the tomatoes between your hands to remove the watery fluid which is to be found near their hearts This, like the seeds, should be discarded.

Put the tomatoes in a casserole with a piece of butter the size of an egg, a bay leaf and a little thyme Put the casserole on a moderate flame and stir the tomatoes until they turn into a purée. While they are cooking, add a spoonful of espagnole sauce or, better still, the fat part of some bouillon. When the tomatoes have reached the right consistency to make a purée, force them through a sieve, and scrape the outside of the sieve with the back of a knife. Put the result of this sieving into a casserole with two spoonfuls of espagnole sauce, and reduce it until it has the consistency of a thin porridge. Add salt to taste; and a little cayenne pepper from the tip of a knife.

[In addition to the above, the following sauces are given in the recipes to which they belong: *beurre noir* and *sauce à l'allemande* (both for calves' brains) on pages 295 and 294; *sauce anglaise* (for saddle of roast lamb), page 156; and *sauce bordelaise* (for mushrooms), page 181; and *sauce aux cerises* (for young wild boar), page 310. There is also a summary recipe for gooseberry sauce (for mackerel) on page 175. Dumas often refers to *sauce remoulade*, without giving a recipe for it. So we explain here that it is a mayonnaise to which mustard, chopped gherkin, capers, chopped spring onions, chervil, chopped tarragon and a little anchovy essence have been added. Dumas also refers often to *sauce à l'hollandaise*. His own recipe for this is not suitable for use, and readers are advised to use their own usual recipe.]

SAUSAGE   *SAUCISSES*

A mixture whose main ingredients are chopped meats, encased either in a piece of caul or in pork or mutton intestines.

and SAUCISSON

Chopped meat encased in the intestines of beef. There are towns whose reputation has been made by good sausages. There are Lyon sausages, Strasbourg sausages and sausages from Arles. But it must be confessed that the beauty of the women of Arles has done more for the reputation of that city than the juiciness of its sausages.

Grimod, in *The Three Musketeers*, owes one of his happiest exclamations to that word 'sausage', which leaps from his memory at the moment when he is passing the inn where, as a prisoner with Athos, he drank the cellar dry and turned the kitchen upside down.

SEA ANEMONE   *ACTINIE*

The *actinie* is popularly called *ortie de mer* (sea nettle) or *anémone de mer* (sea anemone), because of its resemblance to the nettle and the anemone. It consists of a highly contractible mass of flesh, crowned on top by a large number of tentacles. In the middle is an opening which serves both as mouth and as anus. The sea anemone fastens itself by its base either to the sand or to coastal rocks in shallow waters and sticks so fast that it has to be torn away rather than pulled off.

Sea anemones are very numerous on the shores of France, where their brilliant and varied colours often cause them to be mistaken for flowers.

The smell and flavour of the sea anemone are close to those of the crabs and shrimps, whose characteristics they share; and the inhabitants of the southern coasts of France seek it out and eat it with great pleasure. [Consumption of the sea anemone has dwindled since the days of Dumas. It is, however, still used by some people in the south of France to make a sea anemone soup, described on page 238 of my *Mediterranean Seafood* (Penguin, 1972). A.E.D.]

SEA BASS   *BAR*

A marine fish which resembles the familiar mullet. [See page 241. It is not easy to know what Dumas means by *mulet*. Here, however, he must mean the grey mullet, since it would be altogether too fanciful to compare the red mullet with the sea bass.] Those which do not exceed a weight of two or three kilos are very delicate fare; but the sea bass becomes tough and disagreeable to eat when it attains a weight of fifteen to twenty kilos. I caught one at Trouville which weighed twenty three kilos. It was leathery and had lost all its succulence.

There is only one way to eat this fish; that is to prepare it in a court-bouillon incorporating 125 grams of salted butter and five or six large sprigs of parsley with the roots left on. It is to be eaten with a hollandaise sauce.

SEA URCHIN   *OURSIN*

A round shellfish, which is also called *châtaigne de mer* (sea chestnut), since its appearance is exactly like that of a chestnut still enclosed in its prickly shell. Its prickles serve it as feet and, when they become worn down, the animal rolls along like a billiard ball.

When you open this crustacean [echinoderm would be the correct expression, since the sea urchin belongs to a class of creature quite separate from the crustaceans] you find a little red animal, of a salty flavour, who is the owner of the house. Its eggs, which are dark yellow, are attached to the interior walls of the shell. Those who are not disgusted by this sort of living purée eat them as they would an egg, with sippets.

The best sea urchins are those of the Mediterranean. They anticipate storms and withstand them by attaching themselves to the strongest marine plants. They excrete by means of the tiny vents, of which more than twelve thousand have been counted, in their spines.

SHAD   *ALOSE*

The shad is an excellent marine fish which ascends rivers at a certain time of year. It is during this journey that the shad loses its unduly strong saltiness and becomes fatter.

Shad which are presented as a *rôt* are not scaled. They are cooked in a court-bouillon like salmon or Rhine carp, and served on a platter decorated with green parsley and grated horseradish.

For an entrée, the shad are scaled and presented with various sauces; sorrel, tomato or caper. The best way is as follows:

Alose à l'oseille · Shad with sorrel

Scale, gut and wash your shad. Garnish it with fines herbes, wrap it up in buttered cooking paper, cook it on the grill and serve it on a bed of cooked sorrel or in a generous quantity of maître d'hôtel sauce. [See page 256 for a cold maître-d'hôtel sauce. The hot version is made by warming the mixture there described with some velouté.]

SHALLOTS   *ECHALOTES*

The Latin name of the shallot is *ascalonia*. This word is an indication of its provenance; it travelled from Syria to Europe with the crusades.

Like onion and garlic, the shallot is used in sauces; but it brings to them a flavour all of its own which is more delicate than that of the other two condiments which we have just named.

So the shallot is excellent in oil and vinegar based sauces with which artichokes are eaten, either hot or cold. It is impossible to make a good piquant sauce without shallots.

SHARK *REQUIN*

[Dumas has nothing to say about the sharks themselves, but gives the following extraordinary recipe under this heading.]

Croustade de squalles de l'estomac de jeunes requins ·

Shark pie made from the stomachs of young sharks

Take 15 stomachs of young sharks, soak them for 24 hours, then drain them and blanch them for 20 minutes in lightly salted water. Drain them again, rinse them in fresh water and sponge them dry with a cloth.

Line a casserole with strips of bacon and put in your pieces of shark. Add a bay leaf from the Indies, two cloves and three slices of lemon, peeled and pipped. Moisten the dish with a ladleful of good chicken consommé and 3 ounces of butter, and cook all this over a low heat until done.

When you come to serve the dish, make a sauce with a ladleful of *sauce au suprême* [see page 257], a tablespoonful of *sauce soubise* [an onion sauce], and two good pinches of Indian curry; and make sure that when your sauce is reduced it is not too thick.

Now drain your pieces of shark, dip them in the sauce and arrange them in your pie-case.

For people who like shark, or who might imagine themselves eating some, we recommend this recipe. It was given to us by M. Duglerez, chef of the Rothschild household, to whom we are already indebted for several recipes of this kind. However, we state in advance that we cannot give our opinion on this dish, since we have never eaten it and have no wish to do so.

The flesh of the shark is hard, tough, lean, glutinous and difficult to digest; but this does not prevent the Icelanders and the Norwegians from drying it and then cooking and eating it. We recommend to them the recipe given above.

SHRIMPS *CREVETTES*

Everyone is familiar with this little crustacean, which is to be seen on all well-furnished tables but which seems to be there as an ornament rather than for use.

There is no prettier sight than shrimps swimming in a bowl. The creatures themselves are transparent, like the glass enclosing them;

Shrimps

and you see everything inside them, even the beating of the heart.

It is usually women who fish for shrimps, pushing in front of them a net which scrapes along the sea-bed and collects everything to be found thereon.

The shrimp lives for hardly two hours out of its element and needs to be cooked while still alive.

The flesh of a live shrimp seems clammy, but after being cooked it is firm and beautifully white.

The shrimps from the Channel coast are renowned, especially those from the vicinity of Le Havre, which bear the name *bouquet*. We invite tourists who are staying at Le Havre or Étretat to go and eat shrimps at Saint-Jourt, at the establishment of the beautiful Ernestine. She is wise as well as beautiful, twenty-eight years old, owns a hotel and has a reputation which extends all along the coast. At her place you eat the finest shrimps which are fished for ten leagues around. It is the rendezvous for the gourmands of Le Havre, and for painters and poets from Paris, who have left respectively drawings and verses in her album, in praise of her.

When they are to be eaten on the spot, shrimps are simply thrown alive into a casserole full of boiling sea water, to which a thread of vinegar has been added. When they are to be sent to Paris, the shrimps are plunged alive into a cauldron of fresh water, with one kilogram of salt for each four kilograms of shrimps. They are left to boil for five minutes, then taken out and rinsed in cold unsalted water, which does just as much to give them a good appearance as to preserve their flavour.

Potage à la crevette · Shrimp soup

Take six fine tomatoes and six white onions and make a purée of them, half and half. Cook your shrimps in white wine with salt and pepper and a little cayenne pepper. Then peel the tails of the shrimps and put them aside on a plate, about a hundred of them. Keep the bodies and boil them further with the seasoning used in cooking the shrimps, then pound them, bring them back to the boil and pass them through a fine strainer.

Now divide into three equal parts the excellent broth, the shrimp bisque and the purée of tomatoes and onions. Mix them together and bring them to the boil three or four times in order to amalgamate thoroughly the three things. Taste the mixture. If it has been well made and leaves nothing to be desired, throw in your shrimp tails and serve the soup boiling hot.

SMELT   *ÉPERLAN*

The smelt is one of the most delicate fish that one can eat.

Éperlans frits · Fried smelts

Take a sufficient quantity of smelts, gut, scale and wipe them dry one
after the other, then thread them through the eyes on to skewers or
brochettes. Dip them in milk, flour them and fry them until they
have taken on a good colour. Lay a napkin on your serving platter,
dispose the fish thereon and serve them.

SNAILS   *ESCARGOTS*

A large terrestrial gastropod mollusc with a grey shell. The only
distinction which gourmands make between snails depends on the
place where they are collected. Those from vineyards are the most
sought after and the best. The Romans were so partial to them that
they fattened them in *viviers* specially constructed for this purpose.
The snails were fed on wheat and apéritif wines to make them easier
to digest.

Snails should be highly seasoned. A bouillon which is very calming
to consumptives is also made with snails. In several French towns,
particularly in Nancy, they are cooked and eaten like oysters are in
Paris.

Escargots à la provençale

Take three dozen snails and let them soak in a container filled with
cold water, after which you scrub them with a couch-grass brush.
During this time boil enough water in a cauldron to blanch them.
Make a sachet with a handful of sieved wood cinders, tie it with a
string, toss it in the boiling water and let it boil for a quarter of an
hour. When this period has elapsed, toss in the snails and leave them
until it is easy to withdraw the meat from the shells. Twelve or fifteen
minutes later, put them back in cold water in order to take them out
of their carapaces. Put them back in tepid water as you do this.

In a casserole you will have put two spoonfuls of good oil, parsley,
mushrooms, shallots, half a grated clove of garlic, salt, grated nutmeg,
and finally a little green pepper. When these fines herbes are well
softened, add half a spoonful of flour and moisten with a glass of

263

Snails

good white wine. As soon as this sauce starts to bubble, add the
well-drained snails, and let them finish cooking, simmering gently.
The sauce must not be allowed to separate. At this point add the raw
yolks of three eggs. Then fill the shells,* covering them with bread
crumbs. Sprinkle with oil, and put them for a quarter of an hour in
the oven. Serve them while they are still bubbling.

SOLE   *SOLE*

The best soles are those of a linen-grey colour, which are found in the
waters near Dieppe. Soles fished at Calais or Roscoff are distinctly
inferior to these.

Soles au four · Baked soles

Split your soles down the back, lift up the flesh on each side of the
cut, and stuff the back with fines herbes which have been chopped,
fried in butter and allowed to cool. Lay a piece of butter in the bottom
of your dish, and place the soles on it, backs down. Use a feather
dipped in melted butter to give them a golden colour, sprinkle a little
fine salt over them and *fines épices*, then cover them with fine breadcrumbs, moisten them with a little white wine or bouillon and cook
them in the oven.

Filets de sole à la Orly

Clean and gut your soles, split them along the back from head to tail
and lift off the four fillets from each. Trim the fillets and let them
marinate in a terrine with fine salt, sprigs of parsley, chives, sliced

* The instructions are abbreviated. The meaning is that a snail and some sauce
should be placed in each shell.

onion and the juice of one or more lemons. Move them around in the marinade from time to time. They should stay in it for about three quarters of an hour. Just before serving them, drain them, flour them and fry them until they are firm and of a good colour. Arrange them on your platter and pour over them an Italian tomato sauce, also known as *Sauce tomate lisse* [see page 257].

SOUP   *POTAGE*

The name soup is applied to every food whose destiny is to be served in a soup tureen at the beginning of a meal.

During the season of tomatoes, I advise you to make a soup invented by myself. I refer to the soup made with mussels or *praires* [clams of the species *Venus verrucosa*, for which there is no commonly used English name—but other clams would do].

Soupe aux moules · Mussel soup

At eleven o'clock in the morning you must put on your stove a *pot-au-feu* composed in the manner I have already explained [see page 75], but in a small quantity since, as you will see, the resulting bouillon will only account for a third of the soup.

At four o'clock in the afternoon, put a dozen tomatoes and a dozen white onions in a casserole [with water] and let them boil for an hour. Then pass all this through a strainer fine enough to catch the tomato seeds. Season the tomato purée, add a piece of meat jelly weighing three or four ounces, and let the purée reduce and thicken over a very low flame.

Next, put your mussels or clams [in a pot] on the fire, without adding any water. [The mussels or clams will of course still be in their shells, which will have been scrubbed clean.] After a quarter of an hour [or less] they will have opened and yielded their juices. Combine the bouillon, the tomato purée and the [strained] mussel juices.

Now take a large casserole and crush in the bottom of it, with the tip of a knife, half a clove of garlic. Add a little olive oil and let the garlic take colour in this. Then add, gently and with constant stirring, your triple bouillon mixture and cook the whole over a strong flame for a quarter of an hour, until the various heterogeneous elements have been homogenized. At this point, toss in your mussels or clams.

[Dumas also explains that this recipe can be modified to make a shrimp or crayfish soup. He apologizes for giving the instructions in detail, explaining that he is writing here for novices rather than for professional cooks. Most of the other soup recipes which he gives are from other authors or in summary form; but the recipe for onion soup is presented as another of his own.]

Soupe à l'oignon · Onion soup

There are two kinds of onion; the white onion of Spain and the small red one of Florence. The larger, the white Spanish onion, contains a lot of sugary matter, together with a vegeto-animal substance and an element of phosphorus. This onion is not only pleasing to the taste because of its sugar content, but also nourishing because of the vegeto-animal substance and stimulating because of the phosphorus. So this is the onion to be used in soups for hunts-men and drunkards, two classes of people who stand in need of restoration.

Take twenty large onions and chop them very finely. Brown them in a pan with a pound of butter. When they are well browned, pour in three litres of freshly drawn milk (any other kind would 'turn') and let the onions boil in this milk. Then pass everything through a tamis [the kind of strainer illustrated on page 30] so as to produce a purée. Salt and pepper this, add six egg-yolks to bind it, pour the soup over toasted crusts of bread: and there you are!

[Soup recipes given in other entries include *Chou en garbure* (page 85), *Potage aux carottes* (page 91), *Soupe aux cerises à l'allemande* (page 96), *Potage aux tomates et aux queues de crevettes* (page 168), *Soupe à l'oignon à la Stanislas* (page 198) and *Potage à la crevette* (page 262).]

SPINACH   *ÉPINARDS*

A comestible plant, belonging to the orach family, whose leaves are
eaten when cooked.

Lots of jokes are made about spinach, which they say has no
nutritional properties, and which has been styled the stomach's
broom. This is wrong. Spinach, on the contrary, is nutritious and
pleasing to the stomach, for which it is not the broom, if I may use
such an expression, except in the sense that it so suits this organ that
it is digested with remarkable ease.

There are various ways of preparing spinach and we are going to
indicate those which we think the best.

Épinards à la vieille mode · Spinach cooked the old-fashioned way

Once you have blanched and chopped the spinach, you put it in a
casserole with butter and grated nutmeg. When it has been turned in
this, add butter which has been worked with flour, sugar and milk.
Then serve it with a garnish of croûtons fried in butter.

Épinards à l'anglaise · Spinach the English way

Boil water in a cauldron to which you have added a handful of rock
salt. Add the spinach, which you have carefully picked over, washed
and blanched. When it has been cooked in the salted water, chop it
and put it in a casserole with salt and pepper. Stir well, and when it is
hot add a good piece of butter and mix this in well. Serve with fried
croûtons.

SPINY LOBSTER (or CRAWFISH)   *LANGOUSTE*

This crustacean differs from the lobster in having a less delicate
flavour and in lacking the large claws which fishermen call the
lobster's *mordants*. Spiny lobsters are cooked in a court-bouillon and
eaten with a remoulade sauce incorporating capers, or with a mayonnaise made with lemon juice and olive oil.

SPUR-DOG   *AIGUILLAT*

A species of fish popularly known as *chien de mer* (dog of the sea, or dogfish). It has the form of a conger eel. It is found on the Atlantic coast, where specimens weighing more than 10 kilos have been caught. Its flesh is fibrous and tough, and its flavour is not very agreeable. [Dumas makes no mention of other dogfish which are better known in the markets, such as the *Grande roussette* and the *Petite roussette*, the *Émissole*, the *Milandre*, etc. His comparison between the spur-dog and the conger eel is inappropriate; the two creatures are quite dissimilar.]

When I was still at Roscoff, my secretary went fishing one morning with my barber. In the net which they had set on the previous day they found forty-two of these fish, of which the lightest weighed more than 5 kilos, together with two or three red mullet which had been half eaten by their voracious companions in captivity. This catch, which at first sight seemed quite good, turned out to be useless, since, not knowing what to do with these fish and not being able to eat them, they had to take them to the lobster-park, where they provided a tasty meal for the fifteen or eighteen thousand lobsters which were living in it.

STERLET   *STERLET*

There exists in Russia a fish for which the Russians have a predilection similar to that which the Romans had for the red mullet and the gilt-head bream.

We know that at Rome the *amphitryon* (host) would habitually exhibit alive the gilt-head bream and red mullet which were to be served for dinner. Now, as the distance between Rome and the place where the fish were caught was twelve leagues (about 33 miles), relays of running slaves used to carry them, without a change of water, and almost always arrived just in time for the guests to see the gold, purple and azure colours of the fishes' scales fade in their death agonies.

The same situation, but much worse, prevailed in Russia, when the host was offering sterlet to his friends. The sterlet, or small sturgeon (*Acipenser rethenus* [properly *ruthenus*]), was a dish which the seigneurs of Saint Petersburg and the noblemen of Moscow thought incomparable. In their eyes the large, ordinary sturgeon deserved esteem only as a source of caviar.

Before there were railways in Russia, it was sometimes necessary to make a sterlet travel two or three hundred leagues (about a thousand miles) to have the honour of being served at the table of a prince. Now, during the icy perods of winter, when the barometer is at 30 or 32 degrees below zero, and it is necessary to make a fish cover two or three hundred leagues in the same water, at a temperature equal to zero, the task is a difficult one; for it is necessary to reheat the water to the extent and at the rate at which it grows colder. So people had special carriages for the exclusive purpose of transporting sterlets, and it would sometimes happen that a simple sterlet soup, if two or three of the fish were used in making it, would cost from 6,000 to 8,000 francs.

STEWS   *RAGOÛTS*

Stews, above all, were responsible for the brilliance of old French cookery; yet it is stews which bring disgrace on contemporary cuisines, especially that of England.

Never will a cuisine other than our own attain the heights reached by our piquant sauces, or the delicacy of our *blanquettes* or our *poulettes*. [See pages 32 and 34 for the meaning of these terms.]

In the same way, you can take a trip around the world, and you will not find a cook, be he cordon rouge or cordon bleu, who can make you an omelette as good as that made by the mother of a family for her husband's and children's dinner.

First of all, a word about the *salpicons* [see page 35].

These fillings are made with all sorts of meats and vegetables, such as sweetbreads, truffles, mushrooms, artichoke hearts, etc. But if they are to be good, the meats and vegetables used (which should be in equal proportions) must be cooked separately. In this way they can all be cooked to the same extent, according to their nature.

Salpicon ordinaire · An ordinary salpicon

This is made of veal sweetbreads, *foie-gras*, or *demi-gras*, ham, mushrooms and truffles, if they are in season. Dice these into small cubes of the same size. Have ready an espagnole sauce which has been considerably reduced; the quantity to be sufficient for your meat and vegetables. When you are ready, put it all on the stove, stir it without allowing it to boil, and then serve.

One makes this filling in the same way for *quenelles* (forcemeat balls) or a *godiveau* (forcemeat pie) or when using the white meat of spit-roasted poultry, cocks' combs or artichoke hearts. It depends on what is available and what is the season.

Stews

Ragoût de céleri · Celery stew (Recipe of Dr Rocques)

Cook some chopped celery and endive and spinach. Season with pepper, salt and nutmeg, moisten with some good bouillon and serve with golden croûtons. If you are rather partial to them, you can even put a few ortolans or a few fillets of red partridge on this delicate bed. Taste this dish, dear companions in gourmandise, and perhaps you will be satisfied with it.

Ragoût de haricots à la bretonne ·
                Stewed haricot beans as they are prepared in Britanny

Take some beans from Soissons; it doesn't matter whether they are fresh or dried. Pick them over, and wash a litre of them. Put them in a *marmite* with cold water and a piece of unsalted butter. Heat, adding a little cold water from time to time, which will halt the boiling and make the beans softer. When they are cooked, drain them, and put them in a casserole with a bit of butter, one or two spoonfuls of puréed onions in a brown sauce and some espagnole sauce. Season with coarsely ground pepper and salt, sauté them frequently, and finish them with a pat of butter.

STURGEON   *ESTURGEON*

[Dumas begins this entry by remarking that he has already described the sturgeon in his entry on Caviar. This is so. The entry on Caviar, which is oddly sub-titled '*sorte d'esturgeon*', is almost entirely devoted to the fish rather than to its eggs, which constitute caviar. To mitigate the confusion we have combined here all that Dumas has to say about the sturgeon itself in the two entries. We should add, however, that he has yet a third entry, headed Kaviar, in which he remarks that kaviar or caviar—the spellings are given as alternatives—'has the particular virtue of disposing the stomach to food, and for those who like it replaces soup'; an opinion which he attributes to 'the illustrious Meyerbeer'. That is all he says.]

The sturgeon is one of the largest river fish. It weighs up to three or four hundred pounds. In France it has been a rare fish, and very highly esteemed.

    In 1833 I gave a masked ball, which some of my contemporaries will remember, at which were served a whole roast roebuck and a whole sturgeon cooked in a court-bouillon. The roebuck was eaten up, down to the very bones; but, although there were four hundred people taking supper on this occasion, they could not finish off the sturgeon.

*

One day, the Archichancelier Cambacérès, who was competing with Murat, Junot, M. de Cussy and M. de Talleyrand for supremacy at the dining table, received—and this was the very day of a big dinner which he was giving—two monstrous sturgeons, one of which weighed 162 pounds and the other 187.

The butler thought that he had better consult His Highness about this unusual situation. If both sturgeons were served, it was clear that the second would spoil the effect of the first. But if only one was served, the other would be a write-off, since it was out of the question to serve two fish of the same species on two successive evenings to His Highness' guests.

Cambacérès closeted himself with his butler. A quarter of an hour later the latter emerged from His Highness' study, with a beam on his face. They had indeed found an expedient which would permit them, if not to serve both fish, at least to show them both; an expedient which involved sacrificing the first fish in honour of the second, and doing so in such a way as to bring honour to His Highness' table.

Here is the plan which the two of them had worked out.

The sturgeon was to be served as a *relevé du potage*. The smaller of the two fish was laid on a bed of leaves and flowers, and a concerto of violins and flutes announced its entry. The flautist, fully garbed in a chef's costume and followed by two violinists similarly clad, preceded the sturgeon, which came in accompanied by four footmen bearing torches, two kitchen assistants with knives at their sides, and the head porter at the head of the group, holding his halberd. The

sturgeon rested on a small ladder of about eight or ten feet in length, which was supported at its two ends on the shoulders of the two kitchen assistants. The procession began to make its way round the table, to the sound of the violins and the flute and cries of admiration from the guests. Its appearance was so unexpected that these guests quite forgot the respect which they owed to their host, and each climbed up on his chair to have a view of the huge fish.

However, when the tour of the table had been completed, at the moment when the fish was to be taken away, to the accompaniment of applause from the whole gathering, in order to be carved up, one of the porters stumbled and fell on his knee, while the fish for its part slipped downwards from the ladder and fell on to the floor.

A prolonged cry of despair issued from the heart, or rather from the stomach, of everyone present. There was a moment of confusion, during which each person gave his view on what should be done; but the voice of Cambacérès subdued the tumult and he said, with the simple dignity of an ancient Roman: 'Serve the other one'.

Then a second procession was seen coming in, just like the first one except that there were two flautists, four violinists and four footmen. At this, the cries of anguish gave way to applause; and the first fish, which weighed 25 pounds less than the second one, was whisked out of sight.

*

I was present during a period of a month at the caviar fishery on the shores of the Caspian Sea, right along its coastline from the Ural to the Volga. There is nothing more strange than this fishery, in which thousands of fish weighing 300 pounds and twelve to fifteen feet long are killed in a period of six weeks to two months.

In the Danube sturgeon are found which are as much as twenty feet long; they come from the Black Sea and go upstream, in order to spawn, as far as Baden.

The flesh of the caviar [that is to say, of the caviar-producing sturgeon] has a delicate flavour, such as one rarely finds in a cartilaginous fish. It can easily be passed off as veal. We must, however, admit that the nations of today do not show the same enthusiasm for this flesh as did the peoples of classical times. The latter used to garland with flowers not only the sturgeon but also those who served it and those who brought it to table to the sound of flutes. In Greece, according to Athenaeus, the sturgeon was regarded as the best fish for a banquet.

The sturgeon is found in the Atlantic, the Mediterranean, the Red Sea and all the great rivers. It was so common in Provence in the sixteenth century that it was only worth one sou per pound.

The sturgeon grows and becomes fat in the rivers, where it finds the calm conditions, the temperature and the foods which suit it.

In Russia, which is where most of the fishery for the sturgeon takes place, the fish are taken at the time when they are trying to return upstream in the Volga and the Ural rivers. One can form a good idea of the intelligence of the fish from the way in which it is caught. The rivers are closed off by means of barricades, which is all the easier as they are not deep. The sturgeons arrive in shoals of a thousand or two thousand to make their way upstream. Being unable to do this, they swim along in front of the obstruction. Devices like large hooks have been suspended there, at depths of two, three or four feet below the surface of the water, from lines running across the river. Some of the hooks are baited, but that has never seemed to me to be necessary. The fish, in swimming to and fro, come up against an obstacle which they try to push aside; the obstacle pierces their flesh, and they are taken. Men in boats, passing between the lines formed by the beams which are placed crossways in the river, collect the sturgeons which have been caught. When a boat is full, it is taken to the slaughter-house, a real slaughter-house where two or three thousand sturgeons are killed every day by blows from a hammer or sledge-hammer.

The sturgeon, although it is a powerful creature and capable of knocking over even the strongest of men with a blow from its tail, offers no resistance. All it does is to utter a cry when its spinal cord is torn from it. At this moment it leaps four or five feet into the air, then falls down dead.

Pies which are highly esteemed are made with this spinal cord, which is called *visigha*. But what are esteemed even more than these pies are the thousands of eggs which are collected to make *caviar*, a name which is applied especially to a preparation of sturgeon eggs. If they are not exposed to the air, the eggs keep fresh for several days. Apart from these, which are sent off on the same day as they are sealed up in barrels (like our powder barrels, of eight, fifteen and twenty pounds), there are the eggs which are half-salted or fully salted and also despatched in due course.

Sturgeons grow to an enormous size. One was caught in 1769 which was twenty metres long, weighed 1,155 kilograms and yielded 3,030 kilograms of eggs. Having made calculations, people reckoned that the number of eggs was 30,412,860. Henri Cloquet says that sturgeons weighing 1,400 kilograms and measuring thirteen metres are often caught.* The winter fishery takes place in January, with much ceremony. That is the fishery which I witnessed. The date for its commencement is fixed in public assembly. Letters of convocation are sent out and the people assemble ahead of time at the appointed place. One person is designated head of the fishery. Before the fishers set out, he reviews them and their equipment, which consists of a steel hook fixed to a long rod. At sunrise two cannon shots give the signal for setting off; and whoever arrives first has the best position. A volley of muskets announces the start of the actual fishing.

However, to my great astonishment and that of the fishermen too, what we found when we arrived at the shore, was that neither the Volga nor the Caspian Sea were frozen. We beheld, on the contrary, all the arrangements for the summer fishery, which had continued when people saw that the ice was not forming. So it is the summer fishery which I have described, the summer fishery being what I in fact saw.

Esturgeon aux fines herbes

Take a sturgeon of good size [i.e. measuring one or two metres, not a giant of the sort referred to above] and cut it into slices as thick as a finger. Put these slices in a casserole with melted pork fat, salt and pepper, fines herbes, parsley and chopped spring onion, and let them cook and absorb flavour for an hour or two. Then stir them around well, coat them with fine dry breadcrumbs, grill them and serve them on a napkin with a piquant sauce or a remoulade sauce [see page 256 for the former and page 258 for the latter].

SWAN, SWAN PÂTÉ   *CYGNE, PÂTE DÉ CYGNE*

Swans, which several naturalists have classified among the ducks, are placed by Cuvier, to the contrary, in a distinct genus of the order of

---

* Something has gone wrong with the figures in this paragraph. A sturgeon which weighed 1,155 kilograms could not have contained eggs weighing more than twice as much! Official Iranian figures about the yield of eggs from the beluga sturgeon (the largest species) show that the weight of the eggs in a female is usually about one fifth of the total weight of the fish. The largest beluga sturgeon which is recorded as having been taken in the Iranian waters of the Caspian Sea weighed 850 kilograms in all and was 4 metres 20 centimetres long. The Iranian authorities believe, however, that very much larger sturgeons may have been taken in the past and even refer to the possibility of one weighing 1,600 kilograms.

palmipeds. Of all birds, the swan is the one whose neck is composed of the largest number of vertebrae. It has twenty-three of these; eleven dorsal, fourteen sacral and three caudal.

The domestic swan has an elegant build which does not permit any confusion between it and the goose or the duck, to which it is nevertheless so close. One single anomaly causes ornithologists to turn their eyes, or rather their ears, to the swan; and that because the naturalists have given to this animal the name *Cygnus musicus*. Now, whoever has heard the famous song of the swan will avow that it is the most disagreeable of sounds. The swan's song is an expression which one must accept on poetical grounds, and not because of its truth. The swan has maintained its position as virtuoso because of the admirable role it plays throughout *Lohengrin*; but from the culinary point of view none of this would earn it any standing, if the meat of the young swan, and especially the wild swan, was not more tender and more delicious than that of our best palmipeds. Pâtés are made of swan in the same manner as the pâtés from Amiens.

TARRAGON   *ESTRAGON*

An aromatic plant, originally from Siberia and much cultivated in gardens. It is used as a seasoning and is preserved in vinegar. Everyone knows how often it is used in sauces.

I would even add that there is no good vinegar without tarragon; and I invite the reader to put it in his vinegar.

TEA   *THÉ*

It was in 1666, in the middle of the reign of Louis XIV, that tea was introduced into France. Its introduction was opposed no less vigorously than had been that of coffee.

Today, in England and France alone, consumption of tea accounts for more than twenty million pounds sterling. There are seven or eight kinds of tea, but we consume scarcely any but three sorts: pearly tea, whose leaf is rolled up; souchong tea, whose leaves are dark green, even a little black, and well rolled; and finally pekoe tea, with white tips, which is the one with the most aromatic and pleasant smell.

[Dumas' classification of the various teas is difficult to follow, since he employs three different and overlapping systems. The possibilities of confusion can be demonstrated by observing that it would in principle be possible to market a 'pearl soochong Pekoe' tea!]

Besides those listed above, there are five or six other types of tea. There is yellow tea, which is worth from thirty to forty francs a pound in Russia. A single cup is usually drunk after dinner, in the same way as coffee. There is also *camphon* tea, which means tea from selected leaves; it is in fact made up of the best leaves, delicate and of good size, of *bonni* tea. It is greatly preferable to all others, but it is very rare.

Green tea is rarely used in France. It is lightly endowed with a property which is more or less intoxicating and which manifests itself by its effect on the nerves when it is drunk too strong or in too large quantities.

The best tea is drunk at St Petersburg, and in general throughout all Russia. As Siberia confines Russia from China, tea does not have to cross the sea to arrive in Moscow or St Petersburg; sea voyages are very detrimental to tea.

Because of a custom peculiar to Russia, which foreigners find oddly shocking when they first meet it, men drink tea from glasses, while women use cups from China. Here is the legend which relates to this custom. The first tea cups were made in Cronstadt. Now it often happened in cafés that, as an economy measure, less tea was put in the teapot than should have been. So, as there was a picture of Cronstadt in the bottom of the cup, which was much too visible because of the transparency of the liquid, the tea-drinker would call the café proprietor, show him the bottom of the cup and say to him: 'You can see Cronstadt'. The cafe proprietor could not deny that one could see Cronstadt; and since, if the tea had been as strong as it should have been, the view of Cronstadt would have been obscured, he was caught in the very act of fraud. Realizing this, the shopkeeper had the idea of substituting glasses, with transparent bases, for the cups in which one could see Cronstadt.

Tea loses its fragrance easily and is just as easily contaminated by a disagreeable smell. It is therefore important, in order to keep tea in good condition, that it should be kept in porcelain caddies.

Tea is made by being infused. A suitable quantity is put in a tea pot, and half a cup of boiling water is poured over it. After waiting until the leaves have swollen, one then finishes filling up the tea pot.

It is the mistress of the house who puts the tea in the teapot, and puts in the sugar, a whisp of cream, a slice of lemon or a drop of cognac and who takes responsibility for the tea which she offers to her guests.

THRUSHES and BLACKBIRDS *GRIVES et MERLES*

Thrushes and blackbirds and many other birds should only be eaten at the end of November. First of all they fatten in the fields and vineyards, then go to the edges of woods to sweeten their flesh by eating juniper berries. If you are in too much of a hurry to enjoy them, and if you kill them before the right time, you will not find that flavour, that sharp aroma, which is so highly esteemed by real epicures.

Horace, Martial and even Gallienus all recognize the worth of thrushes.

'*Nil melius turdo*', said Horace. The favourite of Augustus and Maecenas ate as many as he wanted, not because he was rich enough to buy them every day—his moderate fortune did not stretch to that —but because banquets were given in his honour everywhere.

Poor Martial, on the other hand, was often on slim rations, and when he was taken by surprise by an invitation to dinner, his eyes sparkled with joy and he said to himself: 'There will probably be thrushes.'

Lucius Apicius and all the famous gourmands in Rome esteemed them greatly. They fattened them in huge aviaries along with blackbirds. Each of these aviaries contained three or four thousand. The thrushes within were unable to see the woods and fields, so that nothing could distract them from the desire to fatten themselves.

Varro cites one country house where they had fattened five thousand thrushes in one year. They were served at the most sumptuous banquets, and were given to convalescents to help them get their strength back.

Grives en ragoût · Ragoût of thrushes

Trim the thrushes appropriately, turn them in a casserole with melted bacon fat, a little flour to bind the sauce well, a glass of white wine, salt, pepper and a bouquet garni. Let it all simmer for a while, and serve with a little lemon.

TOMATOES *TOMATES*

A fruit which comes to us from the people of the south, who treat it with honour. Its flesh is eaten in purée form and its sweet juice is used as a seasoning.

TONGUE   *LANGUE*

Almost all the practitioners who have written about cooking have
advanced the theory that the tongue is the part of the animal which
is superior in taste to all other parts. They regarded ox tongue as an
exception to this rule; yet it was so esteemed in the reign of Louis XII
that a feudal right existed in certain parts of France whereby the
tongues of all oxen which were slaughtered belonged to the local
squire.

Langue de bœuf à la braise · Braised ox tongue

Take an ox tongue and cut away the larynx. Leave it in water for two
or three hours or more, to soak clean, then remove it and scrape it
well with a knife to remove any dirt. Blanch it in a cauldron or a large
pot with onions and carrots; moisten it with some good bouillon and
a glass of white wine; and put in a few trimmings of butcher's meat,
poultry or game so as to give it more flavour. Bring all this to the
boil, then lower the heat and cover the tongue with paper and a lid,
with some coals on the lid. Let it simmer for four and a half hours.

Arrange the tongue on a platter, surrounding it with the vegetables
which you have cooked with it. Strain the cooking liquid through a
silk sieve and add one or two spoonfuls of espagnole sauce. Pour this
sauce over the tongue, and serve.

TRIPE   *TRIPE*

Préparation de la Tripe de Bœuf · The preparation of beef tripe

Seven cities have claimed the honour of being Homer's birth place;
France and Italy argue about who had the honour of discovering how
to prepare beef tripe. For my part, if I had the right to do so, I would
abandon any claim which France might make in this respect. But
duties are imposed on us, and we do not concede our claim on this
score to the inhabitants of Milan.

Scrub and wash the tripe in an ocean of water. Next cut it into
pieces of three fingers' width, boil it with a bouquet of parsley and
thyme, adding butter and garlic, salt, pepper and three or four large
onions. Boil all this for two good hours, then remove the pieces of
tripe from the cooking water and drain them. It is customary to cook
tripe thus before proceeding to whatever particular recipe has been
chosen.

Tripe de Bœuf à la lyonnaise (Recipe of Lucotte)

Fry a dozen onions, cut in quarters, in butter. When they are a good gold colour, put in a spoonful of flour, cook the sauce for a moment and add a bottle of white wine, mushrooms, salt and pepper. Let the tripe cook in the sauce over a low light and then, just before eating it, add lemon juice.

TROUT   *TRUITE*

There are several species of trout, some white, the others with a rosy tint, and of different sizes.

The trout is the fish which most closely resembles the salmon. The best trout are those with reddish flesh, which are called salmon-trout for this reason. Some natural historians claim that this salmon-like colour is something which the fish acquire for themselves by eating crayfish. [The claim was correct, in that both salmon and salmon-trout owe the reddish tint of their flesh to the crustaceans which they eat and from which they absorb a caryatid pigment. But freshwater crayfish are not an important source of this. Prawns and shrimps eaten at sea provide most of it. Nowadays, the same effect can be produced by adding paprika, which contains the same caryatid pigment, to the diet of freshwater trout being reared in trout-farms.]

The trout most highly esteemed in Paris are those from the Meuse and from the Seine. They are never very large, but their flesh has a perfect flavour and is infinitely delicate. The big trout from the Lake of Geneva, on the other hand, almost always have flesh which is dry and tough.

The agility, strength and determination of the trout are all surprising. Not only does it swim back upstream through the fastest torrents; it also throws itself into the loftiest waterfalls and thus makes its way back through the cataracts to the very summits of Mont Blanc and the Great Saint-Bernard. The movements which it makes undoubtedly help to give it a good taste and a very wholesome quality.

Truite à la montagnarde · Trout as cooked in the mountains

Leave the trout for an hour in salted water, then cook it with a bottle of white wine, three onions, a bouquet garni, cloves, two cloves of garlic, thyme, basil, and butter into which you have worked some flour. Boil it over a fierce flame. Then remove the onions and the bouquet and serve the trout with its sauce, sprinkling over it a little blanched parsley.

TRUFFLE   *TRUFFE*

Here we have come to the gastronomes' holy of holies (the *sacrum sacrorum*); to the word which gourmands throughout the ages have never pronounced without lifting their hands to their hats; to the *tuber cibarium*, to the *lycoperdon gulosorum*, to the truffle.

You have questioned scholars, asking them exactly what this tubercle is, and after two thousand years of discussion the scholars reply as they did on the first day: 'We don't know.' You have interrogated the truffle itself, and the truffle has replied to you: 'Eat me and adore God.' To recount the history of the truffle would be to take on the task of relating the history of world civilization. Silent though they are, they have played a greater role in this than the laws of Minos, than the tables of Solon; and they have done so during all the great periods of the nations and throughout the shining hours of the mighty empires. They abounded in Rome, Greece and Libya. The Barbars, coming on them, trampled them underfoot and caused them to disappear. From the time of Augustulus until Louis XV they effaced themselves. They reappeared only in the eighteenth century; and reached their zenith under the parliamentary government between 1820 and 1848.

The *Dictionnaire de la Conversation* states that in France there are several types of truffles; black, grey, violet and garlic-scented. They are gathered in many of our *départements*. The limestone chain which runs through the *départements* of Aube, Haute-Marne and the Côte-d'Or provides the grey truffle which is almost as delicate as the white garlic-scented truffle from Piedmont. The black truffle abounds in Perigord, Angoumois and Quercy. It is also to be found in Gard, Drôme, Isère, Vaucluse, Hérault, Tarn, the eastern Pyrénées and in the Jura mountains, Ardèche and Lozère. Several forests in Touraine produce truffles of good quality.

Brillat-Savarin says that the truffle is the diamond of the kitchen; that it awakens erotic and gourmand memories in the skirted sex, and gourmand and erotic souvenirs in the bearded sex. The truffle is certainly not a positive aphrodisiac, but in certain circumstances it can make women more tender, and men more amiable.

About truffles in general

The truffle holds the first place among the cryptogams: the orange agaric, that mushroom of kings, *Fungus Caesareus*, as it was called by our old botanists, has only second place.

Rather than being indigestible, as has been said repeatedly, the truffle promotes the functions of the stomach (providing that it is used with restraint), and owes its digestive properties to its mildly stimulating molecules. It is nourishing, restoring, warming to cold temperaments. Meats, vegetables, fish and other foodstuffs, whatever they may be, become lighter if they are flavoured with truffles. Nevertheless, there have been some authors whose palates have never been able to savour these delicious tubercles, and who have reproached them for troubling the digestion, causing insomnia and producing a disposition to apoplexy and to nervous diseases. We have consulted a fair number of truffle devotees, some old, others young. They all unanimously acclaim its beneficent action. One of them, a very witty middle-aged man, and of an amiable nature such as all true gastronomes possess, said to me a few days ago:

'When I eat truffles, I become livelier, gayer and more alert; I feel internally, especially in my veins, a sweet and voluptuous warmth, which is not slow to communicate itself to my brain. My ideas are clearer and simpler. If it suits me, I compose verses on the spot for rich poets, I compose speeches for worried savants or for lazy deputies, and then I fall asleep. My digestion works easily, my sleep is untroubled. What is said about certain virtues of the truffle is ancient history for me.'

Beside, who does not know the truffle and its incomparable aroma? Is there a natural product which is more famous amongst ancient and modern peoples? The Romans liked it passionately, and demanded it from Africa.

Truffle

'Libyan,' exclaimed Juvenal, 'unyolk your cattle, keep your harvests, but send us your truffles.'

I belong to the era when truffles have been most in fashion. The Bourbons of the older branch were said to govern with truffles. There were two queens of the stage who particulary acknowledged the influence of these estimable tubercles; Mlle Georges and Mlle Mars.

Every evening when these ladies were acting, and particularly during the period of their greatest successes, supper was available at their homes for some of their intimate friends. They returned to their dwelling with the courtiers from the boxes and found at home the courtiers of the house.

At the house of Georges, truffles were always eaten in the same way.

At the house of Mars, it was up to the cook, and he had carte blanche in this matter.

But at the house of Agrippine [i.e. Mlle Georges], she who embodied every form of sensuality, no mercy was shown to the truffle, it was compelled to yield every sensation which it was capable of giving.

Hardly had she arrived home when perfumed water in a shallow basin of the most beautiful porcelain was brought to Georges, in which she washed her hands. Then the truffles were brought, truffles which had already been subjected to two or three ablutions and the

Mlle Mars

same number of scrubbings; and, in a separate plate, a little vermilion fork and a little knife with a mother-of-pearl handle and a steel blade.

Then Agrippine, with her hand modelled on classical lines, with her fingers of marble and her rosy fingernails, started to peel the black tubercle, an ornament in her hand, in the most adroit fashion in the world. She cut it in thin tiny leaves like paper, poured on some ordinary pepper and a few atoms of Cayenne pepper, impregnated them with white oil from Lucca or green oil from Aix, and then passed the salad bowl to a servant, who tossed the salad which she had prepared.

The rest of the supper, depending on the season, consisted of a roast of game, a chicken from Bresse or from Mans, or a fine turkey from Bourges.

And then came the salad, for which the supper had only been a prologue. It is difficult to imagine the scent which the truffle attained, seasoned merely with oil and pepper.

One scooped out by the forkful from this salad bowl, as one might have from an ordinary salad.

At Mlle Mars, the service was much more complicated, but the salad lacked, in point of dressing, the beautiful hands, the pink fingernails and, more than anything, the abandon and the charming

Mlle Georges

Truffle

permissiveness of Agrippine.

The most ancient recipe for truffles which we can offer to our readers is that of Apicius.

Ragoût de truffes à l'Apicius

First cook your truffles in water, then put them on a skewer, and let them turn five or six times over a fire. Baste them with oil, lemon juice, chervil, pepper and salt. When the sauce boils, bind it with eggs and wine.

[This recipe does not correspond, except in a very general way, to any of the six given by Apicius (VII, xiv). The first of these, given below, may be what Dumas had in mind:

'*Truffles*. Peel the truffles, cook them in water, powder them with salt, impale them on skewers and grill them over a gentle heat. Next, put in an earthenware *marmite* some olive oil, garum (a kind of fish sauce), sweet wine which has been reduced, ordinary wine, pepper and honey. Bring this to the boil, then bind it with (some form of) starch. Take the truffles off their skewers and serve them (with the sauce).']

Salade aux truffes à la toulousaine · A truffle salad from Toulouse

M. Urbain Dubois, an outstanding French cook who practises abroad, gives us the following recipe and accompanying eulogy:

'This dish is a recent creation of Toulousaine science and proves that in France the great art of gastronomy is practised everywhere with equal earnestness and always with success.

'Choose five or six fresh black truffles with a good aroma, and three tender artichokes. Carefully brush the truffles, then wash, peel and chop them up very finely and put them in a closed container. Trim away the tough leaves of the artichokes, leaving only those which are unquestionably tender. Divide them through the middle and lengthwise, slice them as thinly as the truffles and let them macerate with a little salt for ten minutes; then wipe them on a cloth.

'Sieve the yolks of three hardboiled eggs, put them in a terrine, add a little mustard and dilute with half a glass of finest quality oil and a little good tarragon vinegar. Rub the bottom of a salad bowl with garlic, and arrange the artichokes and truffles alternately in layers in this. Season with salt and pepper as well as with a part of the eggs which have been mixed with oil. Ten minutes later toss the truffles and the artichokes in the salad bowl, to blend the seasoning. This salad is worthy of bearing a great name.'

TUNNY

A marine fish which makes migratory journeys in the Mediterranean and is taken on the coasts near Marseilles, on those of Corsica, Elba and Sicily and on those of Africa.

The phrase 'neither meat nor fish' applies with particular aptness to the tunny; and fishermen have given it the nickname of *veau des chartreux*, because parts of its flesh have the taste and white colour of veal. The flesh is eaten fresh, but is most commonly consumed after being preserved in a marinade. Almost all the marinated tunny eaten in France comes from Provence.

The net with which the tunny fishery is conducted is called a *madrague*. A man who keeps watch continuously counts the number of tunny which enter the *madrague*; and, since not a single one can find its way out again among the numerous twists and turns formed by the net, the number which he sees going in is the same as the number caught. When the fishermen think that they have a sufficient number, they close the entrance of the *madrague* and lift the nets up to the surface of the water. Men then go down into the nets and stab the tunny, which give out a huge amount of blood.

Thon frais en salade · Fresh tunny salad
Serve slices of [cold] roast tunny with a remoulade sauce [see page 258].

TURBOT

At a single stroke and in the same Satire, Juvenal delineated both the Emperor Domitian and the turbot which was the cause of his calling a meeting of the Senate. A full-scale session took place, but the matter was so important that the Senators who had been called together went off again without having reached a decision on which sauce should be served with the monstrous creature.

In the absence of a decision by the Roman Senate, we have that of Vincent de la Chapelle, the venerable senator of French cuisine; and, from what we know of the cuisine practised in antiquity, we need not regret too much that, on this occasion, as on so many others, the honourable assembly drew a blank.

Instead of Domitian's turbot—not a specimen to be found every day, if we are to believe the description of Juvenal—take the most handsome and large turbot, without spots, that you can find, especially one which is very thick, very white and very fresh. Make

Turbot

an incision in its back, down to the centre, closer to the head than to the tail, and three or four inches in length, more or less according to the size of the fish. Lift up the flesh from both sides of the cut and break off a section of the bones, as long as the cut, so that you can remove three or four vertebrae of the backbone. Secure the head with a trussing needle and a strong thread passed between the backbone and the bone of the foremost fin; and rub the turbot with lemon juice. Put it in a *turbotière* with some well-salted water and one or one and a half litres of milk. Add two or three lemon peels, sliced and free of flesh and pips.

If it is summer, set the turbot to cook over quite a vigorous flame, since if you start it off on too low a fire you risk seeing it fall apart into pieces. As soon as your seasoned liquid is on the verge of boiling, cover the fire [or turn down the heat] and let your turbot cook without actually boiling. Cover it with a buttered paper and leave it in the seasoned liquid until the time comes to serve it. A quarter of an hour before you do so, drain the turbot. Arrange a napkin on a serving platter, putting beneath it a garnish of bunches of parsley, in such a way that the centre part curves up on the platter. Slip the turbot on top of this, and use a large pair of scissors to trim in a very uniform manner any of the fins which may have been torn. Put sprigs of parsley around the turbot, and, if there were any tears at the edges, cover these with parsley. Serve beside the fish a sauceboat containing a white sauce, with capers; and another sauceboat containing a piquant sauce or a good Hollandaise sauce.

Kadgiori de turbot · Turbot kedgeree

This dish, of Indian origin, is nowadays regularly served in England, which seems to have become a colony of India.

Lift the fillets from a small uncooked turbot, cut them into large cubes and fry these in butter over a lively flame for two minutes only. Then season them and take the casserole off the fire. Chop an onion, cook it in butter without letting it take colour, and mix with this 500 grams of rice which has been washed and left to drain for an hour in a strainer. A few seconds later, pour in enough fish bouillon to increase the volume of the mixture threefold, cook it on a lively flame for 10 to 12 minutes, then remove the casserole and keep it at the mouth of the oven until the rice is just about dry. At this point, mix the pieces of turbot with it, sprinkle a pinch of Cayenne pepper over it, pour on two tablespoons of sauce, and three chopped hard-boiled eggs as well, and finally a piece of butter divided into small bits. Arrange all this at once on a shallow serving dish and moisten it with *beurre à la noisette*.

[Kedgeree was a common breakfast dish in England in the nineteenth century, prepared with cold fish from the previous day, and rice. The above description of how to make it is recognizable, but nevertheless sounds 'not quite right' to the native cooks in India's European colony.

However, we should not blame Dumas for the shortcomings of the recipe. He had lifted it straight out of *La Cuisine de tous les Pays* by Urbain Dubois (1863). All he added was the joke about England becoming an Indian colony and the piece of butter in the penultimate sentence.

The *Amis d'Alexandre Dumas* held a special luncheon at the Hotel Bristol in Paris not so long ago. The menu, composed by Robert J. Courtine, consisted of dishes from Dumas' *Dictionnaire*. Dumas would have been amused to know that the first course was this turbot kedgeree; and to reflect that it should have really been the *Amis d'Urbain Dubois* who ate and applauded it.]

TURKEY   *DINDON*

In ornithology, the terms turkey cock, and hen turkey are used to distinguish the male and female animal. In cookery, one usually uses the word turkey for both the male and the female.

The female is always smaller and more delicate than the male. Turkeys were known to the Greeks, who called them *Méléagrides*, because it was Meleager, King of Macedonia, who brought them to Greece in the 3,559th year after the creation of the world. Some learned men have contested this fact, and have said that the creatures were guinea-hens; but Pliny (book 37, chapter II) describes the turkey in such a way that it cannot be mistaken. Sophocles, in one of his tragedies, which has since been lost, introduced a chorus of turkeys to weep over the death of Meleager.

The Romans professed a particularly great esteem for turkeys; they reared them in their small farms. How did they disappear? What epidemic wiped them out? History does not tell us. The only thing we know is that they became so rare that they ended up being put in cages, just as parrots are nowadays.

In 1432, the vessels of Jacques Cœur (who started out as one of the first wholesale merchants and ended as as King Charles the Seventh's Minister of Finance and Commander of Artillery), in 1432

Turkey

as we were saying, Jacques Cœur's vessels brought back the first turkeys from India. Thus we do not owe this precious bird to the Jesuits, which is the widespread popular belief; the order of the Jesuits was only founded in 1534 by Ignatius Loyola, and only approved by Pope Paul III in 1540.

This belief that it was Loyola's followers who imported the turkey from America has caused some mischievous wags to form the habit of calling turkeys Jesuits. Turkeys have exactly the same right to be cross about this misnomer as the Jesuits would have if they were called turkeys.

So our opinion is not that held by most learned men, who claim that the turkey comes from America. America, discovered in 1492 by Christopher Columbus, could not have been supplying Jacques Cœur's vessels in 1450, which after all was forty-two years earlier, even though his motto had been 'For the brave heart, nothing is impossible'. Its name, *poule d'Inde*, from which the word *dindon* is derived, would seem in any case more natural if it came from India than if it came from America, even though at that time it was customary to call America the West Indies.

Today, the turkey can be found wild in America, particularly in Illinois. Brillat-Savarin, in his *Physiologie du goût*, describes himself as the hero of a hunt when he had the good fortune to kill a turkey. A Canadian huntsman assured me that he had killed one such animal which weighed nearly fifty pounds.

Even though turkey meat, particularly when cold, is excellent, full of flavour, and preferable to that of chicken, there are some gourmets who absolutely refuse to eat it except for the *sot-l'y-laisse* for which the etymology is *sot qui le laisse* ('tis a fool who leaves it). [These are two small pieces of flesh situated above the parson's nose.]

One day, Grimod de la Reynière, the uncle of the famous Count d'Orsay who was the leader of fashion in both England and France for a period of twenty years, was caught by surprise, while on one of his financial rounds, either by nightfall or by bad weather or by one of the other insurmountable problems which force an epicure to stop at a village inn. He asked the landlord what he could give him for supper. The latter confessed with shame and regret that his pantry was completely empty.

A great fire which shone through the panes of a glass door, to wit the kitchen door, attracted the attention of the illustrious gourmand, who was astonished to see seven turkeys turning on the same spit.

'How can you dare to say you have nothing to give me for supper,' exclaimed Grimod de la Reynière, 'when I can see seven magnificent turkeys on the same spit, cooked to a turn?'

'It is true,' replied the landlord, 'but they have been ordered by a gentleman from Paris who arrived before you did.'

'And is this gentleman by himself?'

'He is quite alone.'

'Well, is this traveller a giant, then?'

'No, sir, he is no bigger than you.'

'Oh ho! Tell me the room number of this jovial fellow, and I will be really stupid if I fail to get him to let me have one of his seven turkeys.'

Grimod de la Reynière was given a light and led to the traveller's chamber where he found him seated in front of a blazing fire near the table which had been laid, sharpening two carving knives against each other.

'Well, good Lord! I wasn't wrong,' exclaimed Grimod de la Reynière, 'it's you, my son.'

'Yes, father,' replied the young man, greeting him respectfully.

'So it's you who have ordered seven turkeys to be spit-roasted for your supper?'

'Sir,' replied the amiable young man, 'I can understand that you are disagreeably surprised to see me manifest such vulgar tastes and ones which are so foreign to my noble background. But I had no choice of dishes, this was all that was to be had in this place.'

'By Jove, I'm not reproaching you for eating turkey instead of chicken or pheasant. While travelling one has to put up with whatever is available. But I do reproach you for having seven turkeys spit-roasted for you alone.'

'Sir, I've always heard you say to your friends that the only really good thing about turkey (unless it has truffles in it) is the *sot-l'y-laisse*. I've had seven turkeys put on the spit so as to have 14 *sot-l'y-laisse*.'

'This seems a little costly for an eighteen year old boy,' replied his father, who nevertheless had to respect the young man's intelligence, 'but I cannot say that it is unreasonable.'

*

Avignon has always been a place where one ate marvellously well; it has traditionally been so since the time when it was a papal town.

A worthy president of the tribunal in that town appreciated the qualities of the turkey. One day he said:

'Really, we have just eaten a superb turkey. It was excellent,

Turkey

crammed with truffles up to its beak, tender as a fat pullet, plump as an ortolan, fragrant as a thrush. To be sure, we only left the bones.'

'How many were you?' inquired someone curiously.

'We were two, sir!' he replied.

'Two? . . .'

'Yes, the turkey and me.'

*

The colour red has the property of exciting anger in turkeys, just as it does in bulls; the turkey rushes at the person who is wearing it, and attacks him with pecks. This was the cause of the accident which occurred to the illustrious Boileau.

Boileau, when he was still a child, was playing in a courtyard where, amongst other poultry, there was a turkey. All of a sudden the child fell, his jacket flew back and the turkey saw the abhorred colour. The turkey threw himself on him, and so wounded the poor Nicolas with his pecks that the latter, no longer capable of ever becoming an erotic poet, chose in consequence to be a satirical poet and to slander women.

The poet was inconvenienced throughout his life. This was undoubtedly the reason for his secret aversion to the Jesuits, who he thought, as did most people at the time, had introduced the turkey into France.

Recette de la Dinde aux Truffes, de M. le Marquis de Cussy ·
Recipe of M. le Marquis de Cussy for Turkey with Truffles

You prepare your truffles which you then roll in finely grated bacon and season with pepper, salt and *quatre épices*. Simmer the truffles gently for twenty minutes, and then put them in the cavity of the turkey which you have just killed and gutted. You leave it hanging by its feet in a cool larder, and at the end of three days, having plucked and singed the bird, you replace the first lot of truffles with virgin ones, similarly cleaned and prepared.

M. de Cussy, you must understand, just like Grimod de la Reynière, prefers that truffled turkey should not be plucked. 'Notice well,' he says, 'that by not plucking the animal, all the pores remain closed, and there is no evaporation. The hot truffles combine with the palpitating flesh and the infiltration of their flavour is more active, intense and thorough. But in this combination, the truffles lose what they give.' Ever since reading this, we have taken the view that one should replace the original truffles with fresh ones.

We recognize that either procedure is excellent; but, since it is not everyone who can spend 40 francs on stuffing a turkey with truffles, we are going to give our own recipe. Chop up and mix together some veal, chicken, partridge (if you have some) and add a ¼ *livre* (120 grams) of sausage meat. Cook all this in well-salted water, to which you have added some celery, together with fifteen to twenty beautiful chestnuts from Lyon which you have pounded and reduced to a mush with the minced meat. Add some fine *boudin*, and chop it up with the other ingredients. Put some parsley in the middle of the stuffing and then stuff it all into the turkey's stomach. Close up as far as possible the inner orifice, stuffing into it a piece of butter seasoned with salt and pepper. Put the turkey on a spit and don't take it off until its body emits little jets of smoke, like a volcano, which indicates that it has been cooked to just the right point.

The turkey could be called *Dinde des artistes* (Artists' turkey).

Above all, do not baste your roasts, whatever they are, except with butter into which you have worked salt and pepper. Any cook who puts a single drop of bouillon into his dripping pan deserves to be thrown out on the spot, and banned from France.

TURMERIC (or CURCUMA)
TERRA MERITA ou CURCUMA

This is an oriental root which, like saffron, gives a yellow colour which is used for colouring ragoûts.

Turmeric is one element in curry powder, which is used extensively in India and which is employed in certain dishes in Europe.

We have already remarked that curry powder is made with 120 grams of hot red pepper, 90 grams of turmeric, 30 grams of pepper, 30 grams of cloves and a little nutmeg, all ground to a fine powder.

The English add rhubarb to this. It is well known that one of the gastronomic diversions of the English is to eat little rhubarb tarts and little rhubarb pies. This fashion has been introduced by the English to the pastry-makers of the quarter Saint-Honoré in Paris.

TURNIP   *NAVET*

Vegetables themselves have their own aristocracy and privileges. It is accepted that the three best kinds of turnip which can be grown are

Turnip

those from Cressy, from Belle-Isle-en-Mer and from Meaux. But, whether this results from intrigue or ingenuity, the turnips with which Paris is currently supplied come from Freneuse and Vaugirard.

The first recipe which comes to hand is entitled *Navets à la d'Esclignac*. What can possibly have earned M. d'Esclignac the honour of giving his name to a dish of turnips? In this field, there is no odder subject of study than the books written by cooks and the strange way in which they suddenly make up their minds to make a sauce of, to put on the grill, or to roast our famous men.

This is what we find in one single book, in the section on soups:

Potage à la Demidoff.
— à la John Russell.
— à l'Abd-el-Kader.
— à la ville de Berlin.
— à la Cialdini.
— au 15 septembre 1864.
— au héros de Palestro.
— à la Lucullus.
— à la Guillaume Tell.

Potage au mont Blanc.
— à la Magenta et à la Solferino.
— aux Dardanelles.
— à la Dumas.
— à la Thérésa.
— à la mère l'Oie.
— à la Rothschild.

If we then carry on from soup to hors d'oeuvre, we find the following, the reasons for which again escape us:

Petits soufflés au Caire.
Petits pâtés à la Turbigo.
Petits pâtés Inkermann.
Filets de merlans à la Durando.
Petites timbales à la Garibaldi.
Friture au prince impérial.
— à la Louisiane.
— à la Capodimonte.
— à l'Africaine.

Friture au nouveau monde.
— à la fleuriste Florentine.
Petites timbales à la Titus.
Soufflés à la Marc Aurèle.
Pâtés Omer-Pacha.
Petites bouchées aux vrais amis.
Bâtons à la Palmerston.
Petits soufflés à la Cellini.
Petits soufflés au désir.

[Dumas also gives amusing examples of titles for *relevés*, *entrées chaudes*, *entrées froides* and *rôts*.]

We could carry on giving further lists from this historic writer on cooking, who is at the same time an excellent cook. But in quoting him, it need hardly be said, we will not deprive ourselves of the right to borrow some of his strangely titled recipes.

Let us return to our turnips.

Navets glacés au jus · Turnips with a meat glaze

Choose clean turnips of equal size, suitable to be cut into shapes like pears. Blanch and drain them, and butter the bottom of a casserole which is the right size to take them side by side. Arrange the turnips in this and cook them until golden-brown in butter and sugar. Moisten them with excellent bouillon, and sprinkle over them sugar, a few grains of salt and some bits of cinnamon stick. Bring to the boil on a high heat, cover with a piece of buttered paper, and put at the side of the oven with a flame below. Put the lid on the casserole, and hot embers on the lid. Once the turnips are cooked, uncover them, glaze them, arrange them on a platter, pour a little good bouillon into the casserole to dislodge the pan juices, remove the cinnamon sticks, and pour the sauce over the turnips as you would for a compote.

I notice that I have unfairly skipped over turnips *à la d'Esclignac*, the recipe which was the reason for the lengthy parenthesis from which we have just emerged. I make haste to redress the injustice.

Navets à la d'Esclignac

Take some turnips four or five inches long and cut off their two ends. Split each in two and then, in peeling the halves, shape each like a rope; this is done by using the end of a knife to fashion two little grooves such as one finds on rope.

Blanch the prepared turnips and put them in a casserole in the same manner as in the preceding recipe. Season and cook them in the same way, but do not add any cinnamon. Once they have finished cooking, put a little espagnole in the casserole to help dislodge the pan juices, add a little butter and pour the sauce over the turnips.

VANILLA

An exotic plant belonging to the orchid family. It always grows in the shade, either in the crannies of rocks or at the foot of huge trees. The aroma of vanilla is very delicate and has such perfect fragrance that it is used to flavour creams, liqueurs and chocolates.

VANILLE (Epidendrum vanilla)

VEAL   *VEAU*

The best calves are those of Pontoise, Rouen, Caen, Montargis and Picardy. Calves are also reared in the environs of Paris, and these are not to be despised. The veal eaten in Paris is more succulent than anywhere else. The particular care given to the rearing of those calves which are destined for the table is the first reason for this superiority. A second reason is the strict observance of the rule which forbids the slaughter of these innocent animals before the age of six weeks. Thus veal from Pontoise, at this age, produces the most delicious roast which the butcher can offer.

The choicest parts are the kidney and the part behind it. A serious discussion has taken place among the amateurs of veal to establish which of these two parts is the better. There is one way to reconcile the differing points of view, and that is to serve the whole loin, which combines both these parts. The only trouble is that it needs a large number of people to do it justice, since a really good loin hardly ever weighs less than twelve to fifteen pounds.

Cervelles de veau (1) *à l'allemande*, (2) *au beurre noir* ·
    Calves' brains (1) in the German style, or (2) with black butter

1. *à l'allemande*

Have three brains removed carefully, that is to say without being damaged, and put them in a pan with water to cover. Then remove all the membranes from them, and likewise from the cerebellum. That done, change the water so that they can soak clean. Then rinse them again to remove any remaining bits of membrane.

Blanch the brains for about a quarter of an hour in the following manner. Bring some water to the boil with a pinch of white salt and a glass of white vinegar. Put in the brains, remove them when they are blanched and drain them.

Line a casserole with bacon, put the brains in this and pour over them a glass of white wine and twice that quantity of consommé, so that they are steeped in the liquid. Add a well-seasoned bouquet of parsley and spring onions, with a few slices of lemon from which you have removed rind and pips. Cover all this with some bards of bacon and a round piece of cooking paper, and bring it to the boil on top of the stove. Then leave the casserole for three quarters of an hour on a small *paillasse* (a brick oven with glowing charcoal). When the brains are cooked, arrange them on a platter and mask them with a *sauce à l'allemande*.

The sauce is made thus. Put a little butter and some chopped mushrooms in a pan, cook them thoroughly and add three skimming-spoonfuls of well blended velouté and one of consommé. Reduce, toss in some butter and some blanched parsley, strain it (shaking the strainer as you do so), add the juice of half a lemon and a little ground pepper, strain it again and serve it.

If no velouté is available, proceed as follows. Brown your mushrooms, then pour some really good bouillon over them. Add a well-seasoned bouquet garni; a clove; half a clove of garlic; thyme and a bay leaf. When the sauce is cooked, take out the bouquet (squeezing the liquid out of it) and finish the sauce as indicated above.

2. *au beurre noir*

Prepare and cook the brains in the same fashion as for the recipe above. When you are ready to serve them, drain them and, after arranging them on a platter, dress them with *beurre noir*, prepared as follows.

Put half a pound of butter in a *diable* (a kind of pan with a short handle). Put it on the fire and let the butter turn brown without burning, which can be avoided by shaking the pan. When it is black enough, remove it from the fire and clarify it. After skimming it, wipe your pan clean. Then pour into it two tablespoonfuls of vinegar and a pinch of salt. Heat this mixture, then pour your black butter into it and stir all together.

Pour the sauce over the brains and garnish them with fried parsley, either around them or on top. Serve immediately.

Veal

Ragoût de veau à la menagère · Veal stew

Put a piece of butter in a pan, let it melt, add two spoonfuls of flour
and let this brown. Add your piece of veal and stir it about in the roux
until it has stiffened. Have ready some hot water or stock, which you
now pour over the meat. Stir until it comes to the boil, then add salt,
pepper, a bay leaf and a little thyme. Let it boil for an hour, then add
three onions, mushrooms, carrots or morels [and continue cooking
for another twenty to thirty minutes].

Veau mariné pour servir en hors d'œuvre ·
Marinated veal, to be served as an hors d'oeuvre

Tenderize a beautiful topside of veal (for four days in winter, for only
one in summer—but the weather should not be too hot). Remove
the skin, fat sinews and gristle. Cut the meat into four pieces. Have
ready 125 grams of very dry salt which you have pounded in a
mortar or crushed and sieved. Rub the veal well on all sides with this;
then put it in a stoneware terrine with several slices of onion, sprigs of
parsley, a little thyme, some ginger, a clove of garlic, a dozen fine
juniper berries, crushed black peppercorns and three anchovies
(rinsed and pounded). Stir all this in the terrine, cover it with a white
cloth and tie this in place with string. After four days, turn the veal;
then leave it another four days.

Drain the veal, leaving only one third of the juices which it will
have exuded. Put this, along with the meat and seasonings, in a
casserole. Add a bottle of very good white wine, bring to the boil and
then lower the heat so that it only simmers. When it is cooked,
which you can find out by sticking a fork into it, take it off the fire
and put it back in the stoneware terrine in which it was marinated.
Leave it to cool in its seasonings. Then put it either in a pot or in a
glass jar and pour in enough good olive oil to cover it completely.
Place a piece of cooking parchment on top and use the veal thus
prepared as though it were marinated tuna.

Épaule de veau aux sept racines ·
Shoulder of veal with seven root vegetables

Lard the interior of a boned shoulder with lardoons which have been
seasoned with fine salt, coarsely ground pepper, finely chopped
parsley, two bay leaves, a little thyme well chopped and some mixed
spices. Roll the meat lengthwise and tie it.

Put in the bottom of a braising pan some bards of bacon, a few slices of veal, the bones from the shoulder and the shoulder itself, covered with bacon. Add onions, carrots, turnips, two heads of celery, three parsnips, six Jerusalem artichokes and half a bunch of salsify; and in addition some coarsely ground pepper and a bouquet garni. Cover it all with a circle of buttered cooking paper.

Cook the veal on a low fire, putting some embers on the lid of the braising pan and leaving it to cook thus for three hours. Then untie the string, arrange the meat on an oval platter, glaze it and surround it with all the vegetables which were cooked with it.

WHITE VEAL STOCK   *BLOND DE VEAU*

Voltaire, who was not only always away somewhere, but also always staying with someone, wrote letters from wherever he was, with publication in mind. From Cirey he wrote to his friend Saint-Lambert:

'Do come to Cirey, where Mme Duchatelet will not allow you to be poisoned; there is not a drop of gravy in her kitchen; everything is made with white veal stock. We will live to be a hundred, and no one will ever die any more.'

Now the recipe for this veal stock had been given to Mme Duchatelet by the famous Tronchin, whose lectures on health were encapsulated in these three recommendations: 'Keep your head cold, your feet warm and your stomach happy'. Here then is the recipe of Mme Duchatelet:

Blond de veau à la Duchatelet ·

White veal stock as made chez Mme Duchatelet

'Line the bottom of a casserole with some slices of veal. Add some poultry giblets with a little butter or melted bacon fat, onions, carrots and a bouquet garni. Moisten with a spoonful of bouillon, and allow this to reduce without sticking. Pour on more bouillon, enough to cover the contents of the pan, boil and skim, then moderate the fire and let it keep on cooking gently for two hours.

'Make a white roux separately, turn the mushrooms in this for a few minutes, and pour into it the juices from the meat, stirring all the while so that the roux is thoroughly blended. Boil and skim, and put the casserole on a low heat for a good hour, then strain the stock after having removed the surplus fat.'

VERJUICE   *VERJUS*

The juice of a green grape, the principal variety of which is known under the name of *farineau* or *bordelaise*.

Verjus de grain is the kind which is extracted before the fruit is ripe. It goes without saying that this is the best; and it is above all an indispensable seasoning for green walnuts. *Verjus topette* is the name given to the kind which is made for preserving. It can be improved by adding either a little salt or a few drops of vinegar.

VINEGAR   *VINAIGRE*

This is wine which has undergone acetic fermentation. Vinegar can be adulterated in several ways, all of which have the purpose of making it stronger. To this end, concentrated acetic acid (obtained by the carbonization of wood in sealed vessels) or sulphuric acid is added to it.

VIOLET   *VIOLETTE*

This is a flower whose very name evokes numerous thoughts of Spring. Whoever speaks of the violet speaks of shade, of freshness, of modesty, of a stream running through grass. There is not a poet, whether an erotic like Parny or a romantic such as Hugo, who has not found the word violet at the end of his rhyme; it is a gentle and fragrant name. The cornflour, charming sapphire of the wheat fields, comes after the violet in the poetical ranking of wild flowers. Alive, it is destined to adorn the bodices of young maidens; dead, it lends its fragrance to confectionery, liqueurs, sherbets, preserves, and other household culinary preparations.

Violet ice cream is a dainty dish, among the most esteemed of all delicacies.

Sirope de Violettes · (syrup of violets)

Is there any old person, whatever his age and however close to the grave he may be, who does not see at the other extreme of his life his mother approaching his cradle with a steaming cup in her hand and bringing a perfumed liquid to his lips? This perfumed liquid was syrup of violets.

Pick half a pound of violet flowers (those from the woods are the best) and put them in a terrine or other container which can be stopped up. Boil three half *setiers* ($\frac{3}{4}$ litre) of water, but leave this for ten minutes after you have taken it from the fire before you pour it on the violets, because the infusion, which ought to be of a beautiful violet colour, would become green if the water was too close to the boil. Put the infusion into a drying oven (*à l'étuve*) so that it stays hot until the next day, at which point you take out the flowers, and press them well in a napkin in order to extract the dye. Put this in a terrine with three pounds of powdered sugar, which you then melt. Put the terrine back into the drying oven for a further twenty-four hours, stirring from time to time. Keep the drying oven hot during all this time, as you would for sugar-candy. This produces two bottles of syrup; you must be careful before putting it in the bottles to boil it to the pearl stage, so that the syrup will keep properly and not ferment.

Of all the syrups this is the only one which is made without cooking.

WATER   *EAU*

People who habitually drink water become just as good gourmets about water as wine drinkers about wine.

For fifty or sixty years of my life, I have drunk only water, and no lover of wine has ever felt the same delight in some Grand-Laffite or Chambertin as I have in a glass of cool spring water whose purity has not been tainted by any earthy salts.

Very cold water, even when it has been artificially cooled with ice, acts as an excellent tonic to the stomach, without provoking any irritation and indeed calming any which might already have existed.

But this is not the case with water coming from melted snow or ice, which are heavy because they contain no air. Stir these waters well before drinking, and they will lose their injurious qualities.

Formerly all of Paris slaked its thirst from the river which traverses it. Nowadays the water comes from Grenelle; pipes bring it to the mountain of Sainte-Geneviève, whence it is distributed throughout Paris. For the last five or six years, water from the Dhuys has been competing with this; it comes from the other side, that is to say from Belleville, Montmartre and the Buttes Chaumont.

The water from the Seine was the object of so many calumnies for such a long time, particularly by people from the provinces coming

Water

to pass a few days in Paris, that it grew weary of slaking the thirst of two million ungrateful persons. But when the waters of the Seine were well purified and when it was drawn from above the zoological gardens, and from the middle of the stream, no other water was comparable to it for limpidity, lightness and sapidity. Above all, it was abundantly saturated with oxygen, having been turned over and over by the multiple meanderings which, over a distance of nearly two hundred leagues (eight hundred kilometres), subjected it to the action of the atmosphere's air. Moreover, it flows along a bed of sand all the way from its source until it reaches Paris. Gourmands attribute to this circumstance the superior quality of fish from the Seine to those from other rivers.

Everyone knows that monks have never really liked water very much; here is one more incident which proves their antipathy for this 'dreary liquid'. A Franciscan friar used to visit a bishop's kitchen fairly assiduously, the latter having told his people to look after the good brother. One day, when the prelate was holding a big dinner, the monk happened to be at the bishopric. The monseigneur was talking about the holy man, and recommending him to the assembled company. Right away, several of the ladies exclaimed;

'Monseigneur, you must amuse us by playing a trick on the monk. Summon him, and we will give him a beautiful glass of clear water which we will present to him as a glass of excellent white wine.'

'But you're not seriously thinking of such a thing, ladies!' said the bishop.

'Oh, but it would amuse us, let us do it, Monseigneur.'

So they summoned a manservant, and had him prepare a bottle of water on the spot. This was fastened up properly, and correctly labelled. Then they had the mendicant friar summoned.

'Brother,' said the ladies, 'you must drink to the health of his Grace and to ours.'

The monk was congratulating himself on his good fortune, and prepared himself to receive it well. The bottle was uncorked and a bumper drink was poured out. However, the crafty monk, who immediately saw through the deceit, did not lose his head at all, and said in the most woeful and humble tone to the bishop: 'Monseigneur, I will not drink as you have not given your holy blessing to this nectar.'

'This is quite unnecessary, my brother.'

'But in the name of all the saints of Paradise, I implore you to do so, Monseigneur.'

The ladies joined in the discussion, and implored the prelate to have the good nature to do this for them. The bishop finally bowed to their wishes, and blessed the water. The Franciscan then called a lackey and said to him, smiling: 'Champagne,* take that into the church, a Franciscan has never drunk holy water.'

He was really quite right, wasn't he?

WEEVER   *VIVE*

The weever is the terror of fishermen in the Channel. It is armed on the back, as on the gill covers, with several spines which are exceedingly sharp; and one cannot be too careful in avoiding them when taking the fish out of the net, or preparing it for table. If one is pricked, the first thing to do is to make the wound bleed; and the next is to rub it with a sort of ointment composed of peeled onion and the liver of the fish, with the addition of salt and alcohol. This is the remedy used by all the families who live on the coast around Cherbourg and Barfleur.

Vives à la maître d'hôtel

Cut the formidable spines off the rough backs of your weevers, gut them, wash them and make shallow cuts in both their sides. Marinate them in olive oil with parsley and salt. Then place them on the grill. When they are cooked, arrange them on a platter and cover them with a maître d'hôtel sauce, or a sauce on to which you have rained 'a hailstorm of capers', as Hugo puts it.

WELSH RABBIT (or RAREBIT)   *WELCH-RABBIT*
                                            —lapin gallois

A kind of English toast. Butter some slices of bread and toast them until they are a beautiful colour. Have some English Gloucester

---

* The use of this name presents a pretty problem. At a luncheon held in 1977 at the former home of Alexandre Dumas fils, in Marly-le-Roi, we posed it to a number of members of the Association des Amis de Dumas. Four explanations were advanced: that the lackey's name was in fact Champagne; that his name was not Champagne, but that he came from Champagne and bore that name as his nickname (much as people might adress a Scot as 'Scotty'); that the Franciscan jokingly pretended that the lackey's name was Champagne; or that he was gesturing at the glass of water and pretending, again in jest, that he supposed it to be champagne. The reader may choose between these explanations, or think of a better one.

Welsh Rabbit (or Rarebit)

cheese, or something similar, cut into small pieces. Melt these with a little water in a timbale. Add some Cayenne pepper, spread the melted cheese on the toast, glaze it with a *pelle rouge* (but held at a distance), then delicately place a little fresh butter on top of each toast, with just a touch of English mustard.

WHALE   *BALEINE*

The whale is the largest of the mammals; there are some which are 65 metres long.

The interior of the whale's body is like that of a terrestrial animal. Its blood is warm. It breathes by means of lungs, so cannot remain submerged more than a quarter of an hour. It has sexual intercourse in the manner of viviparous animals and nourishes its *caffre* with milk.

Caffre is the name which whaling men give to a baby whale. The whale has only one udder, placed exactly in the middle of its chest. How the baby whale drinks is not [generally] known. Does it swim on its back and drink while floating upside down? The procedure which it in fact uses is much simpler than that. It jabs the mother's udder with a sharp blow of its snout. The udder then emits a long jet of milk, upon which the baby whale pounces, swallowing it with the water with which it is mixed. It expels the water at once, by the gills or blow-hole, and retains only the milk.

It is strange that the whale, heaviest of fish, travels as quickly as the pigeon, one of the lightest birds; both do 64 kilometres an hour.

It was a whale which resolved the difficult question whether there was a passage from the Atlantic to the Pacific under the Isthmus of Panama. A whale, mortally wounded in the Gulf of Mexico, was found dead in the Pacific Ocean two hours later. Since it had not had time to go round Cape Horn or through the Strait of Lemaire or that of Magellan, given that this would have involved a journey of three thousand leagues, people were obliged to agree that it must have found a submarine passage. It was possible to establish the exact time at which it was wounded, by examining the harpoon which had struck it and which remained fixed in the wound. This harpoon, like all whalers' harpoons, bore its number, and, on board the ship, it was possible to check on what day and at what time it had been shot in the Gulf of Mexico, and twenty-four hours later the whale was found dead in the Pacific. [Two hours or twenty-four—there seems to be a discrepancy.]

[Mr Anthony D. Lilly, the expert on whaling literature, tells us that he has never come across another reference to this story. He adds that, *if* there were a subterranean passage under the Panama Canal, and *if* this were large enough to permit the passage of a whale, it might be possible for a whale to traverse it in two hours, travelling at a speed of 25 or 30 knots (which the sei whale has been known to achieve); but that it would have to come up to breathe every now and then, and that the difficulty in postulating not only an undiscovered subterranean passage, but also a series of large 'breathing holes' by which it would communicate with the air and which had also remained unnoticed strains credulity to breaking point.]

The skin of most whales is black, the flesh red and like beef. This flesh—especially that of the *cébillot*, the largest of the whales—is so good and wholesome that ordinary nautical people attribute to it the perfect health which they enjoy.

WHEAT   *FROMENT*

Here is what M. Aulagnier has to say about this plant, the commonest and the best in existence:

'Wheat, whose origins almost blend in with those of the world itself, is the most precious of all plants. The Egyptians placed Osiris in the ranks of the gods because he taught them agriculture, which has produced the same results in all countries of the world. In the Orient, it was in Babylonia that wheat grew wild. It was also there that the cradle of civilization is thought to lie. Today there are few nations which feed themselves on fruit alone, considering the large number of those which cultivate cereals. Dates and figs certainly continue to serve the Egyptians and Persians as nourishment, but this is only amongst the poor, for wheat is the principal foodstuff in those countries.

'The root of wheat is composed of slender fibres. Its stem grows to four or five feet in height and forms tubes of varying width. These are provided at intervals with knots, to give them strength and to support the long spikelets in which they terminate. From these spring flowers, composed of stamens which in turn are succeeded by oval grains. The grains are soft at both ends, convex on one side and grooved on the other. When ripe, they are yellow and filled with a white floury substance composed of gluten and starch, which is used to make bread.'

France is very rich in wheat of all types. Beauce, Brie, Ille-et-Vilaine and Vexin produce particularly fine examples.

Wheat

The Greeks and Romans paid homage to agriculture by holding festivals, but none of these could be compared with that which from time immemorial has been held annually in China. The emperor, surrounded by the princes and nobles of his court, and by the most worthy agricultural workers, himself works and ploughs the earth, and sows the five types of grain most necessary to life. These are: wheat, rice, broad beans, and two sorts of millet. This festival is celebrated every year in Peking, when spring returns, and likewise throughout the empire. In China the profession of ploughman is more honourable than that of merchant.

WHITEBAIT   *WHITE-BAIT*

Whitebait, a name meaning white fish, is undoubtedly one of the most popular dishes of London.

I recall having been invited, just in the ordinary way and without any special reason, by one of my friends who was back from Indre to go and eat whitebait at Greenwich [spelled *Grennisch* in the French text]. I found the invitation so unusual that I went there at once.

The whitebait is a tiny fish which is called *yanchette* in Italy, *pontin* at Nice and, quite simply, *poisson blanc* at Bordeaux. [This statement is broadly true, in that whitebait are the fry of various clupeoid, i.e. herring-like, fish; and so are the tiny fish sold as *bianchetti* in Italy and as *poutinou* at Nice. But in Britain whitebait are the fry of herring and sprats, whereas the Mediterranean counterpart of whitebait is a mixture of the fry of anchovies and sardines.]

On this occasion the whitebait were the crowning feature of a dinner of three services [each service comprising several different dishes], all of fish. I was curious to see how they prepared this dish, to eat which people would come from two or three hundred leagues away [550 to 800 miles—the meaning is, in effect, from all over England and Wales and parts of Scotland]. Handfuls of the fish were washed in iced water, then laid out on a cloth to drain. They were kept on the cloth, over ice, for twenty minutes. When the time came to serve them, they were rolled in fresh breadcrumbs and then placed in a napkin with a handful of flour. The cook took the napkin by both ends, squeezing it and shaking it in such a way as to propel the fish, in a single avalanche, into a metal sieve so fine that only the flour could pass through it. He shook the sieve and then plunged it, with the fish in it, into very hot frying oil. One minute of cooking was enough. As soon as the fish had taken on a good colour, they were removed from the sieve, dusted with salt and a little cayenne, arranged *en buisson* [in a pyramid—the term is normally used for an arrangement of shrimps or prawns in this fashion] on a folded napkin and served at once. [The description is recognizable, but the rolling in fresh breadcrumbs is unusual and indeed hardly seems possible with such small fish. The reference to handfuls of the fish should not be taken as meaning that they were picked up in handfuls. Great care was taken to avoid handling them.]

WHITING   *MERLAN*

The etymology of the name *merlan* is unknown; but it is quite easy to explain why, in the last century, wig-dressers were known as *merlans*—it was because they were always covered with powder, just as whiting are covered with flour before being fried.

The whiting belongs to the cod family. It is fished in December, January and February. During this period its body is fat and firm. Whitings begin to have roe and milt towards the end of October.

There is no flesh more healthful than that of the whiting; it flakes easily, is tender and light, and is even prescribed for convalescents.

The best whiting are taken in the Mediterranean.

Merlans frits · Fried whitings

Take several whitings and scale them; or rather wipe them with a cloth, using a gentle pressure, and the scales will come off of their own accord. Cut off the end of the tail and the fins, gut the fish and wash them, replace their livers inside them, make incisions on both their sides, flour them and fry them until they are firm and of a good colour. Drain them, sprinkle a little fine salt over them, put a serviette on the serving platter, arrange the fish thereon and serve them.

Merlans aux fines herbes

Scale the fish as described above and prepare them in the same manner. Put them in a shallow cooking vessel which you have lined with butter, parsley, spring onion, salt and nutmeg. Arrange them head to tail alongside each other, sprinkle melted butter over them and moisten them with white wine and bouillon. Once they are cooked on both sides, transfer their cooking liquid to a casserole, leaving the fish where they are. Add to the liquid in the casserole a

Whiting

little butter into which some flour has been worked. Cook and bind
the sauce. Squeeze some lemon juice into it, add a pinch of coarse
pepper, pour the sauce over the fish and serve them.

WIDGEON   *MACREUSE*

This bird can be called Lenten game, for everyone knows that it is
classed among the foods permissible when fasting, as is the teal.

The widgeon has some characteristics of a fish. It looks like a duck,
and lives almost all the time on the sea, where it dives to the bottom
of the water in search of the little shellfish on which it feeds. It also
eats insects, marine plants and little fish which contribute considerably to the savour and flavour of its flesh.

The black widgeon is the best. The grey one, which is the female
and which seamen call *bizette*, is endowed with a certain wild and
marine flavour which no seasoning can mask. The skill of the most
able cooks has never been able to achieve success in dealing with this;
and few people have appreciated *Macreuse au chocolat* (Widgeon with
chocolate), which is the *chef d'œuvre* of the cook's art in this field of
endeavour.

WILD CHICORY   *BARBE DE CAPUCIN*

Wild chicory is a sort of endive whose leaves are eaten in salads. It is
one of the most appreciated salads, very healthy, and one of the most
nutritious, perhaps the best of all, although it is slightly bitter. It is
the only one which doctors sometimes allow their patients during
convalescence.

It is usually eaten with slices of beetroot, seasoned with salt,
pepper, oil and vinegar, but without herbs.

WOODCOCK, SNIPE
BÉCASSE, BÉCASSINE et BÉCASSEAU

This is the best of the black birds, and the queen of the marshes. It is
sought after by gourmets of all classes because of its delicious flavour,
the volatility of its elements, and the delicacy of its flesh. It is, alas,
only a bird of passage. But one can eat it for more than three months
out of the year. Woodcock cooked on a spit is the most distinguished

of roasts, after the pheasant. This precious bird is so venerated that the same honours are paid to it as to the Grand Lhama. Slices of toast, moistened with good lemon juice, receive its trail and are eaten with respect by fervent connoisseurs.

Eléazar Blaze, a great hunter and also a great cook, delivered in these words his opinion of the woodcock:

'Woodcock is excellent game when it is fat; and it is always better during frosts. It is never drawn. If you pound woodcock in a mortar, you make a delicious purée. If you put on this purée some larded partridge wings, you obtain the highest achievement of the culinary art. In former times, when the gods descended to earth, they ate nothing else.

'Woodcock should not be eaten too soon, for its aroma would not be fully developed, and you would have tasteless and flavourless meat. When it is prepared in a *salmis* (ragoût of game), its flavour marries well with that of truffles. Put on a spit, with a cuirass of bacon, it should be supervised by the hunter's own eye, since a woodcock cooked too quickly is worthless. But a perfectly cooked woodcock, placed on its slice of golden and unctuous toast, is one of the most delicate and delicious morsels which a gentleman can eat. And if he takes the precaution of washing it down with an excellent wine from Burgundy, he can flatter himself that he is an excellent logician.

'A president of the Tribunal of Avignon had dined at the house of the Prefect. In his double role as distinguished gourmand and intrepid hunter, he did his duty at table conscientiously. After taking his cup of coffee to facilitate digestion, he had moved on to a third small glass to help down the coffee, when his host accosted him and asked if he had dined well.

' "But ... yes. ..." This reply seemed to be given with some reservations. "I have dined pretty well." '

' "Pretty well doesn't mean well." '

' "Yes, yes, I dined well." '

' "I guess what is on your mind, Monsieur le Président, you are sorry about those two beautiful woodcocks which were not carved." '

' "My goodness, I would certainly have eaten my share of them." '

' "Wait a minute, they will serve them to you." '

' "After the coffee? ... After the liqueur? ... It is impossible." '

' "Nothing is impossible for stomachs like yours." '

'The prefect gave his orders, a small table was set in the adjoining room, the two woodcocks were served, and the happy President ate them.'

It is thought that the woodcock was not known in ancient times. The woodcock is the size of a partridge, has a very long beak, agree-

Woodcock, Snipe

ably variegated plumage and very large eyes. Woodcock is widespread throughout the old world, and is also found in America. In summer it goes to Switzerland to the Savoy over the Pyrenees and the Alps. It is shot in the morning, on the edges of woods. Its flight is sustained, and it flies very quickly. It is stupid, and is said to see nothing except at twilight. The flesh of this black-footed bird is excellent, like that of wild birds. Nevertheless it is not to everyone's taste; it does not suit weak stomachs, nor the bilious, nor the melancholy, but only those who take exercise. It is at its best in autumn. They say that every part of the woodcock is good; it is the game most valued by huntsmen. The smell and taste of this bird are displeasing to dogs, and it is very difficult to get them to retrieve a woodcock.

To M. Alexandre Dumas, at Paris
Dear Master,
Concerning your great work on *l'Art Culinaire*, you ask if I could teach you some original recipes from my country. What could I teach you, the great scholar, who has known for a very long time the little science which my youth has permitted me to acquire? . . . Nothing! Nevertheless, here is a dish which has been much appreciated at my house, and which I have not seen on any restaurant menu. This is not to say that it may not figure in a complete collection of bourgeois cooking. Anyway, I will make it known to you, in the hope of being able to please you.

Bécasses brulées au rhum à la bacquaise ·
Woodcocks flamed with rum *à la Bacquaise*

'The woodcocks, after having been suitably dressed, are skewered underneath the wings, so as not to damage their entrails, and are put in front of a fairly brisk fire. The meat of these birds, like that of the wood pigeon, must be seared if one wishes to keep its flavour.

'In the dripping pan which should catch the juices, you put a piece of toast, rubbed generously with garlic; this piece of toast acts as a sort of sponge, drinking up the trail and the drippings from the animal.

'The flesh of the woodcock, done to a turn, should be slightly red. The carver, having carefully removed the four limbs, withdraws all the interior with a little spoon. He takes great pains to find the gall in order to remove it. And, having crushed the entrails in a shallow bowl with the back of a fork, he spreads it on the toast, adds salt and pepper, and empties over the whole thing a good glass of old rum. As soon as the liquor is alight, the man in charge, usually the oldest of the huntsmen, stirs the rum with a spoon in order to make the flame blaze up, and he takes each piece and passes it through the bluish flame.

'Once this sacrificial rite is accomplished, the toast, divided and put under each quarter, is immediately passed to the gourmets who vie with each other for the last drops of this marvellous sauce.

'The accompaniment for this dish is worth more than the principal ingredient. It is moreover, a dish which could not be more delicate and savory.' B.S.

YOUNG WILD BOAR   *MARCASSIN*

The young wild boar goes by the name of *bête rousse* in hunting terms. It is excellent with any of the sauces normally served with fully grown boar, that is to say spit-roasted or grilled with onions. In olden times young wild boar were not eaten at all, but were castrated and then released in the forest. Thus brought to perfection—and this is the term used of the singers in the Sistine chapel—they become fatter, more delicate, and less wild.

Quartier de marcassin, sauce aux cerises ·
                        Quarter of wild boar with cherry sauce

Choose a fresh tender quarter of young wild boar, without rind. Remove the bone from the chump end and break with a straight cut and bend back the bone protruding at the other end. Salt the quarter and put it in a terrine with a litre of marinade which has been cooked and is now half-cool. Let the quarter macerate for two or three days, then drain it, sponge it off on a cloth and put it in a shallow baking tin with some lard. Cover it with greased paper and cook it for three quarters of an hour, basting it frequently with the fat. Then add a few spoonfuls of the marinade, and cook for an additional half hour, continuing to baste the meat with the pan juices.

When the meat is well 'seized', remove the baking tin from the oven, drain the meat and mask it with a thick layer of grated breadcrumbs (from black bread) which have been dried, pounded, sieved, mixed with a little sugar and cinnamon, and then dampened with some good red wine, but only enough to make them stick together. Over this layer sprinkle breadcrumbs which have not been moistened.

Young Wild Boar

Baste the meat with the fat from the baking tin, put it back on this, and keep it at the front of the oven for a half an hour. When you are about to serve it, take it out of the oven, put a paper frill around the protruding bone, arrange it on a platter and serve the following sauce in a separate vessel.

Sauce aux cerises · Cherry sauce

[In a little water] soften two handfuls of dry black cherries, such as are commonly sold in Germany, that is to say with the stones in. Next, pound them in a mortar, then add a glass of red wine to thin them, and pour the mixture into a vessel which must not be tinned. Add a piece of cinnamon, two cloves, a grain of salt and a piece of lemon zest. Boil the liquid for two minutes, and thicken it with a little starch diluted with water. Put the vessel on the side of the fire, cover it, keep it thus for a quarter of an hour and then strain the sauce.

(Recipe of M. Urbain Dubois, cook to Their Royal Majesties of Prussia.)

YOUNG WILD DUCK   *ALBRAN*

The young wild duck which is shot at the end of August is called *albran*. In September it becomes a duckling and in the month of October finally becomes a duck. The young wild duck is related to the ordinary duck in the same way as the partridge is to the chicken. It is cooked on the spit, and served on canapés [of fried bread] —canapés which have absorbed its unctuous juices and to which has been added the juice of a bitter orange, with a little Indian soya and some coarse ground pepper. It is a delicate and distinguished *plat de rôt*.

ZEST   *ZESTE*

This is what the yellow epidermis of the skin of a lemon is called. The name applies also to oranges and citrons.

Zest is removed in thin slices. The essential oils which give the fruits of this family their aroma are present especially in the zest. The white matter which lies underneath the zest is completely lacking in these, and also has a rather disagreeable bitterness; it is for this reason that it is recommended always to separate the two with care.

APPENDIX 1: Dumas and Vuillemot

The role played by Vuillemot as Dumas' principal adviser on cookery has already been mentioned on page 22.

Denis-Joseph Vuillemot was one of the very few individuals who had entries about themselves in the *Dictionnaire*. Dumas records that Vuillemot was born at Crépy, in Valois, in about 1811. His paternal grandfather was a British Member of Parliament; his father a chef in France. The culinary art also figured on the other side of his family; his maternal grandfather had been maître d'hotel to Mlle de Lescure, a cousin of Louis XVI.

Vuillemot's parents wished him to be a lawyer, but he preferred to follow in his father's steps, and left for Paris at an early age, to train as a cook. He held a junior position in the royal kitchen for a while, and then became the pupil and friend of the illustrious Carême, who completed his culinary education. In 1837 he took over his father's hotel at Crépy. Five years later he and a partner called Morlière acquired the Hôtel de la Cloche at Compiègne, which they ran together for fifteen years.

Dumas had known Vuillemot at Crépy and met him again at the Hôtel de la Cloche, when he and some companions were journeying back from Lille.

'Worn out by fatigue and dying of hunger, I addressed him in the following terms: "Ho, there! Can you serve us some carriage-wheels dressed with sorrel and some meat-chopper handles *à la Sainte-Menehould?*"

'Vuillemot, who had looked through the grille of his door and had recognized me, was quick to reply: "Monsieur, we have nothing left but tiger cutlets and snake with tartare sauce."

'This was enough to identify my friend, whose sallies in this vein used to amuse me in his father's house. I stretched out my hand and thus sealed anew our close friendship.'

Dumas recalls that he was a witness at the marriage of Vuillemot's eldest daughter; and that he finished his *Monte-Cristo* at the great house of Pompadour, which Vuillemot and Morlière rented for a while. He also recounts the story of a ragoût of sixty rabbits' tongues with truffles, which Vuillemot had once prepared. This dish was the subject of an amusing letter from Vuillemot, exemplifying the sort of gastronomic correspondence which passed between him and Dumas.

'Around 1863, after my return from Tiflis, I had a visit from

Vuillemot, who told me that my friends, headed by my son, were giving me an ovation in the form of a banquet, at which Méry, Grisier, Roger du Beauvoir, Léon Bertrand, Noël Parfait and other friends of convivial spirit were to be present.

'The banquet was duly held at the *restaurant de France* in the Place de la Madeleine, which Vuillemot had recently taken over. It was such a splendid meal that I gave to my host, as a token of my gratitude, a knife which I had bought in Tiflis, with the inscription *Alexandre Dumas à son ami Vuillemot* engraved on the blade. A special refinement of the menu was that it contained in culinary guise, from soup to dessert, the list of my principal literary creations.'

Dumas goes on to relate that Vuillemot had sought to retire, a few years later, at Saint-Cloud; but that he had been unable to resist the temptation to buy the *Hôtel de la Tête noire* there and to continue in business. A dinner held to mark the reopening of this establishment was thronged by literary notabilities. Dumas continues as follows:

'There was nothing surprising about this. For a thorough understanding of the culinary art, no one is so well equipped as a man of letters; for he, accustomed to refinements of every kind, knows better than anyone else how to appreciate those of the table. Witness Brillat-Savarin, Grimod de la Reynière, Monselet, etc.

'Before finishing this essay, I must discharge a debt by thanking the excellent Vuillemot for the valuable information which he provided as my collaborator in this *Grand Dictionnaire de la Cuisine*; just as much in the form of original recipes, the formulae of which he had conceived himself, as in pieces of advice, which came from a man who was a perfect practitioner of his art.

'The instructions which I have drawn from him, in conformity with my own taste, have always seemed to me to be based on those great principles which make the cuisine of France superior, as I think I have demonstrated, to those of all other civilized nations.'

APPENDIX 2: Dumas as a Cook

A brief account was given in the introduction of the meal which Dumas cooked when he was staying at the Villa Catinat. Since this is a primary piece of evidence about his activity in the kitchen, we print here a translation of a fuller account—the fullest we have found. It comes from *Les dernières années d'Alexandre Dumas* by the author Gabriel Ferry (Paris, 1883); and is followed by some other relevant quotations from the same source.

(A) The luncheon at the Villa Catinat
'Every Sunday there was a big luncheon at the Villa Catinat. Anyone who had come to see Dumas could stay on for it; and this prospect used often to attract a number of his friends, especially hungry musicians. The dining room would then seem like the scene of a banquet; the conversation was boisterous and appetites were enormous.

'The young woman to whom we referred above [a Neapolitan singer, who was installed in the villa with Dumas] had one fault, besides thinking that she would become a great singer; and this was that she was a poor household manager. She liked to change the personnel of the household frequently, and sometimes in circumstances which were inopportune. Of the three members of the domestic staff, two might thus be dismissed on a Saturday evening. On the following day, when the time came for the famous Sunday luncheon, this reduction in the size of the staff used to cause embarrassment.

'One day—it was a Saturday, as usual—she went one better and dismissed all three simultaneously!

'The next day turned out to be one of those marvellous Sundays when the sunshine is streaming down and people feel the urge to leave Paris for the countryside, especially when the delights of a good luncheon can be counted on to restore them after the fatigue of the journey. So guests began to arrive at the villa around ten o'clock, greeted the 'master', their host, and then spread out in the garden, awaiting the accustomed signal to invade the dining room.

'Dumas, looking out through one of the windows, contemplated with poignant anguish this crowd of hungry people whose appetites had to be satisfied. The situation was critical. The servants had gone without leaving any provisions for the meal, and no preparations for it were in hand.

'What was to be done? Tell the guests the truth? That would have been lamentable. Recruit them to go and look for provisions at Saint-Gratien or Enghien? That would not have been very polite!

'The novelist, tormented by these perplexities, decided to go down and to inform two or three of his closest friends of the peril in which he stood. A discussion ensued immediately, and they all went to the kitchen. The fires of the kitchen range were going out, wanly, and not even the tiniest of cooking pots stood over the last flickers of flame.

'Dumas and his friends opened the drawers and inspected the cupboards. They found several sacks of rice and two or three pounds of cooking butter. Moreover, some of the guests, wishing to make their contribution to the lunch menu, had brought some ham and mortadella and two sausages. All of this was scant fare, however, and barely enough to provide an hors d'oeuvre.

'It was then that they realized that they had overlooked one of the cupboards. They opened it and withdrew a large faience plate on which reposed some fine scarlet tomatoes! This discovery brought a flash of relief to Dumas' face, for it gave him an inspiration. ' "Relight the fires," he said, while going to take down in person an enormous casserole. He flung the tomatoes into this, after cutting them open. "Now," he said to one of his amateur kitchen aides, "two or three glasses of water;" and these were brought to him.

'A few minutes later, the liquid in the bottom of the casserole was bubbling, and the tomatoes quickly transformed themselves into a sauce of an even more beautiful scarlet colour. Dumas then added a large piece of butter, of the saffron yellow kind which is of mediocre quality at table but exquisite in sauces, and let everything go on boiling for a while. Everyone around him kept silent, realizing that he had hit on the best remedy for the situation.

'The author of *The Three Musketeers* had indeed, by means of his own good taste and his studies, become a real artist in the kitchen. He had the faculty of invention, a gift for fantasy, a boldness in mixing ingredients and the memory of a host of recipes which he had learned during his travels. Once the sauce was made, he poured in three or four pounds of rice, added sufficient water and what was left of the butter, sprinkled salt and pepper over everything and put the lid on the huge casserole.

' "Go and help Fanny to lay the table. Lunch will be ready in an hour. What I'm making will be a great success!" The kitchen aides left. When the table had been laid, they came back, curious to see the result of the mixture which the novelist had improvised.

'The rice, swollen in the course of the boiling, had increased its volume to a stupefying extent. Decanted from the casserole on to two large platters, it now presented the appearance of two rose-coloured mountains of superlative flavour. The slices of ham, which had been fried separately, jutted up here and there through the surface of the rice, like islets of appetizing meat. To sum up, Dumas had prepared a dish which is very common in America but unknown in France, and which was copious enough to sate fifteen or twenty hungry guests.

' "Serve it!" said he to his aides, who obediently took hold of the platters. Dumas then opened the kitchen window, which gave on to the garden, and exclaimed in a voice which reverberated like the sound of a trumpet: "Luncheon is ready!"

'Luckily, the cellar of the house was well stocked. The dish of rice and tomatoes was pronounced by all to be excellent. While it was being eaten, Dumas told the true story of its confection; upon which everyone laughed a lot, applauded the idea which he had had and praised above all his talent as a cook. There had never been such a gay meal at the Villa Catinat as on that memorable Sunday.

'But Dumas never again allowed his fair friend to dismiss all three servants at once on a Saturday evening.'

(B) Dumas and his *Causeries culinaires*
Ferry describes the *causeries* (essays intended to seem like a casual conversation with his readers) which Dumas contributed to a periodical of his own creation, *Les Nouvelles*.

'These cosy chats with his readers often turned on the art of cookery. This art had become one of his preoccupations during the last years of the novelist's life. His well-deserved reputation was thus extended in a new direction. People consulted him about this or that foodstuff, and there was much talk about his future book on cookery. It was to be stuffed with marvellous recipes, which would be a revelation for modern gastronomes.

'In this matter of cookery, Dumas was both eclectic and imaginative; but his eclecticism was always buttressed by his own experience, and his strokes of imagination and fantasy were always justified by their success. . . .

'The following lines [taken, presumably, from a piece in *Les Nouvelles*] show how proud the author of *The Three Musketeers* was of this new aspect of his reputation. "I see with pleasure that my culinary reputation is growing and bids fair to eclipse before long my literary reputation. God be praised! I shall then be able to devote myself to

Appendix 2

a respectable calling and to bequeath to my children, instead of books which they would only inherit for fifteen or twenty years, casseroles and marmites which they would inherit for eternity and could bequeath in the same manner to their own descendants. Now, since, it is likely that sooner or later I shall relinquish the pen in favour of the kitchen spoon, I find it no burden at all to be laying down in advance the foundations of what will be the true monument of my fame. Who would claim that the renown of Carême will not outlive that of Horace...? I am already receiving letters from all over France, letters in which people seek my advice about polenta, caviar or birds' nest soup.

'"Now, you are going to ask me whence comes my taste for cookery, and under which master I have studied the art. My taste for cookery, like that for poetry, came to me from the heavens. One was destined to be my ruin—I mean, of course, my taste for poetry—but the other to enrich me; for I still intend to be rich one day. As for who was my master, how do you expect me to answer that question, me, the supreme eclectic? I have studied under all the masters, and especially under the master called necessity. Ask those who accompanied me on my travels through Spain how I managed, throughout those three months, to have them eat salad without oil and vinegar, to such good effect that after their return to France they no longer had any stomach for either. They will tell you!

'"Besides, I have known the great practitioners: Grimod de la Reynière, the uncle of my good friend Dorset; Brillat-Savarin, who is remembered not as a magistrate but as the inventor of omelettes with carp roe; Courchamps, who left behind him the best dictionary of cuisine in existence.... And I have travelled a lot. Wherever I went, I introduced myself to skilled chefs and well-known gourmets."'

(C) Dumas and macaroni

'One day a friend of Dumas wrote and asked him for the authentic recipe for macaroni in the Neapolitan style. For once, the novelist was left in a state of embarrassment. He could not stand eating macaroni; this was a taste which he simply did not have. He had lived in Italy for five years without bringing himself to eat any. The result was that, since he did not like it, he had never bothered to find out how it was made.

'To avoid the embarrassment, and to oblige his friend, he wrote to Rossini. The author of *William Tell*, so people said, was the man who ate the best macaroni in Naples.

'Rossini replied in a friendly letter, inviting Dumas to come and eat a succulent dish of macaroni at his house; and promised that, after he had eaten it, he would be given the recipe. Dumas accordingly went to have dinner with Rossini; but the latter, noticing that his guest ate hardly any of the macaroni which had been prepared in his honour, was offended and decided that Dumas did not deserve to have the recipe.

'Dumas did his best to insist on having it, but was completely unsuccessful. He then began to suspect that Rossini contented himself with eating macaroni, while it was really his cook who prepared it. Indeed he felt free to tell other people that the reputation of the illustrious composer as an expert on macaroni was fraudulent.

'However, he was still embarrassed by not having the recipe. Then, one morning, his doorbell rang and he was told that the marquis del Grillo had come to see him—the husband of Madame Ristori, the famous Italian tragédienne whom everyone in Paris was flocking to see. The marquis entered and Dumas, seeing in him his salvation, held out his arms. "Do you know how to make macaroni?" he asked him.

' "Myself, no," was the reply, "but Madame Ristori has heard of your embarrassment, my dear friend. Come to dinner with her on Monday, even though she is playing in a charity performance on that day. We'll dine early and I'll ensure that, with your own hand on the handle of the casserole, you make the acquaintance of a virtuoso of a quality quite different from Rossini."

' "Bravo! I'll be at your house at three o'clock."

'Dumas did indeed arrive, at three o'clock on the appointed day, at the house of the marquis, and was taken to the kitchen, into the presence of the culinary virtuoso who had been promised. He, warned of the honour which awaited him, was already at work. He had just plunged his macaroni into a *marmite* full of boiling water.

' "There's a start to the making of it," said the novelist, "but now, my friend, I shall be obliged if you will reveal the procedure to me in full detail."

'The artist of the kitchen took up a plate on which reposed a sort of liquid jelly, brown in colour.

' "You see this meat extract?"

' "It looks succulent."

' "Well, that's the indispensable material for moistening, for binding our macaroni."

'Dumas opened his notebook, took a pencil and prepared to write. "Tell me, my friend, with what ingredients you have prepared this appetizing meat extract?"

Appendix 2

' "Four pounds of silverside, a pound of raw smoked ham, four pounds of tomatoes, four big white onions, with thyme, a bay leaf, parsley, cloves of garlic; all moistened with ordinary water and reduced by three hours of cooking."

'The artist of the kitchen went back to his stove, where the macaroni was boiling; then, after a silence, continued. "Remember this well, monsieur Dumas. Macaroni which has been overcooked is worthless. It degenerates into a paste and loses its savour. It is necessary—according to the Neapolitan expression—*che cresca in corpo*, that is to say that it swells in body. How long you cook it is a matter of feeling. After you've done it wrong twice, you'll succeed the third time. And this lot is now exactly ready. Watch closely to see what I do to stop it boiling any longer." Dumas was all eyes and ears.

'The artist, after having removed the *marmite* from the fire, poured a carafe of iced water into it. A cloud of steam rose up and then immediately subsided. Then he emptied the whole contents of the *marmite* into a sieve, so as to drain away all the water. This done, he took a soup tureen, previously warmed, and covered the bottom of it with a handful of finely grated parmesan. On this bed of cheese he placed a layer of macaroni, then one of meat extract, and so on; cheese, macaroni, meat extract, macaroni, cheese. When the tureen was full, he covered it, sealing it hermetically.

' "Now, monsieur Dumas, you know as much about it as I do," he added. "In ten minutes I shall serve it."

'The novelist returned to the salon. This time, he really had the authentic recipe for macaroni *à la napolitaine*!'

*

M. Robert Landru was one of the French *Dumasophiles* to whom we posed the question: how much cooking did Dumas actually do? He provided a remarkably interesting reply, in the form of a transcription of manuscript notes made by M. Henri-François Lhote. These notes have never before been published.

M. Lhote was born at Soissons, about thirteen miles from Villers-Cotterêts, in 1863; and his father was a close friend of Alexandre Dumas. Indeed Dumas gave to the son a small cannon for discharging fireworks; a gift well calculated to make the donor memorable to the small boy. This memory was nourished subsequently by the father's reminiscences of the great novelist, and prompted Henri-François, in later life, to set down his family's *Souvenirs sur Alexandre Dumas père*. The following are extracts from these recollections.

'My father made the acquaintance of Alexandre Dumas at the domaine of Wallu, between Largny and Vauciennes and close to Villers-Cotterêts, around 1862. The intermediary was Darsonville, a friend whom they had in common and who was a miller. Dumas used to visit him every year at the time of the hunting season. Moreover, Dumas used to own a chalet at Wallu, on the banks of a large pond. Wallu was a place where people were never bored, for life there was very happy.

'My father, with his exuberant personality, his natural gift for talking and his taste for hunting big game, quite quickly became one of the intimate friends of the great novelist. The relationship between our family and Dumas continued up to the war of 1870.

'Dumas, when he came to Soissons, used to stay at our very hospitable home in the Rue Saint-Antoine. This house had two large wings, forming two buildings which were separated by the court-yard. We lived in one of them and the other was arranged as guest rooms. When Dumas came, he was always accompanied by two or three secretaries. He used to say that he was coming to spend two or three days, but he usually stayed for a week or more.

'Once installed, Dumas would set off into town with the maid, buying in this shop and that the things which he was planning to cook with her in the evening; for he was a discriminating gourmet and an excellent cook. Depending on whom he happened to meet between purchases, he was accustomed to invite acquaintances quite unceremoniously to "come and share the dinner of his friend Lhote". In short, he considered himself to be thoroughly at home in our house; and the result was that my mother found herself receiving twelve or fifteen of the leading people of Soissons each day.

'Once the guests had gone, Dumas would take over my father's desk and set to work writing. The words flowed from his pen with incredible ease. He never re-read or corrected anything. He had in front of him a packet of large sheets of white paper, wrote on one side of them only and tossed the sheets, once they were covered with writing, to the ground without giving any further thought to them. His secretaries would collect them later and put them in order. This work went on for much of the night. He only slept for a few hours in the morning.

'As I have said, Dumas was an excellent cook. He had an extensive repertoire of recipes, especially exotic ones, which he took pleasure in executing while he was at Soissons.

'One day, in company with Dumas and the Deviolaines, who were close friends of my parents, my father had arranged a party to go

hunting for crayfish in a small river. The fishing was highly successful; several hundreds of crayfish were caught. On that very evening
the entire catch was prepared by Dumas, who made of it a huge
pyramid (*buisson*—see picture) which constituted the main dish at
dinner.

'Madame Deviolaine, who was passionately fond of these crustaceans, did full justice to the dish and, although she found that the
crayfish had an odd flavour, personally made a very large hole in the
pyramid. When dinner was over, she felt unwell and wished to leave
the table. Impossible. . . . Addressing her husband, she said: "I don't
know what's the matter with me, but I feel rather queer—my head is
swimming and I can't get up out of my chair."

'My mother, who was not so partial to crayfish, had eaten only a
few of them and was feeling quite all right. The others at table, who
were men, felt a little "jolly", but nothing more. So no one blamed
the crayfish as the cause of Madame Deviolaine's malaise; which anyway diminished when she came into contact with the fresh air on
returning to her own house shortly afterwards.

'It was on the next day, thanks to our maid, that we had the explanation of our friend's malaise. My mother, in checking the household expenses with the maid, expressed astonishment to her at an
item which represented the purchase of a bottle of old cognac. The

servant replied: "But, Madame, it was Monsieur Dumas who made me buy it, along with some strange kind of pepper and a whole heap of things which I am not accustomed to use. He put all these things in with the crayfish."

'The fact was that Dumas had an excellent recipe for preparing crayfish. Here it is.

'The court-bouillon was made by boiling onions and carrots with a bouquet garni, the whole spiced with cayenne pepper or other fiery condiments.

'Using a cauldron with two handles, Dumas reduced this court-bouillon to such an extent that, after he had added a generous glassful of vinegar, the whole amounted only to a quarter of the volume which he had had to begin with; and this was for two hundred crayfish! It was only then, and after he had strained the concentrated court-bouillon, that he tossed the crayfish into the cauldron. These, of course, given the small amount of court-bouillon, were not covered by it. Dumas then put the cauldron back on to a lively fire, and the cooking proceeded in such a way as to cause the crayfish to jump up into the air, continuously, until they were all cooked. At the end of the cooking, and while the cauldron remained for a few minutes longer on the lively fire, Dumas added the whole contents of a bottle of strong cognac. Then he let the cauldron cool, without disturbing its contents, so that the crayfish could soak up the court-bouillon in its final form and become really tasty. In this manner he produced crayfish of an exquisite flavour, quite different from the dull and tasteless ones which are usually served, even in the best restaurants. The cognac did not give the dish a taste of alcohol, despite the fact that, having been boiled for a few minutes only, it had not evaporated very much.

'Now we understood why Madame Deviolaine, like a thrush which had eaten too many grapes, could not rise from her chair. She had a good laugh over the episode herself and swore that in future she would be very careful when tasting anything which Dumas had cooked.

'Dumas, too, had been laughing to himself up his sleeve when serving his famous dish, and knew very well what made our friend indisposed, but had said not a word about it.

'My mother, subsequently, always served crayfish cooked according to Dumas' recipe, but added only a glass instead of a whole bottle of cognac to the court-bouillon. Her crayfish, I may say, were just as good as his, but did not prevent her guests from rising from their chairs.'

*

Appendix 2

It is interesting to note that Gustave Geffroy, in his *Claude Monet, sa vie, son temps, son œuvre* (Paris, 1922), after describing how Monet and Courbet introduced themselves to Dumas at Le Havre in 1868, states that Courbet and Dumas became close friends during a stay at l'Étretat, where, 'when they were not talking to each other, they were constantly singing and cooking together'.

An especially vivid glimpse of Dumas in the kitchen is afforded by the author of *An Englishman in Paris* (3rd edition, London, 1892), who became involved in a dispute about Dumas' prowess as a cook. He observed that, while few doubted Dumas' literary genius, there were many who suspected his culinary abilities; notably a certain Dr Véron. Dr Véron was in fact misled by his own cook, a woman called Sophie who was jealous of Dumas' success in cooking carp and put it about that the dish was really prepared by other hands. When Dumas heard that Dr Véron was repeating such allegations, he flew into a rage but then calmed down and invited Véron to dine with him on the morrow and to send a representative to his house at three o'clock to watch him prepare the meal.

Albert Vandam (the Englishman in Paris) was the youngest of the company present when the challenge was made, and the choice fell on him. 'That is how my life-long friendship with Dumas began. At three o'clock next day I was at the Chaussée d'Antin, and was taken by the servant into the kitchen, where the great novelist stood surrounded by his utensils, some of silver, and all of them glistening like silver. With the exception of a *soupe aux choux*, at which, by his own confession, he had been at work since the morning, all the ingredients for the dinner were in their natural state—of course, washed and peeled, but nothing more. He was assisted by his own cook and a kitchen-maid, but he himself, with his sleeves rolled up to the elbows, a large apron round his waist, and bare chest, conducted the operations. . . .

'At half-past six the guests began to arrive; at a quarter to seven Dumas retired to his dressing room; at seven punctually the servant announced that "*monsieur était servi*". The dinner consisted of the aforenamed *soupe aux choux*, the carp that had led to the invitation, a *ragoût de mouton à la Hongroise*, *rôti de faisans*, and a *salade Japonaise*. The sweets and ices had been sent by the *pâtissier*. I never dined like that before or after, not even a week later, when Dr Véron and Sophie made the *amende honorable* in the Rue Taitbout.'

The counsel for the defence of Dumas' reputation as a cook may well rest his case on the eye-witness evidence of this young Englishman, who was no casual observer, but the impartial emissary selected by the arch-sceptic Véron to investigate the matter.

BIBLIOGRAPHY

1. Editions of the *Dictionnaire* or parts thereof.

DUMAS, ALEXANDRE: *Grand Dictionnaire de Cuisine*: VI + 1156 pages + Annexe of 24 pages containing advertising matter: Alphonse Lemerre, Paris, 1873.

Petit dictionnaire de Cuisine par Alexandre Dumas, revu et complété par J. Vuillemot: III + 819 pages: Alphonse Lemerre, Paris 1882. (This version, oddly, is sometimes found bearing the shorter title *Dictionnaire de Cuisine*.)

Mon Dictionnaire de Cuisine par Alexandre Dumas: with a Preface by André Maurois and a Foreword by Raymond Oliver: original introductory material omitted: short glossary added at the end: 728 pages: Editions Pierre Grobel, Paris, 1958.

Mon Dictionnaire de Cuisine par Alexandre Dumas: as the preceding version but without Preface and Foreword and with the addition of illustrations by Louis James: 546 pages: Livre club du Libraire, 1960.

Le Grand Dictionnaire de Cuisine: Nouvelle edition annotée par Jean Arnaboldi: original introductory material omitted: many illustrations from other nineteenth-century books added: Cercle du livre précieux, Paris, 1965.

Le Grand Dictionnaire de Cuisine: contents as in the preceding version: Tchou, Paris, 1965.

Le Grand Dictionnaire de Cuisine: contents as in the preceding version: Henri Veyrier, Paris, 1973.

Histoire de la Cuisine: comprising only the original introductory material, with many illustrations added from publications of the nineteenth and earlier centuries: P. Waleffe, Paris, 1967.

2. Other works by Dumas.

It would be impossible to list here all the other works by this prolific author which contain references to food and cookery. As examples, we cite *Capitaine Pamphile* (for the episode of the Englishwoman and the turtle), *Histoires de mes Bêtes* (for a passage about omelettes), *Impressions de Voyage en Suisse* (for the story of the bear steak, etc.) and *Propos d'Art et de Cuisine* (for the *Causeries culinaires*). Dumas also contributed a piece on the roasting of chickens to *La Cuisinière poétique* by Charles Monselet (Michel Lévy frères, Paris, 1859), a book to which other literary figures such as the poets Méry and Théophile Gautier made contributions.

The biography by A. F. Davidson, referred to below, contains a useful list of Dumas' works. The fullest bibliographies used to be those in *Alexandre Dumas et son œuvre* by Charles Glinel (Reims, 1884) and by F. W. Reed (*A Bibliography of Alexandre Dumas père*, London, 1933). But a much fuller bibliography by Douglas Munro, extending to 1900 so as to include the posthumously published works, was brought out by the Association des Amis de Dumas in 1978. A bibliography of works by Dumas translated into English, also prepared by Douglas Munro, was published by Garland Publishing Inc. in New York in the same year. These works are the culmination of over twenty years of research in Europe and North America.

3. Books about Dumas.
These are very numerous. We have used the following.

DAVIDSON, ARTHUR F.: *Alexandre Dumas (père), His Life and Works*: Constable and Co., London, 1902.

DE LAMAZE, JEAN: *Alexandre Dumas*: Editions Pierre Charron, 1972 (short, well illustrated and generally of excellent quality).

FERRY, GABRIEL: *Les Dernières Années d'Alexandre Dumas* (the period from 1864 to 1870): Calmann Lévy, Paris, 1883.

LANDRU, ROBERT: *A propos d'Alexandre Dumas:* published by the author, a resident of Villers-Cotterêts, in 1977.

MAUROIS, ANDRÉ: *Three Musketeers—A Study of the Dumas Family* (tr. Gerard Hopkins): Jonathan Cape, London, 1957.

4. Sources of illustrations. (Dates given are of first editions.)

GOUFFÉ, JULES: *Le livre de cuisine*: Paris, 1867. Illustrations on pages 27, 30 (2nd, 3rd, 4th), 31 (*marmites* only), 34, 36, 45, 49, 148, 195, 204, 255, 266, 280, 294, 312 and 320.

DUBOIS, URBAIN: *Cuisine de tous les pays*: Paris, 1869. Illustrations on pages 29, 30 (first), 31 (centre and bottom), 116, 125, 139, 166, 214, 235 and 245.

DUBOIS, URBAIN: *Cuisine artistique*: Paris, 1872–74. Illustrations on pages 60, 89, 219, 227 and 271.

TROUSSET, JULES (ed.): *Grande encyclopédie illustrée d'Economie domestique et rurale*: Vols 1 and 2, Paris, 1875. Illustrations on pages 68, 90, 97, 115, 117, 129, 137, 141, 150, 179, 189, 207, 228 and 293.

HAGDAHL, DR CH. E. M.: *Kok-konsten*: Stockholm, 1896. Illustrations on pages 72, 94, 151, 158 and 181.

The pictures of fish come from Parnell's *Fishes of the Firth of Forth*, 1838 (that on page 224); from Vol. III of Bonaparte's *Iconografia della Fauna italica*, 1832 (that on page 264); and from Day's *The Fishes of Great Britain and Ireland*, 1880–84 (those on pages 43 and 242).

INDEX

French recipe titles (together with the English titles of those recipes which occur in unexpected places)

Index

Index

OXFORD

MORE OXFORD PAPERBACKS

Details of a selection of other books follow. A complete list of Oxford Paperbacks, including The World's Classics, Twentieth-Century Classics, OPUS, Past Masters, Oxford Authors, Oxford Shakespeare, and Oxford Paperback Reference, is available in the UK from the General Publicity Department, Oxford University Press (JH), Walton Street, Oxford OX2 6DP.

In the USA, complete lists are available from the Paperbacks Marketing Manager, Oxford University Press, 200 Madison Avenue, New York, NY 10016.

Oxford Paperbacks are available from all good bookshops. In case of difficulty, customers in the UK can order direct from Oxford University Press Bookshop, 116 High Street, Oxford, Freepost, OX1 4BR, enclosing full payment. Please add 10 per cent of published price for postage and packing.

FRANCE 1848–1945:

Anxiety and Hypocrisy

Theodore Zeldin

What made French people lonely, self-conscious, worried, bored, hysterical, violent and have more or fewer children? How did they behave as soldiers, colonists and criminals? How can one make sense of their religious and political squabbling? This volume is indispensable to all who are interested not only in France, but in the history of psychology, literature and intellectual life, which it illuminates with a wealth of astonishing insights and amusing detail.

'Brilliant, original, entertaining and inexhaustible' *The Times*

'A very great book . . . A history that is also and above all a great work of sociology and psychology (or psychoanalysis), embracing the whole of life . . . Zeldin's erudition is staggering. His style is deliberately humorous, with a humour that is usually amiable but sometimes ferocious.' *Le Figaro*

'He is a modern Balzac.' *Boston Sunday Globe*

THE ENGLISH GARDENER

William Cobbett

Introduction by Anthony Huxley

'It is a most satisfying read on early gardening, much of Cobbett's advice being as relevant today as it was when he wrote it.' *Yorkshire Evening Post*

'I was surprised and soon delighted at finding *The English Gardener* in paperback . . . (Cobbett's) early writing is a reminder that much about the past has still to be rediscovered.' *Country Life*

'A masterpiece of general gardening.' *Observer*

KNOW AND GROW VEGETABLES

P. J. Salter, J. K. A. Bleasdale, and others
from the National Vegetable Research Station

'One of the very few books which no gardener . . . can afford to be without' *The Guardian*

'A really important gardening book . . . a virtual must for anyone who wants to grow vegetables successfully.' *Birmingham Post*

'The manifesto of a revolution in vegetable growing.' *Country Life*

'An invaluable addition to any gardener's bookshelf.' *Yorkshire Post*

FRANCE 1848–1945:

Ambition and Love

Theodore Zeldin

Ambition and Love, containing the first two sections of Zeldin's outstanding *France 1848–1945,* offers an entertaining, brilliantly original picture of French society. 'Ambition' deals with the aspirations, pretensions and illusions of different sections of French society. The author overturns many commonly accepted generalizations about France; class conflict, 'the bug held responsible for so many of society's ailments', is placed under the microscope, with surprising results.

'Love' is about the attitudes of parents to their children, of husbands to their wives, of women to their place in society. The tensions beneath the facade of family life, the weakness of the movement for female suffrage, the vigour of prostitution and pornography, and the private world of the child are investigated.

'Masterpieces of the historian's art are rare in any generation. Zeldin's *France* belongs in that category. It is a stunning achievement, a monument of scholarship.' *Times Literary Supplement*

THE CHINESE FESTIVE BOARD

Corrine Lamb

The Chinese Festive Board presents a delightful picture of Chinese manners and dining etiquette that is as accurate today as it was when the book was first published in 1935. There are chapters on the conventions of Chinese food, on wine, cooking methods, ingredients, and on how to order a meal. In addition there is a selection of recipes gleaned by the author from twenty years of hospitality at the table of princes, generals, peasants, inn-keepers, and even cameleers. All this is complemented with Chinese proverbs and illustrated with photographs and line-drawings.

The book reflects the Chinese belief that eating is an affair involving pleasant anticipation, careful thought, meticulous selection, and, finally, a wholehearted, if somewhat noisy, gusto during the process itself.

THE CHALLENGE OF SMALLHOLDING

Sedley Sweeny

What is it *really* like to run a smallholding in the modern agricultural world? Sedley Sweeny draws on his own personal experience as a farmer to dispel the romantic mist surrounding the subject.

After a controversial introduction, in which he discusses the economic, social, and ecological implications of current agricultural practices, Sedley Sweeny deals with some of the basic questions: Why run a smallholding? How do you start? And how do you keep going? An examination of the different types of land and enterprise is followed by chapters on the care of soil; crops; livestock; how to organize a dairy; vegetables, fruit, and flowers; and machinery. The last chapter confronts the inevitable financial problems and gives advice on how to make ends meet.

JOURNEYS

Jan Morris

Journeys is a collection of pieces about far-flung and diverse locales. Here she writes about cities as different as Las Vegas and Stockholm, about journeys across Europe and China, about 'romantic re-visits' to such historic sites as the Acropolis and the Taj Mahal. Whether observing the folkways of rural Texans scattered along US 281 or the bustle of humanity on the streets of Bombay, Jan Morris brings her customary passion and wit into full play, producing superbly written essays that are part impressionism, part history, part political interpretation, and part plain travel.

'Morris's reporting is elegant, uncluttered by statistics and intensely personal . . . with great delicacy (she) picks away at the fabric of a place, exposing detail, demonstrating its relevance and aligning it with other vital scraps so that the composition assumes its true form.' *Sunday Times*

A LITTLE TOUR IN FRANCE

Henry James

Foreword by Geoffrey Grigson

One rainy morning in the autumn of 1882 Henry James set out on a trip to the French provinces, which took him from Touraine to the south-west, through Provence, and northwards again along the flooding Rhone to Burgundy.

'James is a knowledgeable guide. His verbal discursions make no pedantic tourists' handbook: and if, as Geoffrey Grigson points out, they lead the reader round not only France but also the country called Henry James, lovers of both countries will find that each in this book exerts an irresistible charm.

'James is the most assumed and well informed of travelling companions and also one of the funniest—this account is a comic delight.' *Sunday Times*

FRANCE 1848–1945:

Intellect and Pride

Theodore Zeldin

In what ways are Frenchmen different from other human beings? Zeldin investigates here the ideas they have had about themselves, their attitudes to foreigners, their peculiar habits as travellers, the nature of their nationalism, the significance of being a Breton or an Alsation, a Provençal or an Auvergnat.

To what extent have the French been fashioned by their schools to think, argue and express themselves in ways that are unique? Zeldin examines their teaching methods at all levels, their cultivation of logic, verbalism and competitiveness, their desperate fights against the rebelliousness of their pupils, the chaos of university life.

'The most perspicacious, the most deeply researched, the liveliest and the most enthralling panorama of French passions.' *Paris Match*

'By general agreement, it is one of the outstanding works of history of our generation.' *BBC World Service*

FRANCE 1848–1945:

Taste and Corruption

Theodore Zeldin

Taste and Corruption looks, in an entirely new way, at France's *joie de vivre*. It is indispensable for both travellers and students who wish to understand better her painting, her good and bad novels, her cinema, the chic of her fashions, the subtleties of her food and wine, the sensationalism of her press, the sarcasm and sentimentality of her singers, the passion for good living, the unique flavour of French laughter, but also the doubts and disputes that torment the French behind the façade they present.

'The world's foremost authority on Frenchness.' *Time Magazine*

'One of the major historical works of our collective lifetime . . . brilliantly stimulating.' *The Listener*

'The most enjoyable book of its kind in nearly forty years.' *New Statesman*

FRANCE 1848–1945:

Politics and Anger

Theodore Zeldin

Politics and Anger is about France's illusions and passions. It surveys the emotions, the ideologies, and the social pressures that lay behind the fragmentation of parties. It presents a multitude of portraits, written with both sympathy and irony, of the individuals who led the country's turbulent internal battles. The author shows how the confusions surrounding these have been partly created by the intellectuals, whose interpretations he pulls apart.

'so fluent and lively that it carries the reader effortlessly along. Zeldin's book is truly a work of genius.' *New Republic*

'a masterpiece' *New York Times* and *TLS*

'one of the most important books ever written about French civilisation' *Le Monde*

'probably the most remarkable social history of a modern European nation which has yet been written' *Sunday Telegraph*

THE CONCISE OXFORD DICTIONARY OF FRENCH LITERATURE

Edited by Joyce M. H. Reid

This abridgement of the classic *Oxford Companion to French Literature* preserves the unique quality of the original work and at the same time extends its scope with the addition of some 150 new entries to bring it up to date. The *Dictionary* retains the distinctive features of the *Companion,* including its coverage of a great variety of major and minor writers, genres, and movements in French literature. Like its parent volume, the *Dictionary* contains entries on other relevant aspects of French history, philosophy, and culture.

TRAVELS THROUGH FRANCE AND ITALY

Tobias Smollett

Edited by Frank Felsenstein

In 1763 Tobias Smollett left England for the Mediterranean. Though claiming to have no quarrel with the French and the Italians he criticized everything from the food ('I . . . abominate garlick') to the 'shockingly nasty' beds and the local inhabitants of Nice where he settled.

Not surprisingly, the *Travels* became notorious and Smollett was ridiculed by Laurence Sterne as 'the learned Smelfungus'. Yet his learning shows to good effect, whether he describes the culture of silk-worms, the French tax system, or the marbles of Florence, Smollett provides many an insight into eighteenth-century taste and into his cantankerous perceptive and intelligent personality. This World's Classics edition includes a letter of Smollett published here for the first time.

'any reader of this edition of his *Travels* . . . will be amused, horrified and aghast—aghast at Smollett (sometimes) as well as at the French of the eighteenth-century (some of them)' *Country Life*

FIVE HUNDRED POINTS OF GOOD HUSBANDRY

Thomas Tusser

The delightful verses of sixteenth-century farmer Thomas Tusser have provided generations of farmers and smallholders with valuable advice about agriculture, gardening, and housekeeping; modern readers may well be surprised at the many English proverbs that find their first publication in Tusser's work. Rivalling Cobbett's *Cottage Economy* as the most famous of English agricultural treatises, it gives a fascinating picture of Tudor and Elizabethan country life.

'A mine of information about the farming practices of Tudor times . . . (a) charming work.' *Observer*

'Garden tips sixteenth-century style . . . Delightful stuff.' *Sunday Times*